中華譯學館

莫言題

中华译学倡立倡宇与

以中华为根 译与学并重

弘扬优秀文化 促进中外交流

拓展精神疆域 驱动思想创新

丁酉年冬月许钧撰 罗卫东书

中华译学馆·中华翻译家代表性译文库

许　钧　郭国良／总主编

杨宪益 戴乃迭 卷

辛红娟／编

ZHEJIANG UNIVERSITY PRESS
浙江大学出版社

总　序

考察中华文化发展与演变的历史,我们会清楚地看到翻译所起到的特殊作用。梁启超在谈及佛经翻译时曾有过一段很深刻的论述:"凡一民族之文化,其容纳性愈富者,其增展力愈强,此定理也。我民族对于外来文化之容纳性,惟佛学输入时代最能发挥。故不惟思想界生莫大之变化,即文学界亦然。"[①]

今年是五四运动一百周年,以梁启超的这一观点去审视五四运动前后的翻译,我们会有更多的发现。五四运动前后,通过翻译这条开放之路,中国的有识之士得以了解域外的新思潮、新观念,使走出封闭的自我有了可能。在中国,无论是在五四运动这一思想运动中,还是自 1978 年改革开放以来,翻译活动都显示出了独特的活力。其最重要的意义之一,就在于通过敞开自身,以他者为明镜,进一步解放自己,认识自己,改造自己,丰富自己,恰如周桂笙所言,经由翻译,取人之长,补己之短,收"相互发明之效"[②]。如果打开视野,以历史发展的眼光,

---

①　梁启超.翻译文学与佛典//罗新璋.翻译论集.北京:商务印书馆,1984:63.
②　陈福康.中国译学理论史稿.上海:上海外语教育出版社,1992:162.

从精神深处去探寻五四运动前后的翻译,我们会看到,翻译不是盲目的,而是在自觉地、不断地拓展思想的疆界。根据目前所掌握的资料,我们发现,在 20 世纪初,中国对社会主义思潮有着持续不断的译介,而这种译介活动,对社会主义学说、马克思主义思想在中国的传播及其与中国实践的结合具有重要的意义。在我看来,从社会主义思想的翻译,到马克思主义的译介,再到结合中国的社会和革命实践之后中国共产党的诞生,这是一条思想疆域的拓展之路,更是一条马克思主义与中国革命相结合的创造之路。

开放的精神与创造的力量,构成了我们认识翻译、理解翻译的两个基点。在这个意义上,我们可以说,中国的翻译史,就是一部中外文化交流、互学互鉴的历史,也是一部中外思想不断拓展、不断创新、不断丰富的历史。而在这一历史进程中,一位位伟大的翻译家,不仅仅以他们精心阐释、用心传译的文本为国人打开异域的世界,引入新思想、新观念,更以他们的开放性与先锋性,在中外思想、文化、文学交流史上立下了一个个具有引领价值的精神坐标。

对于翻译之功,我们都知道季羡林先生有过精辟的论述。确实如他所言,中华文化之所以能永葆青春,"翻译之为用大矣哉"。中国历史上的每一次翻译高潮,都会生发社会、文化、思想之变。佛经翻译,深刻影响了国人的精神生活,丰富了中国的语言,也拓宽了中国的文学创作之路,在这方面,鸠摩罗什、玄奘功不可没。西学东渐,开辟了新的思想之路;五四运动前后的翻译,更是在思想、语言、文学、文化各个层面产生了革命性的影响。严复的翻译之于思想、林纾的翻译之于文学的作用无须赘言,而鲁迅作为新文化运动的旗手,其翻译动机、翻译立场、翻译选择和翻译方法,与其文学主张、文化革新思想别无二致,其翻译起着先锋性的作用,引导着广大民众掌握新语言、接受新思想、表达自己的精神诉求。这条道路,是通向民主的道路,也是人民大众借助掌握的新语言创造新文化、新思想的道路。

回望中国的翻译历史,陈望道的《共产党宣言》的翻译,傅雷的文学翻译,朱生豪的莎士比亚戏剧翻译……一位位伟大的翻译家创造了经典,更创造了永恒的精神价值。基于这样的认识,浙江大学中华译学馆为弘扬翻译精神,促进中外文明互学互鉴,郑重推出"中华译学馆·中华翻译家代表性译文库"。以我之见,向伟大的翻译家致敬的最好方式莫过于(重)读他们的经典译文,而弘扬翻译家精神的最好方式也莫过于对其进行研究,通过他们的代表性译文进入其精神世界。鉴于此,"中华译学馆·中华翻译家代表性译文库"有着明确的追求:展现中华翻译家的经典译文,塑造中华翻译家的精神形象,深化翻译之本质的认识。该文库为开放性文库,入选对象系为中外文化交流做出了杰出贡献的翻译家,每位翻译家独立成卷。每卷的内容主要分三大部分:一为学术性导言,梳理翻译家的翻译历程,聚焦其翻译思想、译事特点与翻译贡献,并扼要说明译文遴选的原则;二为代表性译文选编,篇幅较长的摘选其中的部分译文;三为翻译家的译事年表。

需要说明的是,为了更加真实地再现翻译家的翻译历程和语言的发展轨迹,我们选编代表性译文时会尽可能保持其历史风貌,原本译文中有些字词的书写、词语的搭配、语句的表达,也许与今日的要求不尽相同,但保留原貌更有助于读者了解彼时的文化,对于历史文献的存留也有特殊的意义。相信读者朋友能理解我们的用心,乐于读到兼具历史价值与新时代意义的翻译珍本。

许 钧

2019 年夏于浙江大学紫金港校区

目　录

第三编　中国现当代文学英译

导　言

一、杨宪益、戴乃迭生平

　　杨宪益,原名杨维武,生于天津,著名翻译家、外国文学研究专家、诗人,学贯中西,被认为是"最后一个集'士大夫'、'洋博士'和'革命者'于一身的知识分子"①。

　　1915 年 1 月 10 日,杨宪益出生于天津花园街 8 号大公馆内,按阴历算是甲寅年(虎年)。他后来回忆说,他出生之前母亲曾经梦见一只白虎跃入怀中,故杨宪益晚年应意大利友人约请撰写英文自传,书名便用的是"White Tiger"("白虎")。杨宪益祖上是清朝官员,祖父兄弟八人,其中四人(杨宪益的祖父杨士燮和三位叔祖)通过殿试当上翰林,都曾出任高级地方官,算是典型的封建文人和官僚。杨宪益的父亲和几位叔叔都曾出洋留学,对西方国家,尤其是英、法、德、美等国钦慕不已,算是当时比较有代表性的西方文明拥趸。

　　杨宪益就是在这样的中西学养交融的氛围中开始了他的启蒙学习。年仅 5 岁的杨宪益在家开蒙,几经更换塾师,最终跟定清末秀才魏汝舟读四书五经。魏汝舟学识渊博,思想开通,对杨宪益一生影响深远。他不仅

---

① 蒯乐昊.杨宪益:最后的士大夫、洋博士兼革命者.南方人物周刊,2009(31):66-69.

带着幼年杨宪益熟读儒家经典，还悉心指导他诵读《楚辞》《左传》《幼学琼林》《古文观止》《十三经》《古文释义》《龙文鞭影》和唐诗、唐宋文等。初学对句，杨宪益即能口出"乳燕剪残红杏雨，流莺啼断绿杨烟"这样的佳句。杨宪益虽然受的是传统旧式教育，但在魏汝舟的影响下，对新学思想也不拒斥，阅读了胡适、鲁迅、周作人等新文学作家的许多作品，年仅 11 岁时就写出《驳〈文学改良刍议〉》，批判胡适的文学改革主张，偏爱鲁迅和周作人白话文作品的思想深刻、语言简洁。

杨宪益中学就读于天津新学书院(Tientsin Anglo-Chinese College)，学校的英籍老师均为有大学学位的基督教传教士，英国文学、物理、化学、世界史、地理和数学等课程全部使用英文课本，用英语授课。上高中之前，杨宪益的英文水平已经相当出色，能够直接阅读大量英国文学作品和英译的西方文学作品，如司各特的叙事诗《洛京瓦尔》(*Lochinvar*)、西班牙作家阿索林《西班牙一小时》的英文译本、麦考雷有关古代罗马的叙事诗《贺雷修》(*Horatio at the Bridge*)以及莎士比亚的《凯撒大帝》(*Julius Caesar*)选段。上高中后，杨宪益阅读英文书籍的速度和数量都达到惊人的程度，广泛的阅读使他痴迷上古希腊文学作品，他毅然决定毕业后远赴英伦攻读古典文学课程。1934 年，杨宪益随天津新学书院英籍教员 C. H. B. 朗曼夫妇，取道日本、美国，前往英国伦敦。

初到英国，杨宪益除了花大量时间跟随私人教师学习古希腊文和拉丁文，其他时间全都用在阅读上。仅仅五个月后，杨宪益就顺利通过牛津大学莫顿学院的希腊文和拉丁文笔试，但因考试官的偏见，直到一年后他才得以正式入学。英伦留学期间，杨宪益经挚友伯纳德·梅洛介绍，认识了一位名叫格莱迪斯·玛格丽特·泰勒(Gladys Margaret Tayler)的美丽英国姑娘。与当时的英国女孩不同，格莱迪丝对中国特别感兴趣，热心参加中国学会的一切活动，对日本侵略中国这件事格外愤怒，她就是后来成为杨宪益的终生伴侣和事业上最亲密的同道的戴乃迭(Gladys Yang)。1919 年 1 月 19 日，戴乃迭(格莱迪丝与杨宪益结婚后的中文名字)出生在北京，7 岁时在母亲和姐姐希尔达的陪同下返回英国接受教育，此后在柴郡读了一年女子小学，在肯特郡教会女校沃森斯道霍尔（Walthamstow Hall）学校度过了十年寄宿生涯。1937 年秋，她以优等生身份获得国际奖学金，进入牛津大学攻读法国文学。

　　戴乃迭的父亲约翰·伯纳德·泰勒（John Bernard Tayler，中文名戴乐仁）是一位传教士，大学毕业以后加入伦敦传教士会社，被派到中国。在杨宪益的中学母校天津新学书院和燕京大学执教十多年后，他前往当时十分贫穷的中国甘肃发起社会主义改良运动，收容无家可归的孤儿，为他们提供免费教育。父亲戴乐仁的理想主义情怀和对贫困中国发展的关怀，无形中影响了戴乃迭后来对世界的认识和对中国的无限同情与理解。戴乃迭进入牛津大学时，正值日本大肆侵略中国，战火蔓延到了中国的大部分土地上。英国人的正义感加上她的中国情愫使戴乃迭成了一个坚定的抗日派。杨宪益担任中国学会主席时，戴乃迭担任学会秘书。她帮助杨宪益组织中国学会的会议，记录下每次会议的重要内容。这些活动迅速拉近了两位年轻人之间的距离，这对异国青年很快陷入热恋。为了"才华横溢的杨"，戴乃迭决定放弃法国文学专业，选择中国文学作为她终生的事业。当时，牛津大学刚刚开始设置中国文学荣誉学位，戴乃迭是攻读该学位的第一个学生。戴乃迭的中文导师休斯（Ernest Richard Hughes，中文名：修中诚①）是一位仁慈、开明，具有绅士风度的老先生，对人文主义特别是中国儒家学说怀有浓厚兴趣，致力于向英国及西方全面系统地介绍儒家思想的发展史、著名儒学家和主要儒家经典。在授业导师休斯的指导和杨宪益的影响下，戴乃迭在中国文学方面进步迅速，以优异成绩获得二等荣誉学位。

　　1940 年，杨宪益、戴乃迭从牛津大学毕业，谢绝哈佛大学的任教邀请，

---

① 1939 年，在牛津大学汉学讲座教授空悬的情况下，时任中国哲学和宗教讲师的修中诚主持开展了牛津大学汉学发展史上的一次重大改革，创立汉学科（Chinese Honour School），确定本科四年制的课程内容和考试方法，设置正式学位。戴乃迭为牛津大学汉学科荣誉学位第一人。后来，因翻译《红楼梦》而饮誉世界的英国汉学家霍克思在修中诚指导下专攻中文，是牛津汉学科招收的第二位学生。

回到战火中的中国。此后,二人先后辗转任教于中央大学柏溪分校、贵阳师范学院和成都光华大学。1943年秋,经挚友卢冀野引荐,杨宪益、戴乃迭接受国立编译馆时任馆长梁实秋的聘请前往任职,专门从事将中国经典翻译成英文的工作,正式开启夫妻二人携手合作的职业翻译生涯。

国立编译馆时期是杨宪益、戴乃迭一生中的高产期之一。短短三年时间,除了在内迁北碚的复旦大学(渝校)和国立戏剧专科学校兼职教书以外,夫妻合作翻译了差不多40卷(从战国到西汉部分)的《资治通鉴》、《中国戏剧简史》,晚清小说《老残游记》①;陶渊明、温庭筠和李贺的诗;唐代变文《燕子赋》《维摩诘所述经变文》。他们还从凡百卷的《法苑珠林》里编译了梁武帝时代有关神不灭的辩论,翻译了苗族创世诗《苗本事谣》、艾青和田间的诗若干首、郭沫若历史剧本《屈原》和阳翰笙剧本《天国春秋》……此外,杨宪益将多位时代不同、风格迥异的外国作家、诗人的作品译成中文,如兰姆《伊利亚随笔》中的两篇、辛格的几部独幕剧、赫里克的一些诗等。②

抗战胜利后,杨、戴夫妇随编译馆搬迁到南京,由于时局动荡,他们较少有精力进行翻译,其间的零星译稿大多散失。他们合译的《老残游记》(南京独立出版社,1947)和杨宪益独自翻译的《近代英国诗钞》(中华书局,1948)在这一时期相继刊印。1952年,夫妇俩应新闻总署国际新闻局副局长刘尊棋邀请,调往外文出版社任职,重新回到专职翻译岗位。当时外文出版社创办英文版《中国文学》杂志,开始系统地向西方社会介绍中国文学作品。刘尊棋有一个宏大的计划,打算把从《诗经》《楚辞》到清末的150种古典文学作品和鲁迅以降的100种当代文学介绍给西方世界。把中国独有的文学、文化介绍到西方,促进东西方文化的真正交流和融

---

① 据英国学者比尔·詹纳的研究,夫妇二人在完成牛津大学学业返回中国前就已完成了"20世纪早期的一部巧合丛生、场景鲜明的小说——刘鹗的《老残游记》"的英译,并于归国之际带回。(参见:比尔·詹纳. 戴乃迭. 李晶,译//杨宪益. 我有两个祖国——戴乃迭和她的世界. 桂林:广西师范大学出版社,2003:154.)

② 杨宪益. 杨宪益自传. 薛鸿时,译. 北京:人民日报出版社,2010:154-155.

合,正是杨宪益愿意付出毕生精力的事业,因此,调任北京后,夫妇二人夜以继日,在很短的时间内就翻译出不少中国古代和现代文学作品,这一时期也因此成为杨、戴合作翻译历史上又一个高产期。

1953—1956年,杨宪益夫妇以惊人的速度翻译了大量中文作品,《离骚》《唐代传奇选》《儒林外史》《长生殿》《古代寓言》《宋明评话选》《汉魏六朝小说选》《关汉卿杂剧选》等古典文学,以及《王贵与李香香》《阿Q正传》《太阳照在桑干河上》《白毛女》《鲁迅短篇小说选》《阿诗玛》《三里湾》《李家庄的变迁》《青春之歌》《暴风骤雨》(与他人合译)、《原动力》《朱自清散文》《下一次开船港》《红旗谱》《百合花》《荷花淀》《鲁迅选集》(1—3卷)、《风云初记》《中国小说史略》等译作陆续出版。这段时间里,杨宪益、戴乃迭还与沙博理(Sidney Shapiro,1915—2014)一起承担了英文杂志《中国文学》几乎全部的翻译任务。在浩繁的中译英工作之余,杨宪益从拉丁文翻译了维吉尔的《牧歌》,从希腊文翻译了《阿里斯多芬喜剧二种》(与罗念生合译),从拉丁文翻译了普劳图斯的罗马喜剧《凶宅》(*Mostellaria*)。此外,他还翻译了萧伯纳的戏剧《凯撒和克莉奥佩特拉》(*Caesar and Cleopatra*)和《匹克梅梁》(*Pygmalion*)(收入《萧伯纳戏剧集》),从法文翻译了《地心游记》(与闻时清合译)等,为中国读者了解西方文化打开了一扇大门。这一阶段堪称杨宪益与戴乃迭毕生翻译事业最辉煌的时期。

1960年,得知杨宪益曾在牛津大学攻读过希腊文和拉丁文,中国科学院哲学社会科学部(现在的中国社会科学院)将杨宪益借调过去承担荷马史诗的翻译。《奥德修纪》翻译完成后,杨宪益回到外文出版社与戴乃迭全力投入《红楼梦》的英译工作,全书前一百回初译稿完成时,正值“文革”,夫妇二人蒙冤入狱四年,因此,他们的翻译事业一度中断。1972年出狱恢复名誉后,杨宪益与戴乃迭无怨无悔地继续《红楼梦》的英译工作,终于在1974年译成全书。他们早期的一些译作也在此期陆续出版,包括杨宪益从中世纪法文译出的《罗兰之歌》、从拉丁文译出的《凶宅》,以及夫妇二人合译的鲁迅《野草》和《朝花夕拾》的英译本等。

1981年,杨宪益担任《中国文学》主编,受英国“企鹅丛书”启发,主持发起了旨在弥补西方对中国文学了解空白的"熊猫丛书",重新打开中国文学对外沟通的窗口。这套丛书里既有《诗经》《聊斋志异》《西游记》《三国演义》《镜花缘》等中国古代文学经典,也收录了《芙蓉镇》《沉重的翅膀》以及巴金、沈从文、孙犁、新凤霞、王蒙等人的现当代文学作品。此后,杨宪益忙于主持《中国文学》和"熊猫丛书"的辑定、出版工作,加上多次出访、讲学等,翻译作品少了许多,但在《中国文学》上仍不时有译作,如《龚自珍诗文选》、沈从文的《中国古代服饰研究》、唐弢的《西方影响与民族风格》等。

1989 年,戴乃迭患病卧床,杨宪益基本停止了翻译,悉心照料夫人的饮食起居,并应意大利友人约请开始着手英文自传 *White Tiger：An Autobiography of Yang Xianyi* 的撰写。1999 年 11 月,戴乃迭辞世,失去戴乃迭的杨宪益彻底搁置译笔,仅零星接受媒体、故交和学术界朋友的访谈与探视。2009 年 9 月,因杨宪益在翻译与对外文化传播和文化交流方面做出的巨大贡献,中国翻译协会授予他"翻译文化终身成就奖"。同年 11 月,杨宪益因罹患淋巴癌在北京煤炭总医院溘然离世。

杨宪益和戴乃迭毕生最突出的贡献就是联袂将大量中国文学作品译成英文：从《诗经》到中国现当代文学,时间跨度长达 2600 多年,译著为 70 余种 800 多万字,散见于各文集中的译文几十万字,此外还有已出版的外国文学译成中文的 9 种几十万字,总翻译著作字数逾千万字。他们翻译的《离骚》至今屹立在欧洲各大学的图书馆书架上；他们率先将《史记》推向西方世界；他们翻译的《鲁迅选集》是外国高校教学研究通常采用的蓝本；他们翻译的三卷本《红楼梦》(*A Dream of Red Mansions*),与英国两位汉学家霍克思、闵福德合译的五卷本《石头记》(*The Story of the Stone*)共同成为西方世界最认可的《红楼梦》译本……杨宪益、戴乃迭夫妇为中外文化交流,尤其是中国文化走向世界做出了卓越贡献。他们翻译的中国文学作品,从先秦文学到现当代文学,跨度之大、数量之多、质量之高、影响之深,中国翻译界无人企及。许多外国读者、翻译家,乃至汉学研究者正是通过他们合作翻译的中国文化、文学经典,才得以走近和触摸到厚重、悠远的古代中国,顽强抗争的近代中国和走向复兴的当代中国。

二、杨宪益、戴乃迭翻译思想概述

杨宪益、戴乃迭毕生专注于翻译实践工作,为人低调、谦和,并不认为自己做了多么杰出的贡献,鲜少谈论自己的翻译经验,因此给之后的杨宪益、戴乃迭翻译思想研究带来了不小的困难。目前,学界对杨宪益、戴乃迭翻译思想的梳理相对较少,更遑论形成相对完整的体系。在对两位翻译大家的翻译实践进行梳理和研究的过程中,通过细读他们合作翻译的大量作品及相关序跋、杨宪益译余随笔《零墨新笺》和《零墨续笺》,以及杨宪益参加各类翻译座谈会、接受媒体访谈和在传记中的随感阐发,下文试图在文字的吉光片羽中归纳、提炼出杨、戴二人合作翻译中秉持的观点。由于戴乃迭的翻译之论更加少见,其翻译思想融于杨宪益的思想之中,融于他们的翻译作品中。为行文简洁,下文就概称为杨宪益翻译思想。

1.“信”“达”翻译观

杨宪益为人谦逊,即便参加座谈会或接受访谈,提及夫妇俩的翻译经验,也都是非常低调地几句话带过。比较系统、明确地谈及翻译观点的一共有三次。[①] 一次是 1980 年 3 月,应澳中理事会、澳大利亚文化委员会文学部邀请,与妻子戴乃迭、作家俞林、学者王佐良组成中国作家协会代表团赴澳大利亚参加文化交流活动。接受当地报纸《时代日报》等多家媒体

---

① 这三次分别参见如下文献:

　　a.肯尼思·亨德森.“土耳其挂毯的反面”.陈柏鑫,译//王佐良.翻译:思考与试笔.北京:外语教学与研究出版社,1997:84-89.

　　b.杨宪益.略谈我从事翻译工作的经历与体会//金圣华,黄国彬.因难见巧:翻译名家经验谈.北京:中国对外翻译出版公司,1998:79-84.

　　c.杨宪益.关键是“信”“达”//萧伯纳.凯撒和克莉奥佩特拉.杨宪益,译.北京:人民文学出版社,2002:1-2(译者序).

采访时,被问及"是否认为译者应改写原文",杨宪益表示:"翻译的时候不能作过多的解释。译者应尽量忠实于原文的形象,既不要夸张,也不要夹带任何别的东西。当然,如果翻译中确实找不到等同的东西,那就肯定会牺牲一些原文的意思。但是,过分强调创造性则是不对的,因为这样一来,就不是在翻译,而是在改写文章了。"杨宪益认为,如果在译文中对某一人物所说的话或者对某一事物的描写加进太多的东西,译者就可能会背离原文,"那样一来,翻译就不成其为翻译了,我们必须非常忠实于原文"。即便在谈到译者与目标读者的关系时,杨宪益依然坚持:"我们在竭尽全力把原文的意思忠实地传达给另一读者,使他们能尽量理解原作的内容。我们不应过多地把自己的观点放进去,否则我们就不是在翻译而是在创作了。"能够看出,杨宪益不仅在文学观念上受鲁迅兄弟的影响非常大,在翻译理念上,也始终认同他们所倡导的翻译之"诚",在翻译过程中不能"任情删易",要使译文"弗失文情"。"诚"即是"信",杨宪益力主翻译应当忠实于原文的内容,不能过多阐释或添加,如果还是翻译的话,译者"必须非常忠实于原文",并力争做到不失"信"于译文读者。

第二次是 1994 年,应香港翻译学者金圣华之请,杨宪益撰写《略谈我从事翻译工作的经历与体会》,在文中他秉持一以贯之的低调,说"我的思想从来逻辑性不强,自己也很怕谈理论,所以也说不出什么大道理"。他粗略地描画了从事外译汉和汉译英工作的经历,结合当时译界较多讨论的"翻译是艺术还是科学"问题,杨宪益认为,"从搞文学翻译的角度来说,说翻译是一门科学,不如说它是一种艺术,或者说是一种技巧"。虽然是从其毕生所开展的双向翻译实践中得出的至真经验,杨宪益仍十分谦逊地说,"当然这也可能是我个人的偏见"。在论及外国文学作品汉译时,因他本人翻译出版的外国文学作品多为诗歌、史诗和戏剧等注重节奏、韵律的文学体裁,因此对外国诗歌汉译做了特别说明:

> 翻译外国文学作品为中文,有的译者在翻译诗歌的过程中,有时太注重原作的形式方面。比如说,英国诗过去常用五音节抑扬格,每音节分为轻重两音。这是由于英文同中文不同,每个字不限于一个

音,每个音又分轻重。我们如果一定要按照原文的格律,结果必然是要牺牲原文的内容,或者增加字,或者减少字,这是很不合算的。每国文字不同,诗歌规律自然也不同。追求诗歌格律上的"信",必然造成内容上的不够"信"。我本人过去也曾多次尝试用英诗格律译中文作品,结果总觉得吃力不讨好。现在有许多人还在试图用中文写抑扬格的诗,这是很可惜的。①

从上面的文字,我们能够清晰地看到杨宪益对其始终追求的译文之"信"的具体思考——"信"于原文内容还是"信"于原文格律。

第三次是在 86 岁高龄,完成毕生千万字的翻译实践之后,被问及"翻译经验"时,基于其对中国古代文化史的研究,杨宪益第一次明确提出自己的翻译"信""达"观:

> 我搞中译外和外译中的文学翻译工作一转眼也过了半个多世纪,算是一个老资格了。很多人都来过,问我有什么翻译工作的经验。我很怕谈什么翻译体会,因为我自己实际上觉得没有什么值得一提的新经验。我们中国人不但自己有过几千年的传统文化,而且有过汉唐以来两千年左右的翻译外来文化的好传统。但是过去从鸠摩罗什到玄奘的翻译经验,总结起来,也不过只有两个字,就是"信"与"达",两者都很重要,缺一不可。向我国介绍西方文化名著的严复曾说过:"译事三难信达雅。"其实"雅"只是"达"的一部分。"达"而能"雅",才是真正的"达"。②

虽然已是译界巨擘,杨宪益仍然谦虚地说自己实际上"没有什么值得一提的新经验",主张回到中国古代的翻译事件中寻找翻译智慧,认为"我们中国人不但自己有过几千年的传统文化,而且有过汉唐以来两千年左

---

① 杨宪益. 略谈我从事翻译工作的经历与体会 // 金圣华,黄国彬. 因难见巧:翻译名家经验谈. 北京:中国对外翻译出版公司,1998:84.

② 参见:杨宪益. 关键是"信""达" // 萧伯纳. 凯撒和克莉奥佩特拉. 杨宪益,译. 北京:人民文学出版社,2002:1-2(译者序).

右的翻译外来文化的好传统"。这一主张对于 20 世纪 90 年代国内翻译学界出现的"唯西是从"的理论不自信的做法可谓是有力的反拨。虽然并没有深入展开,也没有使用艰深晦涩的理论性文字,杨宪益归纳说,"过去从鸠摩罗什到玄奘的翻译经验,总结起来,也不过只有两个字,就是'信'与'达'"。在杨宪益看来,"信"与"达"两者同样重要,缺一不可。杨宪益的"信""达"翻译观虽然师法严复,却并非食古不化、照抄照仿,他对严复的"信达雅"三字诀有自己的见地——"雅"只是"达"的一部分,"达"而能"雅",才是真正的"达"。

　　杨宪益非常重视"信",恪守"'信'是第一位,没有'信'就谈不上翻译"①的原则。杨宪益所言的"信",包含三个方面的内容:信于原文形象,信于译文读者,信于原文格律、节奏。杨宪益强调的"信"是对译文终端的关注,与传统意义上"对等"或"忠实"原文的做法不可等同视之。在具体翻译践行中,杨宪益的"信"是"不以形式而损害内容"②。关于这一点,杨宪益在《略谈我从事翻译工作的经历与体会》一文中明确陈述了其对西方诗歌译成中文的观点。基于对中西方语言特点的分析和数十年中西方诗歌鉴赏与写作的经历,杨宪益深信,"追求诗歌格律上的'信',必然造成内容上的不够'信'"。杨宪益对荷马史诗《奥德修纪》有深入研究,认为荷马史诗属六音节格律诗,每行约有十一个轻重音,不用尾韵,但节奏感很强,显然是为朗诵的目的而创造出来的,类似我国的民间弹弦说唱艺术,为了在中国读者中传递出这种等同的效果,他对自己最终采取散文体译诗做了如下说明:"在开始翻译之前也曾考虑是译成诗体好呢,还是译成散文好,最后还是决定译成散文,这是因为原文的音乐性和节奏在译文中反正是无法表达出来的,用散文翻译也许还可以更好使人欣赏古代艺人讲故

---

① 郭晓勇. 平静若水淡如烟:深切缅怀翻译界泰斗杨宪益先生. 中国翻译,2010(1):47.

② 杨清平. 家园的寻觅——隐喻视角下的杨宪益外汉翻译研究. 开封:河南大学博士学位论文,2012:57-60.

事的本领。"①

杨宪益指出："古人说了三个字：信、达、雅。当然，光'信'不'达'也是不可能，那是不要人懂。"②也就是说，光"信"不"达"，令人无法读懂，也就谈不上"信"。由"信"至"达"，翻译者需要具备高超的双语驾驭能力和跨文化体察能力。

杨、戴夫妇的翻译贡献在于"让我们能够对东西方文明的传播做一个学术比较，他们推动了中国文化真正走向世界，他们帮西方读者消除或减少因中西方巨大的历史文化差异而造成的心理隔膜，帮助他们了解中国文明，帮助他们了解当代中国，堪称中华民族的文化英雄"③。他们在文本、文字间留下的翻译智慧，彰显着对中外文学、文明互鉴的诗意思考，这些翻译思考既有对"可译性"的抱持，也有对跨文化传播、读者审美接受与译文质量求真的全面考量。

2."可译性"的思考

杨宪益夫妇虽未著书立说探讨关于翻译的本质问题，但事实上，在千万字翻译实践所蕴藉的翻译诗学思想中，他们始终抱持着"一切都是可以翻译的"这一朴素语言、文化交流信念。杨宪益在不同场合谈过："翻译是沟通不同民族语言的工具。不同地区或国家的人都是人，人类的思想感情都是可以互通的。在这个意义上来说，什么东西应该都可以翻译，不然的话，人类就只可以闭关守国，老死不相往来了。"④在自传和访谈中，杨宪益多次详细介绍过 20 世纪 50 年代初他与毛泽东主席就《离骚》英译的短暂交谈：

　　1953 年或 1954 年初，我和其他科学家、作家、艺术家共计二十人，应邀去会见毛主席。会见的地点是中南海……我至今仍清楚地

① 荷马. 奥德修纪. 杨宪益,译. 北京:中国工人出版社,2008:27.
② 杨宪益. 我与英译本《红楼梦》//郑鲁南. 一本书和一个世界(第二集). 北京:昆仑出版社,2008:2.
③ 赵畅. 杨宪益逝世给我们留下的思考. 观察与思考,2009(24):56.
④ 杨宪益. 去日苦多. 青岛:青岛出版社,2009:99.

记得当时的情景。我们全体人员被领进一个大厅,屏息敛气地在那里等着伟人的到来。首先进来的是周恩来总理,他和我们无拘无束地谈话。……接着我听到有人宣布:毛主席来了。我们站成一排等待接见。毛主席从我们面前的一扇门里走进来。他以缓慢的步伐向我们走来,面露微笑,显得羞涩。他身体早已发福,但看上去非常健康。他走过来,一个一个地和我们握手,周恩来跟在他身边,依次把我们向他一一介绍。当他走到我跟前时,周总理说我是一位翻译家,已经把《离骚》译成英文。毛主席热爱中国古典诗歌,《离骚》是产生在中国南方的一篇古诗,正是毛主席最喜爱的作品之一。他伸出汗津津的手掌和我热烈地握了握说:

"你觉得《离骚》能够翻译吗,嗯?"

"主席,谅必所有的文学作品都是可以翻译的吧?"我不假思索地回答。

他停住脚步,像是想就此问题再说些什么。但他转眼间又不想说了,他微微一笑,再次和我握手后就去和其他人打招呼了。后来我想,他显然不相信像《离骚》这样的伟大诗篇能够翻译成其他语言,当然,他怀疑得有理。尽管我为翻译《离骚》花了心力,但是,就连我都怀疑,翻译诗歌是否能够做到逼真。毛主席本人就写诗,他又不是不懂。真可惜,他那天没有详细说出他对这个问题的想法。他和全体人员都握过手后就离开了,我没有机会和他讨论这个问题。[①]

从上述引文,不难看出,毛主席的话显然透露出对诗歌可译的怀疑态度,然而从青年时期翻译《离骚》开始就秉承着向西方人展示中国文学、文化成就的杨宪益宛如文化场上的勇士,一往直前,不假思索地回应毛主席关于"可译性"的哲学之问——"谅必所有的文学作品都是可以翻译的

---

① Yang, Xianyi. *White Tiger: An Autobiography of Yang Xianyi*. Hong Kong: The Chinese University of Hong Kong Press, 2002: 189-190. 中文译文参见:杨宪益. 漏船载酒忆当年. 薛鸿时,译. 北京:北京十月文艺出版社,2001:178-180.

吧"。杨宪益用简单、直接的方式回答毛主席的提问，并不完全因为会面时间短而仓促，"实乃杨宪益本即不愿将译事复杂化，而主张简单地看问题"①。事实上，杨宪益在此次会面之后，历经困顿始终不曾放弃翻译实践，本身也证明了他始终抱持的翻译理念——"什么东西都可以翻"②。这一论断虽然朴素，却彰显着翻译的本质与本真。

随着人生阅历与翻译实践的丰富，杨宪益意识到"《楚辞》或其他文学作品，尤其是诗歌，能不能翻译成其他文字，而保留其神韵，的确是一个难说的问题"。经历了国内外喧嚣一时的翻译是科学、艺术还是技术的大讨论之后，杨宪益进一步明确阐述他对"可译性"困窘/局限的思考，"人类自从分成许多国家和地区，形成不同文化和语言几千万年以来，各个民族的文化积累又各自形成不同特点，每个民族对其周围事物的看法又会有各自不同的联想，这往往是外国人很难理解的"③。比如，《诗经·小雅·采薇》篇的"昔我往矣，杨柳依依，今我来思，雨雪霏霏"，其中"杨柳"意象所引发的联想和传递的情绪，不熟悉中国文化的外国人也许会对中国园林或绘画中的杨柳图案产生一定的喜好之情，但却很难领会杨柳所寄托的中华民族情思。他还通过对阿瑟·韦利的《诗经》译本评点，指出韦利译本虽然十分了不起，却由于文化传统的隔阂，把许多专属于中国传统的情境弄得过于英国化，频繁使用"城堡""骑士"等中华传统中没有的形象，把中国周朝的农民塑造成田园诗中描绘的欧洲中世纪农民形象。杨宪益对杨柳、城堡、骑士等文化意象和《诗经》整体气氛、情境等的翻译批评，落脚点就在于文化要素的不完全可译问题。

2009 年 8 月 4 日，杨宪益接受《南方人物周刊》记者蒯乐昊采访，被问及"说说《红楼梦》吧，跟《离骚》可不可翻的问题一样，《红楼梦》翻译成另外一种语言，可能难度也很大吧？里面那些多谐音的伏笔、暗示、隐

---

① 李伶伶，王一心. 五味人生——杨宪益传. 哈尔滨：北方文艺出版社，2015：122.
② 参见 2009 年 8 月 4 日《南方人物周刊》对杨宪益的采访.
③ 杨宪益. 略谈我从事翻译工作的经历与体会//金圣华，黄国彬. 因难见巧：翻译名家经验谈. 北京：中国对外翻译出版公司，1998：82-83.

喻……"提问者没有说完的这句话,显然代表了绝大多数阅读、关注《红楼梦》英译的研究者心声。杨宪益对此的回答虽不似五十多年前那般斩钉截铁,答案却也十分积极而明确:"也可以解决,在英语里找到相对应的,能翻的就翻,翻不了的就加注解。"①

正是基于他对"可译性"的认知,杨宪益在毕生的翻译实践中,始终表现出一种举重若轻的大家风范。杨宪益虽然对旧体诗、比较文学和历史学领域都有涉猎,但在世人眼中,他首先是位翻译家,在任何地方、任何人对他的介绍中,排在第一位的永远是翻译家,接下来才是学者、诗人等身份。然而,虽然译作等身,他本人却并不把译事看得过重,认为翻译"无非是把一部作品从某一种文字翻译到第二种文字,就是这么回事"②。对于翻译《资治通鉴》这样的巨著,杨宪益自信地坦言:"一个月翻一万多字是很简单的事情……我以前翻过半白话的书,像《老残游记》《儒林外史》等等,这些都是很简单的,拿过来就翻。《红楼梦》也很简单,我口述,戴乃迭打字机打出一个初稿,然后再把文字改一改,就这样。"③杨宪益如此描述毕生的重大翻译事件和令夫妇二人享誉世界的《红楼梦》英译,并非说翻译可以马虎从事,而只是不愿意把它说得过重,拔擢过高,谈论得过于复杂。这不仅与他为人的淡然与谦逊有关,更主要的是,他毕生卓越的中外文学、文化知识,纵横捭阖的东西交通学识与娴熟的双语表达能力使他有了这份举重若轻的底气。晚年接受采访时,杨宪益谈及翻译更是一以贯之的语气与态度:"翻译没有什么,翻译就跟做木匠一样。"寥寥数语,实则回应了 20 世纪中后期世界范围内展开的那场关于翻译性质的大讨论——翻译是科学还是艺术?于他而言,翻译是一种艺术,更是一种技巧、一门匠艺。

---

① 杨宪益. 从《离骚》开始,翻译整个中国:杨宪益对话集. 北京:人民日报出版社,2011:171.

② 李伶伶,王一心. 五味人生——杨宪益传. 哈尔滨:北方文艺出版社,2015:123.

③ 李伶伶,王一心. 五味人生——杨宪益传. 哈尔滨:北方文艺出版社,2015:170-171.

3.读者审美接受观

牛津留学期间,杨宪益曾以游戏和审美的心态进行过《离骚》的英译。通过自己的考证,杨宪益认定浪漫主义诗篇《离骚》是一部伪作,真正的作者不是屈原,而是比屈原晚几个世纪的汉代淮南王刘安。[①] 因此,杨宪益始终以模仿英雄偶体诗翻译这首诗为得意之事。在他看来,既然原作者身份都存疑,译作就更可以天马行空。虽然杨宪益后来对翻译的认知与思考发生过不少变化,但每每接受访谈,谈及年轻时期的这一创举,杨宪益从未对其使用的翻译策略产生过怀疑或否定。由此能够看出,杨宪益初涉译事就已经有了对读者审美接受和文学翻译传播效果的深刻思考。

20世纪50年代后期,中国的文学、文化建设"逐渐被政治化、计划化、纯洁化,并最终在多种复杂因素的合力之下走向封闭统一的'一体化'时代"[②],杨宪益多次说到自己只是"受雇的翻译匠",该翻译什么并不由自己做主,即便在这样的大气候中,杨宪益仍不愿放弃自己的理念与精神追求。在文本翻译过程中仍然心系读者,竭尽可能行使译者的权利。1960年《中国文学》第1期刊发杨宪益、戴乃迭翻译的《牡丹亭》,以17世纪上半期毛晋《六十种曲》所收录的吕硕园删订版《牡丹亭》[③]为底本。《中国文学》杂志的编辑之所以选择"硕园本"为杨、戴的翻译底本,一则因为"硕园本"相对于通行本减少的戏份多是原作中那些"低下的情愫"、冷闲的场子,二则因为减省的部分以直白的方式影射到与当时道德规范相抵牾的"性"和可能会丑化北方少数民族语言和习俗的表述。应当说,杨、戴翻译《牡丹亭》之时正是国内政治意识形态对文学、文化作品调控作用最强的

---

① 他在20世纪80年代后期写给挚友荒芜的信中,仍然坚持说:"首先我从来不承认屈原真有其人,我认为,那是刘安编造的。"(见:李克玉. 记忆也是货真价实的精神遗产//张世林. 想念杨宪益. 北京:新世界出版社,2016:148.)杨宪益还在信中结合自己的史学、古文学知识进行了分析。对于这一学术论争及其观点准确与否,本书并不着意深入探讨。此处引用,只是为了帮助阐释杨宪益大胆仿拟英雄偶句诗体英译《离骚》的深层理据。

② 吴秀明,等. 当代中国文学六十年. 杭州:浙江文艺出版社,2009:9.

③ 相较于汤显祖原本55出,硕园改本仅43出,是对通行本进行"删""合""调"而成的。

时候,政治意识形态与作品的艺术性之间呈现巨大的张力。作为译者,杨、戴夫妇并无权限选择待译作品,也没有机会参与待译作品版本选择,但二人也绝不是淹没于翻译活动中的抽象主体,而是同时混合两种或两种以上文化信仰的实践主体,有着明确的读者观照意识。

细读"硕园本"《牡丹亭》和《中国文学》上的英译版本,不难发现杨氏夫妇在"硕园本"《牡丹亭》英译的文本内部主要采用了面向译语系统、以可接受性为主导的翻译规范。因《中国文学》版面篇幅限制,杨、戴夫妇在"硕园本"43出剧目中,按照西方爱情小说的模式,留下《标目》《闺塾》《惊梦》《寻梦》《写真》《诘病》《闹殇》《拾画》《幽媾》《回生》《婚走》等11出剧目,按线性推进故事情节:杜丽娘因梦生情,寻梦不得,忧郁而疾,丹青留后,撒手人寰;柳梦梅因缘拾画,艳遇倩魂,开棺救女,收获姻缘。其中最具意味的是译者对《幽媾》和《婚走》这两出剧目的保留,前者是对恋人精神之爱与肉体结合的肯定,后者则按照西方爱情故事"私奔"的浪漫结局改写了东方传奇,在一定程度上迎合了西方读者的心理预期,可谓西方诗学在翻译中的投射。同时,为符合外国读者的阅读习惯和审美期待,杨宪益、戴乃迭还以西方戏剧诗学的标准对《牡丹亭》的戏剧形式进行了文本内操纵与改写。中国戏剧起源于传统说唱艺术,具有程式化特征——人物上场必先自报家门,吟诗作曲一番才切入正题,这也是"唱、念、做、打"在文本层面最粗浅的表现形式。剧中角色,有生、旦、净、末、丑等之分;角色表演,各具特色;每种曲牌表情达意,内涵各异。西方戏剧虽然也起源于祭祀性舞蹈,但其在发展过程中却基本抛弃了歌舞结合的形态。为避免西方读者阅读时感到过分陌生,杨、戴《牡丹亭》英译本中删除了每场的词曲牌名和下场诗,将生、外、末、旦、贴等表演行当名转换成具体的人物姓名。在"唱""念"关系的处理上,按西方话剧的形式进行处理,不分"唱""念",将唱词和诗文统一以诗来对待,从而减少诗学差异给西方读者造成的冲击。①

_____

① 以上论述主要参考:赵征军. 杨宪益、戴乃迭英译《牡丹亭》研究. 三峡大学学报,2015(3):104-109.

翻译不论是从文化角度还是从历史角度来看，都承载着某种利益。有跨文化传播意识的译者，胸怀对目标语读者的接受观照，出于文化译介与传播的目的，多多少少都会对原文进行话语干预，在译文中通过删减、增益、文体润饰等方式塞进各种异于原文的"私货"。为了使译文可以被目标语系统及其读者接受，使译文合乎译语文学系统规范，译者对文本的话语掺杂、修改、删减等操纵不仅是可接受的，而且也值得提倡。孤立的、没有进入读者流通领域的译本是没有生命力的，只有进入目标语社会语境、被目标语读者接受的文本才是"直接生效的"。对此，杨宪益显然有着超前的体认，虽然夫妇二人主要的文化译介活动大多发生在读者接受理论之前，但他们在文本翻译过程中对读者接受的关注，体现了明确的审美接受意识和文化传播意识。

4.超前的文化翻译观

早在世界范围内的翻译研究"文化转向"之前，杨宪益对翻译承载的文化责任、译者的文化立场、意译与直译彰显的文化态度等问题就有着十分明确的思考。可以说，杨宪益的翻译思想是超前的，从译事伊始就蕴含着对文化翻译的承诺。初译《离骚》，杨宪益用实际行动把自己的事业定义在文化输出的更高层面上而非简单的语言转换，将之视为弘扬民族传统文化的责任。入职国立编译馆，开始翻译生涯，杨宪益与戴乃迭是时任负责人梁实秋把中国经典著作翻译成英文介绍给西方这一伟大规划的具体实施人。随后的三年是杨氏夫妇一生中的高产期，他们共同翻译了几十卷《资治通鉴》和一部《中国戏剧简史》，翻译了晚清小说《老残游记》，陶渊明、温庭筠和李贺的诗，唐代变文《燕子赋》《维摩诘所述经变文》……中华人民共和国成立初期，刘尊棋有一个宏伟的对外文化出版计划，力图把中国独有的文化介绍到西方，促使东西方文化真正交流和融合。这个计划令杨宪益为之心动，毅然举家迁居北京，开启了人生的外文出版社时代。

1951年，叶君健受托筹备、创办英文版《中国文学》(*Chinese Literature*)，杨宪益、戴乃迭与沙博理是最初几期的主要译者。《中国文学》创刊号发表沙博理译孔厥、袁静长篇小说《新儿女英雄传》和杨宪益、戴乃迭译李季长诗《王贵与李香香》。1952年,《中国文学》刊发沙博理译赵树理小说《登记》和杨宪益、戴乃迭译《阿Q正传》。1953年出版的两期,先后刊发英译《太阳照在桑干河上》和歌剧《白毛女》以及《离骚》,揭开了《中国文学》登载中国古典文学译作的序幕。从创刊到1953年,《中国文学》不定期出版,1954年改为季刊出版,1958年改为双月刊,次年改为月刊,1964年首次推出《中国文学》法文版(季刊)。其间十余年是杨宪益、戴乃迭合作译介活动的高潮期和丰收期,他们的译介成果均刊发在《中国文学》上,特别值得一提的是,《中国文学》1964年第6、7、8期上接连刊载了彼时他们已完成的《红楼梦》英译稿。

在史无前例的"文革"期间,杨、戴蒙冤入狱。虽然饱受身体和心灵的巨大伤痛,他们出狱后仍矢志不渝地完成《红楼梦》的全译工作,并以全副精力投入中国文学译介事业,共同推动了《中国文学》第二个黄金期的到来。1979年至1986年,杨宪益先后担任《中国文学》的副主编、主编和顾问,负责对外文学推介的选题、编辑和定稿等工作,是此期中国文学走出去的总策划师和有抱负的推手。杨宪益对《中国文学》在内容和形式上进行了大刀阔斧的改革,英、法两个语种的《中国文学》总印数达到6万份以上;订户和读者主要分布区从亚非等第三世界国家逐渐延伸到欧美国家,遍及100多个国家和地区。整整半个世纪,《中国文学》共发行590期,介绍作家、艺术家2000多人次,译载文学作品3200篇。杨宪益与戴乃迭"在《中国文学》这块园地上躬耕近半世纪,在汉籍外译事业中尽力向世界传达出一个真实的中国文化形象,以及中国人鲜活的喜怒哀乐,为大量不同层次的对中国文化抱有兴趣却苦于无法直接阅读中文文本的世界读者,提供了走近中国、感知中国的有效门径"①。《中国文学》作为沟通中外文学、文化交流的重要媒介,极大地激发和满足了国外读者阅读、理解、体

---

① 何琳,赵新宇.*"卅载辛勤真译匠":杨宪益与《中国文学》*.文史杂志,2010(4):57.

味中国文学、文化的诉求,使一个真实而富有时代感的中国得以呈现,许多外国人了解中国文学就是从阅读英文版《中国文学》开始的。

杨宪益发起并主持旨在弥补西方对中国文学了解空白的"熊猫丛书"(The Panda Books),再次打开了中国文学对外沟通的窗口。丛书先将杂志上已译载过但还没单独出过书的作品结集出版,后又增加了新译的作品,主要用英、法两种文字出版中国当代、现代和古代的优秀作品,也出版了少量德、日等文版译本。丛书一推出,立即受到国外读者的广泛欢迎和好评,许多书重印或再版。截至 2009 年①,丛书共出版英文版图书 149种,法文版图书 66 种,日文版图书 2 种,德文版图书 1 种和中、英、法、日四语种对照版图书 1 种,共计 200 余种。介绍的古今作家近 100 位,如果将再版译本算在内,丛书出版的英文版图书共计 219 种。② 作为一个视野开阔的文化学者,杨宪益在选择翻译书目方面表现出卓越的文化战略眼光,"只要把他所翻译的那些作品串联起来便具有了文学史甚而文化史的价值"③。

基于《红楼梦》的英译实践,杨宪益曾说:"翻译不仅仅是从一种文字翻译成另一种文字,更重要的是文字背后的文化习俗和思想内涵,因为一种文化和另一种文化都有差别。"④他深知,翻译不只是语言层面的转换,更是语言背后的文化交流和对话。翻译承担着传播民族文化的责任,参与民族文化资本的积累。作为翻译主体,译者不能只是一台脱离时空的

---

① 2000 年底,中国文学出版社被撤销,杂志停刊,丛书转由外文出版社出版。2009年,德国法兰克福书展上,中国外文局所属外文出版社重新亮出"熊猫丛书"的金字招牌,首批推出 40 种英文版中国现当代作家作品,所有图书统一采用国际流行的开本及装帧风格,熊猫标识重新修改设计,故本文统计截止到 2009 年。

② 耿强. 中国文学走出去政府译介模式效果探讨——以"熊猫丛书"为个案. 中国比较文学,2014(1):67.

③ 叶廷芳. 斯人已去,风范长存//张世林. 想念杨宪益. 北京:新世界出版社,2016:81.

④ 杨宪益. 我与英译本《红楼梦》//郑鲁南. 一本书和一个世界(第二集). 北京:昆仑出版社,2008:2.

简单模仿的"翻译机器",而是所属民族文化的代言人,在翻译文本中言说着本民族的命运和际遇。杨宪益在进行中国文学、文化经典英译时,出于高度的文化自觉,多采用直译法,希冀英语读者借由翻译认识中国、了解中国。在他看来,"译者应尽量忠实于原文的形象,要以忠实的翻译'信'于中国文化的核心、中国文明的精神。这不仅仅是一个翻译中国文化遗产的问题,还涉及忠实传达中国文化的价值、灵魂,传达中国人的人生,他们的乐与悲、爱与恨、怜与怨、喜与怒"①。杨宪益、戴乃迭毕生合作翻译的重心在于中国文学英译,他们"始终将翻译活动置于东西文明互通互惠的发展视野,强调文化研究和文化传承的相互推助,在东西文学文化相互烛照中互勘的思想,才是其翻译思想的真髓所在"②。

三、译文选择原因与理据

新世纪以来,随着中国文学、文化"走出去"的大潮,杨宪益和戴乃迭、沙博理、许渊冲等中国文学外译大家开始吸引越来越多的研究关注,学界从中提炼出的翻译思想在一定程度上推动并丰富了中国翻译话语体系的建设。研究显示,无论是以"翻译家杨宪益",还是以"《红楼梦》英译"为检索项,2010 年至 2015 年间中国知网刊发研究成果均为 1980 年至 2015 年间研究成果总数的 70% 以上。可以说,自 2009 年杨宪益去世以来,这位被盛赞为"翻译了整个中国"的文化巨擘引发了一轮研究热潮。从先秦文学到中国现当代文学,杨宪益、戴乃迭夫妇在中外翻译界创造了一个奇迹,在中外文化交流史上树起了一座难以逾越的丰碑,他们用自己在中西方文化方面的博学,打通了两种语言、文化的障碍,为中国文学、文化"走出去",做出了不可估量的贡献。

杨宪益、戴乃迭夫妇一生完成 70 余种 800 多万字中国文学、文化作

---

① 任生名. 杨宪益的文学翻译思想散记. 中国翻译,1993(4):34.
② 何琳. 杨宪益与东方翻译文学. 文史杂志,2013(5):28.

品的英译,往往令人忽略了杨宪益"业余"承担的外译汉事业。杨宪益谈及一生承担的大部分汉译英工作,多次提到自己是"受雇的翻译匠",在待译文本选择方面有诸多不自由,而"业余"承担的外译汉作品则更多是他真正发自内心热爱、带有情感和温度的翻译作品,也能够更好地体现他对翻译实践和翻译行为的具体观念。此外,由于英译《红楼梦》带来的巨大影响,英译《红楼梦》成为夫妇二人一生翻译事业的代表性标签,常常造成对杨宪益、戴乃迭夫妇所译其他更多类型文学,如诗词曲赋和杂文、时文等的忽略。凡此种种遮蔽与忽略,无法完整勾勒出高山仰止的翻译巨擘形象,对翻译家毕生事业的深度与广度的描绘也因此不完整。有鉴于此,本书力图在有限的版面空间内选取最具"代表性"的译文,既有外国文学汉译,又有中国文学英译,既有先秦文学,也有现当代文学,体裁包括小说、诗歌、戏剧、散文、杂文等,以期管中窥豹,尽可能全面地呈现杨宪益夫妇毕生的翻译努力。

四、编选说明

关于本书中使用的语言文字,有如下几点在此提请读者注意。

(1)新中国成立以来,中国语言文字经历了三次较大规模的"规范化、标准化"调整。本书选编内容中,无论是杨宪益独自完成的外国文学汉译,还是其与夫人戴乃迭合作翻译的中国古代与现当代文学作品,多完成于20世纪60年代以前,在标点符号、一些文字的使用选择上与目前使用规范有所不同,如"的、地、得"不加区分使用,"石像"写作"石象","实验"写作"试验","做得到"写作"作得到","教你讲话"写作"叫你讲话","图像"写作"图象","做了一件错事"写作"作了一件错事","在火上熔化"写作"在火上溶化","痛得够呛"写作"痛得够戗","战栗"写作"战慄","糊涂"写作"胡涂","丁当"写作"叮当","发现"写作"发见","抄写"写作"钞写","辗转"写作"展转","预感"写作"豫感",等等。对于类似的表述,本书原则上保留了原貌,有助于读者更贴近那个时期的文化背景。

(2)杨宪益、戴乃迭译作中所使用的外国人名、地名,如阿里斯多芬(阿里斯托芬)、阿瑟·韦利(亚瑟·韦利)、梭罗门(所罗门)、叶茨(叶芝)、肖伯纳(萧伯纳)、屋大维(乌大维)、莎孚/沙浮(萨福)、凯撒(恺撒)、特罗地方/特洛亚城(特洛伊城)、《哈姆莱特》(《哈姆雷特》)等源自外语的专有名词,虽现在多已有规范译名或广为学术界使用的译名(括号内的表述),但本书并未进行"标准化""当代化"的更改,目的是向读者如实呈现译者的音译选择以及专有名词译名规范化的过程。

(3)对于译者的一些个人修辞表达习惯,比如在《古希腊抒情诗选》"后记"中,杨宪益频繁使用的分号(;),虽基本都作语义表达完成的修辞使用,相当于当下行文表达中使用的句号(。);又比如本书所选的英文翻译里,目前国内用的标准,出现 B.C. 的时候,一般两个年份都加"B.C."(如 476 B.C.—221B.C.),杨、戴的译文遵循了更符合英文世界出版的标准(如 476—221 B.C.)。以上种种,本书全部予以保留,希望能够最真实地呈现原作者、原作以及译者的审美观照意识。

(4)书中涉及的作者、译者姓名的英文表达,因所引述的版本不同而有些微不同,如鲁迅的英文名字有 Lu Xun 和 Lu Hsun 两种,杨宪益的英文名字有 Yang Xianyi 和 Yang Hsien-yi 两种。另外,鲁迅作品以及本书其他的个别选文中出现了一些错讹字,如《狂人日记》中"我翻开历史一查,这历史没有年代,歪歪斜斜的每叶上都写着仁义道德?几个字","每叶"实为"每页"之误;《孔乙己》中,"兼督"为"监督"之误;《祝福》中,四叔"大骂其新党"为"大骂起新党"之误,"匆匆的逃回四叔家中"为"匆匆的逃回四叔家中"之误。为了如实呈现原作与译作的原貌,除个别勘误外,本书基本予以保留。

2019 年是著名翻译家杨宪益(1915—2009)辞世 10 周年、戴乃迭(1919—1999)辞世 20 周年,也是戴乃迭诞生 100 周年。能够用学术的方式缅怀、纪念为中国文学和文化外译做出巨大贡献的"民族文化英雄",让人们铭记这一对"译界合欢花",也让本书有了特别的温度。为致敬杨宪益、戴乃迭为中国翻译事业做出的巨大贡献,本书选目共分为三编,分别是"外国文学汉译""中国古典文学英译"和"中国现当代文学英译",每一编选文尽可能多地涵盖杨、戴翻译实践的文本体裁类型,编排顺序依据译著首次出版刊印的时间先后,力图让读者能够在览阅书稿时感受到译者在数十年的翻译实践中选材和翻译理念的坚持或变化。

最后,感谢浙江大学中华译学馆对本书的经费资助,感谢浙江大学许钧教授多年来的学术引导与推动,感谢冯全功、卢巧丹老师在书稿辑定过程中的细致安排与联络,感谢浙江大学出版社编辑祁潇老师的细致缜密,感谢我所指导的宁波大学外国语学院 2018 级研究生刘园晨、蒋梦缘、单美霞、吴伟、张洁薇、张馨月利用寒假时间每人承担约 3 万字(词)的文本转录和初稿辑定工作,感谢他们以学术的方式与我一同走近、品读杨宪益、戴乃迭翻译文本……

第一编

外国文学汉译

莎士比亚剧中歌词一首[①]

> 尔父深埋五寻水，
> 骸骨依然神已死。
> 森森白骨成珊瑚，
> 沉沉双目化明珠。
> 化为异物身无恙，
> 幽奇瑰丽难名状。
> 鲛人日击丧钟鸣，
> 我今闻之丁当声。

[①] 译者注：此为莎士比亚名剧《暴风雨》中歌辞，予当时读中学，才十七岁，初读此剧，戏译之。

二

希腊女诗人莎孚残句一首[①]

有如林檎丹实滋，

垂垂独在最高枝，

举之不得长叹咨。

有如野蕊深山次，

牧人践过无留意，

紫英残碎枝交坠。

① 　译者注：此亦予十七岁时译作，当时不能读希腊文，只读过英译本，此是从英文
　　转译。
　　编者注：古希腊女诗人 Sappho，现在多译为"萨福"，为保持杨宪益译诗时的音译
　　选择，未统一为当下习见的译名。又："莎士比亚剧中歌词一首"与"希腊女诗人莎
　　孚残句一首"均选自：杨宪益. 银翘集——杨宪益诗集. 福州：福建教育出版社，
　　2007.

三

近代英国诗钞(十八首)^①

A. E. 豪斯曼四首
(A. E. Housman,1859—1936)

最可爱的树

最可爱的树,樱桃,如今
枝上已经垂下了繁英;
孤立在这幽林野径里
为这佳节穿上了白衣。

在我的七十流年里面
有二十年总不会再见,
从七十春天里去二十,
我只余下五十个春日。

五十春天既然是很少
去赏玩开花的树或草,

① 选自:杨宪益,译. 近代英国诗钞. 北京:人民文学出版社,1983.

我要到林径间去玩耍
去看樱桃树如雪的花。

栗树落下火炬似的繁英

栗树落下火炬似的繁英，
从山楂上，花随着风飞逝，
门关上了，雨使窗上模糊，
给我酒杯，这是暮春时季。

又一春天催短我们生命，
又完了一季被风雨摧毁。
明年的春天也许多晴天，
可是我们将是二十四岁。

我们当然并不是第一个
坐在酒店里，当风雨迅雷
把他们乐观的计划打碎，
咒着创世界的什么坏鬼。

是真的，上天是真不公平，
欺我们有限的一点希冀，
减少我们快乐，当你同我
久劳无功的向坟墓走去。

天不公平，可是给我酒杯，
我们母亲生的不是帝王，
我们所能有的属于凡人。
我们不能要天上的月亮。

如果今天此地雷雨阴阴，
明天阴雨将要远去他处，
旁人躯体将要感觉不快，
旁人心中将要感觉忧郁。

我们骄愤的形骸多忧患，
与永古俱来的，不能没有。
我们能受，我们必须忍受。
用肩头撑起这阴天，喝酒！

在我的故乡如我觉得无聊

在我的故乡，如我觉得无聊，
我还有方法安慰我的寂寥，
因为我心苦痛的缘故，大地
也为她所生的儿孙而哀泣。
还有矗立的山丘，千古常存，
分我痛苦，安慰有涯的人生。
在我随意游荡的每条路上。
与我一同走，向同一的方向，
有那幽美而将死去的华年，
很亲密的随从，在我的身边。
有时我在幽暗的山林经过，
我听见山榉实萧萧的下堕，
我又看见绛紫的番红花朵，
在秋天的幽谷里面怒放着，
或看见散在春暮的田野间，
白色的女裙花寂寂的安眠，

有如一湾反映天空的春水，
林里的蓝钟花笼着薄霭睡
在乡间的路上，除这些以外，
有不同季节，来消我的垒块。
可是在城里街上，我无处寻
如此的伴侣，除了那些闲人。
他们同时也不急急来接受，
即使他们情愿，旁人的忧愁
他们已有足够的了。我看见
在许多揣度我的眼睛里面，
因太缺少欢乐，而失了同情，
那一种心理的不治的重病。
为苦痛所逼迫，他们只能够
去怨恨他们的一切的朋友；
在他们自己死前，他们只能
望着你，而希冀你交着恶运。

我的心充满了忧愁

我的心充满了忧愁，
为我在往日的知己。
为许多红唇的女儿。
为许多捷足的孩子。

在宽广难涉的河边，
捷足的孩子们安眠，
红唇的女儿们睡在
红蔷薇花谢的田间。

安德鲁·扬一首
（Andrew Young，1885—1971）

最后的雪

虽然残雪还流连着
堆在鸟萝的钝蹼上，
而把树身一面涂白。
在这有阳光的路上，
新的无名东西出现，
有叶，有苞，下面有茎，
还有土块连在上面，
来指示它们的来因。
无花说出它的名字，
可是一条绿色的箭，
从地下穿过枯叶时，
一下就刺杀了冬天。

埃德蒙·布伦顿一首
（Edmund Blunden，1896—1974）

穷人的猪

已经有黄梅的落英点缀田园；
苹果树干斑斓如老蟾蜍的背，
着了小的红花，在玫瑰未开前
筑着新巢的鸫鸟，看着老人堆

在有阳光的篱上青皮的柳条。
关起的母猪听见他走过,就叫,
要把门闩推开,从里面向外逃,
但它有环的嘴,使它不能乱跑。

后来他放它出来跑,鼻子直喷;
鼓起力量,它就跑到茅舍门口
作出饥饿的呼声,求冷肴残羹;
它有如一阵旋风,又乱撞乱走,
用鼻撩拨着狗,使得鸡雏奔飞;
玩腻时,又如小孩一样撅着嘴。

W. B. 叶茨四首
(W. B. Yeats, 1865—1939)

象　征

风雨飘摇的古楼中,
盲目的处士敲着钟。

那无敌的宝刀还是
属于那游荡的傻子。

绣金的锦把宝刀围,
美人同傻子一同睡。

雪岭上的苦行人

文化是被多端的幻觉圈起,

在一范围内，和平的外表下。
但人的生命是思想，虽恐怕
也必须追求，经过无数世纪，
追求着，狂索着，摧毁着，他要
最后能来到那现实的荒野。
别了，埃及和希腊，别了，罗马。
苦行人在金山雪岭上修道，
深夜时，在山窟中，在积雪底，
或雪与寒风击他们的裸体，
知白昼带来夜，在破晓时候，
他的乐观与华炫将成乌有。

梭罗门与巫女

那天方的巫女如此发言，
"昨夜在荒凉的月色下面，
我正倦卧在蔓草的茵上，
在我怀中睡着梭罗门王，
我忽然发出奇异的喋喋，
非人类语言。"他因能了解
一切飞鸟，或天使的歌声，
就说，"一锦冠的鹦鹉，也曾
在繁花的苹果树上歌啼，
失乐园前三百年的时期。
从那时到现在，就没有唱。
其实本不当唱，可是它想，
'故意'与'偶然'又遇在一处。
那苹果带来的一切痛苦

和这坏的世界,终于死去。
它曾把'永恒'在过去叫走,
以为现在又把它叫回头。
爱恋着的人有蜘蛛的眼,
虽然他眼里充满了爱恋,
每一神经都充满。这两人
还以'故意'和'偶然'的残忍,
来彼此试探。虽两败俱伤,
新婚的床上又带来失望。
因每人都有幻想的形象,
而终发觉了那真的模样。
'故意'和'偶然'二物虽不同,
他为一体时,世界就告终。
当油与灯芯,焚在一火中。
所以昨天夜里,明月多情,
使巫女西跋见了梭罗门。"
"但世界还存在","若是如此,
你的鹦鹉作了一件错事。
可是它想值得它叫一次。
也许那个幻象有如实有,
也许那个幻象象的不够。"
"夜色降下了。也没有声息
在这不可侵犯的灵薮里,
除去有花蕊落地的细声,
在这灵薮里,也没有旁人,
只有我们所卧蔓草的茵。
月色也渐变神异而荒凉。
好不好再试试? 梭罗门王?"

爱尔兰的空军驾驶员

我知道我的生命将结束，
在天上某处,在云层以外。
我所攻击的人我并不恨，
我所护卫的人我也不爱。
我的家乡是吉尔塔坦村，
我的亲友是那里的穷人。
结果怎样他们总无所损，
他们也不会比以前欢欣。
不是法律,义务,使我参战，
不是红会人物,不是民众。
一时忽然的觉得很好玩，
激起我到云层间去活动。
我想过一切,都计算好了，
未来的生活也必是白忙，
过去的岁月也更是无聊。
这个死同这个生活一样。

T. S. 艾略特三首
(T. S. Eliot, 1888—1965)

空洞的人

（过新年,喜事添,给社公社婆一个钱。）

一

我们是空洞的人，

我们是塞草的人。

倚在一起，

头上装满了干草。啊，

我们枯干的声音，当

我们一同私语，

是沉寂而无意义的，

有如风在枯死了的草间，

或老鼠的脚在碎玻璃上，

在我们干的酒窖里。

无形状的东西，无色彩的光影，

僵止的动力，无动作的形势。

那些已到了彼岸的人，

双目直视着，到了死的另一国土的，

记得我们。如果记得的话，不以我们为

流亡的猛厉的魂灵，只是

空洞的人，

塞草的人。

二

在梦里，我不敢遇见的眼睛，

在死的梦幻的国土里，

这些不出现。

在那里，眼睛是

一断柱上的阳光，

在那里，有树在摇动，

声音是，

在风的歌里

比一残星，
更辽远幽肃。

让我不要更接近，
在死的梦幻的国土里。
让我也穿起，
如此故意的伪装，
老鼠的外衣，老鸦的皮，叉形的杖。
在一日里，
随风摇动着，
不更接近。

不要接近最后的会面，
在昏黄的国土里。

三

这是死的土地，
这是不毛的土地。
在这里石像
森立，在这里，他们接受
一死人手的祈求，
在残星的闪光下。

是否如此，
在死的另一国土里？
独行踽踽，
当我们正为
温情而颤动，
将吻的唇

向断石祈祷。

四

那眼睛不在此处，

此处没有眼睛，

在这残星的谷里，

在这空洞的谷里，

我们失去国土的断颚。

在这最后会面的地方，

我们一同摸索着，

避免言语，

集合在这汹涌的河岸边。

看不见，除非

那眼睛再出现，

永久的星

发大光辉，升起，

从死的昏黄的国土里，

空洞的人

的希望。

五

在此处，我们绕着刺梨树，

刺梨树，刺梨树，

在此处，我们围绕着刺梨树，

在清晨五点钟的时候。

在观念

与现实之间，

在动作

与践行之间，

阴影降下了。

　　因为国土是你的。

在怀育

与创作之间，

在情感

与反应之间，

阴影降下了。

　　生命太长了。

在欲望

与满足之间，

在含蓄

与生存之间，

在原子

与降生之间，

阴影降下了。

　　因为国土是你的。

因为国土，

生命是，

因为国土是，

世界就如此终结，

世界就如此终结，

世界就如此终结，

不作大声，只作低声的怨泣。

鹰形的星群在天顶上翱翔

鹰形的星群在天顶上翱翔，
猎人同他的狗循着轨道追，
啊，图象的星群，永久的转动，
啊，定命的时季，永久的来复，
啊，春天，秋天，生与死的世界，
观念与行动，无穷尽的循环，
无尽的发明，和无尽的试验，
给人动作，不给无动的知识，
给人语言，不给无言的知识，
给人道理而不使人明白道，
所有的知识使人更不了解，
不了解，使得人们更近死亡，
离死亡近，并不是离上帝近。
生活中失去的生命在哪里？
知识中失去的智慧在哪里？
见闻中失去的知识在哪里？
在二十世纪里天体的循环
使人更远离上帝，更近尘土。

东方的朝圣者

"我们去的时候天气很冷，
正是一年里最坏的时候，
去朝圣，而且路程这样远，
道路也崎岖，天气也严酷，
因为那正是三冬的时候。"

骆驼也疲乏了,蹄茧,局缩,
都卧倒在溶化的冰雪里。
有的时候,我们也曾后悔,
离弃了山上的行宫庭圃,
和锦衣擎着酒浆的少女。
驼夫们也咒骂埋怨我们,
逃走,要他们的酒和女人。
夜间火炬熄灭,荫盖不足,
每城每镇都敌视着我们,
村庄也都龌龊,要高价钱,
我们那时真是非常困苦,
后来觉得不如夜里走路,
有时候偷点空闲来睡觉,
有声音在我们耳里鸣着,
说这些都是傻子的事情。
黎明,我们来到一个山谷,
潮湿,无雪,有草木的芳馨,
有流泉,水磨撞击着黑暗,
在天低处,远远有三株树,
一匹老白马在草上奔驰,
一家酒店门楣挂葡萄叶,
六只手门前掷骰子赌钱,
又有人脚踢着空的酒囊。
找不到消息,我们继续走,
黄昏才找到,一点也不早,
正好找着,可以说是满意,
这都是很久的事,我记得,
我也愿再来一次,先写下

这事,先写下

这事,我们去那么远,为了

生? 还是为了死? 不错,是生,

我有证据,我看过生和死。

我曾以为是不同,这次生

是我们的苦痛,好象是死。

我们回到我们的王国去,

度着旧生活,再不觉安宁,

看着异族人民抱着偶像,

我真希望再有一次的死。

赫伯特·里德二首
(Herbert Read,1893—1968)

北征的纵队

角声在岩石的谷里蜷曲着,

在鸷鸟的鸣声里得到回响。

迫害又加于苦痛的人群上,

人白白死去,没有光荣事迹。

十一天这纵队走过了荒田,

经过焚毁的农村,空院,断桥。

荒凉在面前有如阴影动摇,

劫灰如雨。他们的焦虑日添。

步入北方的黑暗里,渐走近

一条窄径,山水可怖的冲流,

阴影淤结的恐吓,和多端的

死路,都埋伏好了,等待他们。

最后的前卫吹出凄凉角声,
纵队已迷失了,后继再无人。

在西班牙被炸死的儿童

蜡偶的脸更红,可是这些是小孩子。
他们眼睛不是玻璃,是闪光的纤维。
黑的眸子,在那水银一般的顾盼里,
日光曾颤动过。这些灰白色的嘴唇
曾经是温暖的,而有过灿烂的血色,
可是那时的血
是藏在温润的皮肤里,
而不是纷溅在乱发上。

在这些黑发中间,
红色的花不常是
如此凝成了黑块。

这些是死了的脸,
蜂巢也不更惨淡,
木烬也不更灰白。

他们被列成一行,
如落地的纸灯笼,
经过一夜的狂欢,
干燥晨气中奄灭。

W. H. 奥登三首
（W. H. Auden，1907—1973）

看，异邦的人

看，异邦的人，现在看这个岛，
发现那供你欣赏的动跃的波光。
静立在这里，
也不要发声，
为了在你的耳中
可以如同溪水一般的流荡着，
大海的摇曳的声音。

且略留连于这田畦的终尾，
有白垩的石岩落入浪花，与它的
突起的平岩。
对着潮汐的
牵拽，和它的撞击，
卵石在吸引的海水后匍匐着，
海鸥在峭崖上小息。

远远看来，有如漂着的种子，
船只分去，向着急促自动的目的。
这一切景象
能冲流动荡，
在记忆中，如现在
这些云流过海港的一面明镜，
终夏在海水里徘徊。

和声歌辞

命运比任何海窟还幽秘，
当它落在人身上的时候。
春天，仰慕白昼的花出现，
冰崩，白雪从岩石间落下，
使得他离开了他的家园。
没有女人柔手能留住他，
他还是要经过
驿站的守者，丛林的树木，
到异乡的人间，经过大海，
鱼的居处，令人窒息的水。
或孤独在荒原上如野鹤，
在一多洼穴的石谷中间，
一在石上盘桓烦恼的鸟。

黄昏时，疲倦，头向前垂下，
梦想到了家园，
窗间的招手，欢迎的陈设，
在大被下吻着他的爱妻。
而醒时只看见
一群无名的鸟，傍人门前
不熟习的人声，诉说爱恋。

脱离那仇敌设下的罗网，
脱离那道旁猛虎的突袭，
护佑他的家园，
焦念着数着日子的家园，

避免霹雳下击、
避免蔓延如污点的衰灭，
使模糊的日子变为确定，
带来欢乐，和归家的日期，
幸运的日期，将升的曙光。

空　袭

是的，我们将遭受苦难了，天
悸动如狂热的额。真的痛苦。
摸索着的探照灯光，忽显出
卑微的人性，使得我们乞怜。
因它们存在，我们向未相信，
这里它们突然使我们惊异，
如丑恶的久忘记了的记忆，
而如良心责备，一切炮回应。
每一双和易的眼睛的后背，
都有暗地的屠杀在进行中，
一切妇女，犹太人，富人，人类。
高山不能判断匍匐的我们，
我们住在地上，大地总服从
狡恶的人们，除非人不生存。

四

卖花女(第五幕)[①]

息金斯夫人的客厅。她还是象以前那样坐在写字台前。女仆进来。

女 仆 (在门口)夫人,息金斯少爷来了,在楼下同辟克林上校在一起。

息金斯夫人 叫他们上来吧。

女 仆 他们在打电话。好象是给警察局打电话。

息金斯夫人 什么?

女 仆 (走近几步,低声说)少爷有点精神不正常呢。我想我应该告诉您。

息金斯夫人 你要是告诉我他的精神很正常,那就更奇怪了。他们跟警察局打完交道,叫他们上来。他大概是丢了点什么。

女 仆 是,夫人。(要走出)

息金斯夫人 你上楼告诉杜立特尔小姐,少爷和辟克林上校在这里。叫她先不要下来,等我叫她的时候再来。

女 仆 是,夫人。

息金斯闯进来,正如女仆所说,他的精神是不大正常。

息金斯 妈,这件事真糟糕!

息金斯夫人 是的,孩子,早安。(他忍着火,吻他母亲,同时女仆走出)什么事?

---

① 选自:肖伯纳. 卖花女. 杨宪益,译. 北京:中国对外翻译出版公司,1982.

息金斯　伊莉莎逃走了。

息金斯夫人　（安闲地继续写信）一定是你把她吓跑了。

息金斯　吓跑了！没有的事！昨天晚上和平常一样,我让她最后关灯安歇,可是她不上床睡觉,反而换了衣服一直就走了:她铺好的床都没有睡过。今天早晨七点钟以前她坐了一辆汽车来取她的东西,那个傻瓜别斯太太也不跟我说一声居然把东西都给了她。我现在怎么办?

息金斯夫人　我看只好让她去吧,亨利。这姑娘完全有权利离开,如果她愿意的话。

息金斯　（不安地走来走去）可是我什么东西都找不到了。我也不知道我有什么约会。我是——（辟克林进来。息金斯夫人放下钢笔转过身来。）

辟克林　（同她握手）早安,息金斯夫人。亨利告诉你了么?（他在长榻上坐下。）

息金斯　那个糊涂警长怎么说? 你没答应出赏格吗?

息金斯夫人　（站起来,又惊讶,又生气）你们难道要警察去捉拿伊莉莎?

息金斯　当然了。要不然警察有什么用? 我们不这样还有什么别的办法?（他在伊丽莎白式的椅子上坐下。）

辟克林　那个警长特别跟我们为难。我觉得他是怀疑我们有不正当的企图。

息金斯夫人　当然了。你们有什么权利到警察局去报告她,就象她是个贼,或者是一把丢了的伞什么的? 真是的!（她又坐下来,很不痛快。）

息金斯　可是我们想找她回来呀。

辟克林　你知道,我们不能让她这样走掉,息金斯夫人。我们还有什么办法?

息金斯夫人　你们两个都象小孩子,简直不懂事。你知道——

女仆进来,打断他们的谈话。

女　仆　少爷,一位先生有要紧的事要见你。他是打温波街那儿来的。

息金斯　真讨厌! 现在我不能见任何人。他是什么人?

女　仆　是一位杜立特尔先生。

辟克林　杜立特尔! 你是说那个倒垃圾的吗?

女　仆　倒垃圾的! 啊,不是,是位先生。

息金斯　(兴奋得跳起来)真是的,辟克林,这是她去找的什么亲戚。我们
　　　　还不晓得他是什么人。(对女仆)叫他上来,快。

女　仆　是,少爷。(退出)

息金斯　(满怀希望,走到他母亲那里)她有体面亲戚呢! 现在我们可以
　　　　知道点消息了。(他在契本代尔式椅子上坐下。)

息金斯夫人　你们见过她家里的人吗?

辟克林　只见过她父亲:就是我们和你说过的那家伙。

女　仆　(通报)杜立特尔先生。(她退出。)

　　　　杜立特尔走进来。他穿得很漂亮,好象是要参加盛大婚礼
　　似的,实际上,自己可能就是那新郎。钮孔里插着一朵花,亮晶
　　晶的黑绸礼帽,另外又加上一双漆皮的皮鞋。他太注意自己的
　　事情以致没有看到息金斯夫人。他一直走到息金斯面前,声色
　　俱厉地责备他。

杜立特尔　(指他自己身上)你看! 看见了吗? 这是你干的好事。

息金斯　干了什么事,老兄?

杜立特尔　告诉你,就是这个。你看看,看看这顶帽子。看看这身衣服。

辟克林　伊莉莎给你买衣服了吗?

杜立特尔　伊莉莎! 她可没有。她给咱买衣服干吗?

息金斯夫人　您好,杜立特尔先生。您请坐吧。

杜立特尔　(才知道忘记和女主人打招呼,不好意思)对不起,太太。(走
　　　　过来握她伸出的手)谢谢。(他在长榻上坐下,在辟克林的右边)

咱光想着咱的事了,所以别的都给忘了。

息金斯　你到底是怎么了?

杜立特尔　要单单是咱自己的事倒也算了。什么人都会碰到点意外,你可以说谁也怪不了谁,只能怪老天爷。可是这是你干的:咱就说的是你,亨利·息金斯。

息金斯　你找到伊莉莎了吗?

杜立特尔　她走掉了吗?

息金斯　是的。

杜立特尔　你样样运气都好。咱没找到她;可是你这么一来,她很快就要找咱来了。

息金斯夫人　可是,杜立特尔先生,我的儿子对你作了什么事?

杜立特尔　对我作了什么!他把咱毁了。咱的快活日子全完了。把咱给绑起来,送到满口仁义道德的绅士们手里去了。

息金斯　(不耐烦地站起来,站在他面前)你是胡闹。你喝醉了。你发疯了。我给了你五镑钱。后来又跟你谈过两次话,一个钟头半个克朗。以后我就没有见过你。

杜立特尔　啊,咱喝醉了吗?咱发疯了吗?你说。你是不是写过一封信给美国的一个老家伙,他捐了五百万,要在全世界建立道德改进会,要你给他发明一种世界语?

息金斯　怎么?埃兹拉·狄·万那费勒!他死了。(他又满不在乎地坐下来。)

杜立特尔　是的:他死了;把咱也给毁了。你是不是给他写过一封信,告诉他目前英国最有独特见解的伦理学者,据你所知,就是阿尔弗莱·杜立特尔,一个普通的倒垃圾的?

息金斯　啊,在你第一次来了以后,我好象就开过类似这样一个小玩笑。

杜立特尔　啊!你尽可说它是个小玩笑,可把咱害苦了。你正给他一个机会好表示他们美国人跟咱们不一样:表示他们不管人的地位多么低,他们看得起每一个人的才能。在他的缺德的遗嘱里,息金斯,因为你开的小玩笑,他给咱留下了他的"消化干酪托拉斯"的一笔钱,一年三千镑收入,条件是咱得给他的"万那费勒道德改进世界协会"作讲演,由他们指定,每年不超过六次。

息金斯　真有这样的事!嗨!(忽然高兴起来)这多运气!

辟克林　杜立特尔,这对你来说亏不了。他们听了一次就不会再请你讲第二次了。

杜立特尔　咱怕的不是讲演。咱可以使他们听了脸色大变,咱也毫不在乎。咱反对的是要咱作个绅士。谁让他那样作的?咱本来很快活,很自由自在,咱要用钱的时候差不多见人就要,就象跟你要钱一样,息金斯。现在咱可麻烦了,从头到脚都给绑起来了,什么人都跟咱要钱了。咱那律师说,你运气来了。咱说,是吗?咱说,是你的好运气吧?咱穷的时候也找过一回律师,那回有人在咱的垃圾车里找到了一个小儿车,完了事,他就立刻把咱轰出来了。医生也一样,从前不等咱站稳了,就把咱轰到大门外了,也不用花钱。现在他们说咱身体不好了,要是他们不是一天给咱看两次病,咱就活不成了。在家里咱一件事都不能作;一定要别人来作,完事再跟咱要钱。一年以前咱什么亲戚也没有,只有两三个人肯搭理咱。现在咱有了五十个亲戚,没有一个能象样地挣钱的。咱得为别人活着,不为自己,这就是绅士们的仁义道德。你说伊莉莎丢了。你不用着急;咱敢说这会儿她早到了咱家门口了:要是咱不是绅士,她卖花过活也方便。这以后就该轮着你跟咱要钱了,亨利·息金斯。咱得请你教咱说绅士的话,不能再讲正经英文了。这就是你的买卖,咱敢说你原来就是这个打算。

息金斯夫人　可是,杜立特尔先生,你要是真不喜欢,你就不必受这个罪。也没有人能强迫你接受这笔遗赠的钱呀。你可以拒绝,不是吗,辟克林上校?

辟克林 应该可以。

杜立特尔 (因为对方是女性,态度转得缓和一点)太太,难就难在这里。说不要是容易,可是咱不敢说。谁敢说呢? 咱们都给吓住了。太太,都给吓住了,情况就是这样。咱要是不要这钱,等到老了还不得住孤老院? 咱现在都得把头发染黑才能当个倒垃圾的。咱要是个有人可怜的穷人,也有点积蓄,咱就可以不要了;可是咱又何必呢,那些有人可怜的穷人就是变了百万富翁也享不了福。他们不懂怎么享福。咱可是一个没人可怜的穷人,什么也没有,就得进孤老院,但是这一年他妈的三千镑却硬逼着咱作绅士。(太太,您别怪咱说粗话,您要是碰到咱这种倒霉事也非骂不可)你怎么也逃不了,一边是孤老院,一边是作绅士,前是狼,后是虎,咱也没那进孤老院的勇气。吓住了:就是这么回事。咱算是垮了,把自己出卖了。别的人比咱运气好,可以给咱倒垃圾,跟咱要钱;咱也没法办,白瞪眼,羡慕也没用。这就是你儿子干的好事。(他不胜伤感。)

息金斯夫人 好,我很高兴你没有轻举妄动,杜立特尔先生。因为这样伊莉莎的前途问题就解决了。现在你养得起她了。

杜立特尔 (沮丧而无可奈何)是的,太太,现在什么人都要咱养了,都从这一年三千镑里拿出来。

息金斯 (跳起来)没有的话! 他不能养她。他不应该养她。她不属于他了。我为她付了五镑钱的。杜立特尔,你是要作一个老实人还是要作坏蛋?

杜立特尔 (容忍着他)两样都有点吧,亨利,大家都是这样,两样都有点。

息金斯 你既然为她拿了钱,你就没有权利再把她带走。

息金斯夫人 亨利,别不讲理。你要是想知道伊莉莎在哪儿,她就在楼上。

息金斯　（惊讶）在楼上！！！那我立刻就把她带下来。（他坚决地朝门走去。）

息金斯夫人　（站起来跟着他）安静点，亨利。坐下。

息金斯　我——

息金斯夫人　坐下，孩子，听我说。

息金斯　好吧，好吧，好吧。（他粗鲁地倒在长榻上，脸对着窗户）可是我觉得你本可以前半个钟头就告诉我们这件事。

息金斯夫人　伊莉莎今天早晨到我这儿来的。她告诉了我你们两个对她的粗暴态度。

息金斯　（又跳起来）什么？

辟克林　（也站起来）亲爱的息金斯夫人，她说的话是靠不住的。我们并没有虐待她。我们可以说没有对她说什么话；我们和她分开的时候也特别好。（转身对息金斯）息金斯，我去睡觉以后你欺负她了吗？

息金斯　恰恰相反。她把拖鞋扔到我脸上。她的态度非常无理。我一直都没有惹她。我一进房门拖鞋就砰的一声照着我的脸扔来了——我还没来得及说一句话呢。她还用很难听的话骂我。

辟克林　（惊讶）可是为什么？我们对她有哪点不好？

息金斯夫人　我想我很明白你们是怎么搞的。我想这个女孩子的本性是很多情的。是不是，杜立特尔先生？

杜立特尔　太太，她心肠可软着呢。跟咱一模一样的。

息金斯夫人　对呀。她对你们两个有了感情。亨利，她为你工作很尽心。你大概不太懂她那样出身的女孩子作脑力劳动有多困难。后来呢，看来是等到那重要日子到了，要受考验了，她给你作了那件了不起的事，一点错也没出，可是你们两人坐在那儿，没有对她说一句话，只管说现在事情完了你们多么高兴，这整个的事多么无聊。等到她拿拖鞋来扔你，你倒觉得奇怪了！要是我呀，我就要拿火钳扔你。

息金斯　我们什么也没说,只说我们累了想去睡觉。辟克,不是吗?

辟克林　(耸耸肩)就是这样。

息金斯夫人　(含着讥讽)真的吗?

辟克林　一点不错。真的,就是这样。

息金斯夫人　你们也没有谢谢她,拍拍她肩膀,称赞她,或者说她作得多么好?

息金斯　(不耐烦)可是这些她都知道。你的意思也许是我们没有捧她几句。

辟克林　(良心不安)也许我们是有些不够体贴。她很生气吗?

息金斯夫人　(回到她的写字台前)我恐怕她不愿再回温波街去呢,尤其现在杜立特尔先生可以保持她目前的社会地位了,虽然这地位是你们硬给她的;可是她说她很愿意跟你们作朋友,过去的事一概不提了。

息金斯　(很生气)哦,她真的同意? 嗬!

息金斯夫人　亨利,要是你答应我规规矩矩的,我就请她下来。要是你不答应,就回家去;你在这儿已经耽误我不少时间了。

息金斯　好吧。就这样;辟克,你规矩一点。我们拿出最好的礼貌来招待这个垃圾堆里捡来的贱货吧。(他赌气倒在伊丽莎白式的椅子上。)

杜立特尔　(抗议地)唉,别么说话,亨利·息金斯! 你得顾全一下咱这个绅士的脸面呀。

息金斯夫人　亨利,记住你可是答应了。(她按桌上的铃)杜立特尔先生,您可不可以暂时到凉台上去一下。我不希望伊莉莎听到你的消息而大吃一惊;等她先同这两位和解了再说,好不好?

杜立特尔　听您吩咐,太太。只要亨利能让她不来麻烦咱,咱很愿意效劳。(他从窗口出去。)

　　　　女仆听见铃声走进来,辟克林在方才杜立特尔坐的地方坐下。

息金斯夫人　请杜立特尔小姐下来。

女　仆　是,夫人。(走出)

息金斯夫人　亨利,现在要乖乖的。

息金斯　我不是态度很好吗?

辟克林　息金斯夫人,他在尽力做呢。

　　　　稍停,息金斯把头向后仰着,伸直了腿,开始吹口哨。

息金斯夫人　亨利,好孩子,你这样子实在不好看。

息金斯　(坐好了)我并没有打算作出好看的样子来,妈。

息金斯夫人　没什么,孩子,我是要叫你讲话。

息金斯　为什么?

息金斯夫人　因为你不能同时又说话又吹口哨。

　　　　息金斯叹口气。又是一阵令人难堪的沉寂。

息金斯　(跳起来,不能忍受了)那姑娘到底在哪儿? 我们难道要在这儿等她一整天?

　　　　伊莉莎走进来,和和气气的,态度从容,作出非常自然的样子。她拿着一个小针线篮子,态度安闲自若。辟克林太惊讶了,以致忘记站起来。

伊莉莎　您好,息金斯教授。您身体很好吧?

息金斯　(气得说不出话来)你说我——(他说不下去。)

伊莉莎　当然您身体一定很好;您是从来不生病的。很高兴又看见您,辟克林上校。(他赶快站起来,同她握手)今天天气很凉呢,不是吗? (她在辟克林左边坐下,他也在她的旁边坐下。)

息金斯　你不要跟我要这一套。我教了你,这一套骗不了我。站起来回家去,别装傻了。

　　　　伊莉莎从针线篮子里拿出针线,开始缝纫,对他这种大吵大闹完全没有理睬。

息金斯夫人　说的话真客气,亨利,这样的邀请哪个女人能够拒绝呀?

息金斯　妈,你不要管。让她自己来说。她一说话,你立刻就可以知道,除了我叫她想的说的以外,她自己还有什么思想没有。说真的,这块料是我拿寺院广场的烂菜叶子作成功的,现在她倒在我面前摆起小姐架子来了。

息金斯夫人　(平静地)好吧,孩子。你坐下谈,好不好?

　　　　　　息金斯怒气冲冲地又坐下来。

伊莉莎　(对辟克林,好象毫不注意息金斯似的,同时灵巧地作着针线)辟克林上校,现在试验既然作完了,你打算完全不理我了吗?

辟克林　不要那么说。你千万不要认为这只是一次试验。这样说法我听了很不舒服。

伊莉莎　哦,我不过是一块烂菜叶子——

辟克林　(激动地)不要那么说。

伊莉莎　(继续很平静地)——可是你对我那么好,要是你忘记了我,我会很难过的。

辟克林　杜立特尔小姐,谢谢你这么说。

伊莉莎　这并不是因为你花钱给我买衣服。我知道你对所有的人花钱都是很慷慨的。可是我是从你那里才学到真正的礼貌;也就是这个,才使人成为上等人,不是吗?你知道,有息金斯教授那样的人总在面前,学习礼貌是很困难的事。我过去就象他那样,完全不能控制感情,稍微有一点不高兴就说粗话骂人。要不是有你在那里,我永远也不会明白上等人不是那样的。

息金斯　哦!!!

辟克林　你要知道,他就是那个样子。他不是有什么坏意。

伊莉莎　是呀,我从前卖花的时候也不是有什么坏意呀。这也只是我的习惯。可是我总是那样做了,上等人和下等人的分别也就在这里。

辟克林　对的。可是他教你讲话的;你知道,这我是做不到的。

伊莉莎　(不在意地)当然了,那是他的买卖嘛!

息金斯　混账!

伊莉莎　(继续说)就象学时髦跳舞一样;并没有什么更多的道理。可是你知道我真正受的教育是从什么事情开始的?

辟克林　什么事情?

伊莉莎　(稍微停止一下针线)我才到温波街的那一天你叫我杜立特尔小姐。我的自尊心就是从那件事上开始的。(她继续作针线)还有成百成千的你不注意的小事情,因为那些对你都是很自然的。就象人来了站起来,脱帽,给人开门等等——

辟克林　啊,那都不算什么。

伊莉莎　有关系的:那些事说明你并不拿我当作一个厨房里的小丫头看待;虽然我当然也知道,要是一个厨房丫头到了上房里,你对她也是会同样彬彬有礼的。我在饭厅的时候,你从来没有当着我脱皮靴子。

辟克林　你不要介意,息金斯向来是到处脱皮靴子的。

伊莉莎　我知道。我也不怪他。他的习惯是那样,不是吗?可是你不那样作,使我感觉大不相同。你知道,说真的,除了任何人可以学会的那些东西而外(如同穿衣服讲话等等),一个上等小姐和一个卖花姑娘的分别不在于她怎么作,而在于别人怎么对待她。我在息金斯教授面前永远是个卖花姑娘,因为他一向是那样对待我,将来也是那样。可是我知道在你面前我可以作个小姐,因为你一向是那样对待我,将来也是那样。

息金斯夫人　亨利,请你不要咬牙切齿。

辟克林　杜立特尔小姐,你实在过奖了。

伊莉莎　现在我请你叫我伊莉莎,行不行?

辟克林　谢谢,伊莉莎,当然了。

伊莉莎　可是我要息金斯教授叫我杜立特尔小姐。

息金斯　去你妈的。

息金斯夫人　亨利！亨利！

辟克林　（笑起来）你为什么不回骂他几句？别听他的。骂骂他对他很有好处呢。

伊莉莎　我作不来。从前我可以骂人；可是现在作不来了。你知道，你同我说过的，要是一个小孩子到了外国，几个星期他就能学会当地语言，自己的话就忘记了。唉，我就是你们国家的一个小孩子，把我自己的语言都忘了，现在只能讲你们的话了。这样就和托特汉坊大街的街头真正脱离关系。离开温波街就算毕了业了。

辟克林　（非常惶恐）啊！可是你还要回到温波街的，不是吗？你要原谅息金斯吧？

息金斯　（站起来）原谅！她真会原谅我！去她的，看她没有我们帮忙怎么办！没有我在旁边，要不了三个星期她就又恢复原来的流氓习惯了。

　　　　　　杜立特尔在中间玻璃窗口出现。他很高傲而不以为然地看了息金斯一眼，慢慢地一言不发走到他女儿那里，但伊莉莎背对着窗户，并没有看见他。

辟克林　他这个人总是这样，改不了，伊莉莎。你不会恢复原来习惯的，是不是？

伊莉莎　不会，现在不会了。再也不会了。我已经学好了。我觉得我就是想要发出从前的声音也作不到了。（杜立特尔碰了她左肩膀一下。她看到她父亲的华丽服装不能自制，丢下针线）哎——呀——呀！

息金斯　（感觉胜利而欢笑）哈，哈！对了。（摹仿她的土音）哎——呀——呀！哎——呀——呀！我胜利了！我胜利了！

　　　　　　（他倒在短榻上，交叉着臂，傲慢地叉开腿坐着。）

杜立特尔　你能怪她吗？伊莉莎，别那么瞧着咱。这不怪咱。咱发了财了。

伊莉莎　爹，你这回准是骗了一个百万富翁的钱了。

杜立特尔　是的。可是咱今天是特别打扮的。咱是到汉诺威广场圣乔治教堂去。你的后娘今天要跟咱结婚呢。

伊莉莎　(生气)你跟那下贱女人结婚也不怕丢脸！

辟克林　(平静地)他应该结婚，伊莉莎。(对杜立特尔)她怎么又改变主意了？

杜立特尔　(悲哀地)给吓住了，老爷，给吓住了。绅士的道德把咱们给毁了。伊莉莎，你不戴上帽子到教堂来看咱们的婚礼吗？

伊莉莎　要是辟克林上校说我一定得去，我只好——(几乎要哭)只好忍受耻辱。大概白费一番好意还要受她的气呢。

杜立特尔　别害怕。她真可怜呢，跟谁也不敢顶嘴了！为了要让自己规规矩矩的，她的气势全没了。

辟克林　(轻轻地捏着伊莉莎的膀子)伊莉莎，对他们好一些吧。勉强敷衍一下吧。

伊莉莎　(虽然不高兴但勉强对他稍微一笑)好吧，只是为了表明没有什么恶感。我去一下就来。(她走出去。)

杜立特尔　(在辟克林旁边坐下来)上校，咱这回结婚可是心里嘀咕得很。请您也来参加一下好不好？

辟克林　可是你是结过婚的人了，老兄。你不是跟伊莉莎的母亲结过婚吗？

杜立特尔　谁说的，上校？

辟克林　我没有听谁说。我想自然是——

杜立特尔　不对，上校，那不是自然的办法，那不过是绅士们的办法。咱的办法向来是倒霉的穷人的那一套。可是请您别跟伊莉莎说。她不晓得。咱总觉得告诉她有些不便。

辟克林　　很对,如果你不想说,我们就不提吧。

杜立特尔　　上校,您到教堂来帮咱过了这一关好不好?

辟克林　　我很高兴参加。只要是单身汉能作得到的事。

息金斯夫人　　杜立特尔先生,我也可以来吗? 我很希望能够参加呢。

杜立特尔　　太太,您肯屈尊,那咱太光荣了;咱那可怜的老婆子也要高兴死了。她这会儿正不痛快,觉得过去好日子全完了。

息金斯夫人　　(站起来)我去叫马车,准备一下。(男人们都站起来,除了息金斯)要不了一刻钟我就来。(她走到门口时,伊莉莎正进来,戴好帽子,正在扣她的手套)我也到教堂去看你父亲结婚,伊莉莎。你最好同我一车走吧。辟克林上校可以同新郎一起走。

　　　　　　息金斯夫人走出。伊莉莎走到屋子当中,在中央的窗门和长榻之间。辟克林也走到她那里。

杜立特尔　　新郎! 这个称呼不简单! 真让人想起来他所处的地位呢。

　　　　　　(他拿起帽子走向门口。)

辟克林　　在我没走以前,伊莉莎,希望你还是原谅息金斯,跟我们回去吧。

伊莉莎　　我爹怕不会放我回去呢。你让我去吗,爹?

杜立特尔　　(沉郁但是宽大)伊莉莎,这两位堂堂正正的先生对付你对付得真妙。要是只有一位,你就可以上钩了。可是你瞧,他们是两个人;可以说是一个看住另一个。(对辟克林)上校,你们真鬼,可是咱不怪你;要是咱,咱也这么办。咱一辈子总是吃娘儿们的亏;咱也不怪你们两位占了伊莉莎的便宜。咱不管这事。咱们该走了,上校。亨利,再见吧。伊莉莎,咱们在教堂见面。(他走出。)

辟克林　　(求她)伊莉莎,跟我们在一起,别走吧。(他随杜立特尔走出去。)

　　　　　　伊莉莎为了避免单独和息金斯在一起,走到凉台上。他站起来也走到她那里。她立刻走回来向房门走去,但他也很快地从凉台走回来,在她没到门口之前,他已经背靠着门了。

息金斯　伊莉莎,你可以说是找回一些来了。你报复得够了没有?愿意平心静气地解决问题了吗?还是想再闹下去?

伊莉莎　你要我回去,只是为了好替你拿拖鞋,受你的气,给你取这样拿那样。

息金斯　我也并没有说要你回去呀。

伊莉莎　是吗?那么我们讲这些干什么呢?

息金斯　讲你的事,不是讲我的事。你要是回去,我对待你还跟从前一样,我改变不了我的本性;我也不打算改变我的态度。我的态度跟辟克林上校的态度完全一样。

伊莉莎　这话不对。他对待一个卖花姑娘就象对待一个公爵夫人一样。

息金斯　而我对待一个公爵夫人就象对待一个卖花姑娘一样。

伊莉莎　原来如此。(她平静地走开,坐在长榻上,面对窗门)对任何人都一样。

息金斯　对了。

伊莉莎　跟我父亲一样。

息金斯　(笑起来,觉得有点委屈)伊莉莎,虽然在其他方面未必相同,但你父亲也并不是个乡愿市侩,无论他交了什么怪运,他在任何场合也都能处之泰然。(认真地)伊莉莎,重要的问题不在于对人态度好坏,或采取什么样的对人态度,而在于对任何人都要抱同一态度:简单说,对待人的态度就得象是死后上了天堂那样,在那里没有什么三等车,每人都是平等的。

伊莉莎　阿门!你真是个天才传教士。

息金斯　(不痛快)问题不在于我对你的态度是否粗暴,而是你是否听见过我对别人比对你好些。

伊莉莎　(突然诚恳地)我不在乎你对我的态度怎么样。我不怕你骂我。我也不怕你打我:这我已经受过了。但是(站起来面对着他)我不愿意别人在我面前掠过而不理我。

息金斯　那你就别挡我的路好了；我反正不会为你停下来的。你说得我好象是一辆公共汽车似的。

伊莉莎　你就是一辆公共汽车，只知道横冲直闯，也不考虑人家。可是我没有你也能行，你不要以为非你不可。

息金斯　我知道你可以。我对你说过的。

伊莉莎　(有点伤心，离开他，到长榻的另一边，面对壁炉)我知道你说过，你这个没情感的人。你就是要丢掉我。

息金斯　你说谎。

伊莉莎　好吧。(她绷着脸坐下。)

息金斯　我想你大概从来没有考虑过，我没有你行不行。

伊莉莎　(认真地)你别打算骗我。你不行也得行。

息金斯　(傲慢地)我不需要任何人。我有我自己的灵魂：我自己焕发的才智。可是(忽然谦卑地)伊莉莎，你走了我会想你的。(他在长榻上靠着她坐下)从你的糊涂想法里我也学到一些东西：这点我老实承认，也很感谢。我也习惯了你的声音和外表。我也都很喜欢。

伊莉莎　那你可以把这两种东西用录音器和照相簿保存起来。你觉得闷了，就可以打开机器。也不会伤人家的心。

息金斯　可是我不能打开你的灵魂。你给我留下那些感情；你可以拿去那声音和面貌，那些东西并不是你本人。

伊莉莎　你真是个鬼。你揪女孩子的心，就象别人揪她的膀子去伤害她那么容易。别斯太太叫我提防你的。她好几次都想走，最后一分钟你总是把她骗回来了。可是你一点也不关心她。你也一点不关心我。

息金斯　我关心生活，关心人类；你就是其中的一分子，碰到了我，成为我家的组成部分。你，或者别的任何人，还能要求什么呢？

伊莉莎　我不愿意关心一个对我毫不关心的人。

息金斯　伊莉莎,这是买卖原则。就象(用专家的准确发音摹仿她在寺院广场卖花时的土音)"卖紫地丁呀",对吗?

伊莉莎　别讥笑人。这样很不客气。

息金斯　我从来不讥笑人。讥笑人这件事对于人的外貌和内心都不合适。我是出于义愤蔑视买卖原则。拿感情作交易的事,我从来不作,将来也不会作。你认为我没有情感,因为你替我拿拖鞋找眼镜不能让我承情。你是个傻子:我认为女人给男人拿拖鞋是很不好看的:我给你拿过拖鞋吗? 你拿拖鞋扔我,我觉得倒更佩服你。你给我当奴隶又说要我关心你,这是没有用的:谁关心一个奴隶呢? 你要是回来,那是因为我们合得来,别的是得不到的。我给你的好处比你给我的多一千倍;你要是胆敢破坏我所创造的伊莉莎公爵夫人的形象,搞你那小狗把戏,把拖鞋拿来拿去,我就把你这傻瓜关在门外头。

伊莉莎　你要是不关心我,那你做这事是为了什么呢?

息金斯　(痛痛快快地)为什么? 那是我的工作。

伊莉莎　你从来没有想过这件事给我多少麻烦吧。

息金斯　要是造物主怕麻烦,那世界又是怎么造出来的? 创造生命就是创造麻烦。只有一种办法避免麻烦,就是把东西毁掉。你看,懦夫们总是叫着要把找麻烦的人杀掉。

伊莉莎　我不是传教士,我不注意这些事,我只注意你对我不关心。

息金斯　(跳起来,不耐烦地走来走去)伊莉莎,你是个傻子。我把我的密尔顿一般的宝贵智慧披露在你面前简直是白费。最后一句话,你要明白,我要走我自己的路,作我自己的工作,我们两人谁发生什么事,我也毫不在乎。我不象你爹和你后娘那样,一吓就吓住了。所以你回来也好,见鬼去也好,随你的便。

伊莉莎　我要是回来干什么呢?

息金斯　（一跳跪在长榻上，屈身正对着她）为了好玩。我把你留下也就
　　　　是为这个。

伊莉莎　（转过脸去）要是我每件事都不按着你的意思作，你也许明天就
　　　　把我扔出去？

息金斯　对了。我要是每一件事都不按你的意思作，你也许明天就离
　　　　开我。

伊莉莎　跟我后娘去过吗？

息金斯　对了。卖花也行。

伊莉莎　啊，我要是能够回去卖花就好了。那样我就可以不依靠你，不依
　　　　靠我爹和任何其他的人了。为什么你剥夺了我的独立性？为什
　　　　么我放弃我的独立性？我现在虽穿得漂亮，但我是个奴隶。

息金斯　一点不是。我可以收你作干女儿给你一笔钱，如果你愿意的话。
　　　　或者你愿意嫁给辟克林吧？

伊莉莎　（生气转身向他）就是你要我嫁给你我也不干，虽然你比起他的
　　　　什么来，你同我的年岁还近一些。

息金斯　（温和地）要说"比起他来"，不是"比起他的什么来"。

伊莉莎　（发脾气，站起来）我愿意怎么说就怎么说。你现在不是我的老
　　　　师了。

息金斯　（沉思着）我想辟克林也不会要你。跟我一样，他也是老早决定
　　　　不结婚的了。

伊莉莎　我要的也不是那个，你也不要那么想。要我的小伙子可多着呢。
　　　　佛莱第·希尔就一天给我来两三封信，一写就是好几张纸。

息金斯　（出他意外，不大高兴）真他妈的大胆！（他往后退缩，坐在自己
　　　　脚跟上。）

伊莉莎　可怜的孩子，他愿意那样作，就有那样作的权利。而且他是真爱
　　　　我呢。

息金斯　（离开长榻）你没有权利鼓励他。

伊莉莎　任何一个姑娘都有被人爱的权利。

息金斯　怎么！被那样的傻子爱吗？

伊莉莎　佛莱第也不是傻子。如果他软弱可怜而且需要我，也许比那些比我高明而欺负我不需要我的人更能使我快乐呢。

息金斯　问题在于他能对你有什么用处？

伊莉莎　也许我对他倒有些帮助呢。但我从来不想谁对谁有什么用处，而你只想这一点，不想别的。我只想过自自然然的生活。

息金斯　换句话说，你希望我象佛莱第那样迷上了你，是不是？

伊莉莎　不，我不希望。我要求于你的不是那种感情，你也不要太自信或者过于相信我。我要是愿意的话，我可以做个坏姑娘，你虽然有学问，有些事情我比你见得多。象我这样的姑娘可以很容易勾引男人去爱她。而过不了一分钟，两人就又变成誓不两立的仇人了。

息金斯　自然不错。那么我们究竟还争论什么呢？

伊莉莎　(很烦恼地)我需要一点温情。我知道我不过是个平凡的不学无术的丫头，而你是个有学问的上流绅士；但我也不是你脚底下的泥土。我干这个(改正自己的话)，我作这个并不是为了漂亮衣服和汽车；我作这个是因为我们相处得很好。我也就——也就逐渐对你关心；但并不是要你爱我，我也没有忘记我们中间的不同，我只要求彼此能够友爱一些。

息金斯　当然了。我也希望如此。辟克林也是这样。伊莉莎，你真糊涂。

伊莉莎　你不应该这样回答我。(她在写字台前的椅子上坐下，流着眼泪。)

息金斯　你要是总那么糊涂，你只能得到这样的回答。你要是想作一个上等社会的小姐，你就不要总认为别人不理你，非要你认识的男人用一半的时间对你哭哭啼啼的，另外一半的时间把你打得鼻青眼肿。你要是不能忍受我这种生活的冷淡和紧张，你就回到贫民区去吧。你可以劳动到三分象人七分象兽的地步,然后搂搂抱抱,吵吵闹闹,喝酒喝得昏天黑地。不错,这种下流生活并不坏。那是真实的,温暖的,热烈的;多厚的皮也感觉得到,不用经过训练,也不必下功夫就可以尝得到,闻得到。不象科学,文学,古典音乐,哲学和艺术那样。你觉得我冷淡无情,自私自利,是不是?好吧,你可以回到你所喜欢的那种人里面去。嫁给一个多情而有钱的蠢猪之类的人物。让他的厚嘴唇吻你,让他的大皮靴子踢你。你要是不能欣赏你现在已经得到的东西,那你还是去找你能欣赏的东西去吧。

伊莉莎　(无可奈何)啊,你真是个忍心而专制的人。我没办法跟你辩论:你说话都有理,我说什么都不对。可是你自己始终很明白你不过是欺负人。你知道我没法回到你所说的贫民区去,你知道我在世界上除了你和辟克林上校以外没有真正的朋友。你很清楚在跟你们住过以后,我跟一个下等的普通男人在一起是过不来的,你假装不知道,来侮辱我,你好狠毒。你觉得我非回温波街不可,因为除了我父亲那里,我没有其他地方好去。可是你不要太有把握,以为你可以把我放在脚底下踩,可以欺负。我就要嫁给佛莱第,我决定嫁给他,只要我能养活他。

息金斯　(大吃一惊)佛莱第!!!那个小傻子!那可怜的家伙就是有胆子找工作,作个跑腿的也没有人要!女人,你不知道吗?我已经把你变得足配得上一位国王呢?

伊莉莎　佛莱第爱我:在我看来他就跟国王一样好。我并不要他去工作:他不是在象我那样环境里长大的。我自己可以去当教师。

息金斯　老天爷,你能教什么?

伊莉莎　就是你教我的东西。我要教语音学。

息金斯　哈!哈!哈!

伊莉莎　我可以自荐,去作那大胡子匈牙利人的助手。

息金斯　(站起来,异常生气)什么! 那个冒名顶替的家伙! 那个骗子! 那
　　　　个不学无术的马屁精! 你拿我的东西教给他,把我的发明教给他!
　　　　你只要敢向这方面迈一步,我就要勒死你。(他把手放在她肩上)
　　　　听见没有?

伊莉莎　(倔强,不抵抗)勒死我吧。我怕什么。我知道你迟早要动手打
　　　　我的。(他放下手,知道自己失礼,气得直顿脚,匆忙退后,绊倒
　　　　在长榻上)啊哈! 我现在知道怎样对付你了。我真傻,没有早想
　　　　起这个办法来。你拿不走你教给我的东西。你说过我的耳朵比
　　　　你的还好。我还可以对人客气,这是你所办不到的。啊哈! (故
　　　　意用土音说话,不发 h 音,让他生气)衣(息)金斯呀,这你可没辙
　　　　了吧? 现在我不怕你(捻指作声)再欺负人说大话了。我可以在
　　　　报纸上公开声明,说你的公爵夫人不过是你教出来的一个卖花
　　　　姑娘,而且她可以同样地在半年内教好任何人成为公爵夫人,学
　　　　费是一千畿尼。哈,当我回想我曾经在你脚底下爬,被你拿脚
　　　　踩,受你的骂,而我当时只要一举手之劳就可以和你一样,我自
　　　　己真是该打。

息金斯　(甚为诧异)你这个该死的大胆丫头,你! 可是这样比哭哭啼啼
　　　　要好些,比光会拿拖鞋找眼镜要好些,不是吗? (站起来)确实,
　　　　伊莉莎,我说过要把你改造成人,我现在成功了。我喜欢你象现
　　　　在这样。

伊莉莎　对啦,你现在转过来向我讨好了,因为我不怕你了,可以用不着
　　　　你了。

息金斯　当然了。你这小傻瓜。五分钟以前你是我的一块绊脚石,现在
　　　　你是独当一面,一艘护航的军舰了。你和我和辟克林将要是三
　　　　个独身汉而不是两个男人和一个傻姑娘了。

　　　　　息金斯夫人走进来,穿着参加婚礼的衣服。伊莉莎立刻变
　　　　得沉着文雅起来。

息金斯夫人　伊莉莎，马车在等着我们。你预备好了吗？

伊莉莎　都好了。教授也来吗？

息金斯夫人　当然不要他来。他在教堂里不会守规矩的。他总要大声评论牧师的口音。

伊莉莎　那样我们就不能再见了，教授。再见。(她走到门口。)

息金斯夫人　(走向息金斯)再见，孩子。

息金斯　再见，妈妈。(他正要吻息金斯夫人，忽然想起几件事)哦，我想起来了，伊莉莎，请你叫店里送一只火腿和一块斯提尔敦干酪来好吗？再给我买一双鹿皮手套，要八号大小的，还要一条新领带来配我那身新衣服。你可以挑选颜色。(他那高高兴兴，无忧无虑，健强有力的声音说明他毫无改悔之意。)

伊莉莎　(鄙视地)你穿八号的太小了，要是你要里面衬羊毛的话。你的洗脸台抽屉里还有三条新领带，你忘记了。比起斯提尔敦干酪来，辟克林上校更喜欢双料格罗塞斯特干酪；你也分别不出来。今天早晨我已经给别斯太太打过电话，叫她不要忘记了火腿。我真不知道你没有我怎么办？(她飘然走出。)

息金斯夫人　恐怕你把这姑娘惯坏了，亨利。要不是她比较喜欢辟克林的话，我就要为你们担心了。

息金斯　辟克林！哪里的话：她要嫁给佛莱第呢。哈！哈！佛莱第！佛莱第！！哈哈哈哈哈！！！！！(他大笑，全剧结束。)

五

牧歌(其四、其五)①

其　四②

让我们唱雄壮些的歌调,西西里的女神,

荆榛和低微的柽柳并不能感动所有的人,

---

① 选自:维吉尔. 牧歌. 杨宪益,译. 北京:人民文学出版社,1957.

② 译者注:这篇的内容曾引起很多的猜测和争论。这篇是说在维吉尔的好友及庇护者波利奥作罗马执政官(Consul,诗中译作都护)的时候,有一小孩刚刚诞生,而这将是新的黄金时代的开始。在这里,一些简单的考证还是必要的;波利奥作执政官是在纪元前四〇年,这初生的小孩所指是谁,有几个可能:(一)可能是指波利奥的儿子,(二)可能是指屋大维的孩子,(三)屋大维的妹妹屋大维亚(Octavia)和屋大维的政敌安东尼的孩子,(四)屋大维亚和她前夫马切鲁斯(Marcellus)的儿子。从这首诗把这孩子尊如神明,认为是未来的统治者这一点看来,这孩子似乎不可能是指波利奥的儿子,而应该是和屋大维家有关;这孩子又似乎不可能指屋大维或安东尼的孩子,因为诗里很明显说是男孩子,而屋大维和安东尼这时所生的孩子都是女的;因此据我看来,这孩子应该指屋大维亚和她前夫的儿子。这孩子全名叫马库斯·克劳狄乌斯·马切鲁斯(Marcus Claudius Marcellus),约生于纪元前四十三年;屋大维非常宠爱他,并打算以之为嗣,在纪元前二十五年把自己的女儿嫁给他,但不幸在两年后他突然死了;据说是屋大维的妻子妒忌他,怕他继承帝位,而把他毒死的;维吉尔在史诗"伊尼特"第六卷第八百六十行起也提到此子,可以参看。诗人写这首诗时,内战初停,因此诗人想像在屋大维及其继承者的统治下将出现新的黄金时代。这种对未来的希冀本来是很自然的;但过去西方一些基督教学者认为这是诗人对耶稣基督的诞生的一种预言;这种穿凿附会是很可笑的。

要是还歌唱山林，也让它和都护名号相称。

现在到了库玛谶语①里所谓最后的日子，

伟大的世纪的运行又要重新开始， 5

处女星已经回来，又回到沙屯②的统治，

从高高的天上新的一代已经降临，

在他生时，黑铁时代就已经终停，

在整个世界又出现了黄金的新人。

圣洁的露吉娜③，你的阿波罗今已为主。 10

这个光荣的时代要开始，正当你为都护，

波利奥啊，伟大的岁月正在运行初度。

在你的领导下，我们的罪恶的残余痕迹

都要消除，大地从长期的恐怖获得解脱。

他将过神的生活，英雄们和天神他都会看见， 15

他自己也将要被人看见在他们中间，

他要统治着祖先圣德所致太平的世界。

孩子，为了你那大地不用人力来栽，

首先要长出那蔓延的长春藤和狐指草，

还有那埃及豆和那含笑的莨苕； 20

充满了奶的羊群将会得自己回家，

巨大的狮子牲口也不必再害怕，

---

① 译者注：库玛（Cume）谶语是古代罗马人的一种迷信；据说在库玛地方有一山洞，洞里住一女巫，能作种种预言，这些谶语就是记录下来的预言；当时罗马统治阶级这种迷信和我们东汉初年光武帝等迷信谶纬图书是一样的。

② 译者注：沙屯（Saturn），神名，又见第六首第四十一行。据说这是最早的神王，在他的统治下开始了黄金时代；当时罗马正在进行更改历法；这种认为时纪运行周而复始和统治阶级的历数中衰应该改元的迷信也是同我们东汉初年的说法很相像的。

③ 译者注：露吉娜（Lucina）是罗马神话里的"送子娘娘"，也就是狄安娜女神（Diana），阿波罗的妹妹。这里显然指屋大维的妹妹，而阿波罗神当即指屋大维。

你的摇篮也要开放花朵来将你抚抱，

蛇虺将都死亡，不再有骗人的毒草，

东方的豆蔻也将在各地生得很好。　　　　　　　　25

当你长大能读英雄颂歌和祖先事迹，

当你开始能够了解道德的意义，

那田野将要逐渐为柔穗所染黄，

紫熟的葡萄将悬挂在野生的荆棘上，

坚实的栎树也将流出甘露琼浆。　　　　　　　　30

但是往日罪恶的遗迹那时还有余存，

人还要乘船破浪，用高墙围起城镇，

人也还要把田地犁成一条条深沟，

还要有提菲斯，还要有阿戈的巨舟①

载去英雄的精锐，还要有新的战争，　　　　　　35

还要有英雄阿喀琉②作特洛亚的远征。

但当坚实的年代使你长大成人的时候，

航海的人将离开海，那松木的船艘

将不再运货，土地将供应一切东西，

葡萄将不需镰刀，田畴将不需锄犁，　　　　　　40

那时健壮的农夫将从耕牛上把轭拿开；

羊毛也不要染上种种假造的颜色，

草原上的羊群自己就会得改变色彩，

或者变成柔和的深紫，或鲜艳的黄蓝，

吃草的幼羔也会得自己带上朱斑。　　　　　　　45

---

① 译者注：提菲斯（Tiphys）和阿戈（Argo）的巨舟都见著名的金羊毛故事；阿戈就是
载着英雄们到黑海去寻找金羊毛的船；提菲斯是船上的掌舵人。

② 译者注：阿喀琉（Achilles）是荷马史诗里的著名英雄，他攻打特洛亚城并杀了它的
主将赫克托（Hector）。

现在司命神女①根据命运的不变意志，

对她们织梭说，"奔驰吧，伟大的日子。"

时间就要到了，走向伟大的荣誉，

天神的骄子啊，你，上帝的苗裔，

看呀，那摇摆的世界负着苍穹，　　　　　　　　　　50

看那大地和海洋和深远的天空，

看万物怎样为未来的岁月欢唱，

我希望我生命的终尾可以延长，

有足够的精力来传述你的功绩，

色雷斯的俄耳甫的诗歌也不能相比，　　　　　　　55

林努斯②也比不过，即使有他父母在旁，

嘉流贝③帮助前者，后者美容的阿波罗帮忙，

甚至山神以阿卡狄④为评判和我竞赛，

就是山神以阿卡狄为评判也要失败；

小孩子呀，你要开始以笑认你的生母，　　　　　　60

(十个月的长时间曾使母亲疲乏受苦)，

开始笑吧，孩子，要不以笑容对你双亲，

就不配与天神同餐，与神女同寝。⑤

---

① 译者注：司命神女(Fatae)是罗马神话中掌管人类命运的神；她们共有三个，用纺梭织着人类的命运。

② 译者注：林努斯(Linus)是神话中著名的歌手，他的父亲就是阿波罗神。

③ 译者注：嘉流贝(Calliope)是司诗歌的神女之一，她是著名歌手奥尔菲的母亲。

④ 译者注：阿卡狄(Arcadia)又见下面第七首和第十首，是希腊南部地名，是著名的牧地，相传是山神潘(Pan)的居地。

⑤ 译者注："与天神同餐，与神女同寝"是指神话里著名的半神英雄赫库雷(Hercules)的故事。他在人世上建立了十二件功劳，终于得参加天神的行列，并以女神希贝(Hebe)为妻。

其　五^①

梅　莫勃苏呀，我们两个高手今天既然见面，
　　你会吹轻快的芦笛，我长于歌诵诗篇，
　　我们何不就在榛莽和榆树中间小坐一番？

莫　你是老前辈，我一切遵命，梅那伽，
　　或去到树荫，在那风摇不定的阴影下，　　　　　　　5
　　或到岩穴间去；看那山间的藤蔓
　　已经在岩穴上纷披着果实斑斓。

梅　我们山里只有阿敏塔能同你比赛唱歌，

莫　什么？他不是夸口要胜过阿波罗？

梅　你先开始，莫勃苏，唱那"菲利丝的爱恋"，　　　　　10
　　或唱那"阿尔康的赞扬"或"考德鲁的埋怨"^②，
　　开始唱吧，提屠鲁在看守着吃草的羊。

莫　不，最近我在一株榉树的青皮上
　　曾刻过一首歌，并且加上了音乐节奏，
　　让我先试试，然后你再叫阿敏塔来对口。　　　　　　15

梅　正如垂杨总比不上淡绿的橄榄，

---

①　译者注：这篇体裁是两个牧人梅那伽和莫勃苏（Mopsus）的对话，然后两人歌唱了
　　一个牧人达芙尼的惨死和升天；过去不少注释家认为这里的达芙尼实在是指的恺
　　撒，这是很可能的；恺撒被刺死是在纪元前四十四年，次年屋大维隆重纪念他，据
　　说当时天空发现了一个新星，证明恺撒已成为天神。据说恺撒曾把纪念酒神巴库
　　斯（Bacchus）的礼仪歌舞从东方带到意大利，这里说的"达芙尼开始用阿曼尼亚
　　（Armenia）的猛虎驾车，并带来了巴库斯的神舞神歌"应即指此。后面又说设立
　　四座祭坛，两座为达芙尼，两座为阿波罗；按在维吉尔诗里屋大维常比作阿波罗，
　　所以达芙尼即指恺撒也是符合的。

②　译者注："菲利丝的爱恋""阿尔康（Alcon）的赞扬""考德鲁（Condrus）的埋怨"都是
　　歌名。

卑微的缬草也不能和紫玫瑰作伴，

照我看来同样阿敏塔也与你不同，

但是不要说了，孩子，我们已到了岩洞。

莫　达芙尼死了，山林神女都为他惨死啼哭，　　　　20

（你们丛榛和溪水也都曾经目睹），

当他母亲抱着她儿子可怜的尸首，

向天神和星辰诉说他们残忍的时候，

那些日子里，没有一个牧人赶着牛

走向清冷的溪水，也没有任何牲口　　　　25

肯去喝水或者碰一碰一根草豆；

达芙尼，为你的死连非洲狮子也在呻吟，

连荒野的山峰和树林也在回声相应。

达芙尼开始用阿曼尼亚的猛虎驾车

并带来了巴库斯的神舞神歌，　　　　30

在柔软的戈矛上绕着薛荔女萝。

正如藤蔓使老树，葡萄使藤蔓更加漂亮，

牡牛为畜群增光，谷子为肥沃的田野增光，

你使你周围一切生色，自从命运把你带走，

巴雷斯①和阿波罗都离开了我们的田畴。　　　　35

常当我们在田里种下了丰满的大麦，

却长出来没有用的莠草和不实的萧艾；

只有荒荆和有刺的野棘到处丛生，

代替了深紫的水仙花，柔美的地丁。

在地上撒满绿叶，在清泉上植树成荫，　　　　40

牧人们要这样作，这是达芙尼的命令；

给他造一个坟，并且在坟上加上墓铭：

---

① 　译者注：巴雷斯（Pales）是司农耕的女神。

　　"我是山林的达芙尼,我的名声远达星霄,

　　美好的羊群的看守人,我自己却更美好。"

梅　神圣的诗人啊,你的诗歌对于我　　　　　　　　　　　45

　　正如疲倦时在草地上睡眠,正如苦渴

　　在炎暑中得到了流泉的清甜的水。

　　你不但在吹笛上,连唱歌也赶上了前辈;

　　幸运的孩子,你现在和他并驾齐驱,

　　可是我还要尽我所能把歌辞继续,　　　　　　　　　50

　　把你的达芙尼高高的举向星霄,

　　把他举向星霄,因为他也跟我相好。

莫　没有别的礼物比这个对我更有用,

　　那孩子值得赞扬,而且斯提米空①

　　也已经把你的诗才对我称颂。　　　　　　　　　　　55

梅　他辉煌的新来到天门前充满惊奇,

　　看着那云彩和星辰都在他脚底,

　　为了这个,山林田野和那山神,

　　牧人和林中神女都觉得无限欢腾,

　　豺狼不再为羊群设伏,也不再有人　　　　　　　　　60

　　用罗网捕鹿,善良的达芙尼爱好和平。

　　多发的青山由于快乐而昂首高歌,

　　直达星霄,就连岩石也唱歌相和,

　　丛树也唱着,"他是神啊,是神啊"。

　　赐福给我们和你朋友,这里祭坛四座,　　　　　　　65

　　两座是为你而设,两座是为阿波罗。

　　每年我将为你放上有泡沫的鲜奶两罐,

　　还有肥美的橄榄香油两大碗;

---

①　译者注:斯提米空(Stimichon)大概是一个知音的牧人。

而且首先要喝很多酒来庆祝欢宴，

收割时就在树荫下，天冷就在灶前，　　　　　　　　70

让酒瓶流出来阿里乌西①的新酿，

达摩埃塔和利克托斯的埃贡将为我歌唱，

阿菲西伯②也要舞蹈像羊神那样。

你将永享祭祀，每当我们以神圣誓言

向神女们祈祷，或当我们祓除土田。　　　　　　　75

正如野猪爱在山岭上，鱼爱在水里住，

正如蜜蜂爱吃茴香，蝉爱吃清露，

你的荣耀，声名和颂扬将永世长存，

每年我们农人们像对酒神和谷神

都要向你祈求，你也要为我们作证。　　　　　　　80

莫　这样好的歌我要用什么礼物回敬？

无论南风的絮语或浪涛击岸的嚣音，

或是清泉涌下幽谷的乱石崚嶒，

我认为都不如你的歌那样好听。

梅　我要先送给你这个纤细的芦笛，　　　　　　　　85

它曾教我唱了"柯瑞东热恋着漂亮的阿荔吉"，

和"这是谁的羊，是否梅利伯所有？"

莫　那你就拿去这个安提根尼③常要的羊钩，

虽然他那时也讨人喜欢，可是我没给他；

羊钩是漂亮的，有均匀的竹节和铜饰，梅那伽。　　90

---

①　译者注：阿里乌西（Ariusis）希腊（地名），当地的葡萄酒最为著名。

②　译者注：埃贡，达摩埃塔和阿菲西伯（Alphesiboeus）都是擅长歌舞的牧人。

③　译者注：安提根尼（Antigenes）也是一个年轻的牧人。

六

地心游记(第九、十章)[①]

第九章　在冰岛

　　我们离开的日子到了。前一天,和善的汤孙先生把致冰岛统治者特朗勃伯爵、大主教的助手匹克吐孙先生和雷克雅未克市长芬孙先生的热情的介绍信带来给我们。为了表示谢意,叔父至诚地和他握手。

　　6月2日早晨六点钟,我们宝贵的行李被装入伏尔卡利的船舱,船长把我们带到略微显得狭窄的尾部。

　　"是不是顺风?"叔父问道。

　　"风向不能再好了,"船长布加恩回答,"刮东南风。我们将张起全部风帆离开波罗的海峡。"

　　几分钟以后,我们果然扬帆启航,一小时之内我们就穿过了埃尔西诺尔港口。我神经质地期望在那块著名的平台上见到《哈姆莱特》(莎士比亚的剧作)一剧中出现的鬼魂。

---

①　选自:儒勒·凡尔纳. 地心游记. 杨宪益,闻时清,译. 上海:上海人民出版社,2019.
　　编者注:本书为杨宪益与闻时清合译,虽然目前并无相关文献显示两位译者合作翻译的模式,但考虑到杨宪益外译汉作品的类型,加之2019年上海文化发展基金会将该译作纳入《杨宪益中译作品集》(全五卷),故此,本卷选集也将此作列入杨宪益外国文学汉译系列。

"崇高的狂人!"我说,"你无疑会赞同我们! 你或许会跟随我们,在地心找到解决你的永恒的问题的答案!"

然而在那古老的墙垣上,什么也没有出现;那古堡也比英勇的丹麦王子要年轻得多。它现在是这个每年有一万五千条各国船只经过的海峡的管理人的豪华寓所。克朗葛保古堡很快地消失在浓雾中了,矗立在瑞典岸上的海尔新堡塔也消失了。在卡特加特①的微风的吹拂下,我们的帆船稍稍有点倾侧。

伏尔卡利是一条很好的帆船,但是坐在帆船里任何人都不能肯定会遭遇到些什么。这条船把煤、日用品、陶器、羊毛衣和小麦带到雷克雅未克去;全船人员都是丹麦人,一共只有五人。

"要多久才能到达?"叔父问船长。

"十来天,如果在穿过弗罗埃②时不遇到太多风暴的话。"船长回答说。

"即使遇到也不至于耽搁很多天吧?"

"不会的,黎登布洛克先生,你放心好了,我们一定会到那儿的。"

傍晚时刻,帆船围绕着丹麦北端的斯卡根海角航行,晚上穿过了斯卡格拉克,接近了挪威南端名叫那池的海角,并且到达了北海。

两天以后,我们在苏格兰港湾见到了彼得黑德,然后我们从奥克尼和设得兰的中间驰过,并向费罗群岛进发。到了费罗群岛以后,我们又一直驰向冰岛南岸的波得兰岬角。

不一会儿,我们的船就受到大西洋海浪的冲击了;它逆着北风,困难地到了费罗群岛。3日那天,看见了这个群岛最东面的岛屿——米刚奈斯岛。这以后,船就一直驰向位于冰岛南岸的波得兰海峡。

全段航程中没有发生意外。我没有晕船,可是叔父却完全被晕船所折磨,这使他感到很大的烦恼和更大的惭愧。

因此他无法向船长询问有关斯奈弗、交通工具和旅行上种种方便的

---

① 译者注:卡特加特(Cattègat),丹麦瑞典间的海峡。
② 译者注:弗罗埃(Feroê),丹麦的岛屿,气候恶劣,多雾和大风。

问题,这一切只得等上岸时再问了。他一直躺在船舱中,船的颠簸把船舱的板壁震得咯吱咯吱直响。我认为他活该受罪。

11 日,我们驰过了波得兰海角,并且见到了高出在波得兰海角的米杜斯·姚可。这里的海峡十分昏暗,岸很陡,孤零零地突出在海滩上。然后伏尔卡利从距离港湾还有相当一段间隔的地方,在大量鲸鱼和鲨鱼之间继续向西航行。不久我们见到一块仿佛凿穿了的大岩石,汹涌的浪涛在裂缝中穿过去。西萌小岛看来似乎是浮在清澄的海面上一般。我们的帆船从这里围绕着形成西萌小岛西南角的雷克牙恩斯海角航行。海浪很大,它使得叔父无法到甲板上去欣赏那在西南风吹拂下的锯齿形的海岸。

四十八小时以后,一阵暴风雨迫使我们收下所有的帆,暴风雨平静了以后,我们在危险的斯卡根见到了浮标。斯卡根的危崖长长地延伸在海中。一位冰岛的领港员登上了我们的船,三小时以后,伏尔卡利在雷克雅未克以外的法克萨港口抛锚。

教授终于走出了船舱,脸色有点苍白,有点憔悴,但仍旧很兴奋,两眼现出满意的神色。

镇上的人们都聚集在码头上,对一条给他们每一个人带来一些东西的帆船,感到很大的兴趣。

叔父赶紧离开这个浮在水面上的监狱,可是在他离开以前,他向北指给我看一座双峰高山,有一个重叠的尖峰上盖满了积雪。"斯奈弗!"他喊道,"斯奈弗!"

这时候,叔父做了一个手势,叫我保持绝对安静,于是他爬进一只小艇,小艇把我们带到了冰岛海岸。统治者特朗勃先生立刻出现;叔父把来自哥本哈根的介绍信交给他,接着他们就以丹麦语作了一次简短的谈话,我有足够理由不参加这次谈话。结果这位统治者完全满足了黎登布洛克教授的要求。

叔父受到了市长芬孙先生的热情接待。市长不仅和统治者一样穿着军装,性情也同样十分温和。大主教的助手匹克吐孙先生正在冰岛的草原上旅行,我们暂时不能见到他。但是我们遇到了一位十分讨人喜欢和最有帮助的弗立特利克孙先生,他在雷克雅未克学校里教自然科学。他只能说冰岛语和拉丁语,他和我以拉丁语相处得很好,并且成了我在冰岛逗留期间唯一能交谈的人。

这位善良的人把我们安顿在他家的三间房子中的两间里面。我们立刻把行李搬进去,在那里住下来,我们行李之多有些引起当地居民的惊讶。叔父对我说:"现在最困难的事情也解决了!"

"最困难的事情?"我说道。

"当然,"他回答,"我们一到了那地方,就得下去!"

"可是怎么上来呢?"

"哦!别管那些。来吧,别浪费时间。我要到图书馆去,那里可能有萨克奴姗的手稿,如果真能找到一些手稿,我还得仔细查考一下。"

"啊!对这个我不大感兴趣。在这块土地上,有趣的东西不是在地底下,而是在地面上。"

我走了出去,无目的地走着。

雷克雅未克一共只有两条街,不至于迷路,所以我就不必指手画脚地问路而惹来很多麻烦了。

这个长形的市镇躺在两座小山之间,地势相当低,土地潮湿。小镇的一边覆盖着一大片火山喷石,缓缓地伸入海去。小镇的另一头就是宽阔的法克萨海湾,北面是巨大的斯奈弗冰山,海湾中现在只停泊着伏尔卡利。平时英国和法国的渔业巡逻船都停在那里,但是现在它们正在东部岛岸巡逻。雷克雅未克仅有的两条马路中比较长的那条是和海岸平行的,两边尽是商人和店员住的、用横叠起来的红木柱头造成的房子;另一条马路比较偏西,通向小湖,每边都住着主教和非商人家。

我迈着大步在那荒凉寂静的路上走着。不时看见一块好像旧地毯似的发黄的草坪或者一个果园。园中的那一点点蔬菜、土豆和莴苣只能做一些简单的饭菜,园中还有几株瘦瘦的丁香也在生长。

靠近那条没有店铺的街,有一个用土墙围起来的公墓,它的面积倒不小。再过去几步,就到了统治者的住所,它跟汉堡的市政大厦比起来只是一幢破屋而已,但在冰岛居民的茅屋相映之下,却如一座宫殿。

在小湖和市镇之间矗立着一座礼拜堂,是基督教堂的风格,它是用火山爆发时开采出来的石灰石建成的。屋顶铺着红瓦,一旦遇到巨大的西风,必然会被刮得向四处飞散,使教徒们遭受巨大损失。

在礼拜堂旁边一块隆起的高地上,我看见了国立学校,后来我从我们的房东那里知道,这所学校里有希伯来文、英文、法文和丹麦文四种语言课。惭愧得很,对于这几种语言,我连一个字母都不知道。和这所小小的学校里的四十个学生比起来,我算是成绩最坏的学生。我也不配和他们一起睡在那些象衣柜似的双人床上——在这种床上,娇气些的人睡一夜就会闷死的。

不到三个小时,我把这座小镇连它的四周围全都参观完了。整个小镇显得异乎寻常地惨淡。没有树木,也没有花草。到处是尖耸的火山岩。当地居民的茅屋是用土和草盖起来的,墙往中间倾斜,好像是些直接放在地上的屋顶。不过这些屋顶却像一片田野,由于里面住着人,比较暖和,所以草在屋顶上长得比在寒冷的土地上要繁茂得多。而且每到割草期,人们就小心地把草割下来,要不然家畜就必然会把这些绿色的屋顶当作牧场了。

我回来的时候,看见大部分人都在晒、腌和包装他们主要的出口货——鳘鱼。这些人看来很结实但很笨拙,头发比德国人的还黄,神色忧郁,仿佛他们觉得自己和人类几乎没有接触似的。他们偶然大笑一下,可是我从来没有看见任何一个人微笑过。

他们的服饰包括一件用大家都称为"瓦特墨尔"的粗糙的黑羊毛织成的卫生衫、一顶阔边帽子、红条子裤子和盖着脚的一块折叠起来的皮。

女人们的脸都显得忧愁而消沉,可是很随和,也没有面部表情,她们穿着紧身胸衣和用暗色的"瓦特墨尔"做的裙子。女孩子们都梳着辫子,头上戴着棕色羊毛织成的帽子,出嫁了的女子都用彩色的头巾包着头,头巾上面还有一块亚麻布。

散步回来,我看见叔父和我们的主人在一起。

第十章　冰岛的一次晚餐

晚饭准备好了，叔父由于在船上被迫吃素，这次他饱餐了一顿。这顿算是丹麦式而不是冰岛式的饭，并不怎么出色；可是我们这位是冰岛而不是丹麦的主人却使我想起古老的好客的故事来了。显然我们已经比主人更显得没有拘束了。

谈话是用冰岛语进行的，叔父夹进几个德语，弗立特利克孙则夹进几个拉丁语，好让我也能听得懂。谈话以科学为话题，可是谈到我们自己的计划时，叔父就完全保留了。

弗立特利克孙先生立刻就问起叔父在图书馆里研究工作的结果。

"你们的图书馆啊！"叔父喊道，"那些差不多空空的书架子上只有几本古怪的书！"

"哦，"他的主人答道，"我们有八千卷书，其中有许多是贵重而稀罕的书。"

"我不知道你能用什么来证明你这句话，"教授说道，"据我估计——"

"哦，黎登布洛克先生，它们大都被借走了。我们古老的冰岛上面的人都爱看书！农民和渔夫都是看了再看。所以这些书不是老放在门后面，而是由一个人传给另一个人看；他们看了再看，经常是一两年以后才回到书架上。"

"同时，"叔父有些恼怒地说，"一些外地人——"

"首先，外地人都有他们自己的图书馆，最重要的是我们的农民也要受教育。我再说一遍：对学习的爱好是渗透在冰岛人的血液中的。所以在1816年，我们成立了一个文学协会，它发展得很好，也有外国学者参加。协会也出版书籍，都是些能教育我们的同胞和真正为我们国家服务的书，如果您也加入，黎登布洛克先生，我们将感到很荣幸。"

叔父已经至少是一百个科学协会的会员了，这次他还是欣然加入，所以感动了弗立特利克孙先生。

"那么，"他说，"告诉我你要找什么书，我可以帮助你找。"

我瞧着叔父。他犹豫着没有回答，因为这直接涉及他的计划。但是经过考虑后，他还是回答了："你那些古书里面，有没有阿恩·萨克奴姗的著作？"

"你指的就是那位十六世纪的人，他是一位伟大的博物学家、炼金术士和旅行家？"

"对。"

"冰岛文学和科学的光荣之一，一位著名人士？"

"正如你所说的那样。"

"他的勇气能和他的天才相比？"

"是的；我觉得你很熟悉他。"

叔父又说道："你有他的作品吗？"这时候他的眼睛炯炯有光。

"不，没有。"

"冰岛没有？"

"冰岛或别的地方都没有。"

"为什么呢？"

"因为阿恩·萨克奴姗当时被当作异教徒处死刑了，他的作品都在哥本哈根被绞刑吏烧光了。"

"好——太好了！"叔父喊道，把这位冰岛的教授吓了一跳。

"请再说一遍？"这位冰岛教授说道。

"对，这说明了一切。我现在知道萨克奴姗为什么被排斥并且被迫隐瞒了他的发现，还不得不把他的秘密藏在密码里面——"

"什么秘密？"弗立特利克孙先生有兴趣地问道。

"一个秘密……它……"叔父吞吞吐吐地说。

"您是不是有些什么特别的文件？"我们的主人问。

"不……我说的完全是一种假定。"

"我明白了，"弗立特利克孙先生说，他太客气了，所以不敢坚持，"我希望，"他又加上一句，"你能去调查一下我们岛上的一些矿藏。"

"当然，"叔父答道，"但是我来得已经晚了一些，这里已经有学者来过了吧？"

"是的，黎登布洛克先生，已经到这里来考察过的有奉王命而来的奥拉夫生和鲍弗尔生两位先生，有特罗伊尔先生，有坐法国'搜索'号军舰①来的盖马尔和罗勃特先生的科学调查团，最近还有坐'奥当斯皇后'号军舰来的一些学者，他们对冰岛的历史地理作了不少贡献。不过，请相信我，这里还有考察工作可做。"

"您这样想吗？"叔父装作若无其事地问，一面竭力压住眼中的闪光。

"是的。还有人们不太知道的很多山岭、冰山和火山值得考察！不用说远的，您就看突出在那边的那座山吧，那是斯奈弗山。"

"啊，斯奈弗。"叔父说。

"不错，这是最奇怪的火山之一，它的火山口很少有人访问过。"

"是死火山吗？"

"哦，是的，已经有五百年了。"

"那么，"叔父说，他把腿交叉起来，竭力使自己不跳起来，"我想我应该到赛弗——哦，斯奈弗——究竟是什么——去进行地质研究？"

"斯奈弗，"好心的弗立特利克孙先生重复着说。

这一段对话是用拉丁语进行的，所以我能听懂，当我看到叔父心中得意扬扬，可是表面想不露声色而又掩饰不住的时候，我自己的面部表情简直也很难控制。

"是的，"他说，"你的话使我决定登上这座山，甚至于还要研究这个陷口！"

"我很抱歉，"弗立特利克孙先生答道，"我的职务不允许我陪你去。如果能陪你去，我既感到高兴，又能获得利润。"

---

① 译者注："搜索"号军船，1835 年法国杜贝莱海军大将为了寻访一支失踪的远征军而派出去的一艘军舰。关于这支由勃洛斯维勒和拉里洛阿斯率领的远征军，一直没有得到任何消息。

"哦,不,不!弗立特利克孙先生,"叔父喊道,"当然你的职务要紧,虽然你那渊博的学问对我们极有帮助。"

"我非常赞成你从这座火山着手,黎登布洛克先生。"他说,"你这番考察一定会得到很多收获,发现很多新鲜东西。不过,请你告诉我,你们打算怎么样到斯奈弗半岛去呢?"

"穿过海湾,渡海过去。这是最短的一条路。"

"也许是的,不过这条路没有办法走。"

"为什么?"

"因为我们这儿一条汽船也没有。"

"真糟!"

"只有沿着海岸打陆地上过去。这条路长一点,不过一路上更有趣些。"

"好吧,我想法去找一个带路的。"

"我正好有一个可以介绍给你。"

"是靠得住的机灵人吗?"

"是的。他是半岛上的居民。是个非常熟练的猎手。你一定会满意的。他丹麦话讲得非常好。"

"那么我什么时候可以看见他呢?"

"明天,如果你同意的话。"

"为什么不是今天呢?"

"因为他要明天才能来。"

"那就明天吧。"叔父叹了一口气回答。

晚饭结束了,这位德国人对冰岛教授衷心感谢。这位德国人已经知道了许多最重要的事情——其中包括萨克奴姗的历史、文件神秘的原因。我们的主人不能陪我们一同去,但明天我们将能找到一位向导。

七

古希腊抒情诗选（二十七首）①

童 谣

哪儿有玫瑰和紫地丁？
哪儿有芜菱青又青？
这儿有玫瑰和紫地丁，
这儿有芜菱青又青。

屠尔泰欧斯（一首）

战 歌

前进啊，斯巴达人的子弟，
你们是勇敢的人民的后裔；
伸出左手，拿起你们的坚盾，
有力的扔出长矛，向着敌人；
对你们的生命决不要吝惜，
那样不是斯巴达人的惯例。

---

① 选自《世界文学》1961 年 Z1 期（八·九月号）。

阿克曼（二首）

歌

我要给你一口大鼎，
里面能装一大锅饭，
现在还没生火，但是就要装满，
好给贪吃的阿克曼一顿饱餐；
他喜欢饭煮得热热的，
当白天不再是那么短；
他并不要吃那些细巧的点心，
同老百姓一样，只愿吃得平凡。

歌

啊，少女们，你们的歌声甜蜜而温柔，
我的身体不行了，真希望能象那海鸥，
随着春天的翡翠鸟，如海水那样幽蓝，
毫无畏惧的飞过象花朵一般的波澜。

阿尔凯欧斯（三首）

暴　君

他迈开了大步，跨过你们头上，
你们召来了鬼，却一声不敢响；

乡亲们,冒烟的木柴要早灭掉,
越快越好,不要让火继续延烧。

壁　　垒

要建立壁垒并不在于
木头石块,工匠的技巧;
只要人知道要保卫自己,
那就有了可靠的城堡。

饮酒歌

我们喝酒吧,何必等到点灯?
我们只有一个手指长的光阴。
朋友,从架上拿下巨大酒罍;
天帝和塞美娜的儿子给人类
忘忧的酒;一成酒掺两成水,
让我们循环痛饮,彼此传杯。

沙浮(九首)

献给司爱女神

宝座璀璨,永生的司爱神女,
织作迷网的帝子,我向你求诉,
不要使我的心充满悲哀、痛苦,
我的女主;

请你降临，如果你曾从远方
听到过我的呼声，我的渴望，
请你就从你父亲的殿宇飞降，
神辇金黄，
灵巧而快捷的鹊鸟鼓着健翼，
驾着车，飞降到玄色的土地，
回旋着，经过了苍穹无际，
穿过大气；
啊，女神，你就很快的来到，
你那不朽的面庞上带着微笑，
问我为什么悲伤，有什么需要，
为什么呼叫；
问我这狂乱的心有什么希冀，
"啊，沙浮，你要我怎样施力？
要叫哪一个人从心里爱你？
谁对你不起？
跑开的人将很快反过来追逐，
不接受馈赠的将给你礼物，
不爱你的将很快转成爱慕，
不由她自主。"
现在请你降临吧，我的忧愁
请给我解脱，并且请你成就
我心愿成就的事，作我的战友，
帮助我奋斗。

歌

我觉得同天上神仙可以相比，

能够同你面对面的坐在一起，
听你讲话是这样令人心喜，
是这样甜蜜：
听你动人的笑声，使我的心
在我的胸中这样的跳动不宁，
当我看着你，波洛赫，我的嘴唇
发不出声音，
我的舌头凝住了，一阵温柔的火
突然间从我的皮肤上面溜过，
我的眼睛看不见东西，我的耳朵
被噪声填塞，
我浑身流汗，全身都在战慄，
我变得苍白，比草叶还要无力，
好象几几乎我就要断了呼吸，
在垂死之际。

断　章

有若娇红的苹果悬在树梢，
在最高枝头，被采果的人忘了，
不是忘了，而是要采采不到。

断　章

有若山里的风信子被牧人践踏，
虽然倒在地上，但还开着紫花。

午　夜

现在月亮已经开始西沉，
昴星已落下，是午夜时分，
时间还是在飞驶不停，
我一个人睡着，还在空等。

黄　昏

白昼把世间万物随意散置，
而黄昏把一切又重新聚起，
它带回来那些绵羊和山羊，
又把孩子带到他母亲那里。

断　章

在清冷的水边，
风从林檎间吹过，
树叶在轻颤，
摇落下幽梦朵朵。

断　章

在皓月旁边，
繁星失去了光采，
银光遍照着，
是这样无所不在。

歌

啊,处女的年华,你去到哪里?
去到哪里?
新娘,我走了,同你不再在一起,
不再在一起。

梭伦(一首)

警　惕

对每一个人你都要提防,
看他心里是否有暗剑隐藏;
他对你也许笑着脸讲话,
但心是黑的,话里两种心肠。

阿那克雷翁(一首)

歌

爱情象铁匠给我沉重打击,
又把我浸在冰凉的泉水里。

西摩尼底斯(六首)

祖　国

要作完全幸福的人而生活，
首先要有威名远扬的祖国。

温　关

在这里斯巴达子弟四千，
曾经抗击了敌军三百万。

温　关

过客请传告斯巴达人，在这里
我们长眠，遵守着他们的指示。

温　关

埋在这块土地里的人永享荣光，
他们同你，斯巴达广士的名王，
死在一起，在战斗中终于遏止
无数波斯人锐矢和枭骑的攻势。

墓　铭

永别了，享大荣光的战争英雄们，

永别了,雅典人民的子弟骑兵,
你们面对大半个希腊进行了斗争,
为祖国的清歌妙舞抛掷了青春。

墓　铭

让我们记住这些善战的勇士在此长眠,
他们战死是为了保卫特竭亚的丰原;
用戈矛捍护了城国,这样就使得希腊
不必从光荣的头上把自由华冠掷下。

柏拉图(一首)

歌

我把苹果丢给你,你如果对我真心,
就接受苹果,交出你的处女的爱情,
如果你的打算不同,也拿起苹果想想,
要知道你的红颜只有短暂的时光。

阿斯克雷比阿底斯(二首)

歌

你舍不得处女年华么? 那有什么关系?
当你到了阴间,你将找不到人爱你,

爱情的欢乐属于人世,等你到了幽府,

处女啊,我们长眠,只留下白骨和尘土。

歌

狄杜密用她的柔枝将我紧紧擒拿,

看见她的美貌,我象蜡在火上溶化,

皮肤黑有什么关系？ 看那黑色的炭

燃着了它,就变得象玫瑰一般红艳。

后　记[①]

　　说起古希腊的诗歌,相传最早的和最重要的作品当然是荷马的两部史诗;我们都知道这两部史诗从口头传述到写成定稿经过了很长时期,但是至少在公元前八、九世纪就已经有职业歌人演唱这两部史诗中的若干片段章节了;至于抒情诗歌,一般西方文学史家都喜欢把它在时代上列在史诗之后,这主要是因为名字为我们所知的古希腊的抒情诗歌的作者,传说中的人物除外,都是公元前六、七世纪和以后的人。但是实际上,在任何古代民族中,抒情诗歌的起源也并不会比英雄史诗更晚,只是史诗是由职业歌人演唱的,而且这种歌人世代互相传授他们的技术,因此我们就听说古代有个叫作荷马的史诗作家;抒情诗歌最初只是劳动人民自然的感情流露,创造诗歌的人并没有把名字流传下来,最早的抒情诗人的名字因此就无人知道了。在现存的古希腊诗歌里,有一首歌谣《燕子来了》,其中保存了不少原始人的宗教信仰,看来其来源是相当古老的;这一类的诗歌

---

① 　编者注:此"后记"为译者杨宪益关于古希腊抒情诗歌评介性短文,是杨宪益比较文学研究和诗歌翻译研究的重要内容。

完全可能比荷马史诗和早期神颂还要早一些;再如《哪儿有玫瑰和紫地丁?》这首童谣,大概也可以追溯到公元前七、八世纪或者更早的时代。

最早的抒情诗大概都是用来歌唱的,歌唱时又往往伴有乐器;我国古代常常用"管弦"来代表器乐,弦乐是琴瑟之类,管乐是箫管之类,古代希腊也是这样;如果按伴奏的乐器来说,可以分作笛歌和琴歌两大支;在公元前七世纪前后,有一种抒情诗体叫作"埃列高斯"(Elégos),有人说这字的原意是"悲歌",也有人说是"笛歌"的意思;姑且不管原来字义是什么,总之这种歌是用笛子伴奏的,是一种六音节和五音节混合的诗体,不同于全用六音节诗句的荷马史诗。这种歌曲多半是宴席上的乐曲或出征时的战歌;我们可以举公元前七世纪初年或中叶的屠尔泰欧斯(Tyrtaeus)的歌曲为例;相传屠尔泰欧斯是雅典的一个跛足的教师,他去到斯巴达,写了一些战歌,帮助斯巴达人战胜他们的敌人;我们从他的残存的战歌可以看到他的诗是质朴而有力的;这些歌曲帮助培养了斯巴达人民勇武刚强的传统。古代记载说,"每当斯巴达人要出征的时候,根据法律每人都要先到国王的营帐去听屠尔泰欧斯的战歌,这样就使得每一个人都愿意为他的祖国牺牲了。"屠尔泰欧斯的声名不仅限于斯巴达地方;一直到柏拉图的时代,据说年轻的雅典人还能背诵他的诗歌。

除了屠尔泰欧斯而外,公元前七世纪的"笛歌"诗人还有阿尔希洛科斯(Archilochos);这是一个多才多艺的诗人,据说他创造了一些新的格律,如抑扬格和四音节诗等;他的诗歌的内容也是多种多样的,有歌颂战斗的诗;也有表达个人情感的抒情诗和讽刺诗,可惜都没有保存下来。还有加利诺斯(Callinos)和密勒摩斯(Mimnermos)也是这时代的著名"笛歌"诗人。

与用笛子伴奏的歌曲同时或略晚,出现了用弦琴伴奏的歌曲;古希腊的琴是拿在手里弹奏的,有如我国古代的箜篌;开始也只有两三根弦,逐渐发展到五弦和七弦;在公元前七世纪的斯巴达,著名的"琴歌"诗人有特盘得(Terpender);据说他是从东方的莱斯伯斯岛来的;根据传说,当时斯巴达正闹内战,但是特盘得的和谐的歌声使得他们恢复了和平。据说特盘得在音乐和格律方面也有不少新的创造。

比特盘得略晚，又有阿克曼（Alcman），这是公元前七世纪斯巴达最重要的"琴歌"诗人；相传他也是从东方迁居斯巴达的。他的诗歌大部是相和歌；根据传说，他原来是个奴隶；从残存的一些诗歌断章看来，他很富于劳动人民的幽默感，喜欢朴素平凡的生活，所以这个说法也许是有些根据的。他一共留下来六卷抒情诗歌，但今天我们只能看到一些断片。

在公元前六百年左右，靠近亚洲大陆的莱斯伯斯岛上有两个著名诗人，这就是阿尔凯欧斯（Alcaios）和沙浮（Sappho）；他们的抒情诗是古希腊诗歌的高峰，尤其是女诗人沙浮的诗一直被后世认为是不可企及的楷范；这时的"琴歌"，除了相和歌以外，又有了独唱的诗歌，就诗的内容来说，也更多抒发个人的情感。

阿尔凯欧斯是一个有些象我们唐代李白的诗人；他歌颂战争，爱喝酒，不能忘情于政治，失意时又变得有些消极颓废；从他残存的诗歌看来，他的十卷诗歌里有颂歌，有歌颂战争的歌，有关于政治的歌，有关于爱情的歌，而最多的大概是喝酒的歌。他同当时莱斯伯斯岛的统治者不断展开斗争，也曾遭到放逐；他在《暴君》一诗中所攻击的辟塔科斯（Pittacos）是否真是象他所说那样坏的暴君，这很难说；当时希腊东部正在商业经济繁荣、奴隶制上升阶段，阿尔凯欧斯的政敌大概是代表新兴势力的，而阿尔凯欧斯在政治上却大概是代表保守势力方面的。但不管他政治见解怎样，他的诗歌倒是洋溢着一种乐观的战斗精神和年轻人的锐气，也有一些热爱人民、热爱家乡的思想。

沙浮是一个女诗人，她与阿尔凯欧斯同时，大概略为年轻一些。她留下的诗篇，除了两首比较完整的而外，也都是一些断章零简，但是她一直被认为是西方文化中最伟大的女诗人；英国的拜伦曾把她的诗歌比作炽热的火焰。西方古代文学评论家对她一直是赞不绝口的。据说公元前六世纪雅典的著名政治家和诗人梭伦（Solon），在他老年一天晚上听了他侄子唱了一首沙浮的歌，他就叫他侄子教他唱；旁人问他为什么，他说他希望唱着这样美妙的歌离开人世。沙浮留下九卷诗，多半是抒发个人情感的爱情诗,还有一些婚礼用的乐曲。她的诗名是历代所公认的。我们今天从残存的断章来看,也可以看到她的诗歌的优点,主要是语言朴素而自然,感情真挚,音乐性很强,所以她的诗歌才有那样感人的力量。

沙浮以后,希腊抒情诗歌的中心从东方转到南方西西里岛和雅典一带。公元前六世纪西西里岛的斯提西考瑞欧斯(Stesichoreios)也是一个重要的抒情诗人;他写了二十六卷诗,对希腊抒情诗的发展有不少影响,但他的诗留到今天的只有很少残句。他的诗大部都是以神话传说作为题材的,比较接近叙事诗。意大利南部当时还有伊布科斯(Ibycos),也是著名的抒情诗人;据说他留下七卷诗歌,多半是爱情诗。

公元前六世纪雅典的著名政治家梭伦也留下一些短诗;这种带教训味道的短诗也是古希腊抒情诗的一个特点。古代希腊人是年轻的民族;他们有时在诗歌中显得很随便大胆,思想上毫无顾忌,但有时对待生活的态度却又十分严肃认真,很喜欢在诗中谈谈哲理和对人生的体会。

阿那克雷翁(Anacreon)是以饮酒歌和爱情诗著名的希腊抒情诗人;他来自靠近亚洲大陆的提奥斯岛,在萨摩斯岛住了一些时候,最后到了雅典;他留下五卷诗;他在古代是最著名的抒情诗人之一,公元前五世纪雅典人曾为他建立石象,在公元前三世纪的亚历山大城有不少诗人摹仿他的诗歌。今天我们还可看到许多摹仿他的作品,但是他自己的抒情诗可惜只留下一些断章。

公元前六世纪后半和五世纪的雅典是古代希腊文化的全盛时期。除了大家都知道的悲剧诗人外,西摩尼底斯(Simonides)和屏达罗斯(Pindaros)的诗歌都是雅典文化高潮的代表作品。屏达罗斯的诗歌今天还保留下来较多,但是留下来的绝大部分都是歌赞当时体育竞赛中优胜者的颂歌,很少是抒发个人情感的;他的诗歌凝炼庄重,很喜欢搬用古典,在当时是很受欢迎的,但是这些颂歌对今天读者却没有多大意思,因为里面看不到多少个人的感情。西摩尼底斯侄子巴克库利底斯(Bacchylides)也写了一些歌赞优胜的颂歌,从流传下来的十六首颂歌来看,他的诗好象比屏达罗斯活泼一些,但是在当时他的名声却远不如屏达罗斯。

西摩尼底斯给我们留下来一些非常著名的短诗；这些短诗多半是墓碑上的铭文，纪念对波斯人的战争中战死的勇士们。西摩尼底斯的诗歌也是很凝炼庄重的，但是他善于用极简略又极准确的语言激起人们的爱国感情和民族自豪感；在这方面，他是一个楷范。在公元前四八〇年波斯大军向雅典等地进攻，在温关(德摩比利)防守的斯巴达军全部战死，但希腊人终于遏止了波斯人的攻势；西摩尼底斯为这次战役所写的短铭是举世传诵的，尤其是下面这一首：

> 过客请传告斯巴达人，在这里
> 我们长眠，遵守着他们的指示。

原文的精炼和音节的铿锵在翻译中无法表达；我们可以说在运用文字技巧方面西摩尼底斯达到了惊人的艺术高度。

以雅典为代表的古希腊文化，从公元前四世纪起，开始走向衰落：在抒情诗歌方面也是这样。从公元前四世纪到公元后六世纪左右这一千年间，古希腊抒情诗歌的传统虽然是一直在延续着，也有不少有才能的诗人写出了一些美妙的篇章，但是在这一千年间的抒情诗歌中，我们只能看到一些巧妙的设想，一些精炼的辞藻，却找不到象沙浮或西摩尼底斯的那样震撼心弦的诗句。早期的古希腊抒情诗歌很少有完整被保留下来的；中古欧洲的教会统治对古典文学遗产曾大加摧残；沙浮等人的诗集都被列为禁书烧掉，所以今天我们只能看到一些断章残句。从公元前四世纪到公元后六世纪左右的后期希腊抒情诗歌却有着不同的命运；这一千年左右的许多短篇诗歌被保存得较好；从公元前后开始，曾有若干选集；后来这些诗歌选辑成了一部总集，被称为《安托洛吉亚》(Anthologia)，这个希腊字的意思就是"诗苑英华"。这部诗集共收进了四千来首短诗，多半是铭辞之类。欧洲文艺复兴以后，古希腊罗马文学成为欧洲作家学习的典范；这部《诗苑英华》对近代欧洲的抒情诗歌曾起过很大的影响。

在后期的古希腊抒情诗歌里也还有不少重要的名字，这里应该略要地提一下。公元前四世纪的柏拉图，大家都知道是重要的散文作家和哲学家,苏格拉底的学生;但是他也留下来一些很不坏的抒情短诗,这里也选译一首。公元前三世纪起,希腊文化的中心转到非洲北部的亚历山大城。在罗马帝国兴起以前,亚历山大城的文艺是很兴盛的;这时最著名的一位诗人是卡利马克斯(Callimachos),他的诗歌虽以新奇取胜,却并不怎样好,对后世也没有多少影响。差不多与他同时,公元前三世纪的阿斯克雷比阿底斯(Asclepiades)和雷昂尼达斯(Leonidas)等却留下一些很优美的抒情短诗。

但是在亚历大城文坛上,最重要的抒情诗人恐怕要算提奥克利托斯(Theocritos)了。他大概是西西里岛人,至少他的诗都是以西西里岛为背景的;他约生于公元前四世纪末到三世纪中叶;他留下了不少美妙的牧歌;这些歌有些采用对话形式,有些叙述一段事。他的诗当然也受当时文风的影响,可以看出来有些雕琢,讲究词藻;他是在有意识的写诗,不象早期抒情诗那样纯粹是自然感情的流露。但他的诗比一般亚历山大城诗人要好,因为时时也带着真挚的情感。他的这些牧歌应该算作古希腊文学中有价值的东西,对后世影响也很大;举例说,罗马维吉尔的牧歌就是摹仿他的;此外后世摹仿他的牧歌体裁的还很多。由于这些牧歌体裁较长,而且好象已经成为一种特殊文学形式,与一般抒情诗不同,所以这里没有选译。

模仿提奥克利托斯的诗人还有公元前二世纪的摩斯科斯(Moschos)和彼翁(Bion);这两个诗人所写的牧歌也很清新美妙。

公元前一世纪还有一个叙利亚地方的希腊抒情诗人梅利亚格罗斯(Meleagros),也是值得一提的;在后期抒情诗歌中,他的诗还是比较清新真挚的;他也作了一些保存希腊抒情诗歌的工作;他集选了一些短诗,这些后来都收到后期希腊短诗的总集里去了。

在罗马帝国和东罗马时代,希腊抒情诗歌的传统虽然还继续了几百年,但是已经看不到早期诗歌的健康真朴的气氛,只反映出一些享乐主义和颓废的人生观。公元后四世纪的巴拉达斯(Palladas)是这方面的代表。从语言形式方面来看,晚期的希腊抒情诗歌还是语言精炼、技巧纯熟的,设想也往往很巧妙,对文艺复兴以后的欧洲诗歌也曾有不少影响;这里就不详细介绍了。

古代希腊抒情诗歌发展的大致轮廓就是这样;关于希腊诗的形式体裁方面,不容易说得清楚,这里不打算多谈;简单的说,希腊的诗同我们的传统不同,不用尾韵;但是不同体裁的诗,每句里轻重音的变换也是按照严格规律的,象我们旧诗里运用平仄达到音乐效果一样。抒情诗歌有多种体裁,有不同的长短句排列,也有每句长短一律的。

古希腊文学是人类幼年时期的文学;我们不能拿今天的标准去看它,也不能拿封建时代的标准去看它;但是从这些抒情诗歌里,我们也可以看到当时人对美好的追求,对邪恶的谴责,对和平生活的渴望,对自己乡土的热爱;而这一切在今天也还是有积极意义的,因此介绍古希腊的抒情诗还不仅是为了增加一些历史知识而已,这里面也还有不少值得我们学习的东西。

——杨宪益

八

奥德修纪(卷一)[①]

卷 一

女神啊,给我说那足智多谋的英雄怎样,

在攻下特罗神京后,又飘游到许多地方,

看到不少种族的城国,了解到他们心肠;

他心中忍受很多痛苦,在那汪洋大海上,

争取自己和同伴能保全性命,返回家乡;

他终于救不了他的同伴,虽然这样希望;

他们由于自己的愚蠢,结果遭遇到死亡;

那些人真胡涂,他们拿日神的牛来饱飨,

因此天神就剥夺了他们返回家乡的时光。

天帝的女儿缪刹,请你随便从哪里开讲。

且说所有其他英雄这时都已离开战争和海洋,逃脱凶险的死亡命运,回到了自己家乡;只有奥德修一个,苦苦怀念着归程和他的妻子,却被那有魔力的女神卡吕蒲索洞主留在她的山洞里,要他同她成亲;但是岁月流转,上天注定奥德修回到伊大嘉岛的一年终于到来,只是他回到亲人中间的时候,还免不了要受些艰难考验。天神们都对奥德修表示同情,只有波

---

① 选自:荷马.奥德修纪.杨宪益,译.上海:上海译文出版社,1979.

塞顿还是不停的对这位英雄发泄怒气，一直到他到达陆地上才肯罢休。可是这时候波塞顿到远方的埃塞俄比亚人那里去了；那个种族居住在人类最远的地区，分为两部，一部在日落之地，另一部在日出之地。波塞顿去到那里接受牛羊牺牲。就当他在席上享受盛宴的时候，其他天神都在奥仑波山上，在天帝宙斯宫中聚会。这时世人和众神之父在群神当中首先讲了话；他心里想起那材力非凡的埃吉斯陀被阿加曼农的儿子，威名远扬的奥瑞斯提杀掉的故事，就对大家说道："唉，世人总喜欢埋怨天神，说什么灾祸都是我们降下的；实际上他们总是由于自己胡涂，才遭到注定命运之外的灾祸的。当前一个例子就是埃吉斯陀。他违反天命，霸占了阿特留之子的妻子；阿加曼农回家时，埃吉斯陀又把他杀掉；埃吉斯陀很清楚他要遭到凶死；这是我们事先警告过他的；我们派遣了眼观千里的斩魔神赫尔墨去警告他，不要谋害阿加曼农，也不要霸占阿加曼农的妻子，因为奥瑞斯提一旦长大成人，怀念乡土，就会去给阿特留之子报仇。赫尔墨曾经这样警告过他，可是我们一番好意却说不服埃吉斯陀；他结果还是彻底的付出了代价。"

明眸女神雅典娜回答他说道："我们的父亲，闶闾之子；至高的尊神，埃吉斯陀死了是罪有应得，旁的人作出这种事也应该遭到毁灭的；可是我却为多智的奥德修悲伤；他真是命运不好，那么多年头离开亲人，留在大海中心、四面是水的一个岛上，受着苦难；那个树木阴森的海岛上住着一位女神；凶暴的阿特拉手擎巨柱，撑着大地和苍穹，所有海洋的深度他都清楚；就是阿特拉的女儿留下了那不幸的忧伤的奥德修，不断用甜言蜜语媚惑他，要他忘掉伊大嘉；可是奥德修渴望能够看见故乡升起的炊烟，觉得不如死掉还好些。你是主管奥仑波山的天帝，对这件事却毫不动心；奥德修在特罗广野，在阿凯人的船边，不是也给你献过牺牲，使你喜悦么？宙斯啊，你为什么对他这样狠毒啊？"

聚云者宙斯回答她说道："我的孩子，你嘴里说出了什么话？我怎么会忘记英雄奥德修呢？他比一切凡人都更聪明，他向主掌广天的永生神祇献上的祭礼也比旁人更丰盛。问题在于环绕大地的寰海之神波塞顿，为了独目巨人的事一直怀着怨恨；奥德修弄瞎了大圣波吕菲谟的眼睛；波吕菲谟是威力最大的巨人，是主宰荒茫海水之神伏尔鸠的女儿托欧沙的儿子；托欧沙在中空的岩洞里同波塞顿交合，生了波吕菲谟。摇撼大地之神波塞顿虽然没有杀死奥德修，但是让他远离乡土到处飘游，就是为了这件事。现在我们大家可以计划一下怎么让他回到家乡；波塞顿总要停止发怒的；他总不能单独违抗全体永生天神的意旨。"

明眸女神雅典娜回答说道："好吧，我们的父亲，阃阃之子，至高的尊神，既然现在极乐的天神都愿意让多智的奥德修还乡，我们可以派遣天神的使者斩魔神赫尔墨到奥鸠吉岛去，让他立刻把我们的决定告诉那华鬘女神，放那意志坚定的奥德修回家。我自己也要到伊大嘉岛，去激励他的儿子，在他心里增加勇气，要他召集长发的阿凯人去到会场，要他对那些每天杀食他的羊群和肥牛的求婚子弟们讲话。我还要派奥德修的儿子到斯巴达和蒲罗沙滩去，打听一下关于他父亲还乡的消息；那样他就会得到众人称赞了。"

她说完话，就把她的华履在脚上系好，那是一双具有神奇力量的，金光闪耀的鞋子，可以带着她象一阵风似的渡过海洋和无边陆地；她又拿起她的巨矛，矛头有青铜的尖锋，那矛非常粗大，又长又重；当这位威严的天帝女发怒的时候，她曾经用这支矛摧毁英雄们的队伍。她离开众神，从奥仑波山上飞下，降落到伊大嘉岛上，来到奥德修的家门，外院的门口；她手里拿着青铜矛，外表象一个外乡人，扮作达菲人的首领曼提的模样。

她发现那些傲慢的求婚子弟们正在门口，坐在他们所宰杀的牛的皮革上，下棋取乐；他们的随从奴仆都在忙碌工作，有些人在酒爵里用水搀酒，有些人正用多孔的海绵擦洗餐几，把餐几摆好，有些人正在切着大块的肉。高贵的帖雷马科首先看到了来人；他这时正坐在求婚子弟们当中，心中闷闷不乐，梦想他的尊贵父亲从外面走进来，把家里的求婚人赶得东逃西窜，赢得光荣，再度成为一家之主。他坐在求婚子弟当中，正想着这些，就看到了雅典娜。他立刻走到门口，因为他感觉让来客在门口久等是不礼貌的；他来到她面前，抓住她的右手，把铜矛接过来，对她认真的说道："客人，你好，欢迎你来我们家里作客；等到你用过餐之后，你可以告诉我们你需要什么。"他说着，就在前面带路，帕拉雅典娜跟着他走进来。

他们走进这座高大的宫邸；帖雷马科把长矛放到大柱旁边精雕的矛架上，那里放着许多铜矛，都是英雄奥德修使用的。他领着雅典娜，请她在一个精雕的椅子上坐下，椅子上铺着毛毡，下面有放脚的凳子；他自己也搬过来一把华饰的便椅，远远离开那些求婚子弟，免得客人坐在那些狂妄胡闹的人当中，听到他们喊叫，感觉厌恶，因而吃不好饭；还为了他这样可以向她打听他在外的父亲的消息。一个侍女拿来美丽的金壶，把水倒在银盆里给他们洗手，在他们面前又摆好光滑的餐几；庄重的女仆拿来面食，放在餐几上，还摆好许多菜肴，殷勤的招待客人；厨役也拿来很多盘各种烤肉，放在他们面前，又摆好黄金的酒杯；还有侍从跑来跑去给他们斟酒。那些高贵的求婚子弟也入了座，一排排坐在椅子上，仆役在他们手上倒了水，女奴用篮子装来成堆的麦饼，侍童在他们的酒爵里盛满了酒；他们就伸出手来，尽兴取食面前的酒肉。

求婚子弟们吃饱喝够，兴趣就转到另一方面；他们想听音乐和歌曲，那些娱乐是宴会的冠冕；一个侍从把美妙的鸣筝放到菲弥奥手里，强迫他在求婚子弟面前歌唱，他就开始弹筝，准备唱个美妙的歌曲。这时帖雷马科对明眸女神雅典娜讲了话；他的头靠近女神耳边，免得让旁人听到；"亲爱的客人，希望你对我说的话不见怪。这些人现在又要欣赏鸣筝和歌曲这些娱乐了；他们毫无顾虑，无偿的消耗别人的家财，不管这家主人的白骨是否横陈在地上被雨泡烂，或是在海里随着波浪飘浮。如果他们能看到他回到伊大嘉岛，他们那时就要祷告天神，希望能跑得更快一些，不想占有更多的黄金和衣饰了；可是现在我们已经绝望；他一定已经不幸死掉；虽然世上还有人说他还会回来，我看他是不会还乡的了。可是请你告诉我，要老老实实的对我说，你是什么人？从哪里来的？居住什么城镇？你的父母是谁？你坐的什么船？航海的人怎样把你带到伊大嘉的？他们又自称是什么人？我看你总不会是步行来的。还有请你老实告诉我，让我弄明白；你是第一次来这里呢，还是从前就作过我父亲的客人？因为许多客人都到过这里,正如我父亲自己也访问过许多地方的人一样。"

明眸女神雅典娜对他说道:"好吧,我就老老实实的同你说:我名叫曼提,是智慧的安奇阿洛的儿子;我统领着喜欢航海的达菲人。我现在同我的船只和伙伴路过这里,要渡过葡萄紫的大海,访问说不同语言的种族,装载着明亮的铁器,到帖眉息地方去买铜。我的船停在城郊,在林木阴翳的奈依翁附近的瑞特隆港口。我们是世交,你可以去问年老的英雄拉埃提。我听说拉埃提不在城里,而是住在乡下,生活很俭朴;他在葡萄园里从事劳动;身体疲乏的时候,就爬上山坡,有一个年老的女奴侍候着他,给他安排饮食。我这次来这里,因为据说你父亲确实还在,大概是天神们阻碍了他的归程;我听说英雄奥德修并没有离开人世;他还活着,在波涛汹涌的大海上,被凶恶的人捉住,强迫留在一个四面是海的孤岛上。我现在要对你作一个预言;永生的天神给我这个想法,我认为一定要实现的,虽然我并不是个预言家,也不是用鸟占卜的人。奥德修不会离开他亲爱的故乡很久了;就是用铁打的锁链束缚他,他也会想办法回来,因为他是很有智谋的。可是你也老老实实的同我说吧;你真的是奥德修的儿子吗?怎么长得这么大了?你的头和漂亮的大眼睛倒是非常象他的。我们过去经常在一起,那是在他航海到特罗去之前;自从那些勇敢的阿凯人乘着弯船远征之后,我同奥德修就彼此没有再见过面呢。"

谨慎的帖雷马科对她说道:"客人,我也老老实实的告诉你。据我母亲说,我是奥德修的儿子;可是我自己不知道是否是这样,因为谁也不能知道自己的来历。我真希望我父亲是个幸运的人,可以守着家业安度晚年;你既然要问我这件事,我只能说人们都认为我是那位最不幸的人的儿子。"

明眸女神雅典娜对他说道:"天神不会让你家失掉荣名的,既然潘奈洛佩生了你这样一个好儿子。可是你要老老实实的告诉我这件事;这里的酒宴和客人是为了什么?你为什么要这么铺张?是请客还是举行婚礼?我看这不象是一般聚餐;看起来这些高贵的人在你家里吃喝,都很嚣张狂妄;一个正派人来到这里,看到这些无礼的事,会感到气愤的。"

　　谨慎的帖雷马科对她说道："客人，你既然要问我这件事，我就要说明，当奥德修在这里的时候，我们家曾经是富裕高贵的；可是现在天神们变了心，不喜欢我们了；在众人中偏偏让他下落不明；如果他是和同伴一起在特罗战死，或者在战争结束后死在朋友手里，我还不会为他的死亡这样感觉伤心；在那种情景下，全体阿凯人会给他造个坟墓，他的后代将来也可以分享光荣；现在一阵狂风把他吹得无影无踪，没有下落，也没有消息，只给我留下悲伤痛苦。我悲伤叹息还不是仅仅为了他的缘故；天神们又为我降下来别的灾祸。那些统治各个海岛的王侯，包括杜利奇岛、萨弥岛和林木茂盛的查昆陀岛，以及山岭绵延的伊大嘉岛的首领们，都来向我母亲求婚，浪费我们家财；我母亲虽然讨厌这件婚事，却没有拒绝他们，也没有能力结束这件事；那些人大吃大喝，消耗我的产业，要不了许久时间就要把我毁了。"

　　帕拉雅典娜气愤的对他说道："唉！你真需要远在异乡的奥德修回来，好让这群无耻的求婚子弟落到他的手里。我希望他现在就回来，穿戴盔甲，带着盾牌，拿着两根枪，站在门口，就象我最初见到他那样。那时他从埃甫瑞的眉美洛之子伊罗那里转回来，曾经在我家里受过酒宴招待。奥德修乘着快船去找伊罗，向他索取一种致命的毒药，来涂他的青铜箭镞，可是伊罗畏惧永生天神的谴责，拒绝给他这种药；结果我的父亲还是把这种药送给他了，因为我父亲同奥德修非常要好。奥德修要是那样在求婚子弟当中出现，他们就要立刻遭殃，求婚的事就要变成找死了。当然这一切都由天神决定；他也许能回来，在堂上报仇雪恨；也许他不能这样做；可是我还是劝你考虑一下，有没有办法把求婚人赶走。你要听我的话，好好想想：明天清早你召集阿凯首领们，在会场对大家讲清楚，天神会给你作证。你可以叫求婚子弟们各自回家；至于你母亲，如果她心想再嫁，就让她回到她那尊贵的父亲家去；他们可以在她家里安排婚事，准备丰盛聘礼，送走他们的爱女。我还有一个经过周密考虑的建议，希望你能采纳：你找一只最好的船，配备二十个桨手，然后去寻找你长久在外的父亲；也许有人会告诉你一些消息，再不然你也许会听到天帝的意旨，他是常常给人指示的。你可以先到蒲罗去,问问英雄奈斯陀;从那里再到斯巴达去见黄发的曼涅劳;他是披甲的阿凯英雄里最后回来的。如果你听说你父亲还活着,快要回来了,那样你虽然受着苦难,也可以再忍受一年;如果你听说他已经死掉,不在人世,你就可以回到故乡,给他造一座坟,按照礼节,隆重办理丧事,让你母亲再嫁。在你结束了这一切事务之后,你应当仔细计划一下,怎样把你家里的求婚子弟们杀掉,用计谋还是公开进行。你不能再有孩子气了,因为你的年龄已经不小了。你难道没有听说吗?英雄的奥瑞斯提在世人中赢得了荣名,因为他杀了他的杀父仇人,就是那个用阴谋害死他的威名显赫的父亲的埃吉斯陀。朋友,我看你长得很强壮魁伟;你也应该鼓起勇气,在后世传下美名。我现在要回到我的快船和伙伴那里去了;他们已经等得不耐烦;你要好好考虑我嘱咐你的事。"

谨慎的帖雷马科对她说道:"客人,你说的都是为我好,真象父亲对孩子那样;我绝不会忘记你的话。现在你还是多留一些时候吧,虽然你急着要上路;还是先洗个澡,吃得饱饱的,然后高高兴兴的带一些礼物回船去;你可以拿一件值钱的、十分美好的礼物,作为纪念,就象亲爱朋友互相赠送的那样。"

明眸女神雅典娜对他说道:"你不要留我,因为我急着要上路;如果你想送我什么礼物,给我带回家去,那就等我回来的时候再送吧;你可以挑一件最好的纪念品;你也会得到适当报答的。"

明眸女神雅典娜说完就走了,象飞鸟一样穿云而去;女神在他心里增加了力气和胆量,使他比以前更加想念他的父亲。帖雷马科看见这件事感觉惊奇,明白这是一位天神显圣。他精神振奋,立刻回到求婚子弟中间。

这时那位著名的乐师正为求婚子弟们歌唱;他们都安静的坐在那里听他的歌;他歌唱阿凯人怎样离开特罗地方,走上他们的悲惨归程,帕拉雅典娜怎样给他们降下不同遭遇。聪明的潘奈洛佩,伊加留的女儿,在楼上也听到这神妙的歌声;她步出房门,走下高高楼梯;她不是单独前来,旁边有侍女随从着。这位高贵的夫人来到求婚子弟那里,站在坚固的殿宇的堂柱旁边,用柔滑的面纱遮住了脸,两边站着两个侍女小心服侍;她流着泪向那神妙的乐师说道:"菲弥奥,你知道许多使人听了高兴的事,许多大家传诵的人神事迹;请你坐在这里给他们唱那些故事吧,好让他们安安静静的喝酒;可是我请你停止唱这个悲惨的歌;它每次都使我的心里悲痛;我怀着难忘的痛苦,永远怀念着那个人的容貌;他的声名传遍全希腊和阿凯地方。"

谨慎的帖雷马科对她说道:"妈妈,你为什么要阻止这位好乐师按照自己心意给人娱乐?唱什么不唱什么,这不是乐师而是天帝决定的;上天愿意赐给劳动人民什么就给什么。你不应该反对他歌唱达菲人的悲惨遭遇;世人总是喜欢听最新的故事。你应该坚强一些,打起精神;奥德修也并不是唯一的没有从特罗地方回来的人;还有很多英雄也都死在那里哩。你还是回到自己房间里作你的事去吧,回到你的织机和纺梭那边,命令女奴们干她们的活;讲话是男人们的事,首先是我的事,因为我是这家的主人。"

她感到惊奇,就走回自己的房间,心里考虑着她儿子的有道理的话;她同侍女一道上了楼,为她亲爱的丈夫奥德修悲伤啼泣,一直到明眸女神雅典娜把酣梦降到她眼睫上的时候。

这时求婚子弟都在阴暗的殿堂上大声喊嚷,希望能同潘奈洛佩同床睡觉。谨慎的帖雷马科就对他们说道:"向我母亲求婚的诸位先生,你们未免太放肆无礼;还是吃喝取乐吧,不要这样吵闹;你们能够听到有这样神妙歌喉的人讲故事还不知足吗?明天早晨我们可以到会场去,各就各位,我要正式通知你们离开这所房子,到旁的地方聚餐,到你们自己家里去,吃你们自己的东西。如果你们愿意这样消耗旁人的财产,不付出任何代价,认为这样对你们更有利,当然你们也可以这样继续下去,可是我要向永生的天神祷告,让上天降下报应,让你们在这所房子里遭到灭亡,也得不到任何赔偿。"

他这样说了,求婚子弟们都很惊讶,咬着嘴唇,因为他说的很大胆。尤培塞之子安提诺就对他说道:"帖雷马科,天神把你教导成一个会说大话的家伙了;你说话好大胆,我希望闶阖之子不让你成为四面环海的伊大嘉岛的国王,虽然这是你的祖产。"

帖雷马科对他说道:"安提诺,你也许不爱听我说的话;我正是希望上天降给我这个命运。你难道认为这是世人最坏的命运吗?作个国王并不坏呀;立刻家里就有钱了,而且还更加受人尊敬呢。当然目前在四面环海的伊大嘉还有很多其他阿凯王侯,有些是旧有的,有些是新来的,其中任何一位都可能统治这块地方,因为英雄奥德修已经不在了;可是我总是我自己家园的主人,管理着这些奴隶,那是英雄奥德修为我赢来的。"

波吕伯之子尤吕马科对他说道:"帖雷马科,关于谁将在四面环海的伊大嘉作阿凯人的国王,那是只有天神们才能决定的事;至于你的财产,当然应该属你所有;你将作自己家园的主人;只要有我们在伊大嘉居住,就不会有旁人用暴力欺负你,抢去你的财产。可是,朋友,我想问问,方才那位客人是谁?是从哪里来的?他自称是什么地方的人?他的部族和祖产在哪里?他是给你带来你父亲还乡的消息,还是为了自己事到这里来的?怎么他一下就不见了,也没有让人认识他?从他外表看来好象不是个下等人哩。"

谨慎的帖雷马科对他说道:"尤吕马科,我的父亲肯定是不会回来了;就是有什么传闻,我也不会相信;如果我母亲叫来这样的人到家里来问卦,我也不会受这样的人的欺骗,方才那位客人是从达菲地方来的一位世交;据他说他是智慧的安奇阿洛的儿子曼提;他统治着喜欢航海的达菲人。"帖雷马科这样说,可是他心里明白那是一位永生的天神。

他们的兴趣又转到舞蹈和令人欢畅的歌曲方面,一直玩到黄昏时分;在欢娱中不觉阴暗的暮色已经降临;这时他们就各自回家睡觉去了。帖雷马科心事重重,也回到这所美好府邸中他的卧房去休息;那所房子建筑在高地,可以向远方眺望。他的忠诚的保姆尤吕克累拿着明亮的火炬领路;她是培西诺之子奥普的女儿,过去拉埃提在她年轻的时候出钱将她买下来,出了二十头牛的代价;在家里,拉埃提对待她同对待他忠贞的妻子一样,只是没有同她睡过觉,因为怕他妻子生气。现在就是这个尤吕克累给帖雷马科拿着明亮火炬,在女奴中只有尤吕克累最爱护帖雷马科,当他还是个婴孩的时候就抚养过他。

　　帖雷马科打开精筑的卧房的门,坐在床上,脱掉他的柔软的外衫,交到那聪明的老妇人手里。她把衣服叠好放平,挂在绳床旁的钩上,走出去,抓着房门的银环,把门带上,又用皮带把门拴好。帖雷马科在房间里盖上羊毛毡子,通宵盘算着雅典娜给他计划的旅程。

九

罗兰之歌(一五六——一七〇首)[①]

一五六

伯爵罗兰打得很漂亮，

可是他的身上热汗直淌，

他的头也痛得够戗，

他迸裂了天灵盖把号角吹响；

可是他想知道查理是否转回，

他拿起号角，竭力再吹。

皇帝停下来，又一次听到，

他说，"诸公，我们的情况很糟，

今天我的外甥罗兰我要失掉，

我从号角声中听出他性命难保。

你们一定要催马快跑，

还要吹起全军的所有号角。"

六万人吹起号角，宏音远震，

在山上谷中都响起回声。

异教徒也听到了，他们不敢开玩笑，

---

① 选自：杨宪益，译．罗兰之歌．上海：上海译文出版社，1981.

他们彼此说道,"查理王就要到了。"

一五七

异教徒说,"皇帝就要来到,
你听法兰西人都吹起了号角。
如果查理来到,我们性命难保;
罗兰要是生还,战争就会再起,
我们就要丢掉西班牙,我们的土地。"
四百个戴着头盔的人集合一起,
他们都被认为是最好的战士,
他们对罗兰展开凶猛攻击,
伯爵对付他们要费些力气。

一五八

当罗兰伯爵看到他们又来进攻,
他打起精神,变得非常勇猛;
只要他还活着,他就不会退让。
他骑在名为维昂提的马上,
用精金的马刺催着马去打仗,
向着层层敌阵里直闯。
主教屠宾也同他一样;
敌人彼此说,"朋友们,快跑,
法兰西人的号角我们已经听到,
那威力强大的大王查理就要来到。"

一五九

罗兰伯爵不喜欢人贪生怕死，
不喜欢人骄傲自大，和坏人坏事，
也不喜欢不能奋勇作战的骑士；
他叫主教屠宾，同他说话，
"你是站在地上，我却骑着马，
为了我们友爱，我也要停下；
我们要在一起祸福同享，
我不会为旁人把你遗忘。
今天异教徒的进攻我们要阻挡，
杜伦达宝剑要作出最好榜样。"
主教说道，"谁不好好作战，谁就最可羞！
查理就要回来，他要给我们好好报仇。"

一六〇

异教徒们说，"我们真糟糕，
这一天对我们非常不好！
我们的公侯将军都损失殆尽。
查理王又带回他的大军。
我们听到法兰西人响亮的角声，
他们高呼着'蒙鸠依'，声音远震，
罗兰伯爵又是这样精神振奋，
世上没有人能把他战胜。
让我们向他投枪，然后离开他们。"

他们就射出许多短镖，
带羽的箭和各种枪矛；
罗兰的盾牌被他们刺穿，
他的铠甲也被他们打烂，
可是他们没有伤到他的身躯，
可是战马维昂提受伤三十处，
它被打死，倒在伯爵身底。
异教徒都跑掉，留下他在那里。
罗兰伯爵被留下，失去坐骑。

一六一

异教徒都跑了，愤怒慌张，
他们匆忙逃向西班牙地方；
伯爵罗兰也不能去追，
他失去了维昂提，他的坐骑，
不管怎样只好留在原地。
他去把主教屠宾扶起，
把他镀金的盔从头上脱下，
又脱掉他的白色轻甲，
把他衬衫全部撕掉，
用布把他巨大的伤口塞好，
又抱着他身体，靠着自己胸膛，
然后轻轻把他放倒在绿草上。
罗兰非常温柔地对他讲，
"啊，我的好人，允许我离开你，
我们最亲爱的伙伴们在那里

都已战死,我们不能把他们抛弃,
我要前去把他们寻觅,
在你面前把他们排列整齐。"
"你快去快回,"主教说道,
"感谢上帝,这战场属于你我二人了!"

一六二

罗兰转身单独穿过战场,
他巡视谷里又巡视山上,
他找到解林和他的伙伴解瑞,
又找到了阿屯和贝伦吉,
又找到安歇依和桑申,
又找到解拉,那鲁西荣的老人,
侯爷将他们一个又一个抬起,
把他们都带到主教那里,
放在他膝前摆整齐;
主教不能遏止他自己啼哭,
他举起了手,给他们祝福,
他又说道,"你们的命真苦,
望荣耀的上帝把你们的魂灵保护,
带到乐园里,同圣洁的花放在一处;
我非常痛苦,我就要死亡,
我将见不到那强大的君王。"

一六三

罗兰又转身去到战场寻找，
他把伙伴奥利维也找到，
靠着胸膛，把奥利维紧抱；
他用尽力气回到主教身旁，
把奥利维放倒在旁边盾牌上。
主教给他赎了罪，作了十字记号。
他们这时更加哀悼，
罗兰说道，"好伙伴，奥利维，
你是瑞奈公爵的后裔，
他拥有卢奈山谷封地。
你曾把枪矛打断，盾牌打碎，
战胜狂妄敌人，使他们丧气，
你支持正义的人，给他们出主意，
打败贪恶的人，使他们战栗，
在任何地方没有战士能胜过你。"

一六四

伯爵罗兰看到牺牲了这些英豪，
他最亲爱的奥利维也死掉，
他为他们伤心，开始悲泣哀悼，
面容变得苍白枯槁，
他是那样伤心，他支持不住了，
他不由得在地上晕倒，

"将军,你多么不幸,"主教说道。

一六五

主教看见罗兰晕倒过去,
他的悲痛达到最大程度。
他伸出手来把号角抓住;
在昂赛瓦有一条小河,
他想到那里去给罗兰取点水喝,
他就离开罗兰,一步一步向前挪,
他太虚弱了,不能走到小河,
他没有气力,失血过多,
他走了还不过一里之遥,
心跳停止,就向前扑倒,
在非常痛苦中死掉。

一六六

罗兰伯爵从昏迷中苏醒,
他站立起来,但是非常悲痛,
他看看山谷又望望山顶,
在青草上,在他的伙伴尸体附近,
他看见那位死掉的高贵将军,
就是那主教,上帝的代言人。
他作了忏悔,他向上看,
他合起双手,举手向天,

向上帝祷告让他进入乐园。
屠宾死了,查理王的伙伴,
无论高明的讲道还是激烈征战,
他永远是反对异教徒的骨干,
愿上帝赐给他神圣恩典!

一六七

罗兰伯爵看见主教躺在地上,
从他身体里流出了肚肠,
他前额涌出了脑浆,
他合起他的白手,手很漂亮,
在他锁骨中间,正当胸膛。
罗兰就按照家乡习惯为他悼丧。
"啊! 好伙伴,名门的骑士,
今天我把你交给上帝的恩慈。
从来没有人更积极把上帝服侍,
在十二门徒之后从没有过这样先知,
你引人为善,又坚持真理,
愿你的灵魂平安无恙,
愿乐园的门为你开放。"

一六八

罗兰感到死亡已经临近,
他的脑浆从双耳向外喷进,

他为将军们向上帝祈祷，
然后又为自己向天使加伯里祷告。
为了不让人责备他，他拿起号角，
另一只手又抓住杜伦达，他的宝刀，
他走过弓弩能射到的距离，
朝着西班牙方向，到了一块荒地，
他登上山巅，在两株美好的树后，
那里有四块白色的石头，
在绿草上面他仰身躺倒，
死亡就要来临，他又晕倒了。

一六九

山峰高耸，树木阴森，
有四块白石亮晶晶，
罗兰晕倒在绿草中心。
这时一个大食人正对他观望，
那人假装死掉，躺在别人身旁，
用血涂满身体和脸上，
现在他站起身来，奔跑匆忙。
这人很勇敢，身躯强壮，
他的骄傲要使他遭到灭亡。
他触动罗兰身体和兵仗；
就说道，"查理的外甥已被打败，
这把宝刀我要带回大食地带。"
他拔刀的时候，伯爵又醒了过来。

一七〇

罗兰觉到有人在拔他的宝刀，
他睁开眼，对那人说道，
"我看得出，你同我们不是一道。"
罗兰抓起号角，他不愿把它丢掉，
向着敌人镶着金宝的头盔猛砍，
把铁盔和他的头骨打烂，
从敌人头上迸出他的双眼，
敌人被打死，倒在脚边。
罗兰对他说道，"奴才，你怎么敢？
你敢碰我？道理你都不管，
任何人听到都会说你太大胆，
我的号角也被打坏了一边，
上面的水晶和黄金落到地面。"

第二编

中国古典文学英译

离　骚[①]

帝高阳之苗裔兮,朕皇考曰伯庸。

摄提贞于孟陬兮,惟庚寅吾以降。

皇览揆余初度兮,肇锡余以嘉名:

名余曰正则兮,字余曰灵均。

纷吾既有此内美兮,又重之以修能。

扈江离与辟芷兮,纫秋兰以为佩。

汩余若将不及兮,恐年岁之不吾与。

朝搴阰之木兰兮,夕揽洲之宿莽。

日月忽其不淹兮,春与秋其代序。

惟草木之零落兮,恐美人之迟暮。

不抚壮而弃秽兮,何不改此度?

乘骐骥以驰骋兮,来吾道夫先路!

昔三后之纯粹兮,固众芳之所在;

杂申椒与菌桂兮,岂维纫夫蕙茝?

---

① 中文选自:屈原. 楚辞:汉英对照(古诗苑汉英译丛). 杨宪益,戴乃迭,译. 北京:
外文出版社,2001.
英语译文依据 *Li Sao and Other Poems of Chu Yuan*. Yang Hsien-yi & Gladys
Yang. Trans. Beijing: Foreign Languages Press,1953.

彼尧舜之耿介兮,既遵道而得路;
何桀纣之猖披兮,夫唯捷径以窘步。
惟夫党人之偷乐兮,路幽昧以险隘。
岂余身之惮殃兮,恐皇舆之败绩!

忽奔走以先后兮,及前王之踵武。
荃不察余之中情兮,反信谗而齌怒。
余固知謇謇之为患兮,忍而不能舍也。
指九天以为正兮,夫唯灵修之故也!
曰黄昏以为期兮,羌中道而改路。
初既与余成言兮,后悔遁而有他。
余既不难夫离别兮,伤灵修之数化。

余既滋兰之九畹兮,又树蕙之百亩。
畦留夷与揭车兮,杂杜衡与芳芷。
冀枝叶之峻茂兮,愿俟时乎吾将刈。
虽萎绝其亦何伤兮,哀众芳之芜秽!

众皆竞进以贪婪兮,凭不厌乎求索。
羌内恕己以量人兮,各兴心而嫉妒。

忽驰骛以追逐兮,非余心之所急。
老冉冉其将至兮,恐修名之不立。
朝饮木兰之坠露兮,夕餐秋菊之落英。
苟余情其信姱以练要兮,长顑颔亦何伤!
揽木根以结茝兮,贯薜荔之落蕊。
矫菌桂以纫蕙兮,索胡绳之𪾢𪾢。
謇吾法夫前修兮,非世俗之所服。

虽不周于今之人兮,愿依彭咸之遗则。

长太息以掩涕兮,哀民生之多艰。
余虽好修姱以靰羁兮,謇朝谇而夕替。
既替余以蕙𫄸兮,又申之以揽茝。
亦余心之所善兮,虽九死其犹未悔!

怨灵修之浩荡兮,终不察夫民心。
众女嫉余之蛾眉兮,谣诼谓余以善淫。
固时俗之工巧兮,偭规矩而改错;
背绳墨以追曲兮,竞周容以为度。

忳郁邑余佗傺兮,吾独穷困乎此时也。
宁溘死以流亡兮,余不忍为此态也!
鸷鸟之不群兮,自前世而固然。
何方圜之能周兮,夫孰异道而相安!
屈心而抑志兮,忍尤而攘诟。
伏清白以死直兮,固前圣之所厚。

悔相道之不察兮,延伫乎吾将反。
回朕车以复路兮,及行迷之未远。
步余马于兰皋兮,驰椒丘且焉止息。
进不入以离尤兮,退将复修吾初服。
制芰荷以为衣兮,集芙蓉以为裳。
不吾知其亦已兮,苟余情其信芳。
高余冠之岌岌兮,长余佩之陆离。
芳与泽其杂糅兮,唯昭质其犹未亏。
忽反顾以游目兮,将往观乎四荒。

佩缤纷其繁饰兮，芳菲菲其弥章。

民生各有所乐兮，余独好修以为常。

虽体解吾犹未变兮，岂余心之可惩！

女媭之婵媛兮，申申其詈予。

曰："鲧婞直以亡身兮，终然殀乎羽之野。

汝何博謇而好修兮，纷独有此姱节？

薋菉葹以盈室兮，判独离而不服。

众不可户说兮，孰云察余之中情？

世并举而好朋兮，夫何茕独而不予听？"

依前圣以节中兮，喟凭心而历兹。

济沅湘以南征兮，就重华而陈词：

"启九辩与九歌兮，夏康娱以自纵。

不顾难以图后兮，五子用失乎家巷。

羿淫游以佚畋兮，又好射夫封狐。

固乱流其鲜终兮，浞又贪夫厥家。

浇身被服强圉兮，纵欲而不忍。

日康娱而自忘兮，厥首用夫颠陨。

夏桀之常违兮，乃遂焉而逢殃。

后辛之菹醢兮，殷宗用而不长。

"汤禹俨而只敬兮，周论道而莫差，

举贤而授能兮，循绳墨而不颇。

皇天无私阿兮，览民德焉错辅。

夫维圣哲以茂行兮，苟得用此下土。

瞻前而顾后兮，相观民之计极。

夫孰非义而可用兮，孰非善而可服？

阽余身而危死兮，览余初其犹未悔，
不量凿而正枘兮，固前修以菹醢。"
曾歔欷余郁邑兮，哀朕时之不当。
揽茹蕙以掩涕兮，沾余襟之浪浪。

跪敷衽以陈辞兮，耿吾既得此中正。
驷玉虬以乘鹥兮，溘埃风余上征。
朝发轫于苍梧兮，夕余至乎县圃。
欲少留此灵琐兮，日忽忽其将暮。
吾令羲和弭节兮，望崦嵫而勿迫。
路漫漫其修远兮，吾将上下而求索。

饮余马于咸池兮，总余辔乎扶桑。
折若木以拂日兮，聊逍遥以相羊。
前望舒使先驱兮，后飞廉使奔属。
鸾皇为余先戒兮，雷师告余以未具。
吾令凤鸟飞腾兮，继之以日夜。
飘风屯其相离兮，帅云霓而来御。
纷总总其离合兮，斑陆离其上下。

吾令帝阍开关兮，倚阊阖而望予。
时暧暧其将罢兮，结幽兰而延伫。
世溷浊而不分兮，好蔽美而嫉妒。
朝吾将济于白水兮，登阆风而绁马。
忽反顾以流涕兮，哀高丘之无女。

溘吾游此春宫兮，折琼枝以继佩。
及荣华之未落兮，相下女之可诒。

吾令丰隆乘云兮，求宓妃之所在。
解佩纕以结言兮，吾令蹇修以为理。
纷总总其离合兮，忽纬繣其难迁。
夕归次于穷石兮，朝濯发乎洧盘。
保厥美以骄傲兮，日康娱以淫游。
虽信美而无礼兮，来违弃而改求。

览相观于四极兮，周流乎天余乃下。
望瑶台之偃蹇兮，见有娀之佚女。
吾令鸩为媒兮，鸩告余以不好。
雄鸠之鸣逝兮，余犹恶其佻巧。
心犹豫而狐疑兮，欲自适而不可。
凤皇既受诒兮，恐高辛之先我。
欲远集而无所止兮，聊浮游以逍遥。
及少康之未家兮，留有虞之二姚。
理弱而媒拙兮，恐导言之不固。

世溷浊而嫉贤兮，好蔽美而称恶。
闺中既以邃远兮，哲王又不寤。
怀朕情而不发兮，余焉能忍与此终古？

索琼茅以筳篿兮，命灵氛为余占之。
曰："两美其必合兮，孰信修而慕之？
思九州之博大兮，岂唯是其有女？"
曰："勉远逝而无狐疑兮，孰求美而释女？
何所独无芳草兮，尔何怀乎故宇？

世幽昧以炫曜兮，孰云察余之善恶？

民好恶其不同兮,惟此党人其独异。
户服艾以盈要兮,谓幽兰其不可佩。
览察草木其犹未得兮,岂珵美之能当?
苏粪壤以充帏兮,谓申椒其不芳。"
欲从灵氛之吉占兮,心犹豫而狐疑。
巫咸将夕降兮,怀椒糈而要之。
百神翳其备降兮,九疑缤其并迎。
皇剡剡其扬灵兮,告余以吉故。

曰:"勉升降以上下兮,求矩矱之所同。
汤、禹严而求合兮,挚、咎繇而能调。
苟中情其好修兮,又何必用夫行媒?
说操筑于傅岩兮,武丁用而不疑。
吕望之鼓刀兮,遭周文而得举。
宁戚之讴歌兮,齐桓闻以该辅。
及年岁之末晏兮,时亦犹其未央。
恐鹈鴂之先鸣兮,使夫百草为之不芳。"

何琼佩之偃蹇兮,众薆然而蔽之。
惟此党人之不谅兮,恐嫉妒而折之。
时缤纷其变易兮,又何可以淹留。
兰芷变而不芳兮,荃蕙化而为茅。
何昔日之芳草兮,今直为此萧艾也!
岂其有他故兮,莫好修之害也。

余以兰为可恃兮,羌无实而容长;
委厥美以从俗兮,苟得列乎众芳。
椒专佞以慢慆兮,樧又欲充夫佩帏。

既干进而务入兮，又何芳之能只？
固时俗之流从兮，又孰能无变化？
览椒兰其若兹兮，又况揭车与江离？

惟兹佩之可贵兮，委厥美而历兹。
芳菲菲而难亏兮，芬至今犹未沫。
和调度以自娱兮，聊浮游而求女。
及余饰之方壮兮，周流观乎上下。

灵氛既告余以吉占兮，历吉日乎吾将行。
折琼枝以为羞兮，精琼蘼以为粻。
为余驾飞龙兮，杂瑶象以为车。

何离心之可同兮，吾将远逝以自疏。
邅吾道夫昆仑兮，路修远以周流。
扬云霓之晻蔼兮，鸣玉鸾之啾啾。
朝发轫于天津兮，夕余至乎西极。
凤皇翼其承旂兮，高翱翔之翼翼。
忽吾行此流沙兮，遵赤水而容与。
麾蛟龙使梁津兮，诏西皇使涉予。

路修远以多艰兮，腾众车使径待。
路不周以左转兮，指西海以为期。
屯余车其千乘兮，齐玉轪而并驰。
驾八龙之蜿蜿兮，载云旗之委蛇。
抑志而弭节兮，神高驰之邈邈。
奏九歌而舞韶兮，聊假日以媮乐。
陟升皇之赫戏兮，忽临睨夫旧乡，

仆夫悲余马怀兮,蜷局顾而不行。

乱曰:已矣哉!

国无人莫我知兮,又何怀乎故都?

既莫足与为美政兮,吾将从彭咸之所居。

Li Sao

A Prince am I of Ancestry renowned,
Illustrious Name my royal Sire hath found.
When Sirius did in Spring its Light display,
A Child was born, and Tiger marked the Day.
When first upon my Face my Lord's Eye glanced,
For me auspicious Names he straight advanced,
Denoting that in me Heaven's Marks divine
Should with the Virtues of the Earth combine.
With lavished innate Qualities indued,
By Art and Skill my Talents I renewed;
Angelic Herbs and sweet Selineas too,
And Orchids late that by the Water grew,
I wove for Ornament; till creeping Time,
Like Water flowing, stole away my Prime.
Magnolias of the Glade I plucked at Dawn,
At Eve beside the Stream took Winter-thorn.
Without Delay the Sun and Moon sped fast,
In swift Succession Spring and Autumn passed;
The fallen Flowers lay scattered on the Ground,
The Dusk might fall before my Dream was found.

Had I not loved my Prime and spurned the Vile,
Why should I not have changed my former Style?

My Chariot drawn by Steeds of Race divine
I urged; to guide the King my sole Design.

Three ancient Kings there were so pure and true
That round them every fragrant Flower grew;
Cassia and Pepper of the Mountain-side
With Melilotus white in Clusters vied.
Two Monarchs then, who high Renown received,
Followed the kingly Way, their Goal achieved.
Two Princes proud by Lust their Reign abused,
Sought easier Path, and their own Steps confused.
The Faction for illicit Pleasure longed;
Dreadful their Way where hidden Perils thronged.
Danger against myself could not appal,
But feared I lest my Sovereign's Sceptre fall.

Forward and back I hastened in my Quest,
Followed the former Kings, and took no Rest.
The Prince my true Integrity defamed,
Gave Ear to Slander, high his Anger flamed;
Integrity I knew could not avail,
Yet still endured; my Lord I would not fail.
Celestial Spheres my Witness be on high,
I strove but for His Sacred Majesty.
Twas first to me gave his plighted Word,
But soon repenting other Counsel heard.
For me Departure could arouse no Pain;
I grieved to see his royal Purpose vain.

Nine Fields of Orchids at one Time I grew,
For Melilot a hundred Acres too,
And fifty Acres for the Azalea bright,

The Rumex fragrant and the Lichen white.
I longed to see them yielding Blossoms rare,
And thought in Season due the Spoil to share.
I did not grieve to see them die away,
But grieved because midst Weeds they did decay.

Insatiable in Lust and Greediness
The Faction strove, and tired not of Excess;
Themselves condoning, others they'd decry,
And steep their Hearts in envious Jealousy.

Insatiably they seized what they desired,
It was not that to which my Heart aspired.
As old Age unrelenting hurried near,
Lest my fair Name should fail was all my Fear.
Dew from Magnolia Leaves I drank at Dawn,
At Eve for Food were Aster Petals borne;
And loving thus the Simple and the Fair,
How should I for my sallow Features care?
With gathered Vines I strung Valeria white,
And mixed with blue Wistaria Petals bright,
And Melilotus matched with Cassia sweet,
With Ivy green and Tendrils long to meet.
Life I adapted to the ancient Way,
Leaving the Manners of the present Day;
Thus unconforming to the modern Age,
The Path I followed of a bygone Sage.

Long did I sigh and wipe away my Tears,
To see my People bowed by Griefs and Fears.
Though I my Gifts enhanced and curbed my Pride,
At Morn they'd mock me, would at Eve deride;

First cursed that I Angelica should wear,
Then cursed me for my Melilotus fair.
But since my Heart did love such Purity,
I'd not regret a thousand Deaths to die.

I marvel at the Folly of the King,
So heedless of his People's Suffering.
They envied me my mothlike Eyebrows fine,
And so my Name his Damsels did malign.
Truly to Craft alone their Praise they paid,
The Square in Measuring they disobeyed;
The Use of common Rules they held debased;
With Confidence their crooked Lines they traced.

In Sadness plunged and sunk in deepest Gloom,
Alone I drove on to my dreary Doom.
In Exile rather would I meet my End,
Than to the Baseness of their Ways descend.
Remote the Eagle spurns the common Range,
Not deigns since Time began its Way to change;
A Circle fits not with a square Design;
Their different Ways could not be merged with mine.
Yet still my Heart I checked and curbed my Pride,
Their Blame endured and their Reproach beside.
To die for Righteousness alone I sought,
For this was what the ancient Sages taught.

I failed my former Errors to discern;
I tarried long, but now I would return.
My Steeds I wheeled back to their former Way,
Lest all too long down the wrong Path I stray.
On Orchid-covered Bank I loosed my Steed,

And let him gallop by the flow'ry Mead
At Will. Rejected now and in Disgrace,
I would retire to cultivate my Grace.
With Cress Leaves green my simple Gown I made,
With Lilies white my rustic Garb did braid.
Why should I grieve to go unrecognised,
Since in my Heart Fragrance was truly prized?
My Headdress then high-pinnacled I raised,
Lengthened my Pendents, where bright Jewels blazed.
Others may smirch their Fragrance and bright Hues,
My Innocence is proof against Abuse.
Oft I looked back, gazed to the Distance still,
Longed in the Wilderness to roam at Will.
Splendid my Ornaments together vied,
With all the Fragrance of the Flowers beside;
All men had Pleasures in their various Ways,
My Pleasure was to cultivate my Grace.
I would not change, though they my Body rend;
How could my Heart be wrested from its End?

My Handmaid fair, with Countenance demure,
Entreated me Allegiance to abjure;
"A Hero perished in the Plain ill-starred,
Where Pigmies stayed their Plumage to discard.
Why lovest thou thy Grace and Purity,
Alone dost hold thy splendid Virtue high?
Lentils and Weeds the Prince's Chamber fill:
Why holdest thou aloof with stubborn Will?
Thou canst not one by one the Crowd persuade,
And who the Purpose of our Heart hath weighed?
Faction and Strife the World hath ever loved;
Heeding me not, why standest thou removed?"

I sought th'ancestral Voice to ease my Woe.
Alas, how one so proud could sink so low!
To barbarous South I went across the Stream;
Before the Ancient I began my Theme:
"With Odes divine there came a Monarch's Son,
Whose Revels unrestrained were never done;
In Antics wild, to coming Perils blind,
He fought his Brother, and his Sway declined.
The royal Archer, in his wanton Chase
For Foxes huge, his Kingdom did disgrace.
Such Wantonness predicts no happy End;
His Queen was stolen by his loyal Friend.
The Traitor's Son, clad in prodigious Might,
In Incest sinned and cared not what was right.
He revelled all his Days, forgetting all;
His Head at last in Treachery did fall.
And then the Prince, who Counsels disobeyed,
Did court Disaster, and his Kingdom fade.
A Prince his Sage in burning Cauldrons tossed;
His glorious Dynasty ere long was lost.

"But stern and pious was their ancient Sire,
And his Successor too did Faith inspire;
Exalted were the Wise, the Able used,
The Rule was kept and never was abused.
The august Heaven, with unbiassed Grace,
All Men discerns, and helps the virtuous Race;
Sagacious Princes through their virtuous Deed
The Earth inherit, and their Reigns succeed.
The Past I probed, the Future so to scan,
And found these Rules that guide the Life of Man:

A Man unjust in Deed who would engage?
Whom should Men take as Guide except the Sage?
In mortal Dangers Death I have defied,
Yet could look back, and cast Regret aside.
Who strove, their Tool's Defects accounting nought,
Like ancient Sages were to Cauldrons brought."
Thus I despaired, my Face with sad Tears marred,
Mourning with Bitterness my Years ill-starred;
And Melilotus Leaves I took to stem
The Tears that streamed down to my Garment's Hem.
Soiling my Gown, to plead my Case I kneeled;
Th'ancestral Voice the Path to me revealed.

Swift jade-green Dragons, Birds with Plumage gold,
I harnessed to the Whirlwind, and behold,
At Daybreak from the Land of Plane-trees grey,
I came to Paradise ere close of Day.
I wished within the sacred Grove to stay,
The Sun had dropped, and Darkness wrapped the Way;
The Driver of the Sun I bade to stay,
Ere with the setting Rays we haste away.
The Way was long, and wrapped in Gloom did seem,
As I urged on to seek my vanished Dream.

The Dragons quenched their Thirst beside the Lake
Where bathed the Sun, whilst I upon the Brake
Fastened my Reins; a golden Bough I sought
To brush the Sun, and tarried there in Sport.
The pale Moon's Charioteer I then bade lead,
The Master of the Winds swiftly succeed;
Before, the royal Blue Bird cleared the Way;
The Lord of Thunder urged me to delay.

I bade the Phoenix scan the Heaven wide;
But vainly Day and Night its Course it tried;
The gathering Whirlwinds drove it from my Sight,
Rushing with lowering Clouds to check my Flight;
Sifting and merging in the Firmament,
Above, below, in various Hues they went.

The Gate-keeper of Heaven I bade give Place,
But leaning on his Door he scanned my Face;
The Day grew dark, and now was nearly spent;
Idly my Orchids into Wreaths I bent.
The Virtuous and the Vile in Darkness merged;
They veiled my Virtue, by their Envy urged.
At Dawn the Waters white I left behind;
My Steed stayed be the Portals of the Wind;
Yet, gazing back, a bitter Grief I felt
That in the lofty Crag no Damsel dwelt.

I wandered eastward to the Palace green,
And Pendents sought where Jasper Boughs were seen,
And vowed that they, before their Splendour fade,
As Gift should go to grace the loveliest Maid.
The Lord of Clouds I then bade mount the Sky
To seek the Stream where once the Nymph did lie;
As Pledge I gave my Belt of splendid Sheen,
My Councillor appointed Go-between.
Fleeting and wilful like capricious Cloud,
Her Obstinacy swift no Change allowed.
At Dusk retired she to the Crag withdrawn,
Her Hair beside the Stream she washed at Dawn.
Exulting in her Beauty and her Pride,
Pleasure she worshipped, and no Whim denied;

So fair of Form, so careless of all Grace,
I turned to take another in her place.

To Earth's Extremities I sought my Bride,
And urged my Train through all the Heaven wide
Upon a lofty Crag of jasper Green
The beauteous Princess of the West was seen.
The Falcon then I bade entreat the Maid,
But he, demurring, would my Course dissuade;
The Turtle-Dove cooed soft and off did fly,
But I mistrusted his Frivolity.
Like Whelp in Doubt, like timid Fox in Fear,
I wished to go, but wandered ever near.
With nuptial Gifts the Phoenix swiftly went;
I feared the Prince had won her ere I sent.
I longed to travel far, yet with no Bourn,
I could but wander aimless and forlorn.
Before the young King was in Marriage bound,
The Royal Sisters Twain might still be found;
My Plea was weak, my Mission was but frail;
I knew that my Demand could not avail.

The World is Dark, and envious of my Grace;
They veil my Virtue and the Evil praise.
Thy Chamber dark lies in Recesses deep,
Sagacious Prince, risest thou not from Sleep?
My Zeal unknown the Prince would not descry;
How could I bear this harsh Eternity?

With Mistletoe and Herbs of magic Worth,
I urged the Witch the Future to show forth.
"If Two attain Perfection they must meet,

But who is there that would thy Virtue greet?
Far the Nine Continents their Realm display;
Why here to seek thy Bride doth thou delay?
Away!" she cried, "Set craven Doubt aside,
If Beauty's sought, there's none hath with thee vied.
What Place is there where Orchids flower not fair?
Why is thy native Land thy single Care?

"Now darkly lies the World in Twilight's Glow,
Who doth your Defects and your Virtue know?
Evil and Good herein are reconciled;
The Crowd alone hath Nought but is defiled.
With stinking Mugwort girt upon their Waist,
They curse the others for their Orchids chaste;
Ignorant thus in choice of Fragrance rare,
Rich Ornaments how could they fitly wear?
With Mud and Filth they fill their Pendent Bag;
Cursing the Pepper sweet, they brawl and brag."
Although the Witches Counsel I held good,
In foxlike Indecision still I stood.
At Night the Wizard great made his Descent,
And meeting him spiced Rice I did present.
The Angels came, shading with Wings the Sky;
From Mountains wild the Deities drew nigh.
With regal Splendour shone the solemn Sight,
And thus the Wizard spake with Omens bright:

"Take Office high or low as Days afford,
If One there be that could with thee accord;
Like ancient Kings austere who sought their Mate,
Finding the one who should fulfill their Fate.
Now if thy Heart doth cherish Grace within,

What Need is there to choose a Go-between?

A Convict toiled on Rocks to expiate

His Crime; his Sovereign gave him great Estate.

A Butcher with his Knife made Roundelay;

His King chanced there and happy proved the Day.

A Prince who heard a Cowherd chanting late

Raised him to be a Councillor of State.

Before old Age o'ertake thee on thy Way,

Life still is young; to Profit turn thy Day.

Spring is but brief, when Cuckoos start to sing,

And Flowers will fade that once did spread and spring. "

On high my Jasper Pendent proudly gleamed,

Hid by the Crowd with Leaves that thickly teemed;

Untiring they relentless Means employed;

I feared it would through Envy be destroyed.

This gaudy Age so fickle proved its Will,

That to what Purpose did I linger still?

E'en Orchids changed, their Fragrance quickly lost,

And midst the Weeds Angelicas were tossed.

How could these Herbs, so fair in former Day,

Their Hue have changed, and turned to Mugworts grey?

The Reason for their Fall, not far to seek,

Was that to tend their Grace their Will proved weak.

I thought upon the Orchids I might lean;

No Flowers appeared, but long bare Leaves were seen;

Their Grace abandoned, vulgar Taste to please,

Content with lesser Flowers to dwell at Ease.

To Boasts and Flattery the Pepper turned;

To fill the Pendent Bag the Dogwood yearned;

Thus only upon higher Stations bent,

How could they long retain their former Scent?
Since they pursued the Fashion of the Time,
Small Wonder they decayed e'en in their Prime.
Viewing the Orchids' and the Peppers' Plight
Why blame the Rumex and Selinea white?

My Jasper Pendent rare I was beguiled
To leave, and to this Depth then sank defiled.
It blossomed still and never ceased to grow;
Like Water did its lovely Fragrance flow:
Pleasure I took to wear this Bough in Sport,
As roaming wild the Damsel fair I sought.
Thus in my Prime, with Ornaments bedecked,
I roved the Earth and Heaven to inspect.

With Omens bright the Seer revealed the Way,
I then appointed an auspicious Day.
As Victuals rare some Jasper Twigs I bore,
And some prepared, Provision rich to store;
Then winged Horses to my Chariot brought
My Carriage bright with Jade and Ivory wrought.

How might two Hearts at Variance accord?
I roamed till Peace be to my Mind restored.
The Pillar of the Earth I stayed beside;
The Way was long, and winding far and wide.
In Twilight glowed the Clouds with wondrous Sheen,
And chirping flew the Birds of jasper Green.
I went at Dawn high Heaven's Ford to leave;
To Earth's Extremity I came at Eve.
On Phoenix Wings the Dragon Pennons lay;
With Plumage bright they flew to lead the Way.

I crossed the Quicksand with its treach'rous Flood,
Beside the burning River, red as Blood;
To bridge the Stream my Dragons huge I bade,
Invoked the Emperor of the West to aid.

The Way was long, precipitous in View;
I bade my Train a different Path pursue.
There where the Heaven fell we turned a Space,
And marked the Western Sea as Meeting-place.
A thousand Chariots gathered in my Train,
With Axles full abreast we drove amain;
Eight Horses drew the Carriages behind;
The Pennons shook like Serpents in the Wind.
I lowered Flags, and from my Whip refrained;
My Train of towering Chariots I restrained.
I sang the Odes. I trod a sacred Dance,
In Revels wild my last Hour to enhance.
Ascending where celestial Heaven blazed,
On native Earth for the last Time we gazed;
My Slaves were sad, my Steeds all neighed in Grief,
And, gazing back, the Earth they would not leave.

Epilogue

Since in that Kingdom all my Virtue spurn,
Why should I for the royal City yearn?
Wide though the World, no Wisdom can be found.
I'll seek the Stream where once the Sage was drowned.

二

杜十娘怒沉百宝箱①

话中单表万历二十年间,日本国关白作乱,侵犯朝鲜。朝鲜国王上表告急,天朝发兵泛海往救。有户部官奏准:目今兵兴之际,粮饷未充,暂开纳粟入监之例。原来纳粟入监的,有几般便宜:好读书,好科举,好中,结末来又有个小小前程结果。以此宦家公子,富室子弟,到不愿做秀才,都去援例做太学生。自开了这例,两京太学生,各添至千人之外。内中有一人,姓李名甲,字干先,浙江绍兴府人氏。父亲李布政所生三儿,惟甲居长。自幼读书在庠,未得登科,援例入于北雍。因在京坐监,与同乡柳遇春监生同游教坊司院内,与一个名姬相遇。那姬姓杜名媺,排行第十,院中都称为杜十娘,生得:

> 浑身雅艳,遍体娇香。两弯眉画远山青,一对眼明秋水润。脸如莲萼,分明卓氏文君;唇似樱桃,何减白家樊素。可怜一片无瑕玉,误落风尘花柳中。

那杜十娘自十三岁破瓜,今一十九岁,七年之内,不知历过了多少公子王孙,一个个情迷意荡,破家荡产而不惜。院中传出四句口号来,道是:

> 坐中若有杜十娘,斗筲之量饮千觞;院中若识杜老媺,千家粉面都如鬼。

---

① 中文、英译文选自:(明)冯梦龙,凌濛初. 宋明评话选I(大中华文库·汉英对照). 杨宪益,戴乃迭,译. 北京:外文出版社,2007.

却说李公子,风流年少,未逢美色,自遇了杜十娘,喜出望外,把花柳情怀,一担儿挑在他身上。那公子俊俏庞儿,温存性儿,又是撒漫的手儿,帮衬的勤儿,与十娘一双两好,情投意合。十娘因见鸨儿贪财无义,久有从良之志;又见李公子忠厚志诚,甚有心向他。奈李公子惧怕老爷,不敢应承。虽则如此,两下情好愈密,朝欢暮乐,终日相守,如夫妇一般,海誓山盟,向无他志。真个:

恩深似海恩无底,义重如山义更高。

再说杜妈妈女儿被李公子占住,别的富家巨室,闻名上门,求一见而不可得。初时李公子撒漫用钱,大差大使,妈妈胁肩谄笑,奉承不暇。日往月来,不觉一年有余,李公子囊箧渐渐空虚,手不应心,妈妈也就怠慢了。老布政在家闻知儿子嫖院,几遍写字来唤他回去。他迷恋十娘颜色,终日延挨。后来闻知老爷在家发怒,越不敢回。古人云:"以利相交者,利尽而疏。"那杜十娘与李公子真情相好,见他手头愈短,心头愈热。妈妈也几遍教女儿打发李甲出院,见女儿不统口,又几遍将言语触突李公子,要激怒他起身。公子性本温克,词气愈和,妈妈没奈何,日逐只将十娘叱骂道:"我们行户人家,吃客穿客,前门送旧,后门迎新,门庭闹如火,钱帛堆成垛。自从那李甲在此,混帐一年有余,莫说新客,连旧主顾都断了,分明接了个钟馗老,连小鬼也没得上门。弄得老娘一家人家,有气无烟,成什么模样!"杜十娘被骂,耐性不住,便回答道:"那李公子不是空手上门的,也曾费过大钱来。"妈妈道:"彼一时,此一时,你只教他今日费些小钱儿,把与老娘办些柴米,养你两口也好。别人家养的女儿便是摇钱树,千生万活,偏我家晦气,养了个退财白虎,开了大门,七件事般般都在老身心上。到替你这小贱人白白养着穷汉,教我衣食从何处来?你对那穷汉说:"有本事出几两银子与我,到得你跟了他去,我别讨个丫头过活却不好?"十娘道:"妈妈,这话是真是假?"妈妈晓得李甲囊无一钱,衣衫都典尽了,料他没处设法。便应道:"老娘从不说谎,当真哩。"十娘道:"娘,你要他许多银子?"妈妈道:"若是别人,千把银子也讨了,可怜那穷汉出不起,只要他三百两,我自去讨一个粉头代替。只一件,须是三日内交付与我,左手交银,右手交人。若三日没有银时,老身也不管三七二十一,公子不公子,一顿孤拐,打那光棍出去。那时莫怪老身!"十娘道:"公子虽在客边乏钞,谅三百金还措办得来。只是三日忒近,限他十日便好。"妈妈想道:"这穷汉一双赤手,便限他一百日,他那里来银子。没有银子,便铁皮包脸,料也无颜上门。那时重整家风,嬡儿也没得话讲。"答应道:"看你面,便宽到十日。第十日没有银子,不干老娘之事。"十娘道:"若十日内无银,料他也无颜再见了。只怕有了三百两银子,妈妈又翻悔起来。"妈妈道:"老身年五十一岁了,又奉十斋,怎敢说谎? 不信时与你拍掌为定。若翻悔时,做猪做狗。"

> 从来海水斗难量,可笑虔婆意不良。
>
> 料定穷儒囊底竭,故将财礼难娇娘。

是夜,十娘与公子在枕边,议及终身之事。公子道:"我非无此心。但教坊落籍,其费甚多,非千金不可。我囊空如洗,如之奈何!"十娘道:"妾已与妈妈议定只要三百金,便须十日内措办。郎君游资虽罄,然都中岂无亲友可以借贷? 倘得如数,妾身遂为君之所有,省受这虔婆之气。"公子道:"亲友中为我留恋行院,都不相顾。明日只做束装起身,各家告辞,就开口假贷路费,凑聚将来,或可满得此数。"起身梳洗,别了十娘出门。十娘道:"用心作速,专听佳音。"公子道:"不须分付。"

公子出了院门,来到三亲四友处,假说起身告别,众人到也欢喜。后来叙到路费欠缺,意欲借贷。常言道:"说着钱,便无缘。"亲友们就不招架。他们也见得是,道李公子是风流浪子,迷恋烟花,年许不归,父亲都为他气坏在家。他今日抖然要回,未知真假。倘或说骗盘缠到手,又去还脂粉钱,父亲知道,将好意翻成恶意,始终只是一怪,不如辞了干净。便回道:"目今正值空乏,不能相济,惭愧! 惭愧!"人人如此,个个皆然,并没有个慷慨丈夫,肯统口许他一十、二十两。李公子一连奔走了三日,分毫无获,又不敢回决十娘,权且含糊答应。到第四日又没想头,就羞回院中。

平日间有了杜家,连下处也没有了,今日就无处投宿。只得往同乡柳监生寓所借歇。柳遇春见公子愁容可掬,问其来历。公子将杜十娘愿嫁之情,备细说了。遇春摇首道:"未必,未必。那杜媺曲中第一名姬,要从良时,怕没有十斛明珠,千金聘礼?那鸨儿如何只要三百两?想鸨儿怪你无钱使用,白白占住他的女儿,设计打发你出门。那妇人与你相处已久,又碍却面皮,不好明言。明知你手内空虚,故意将三百两卖个人情,限你十日。若十日没有,你也不好上门。便上门时,他会说你笑你,落得一场褒渎,自然安身不牢。此乃烟花逐客之计。足下三思,休被其惑。据弟愚意,不如早早开交为上。"公子听说,半晌无言,心中疑惑不定。遇春又道:"足下莫要错了主意。你若真个还乡,不多几两盘费,还有人搭救。若是要三百两时,莫说十日,就是十个月也难。如今的世情,那肯顾缓急二字的。那烟花也算定你没处告债,故意设法难你。"公子道:"仁兄所见良是。"口里虽如此说,心中割舍不下。依旧又往外边东央西告,只是夜里不进院门了。公子在柳监生寓中,一连住了三日,共是六日了。

杜十娘连日不见公子进院,十分着紧,就教小厮四儿街上去寻。四儿寻到大街,恰好遇见公子。四儿叫道:"李姐夫,娘在家里望你。"公子自觉无颜,回复道:"今日不得功夫,明日来罢。"四儿奉了十娘之命,一把扯住,死也不放,道:"娘叫咱寻你,是必同去走一遭。"李公子心上也牵挂着婊子,没奈何,只得随四儿进院。见了十娘,嘿嘿无言。十娘问道:"所谋之事如何?"公子眼中流下泪来。十娘道:"莫非人情淡薄,不能足三百之数么?"公子含泪而言,道出二句:"不信上山擒虎易,果然开口告人难。一连奔走六日,并无铢两,一双空手,羞见芳卿,故此这几日不敢进院。今日承命呼唤,忍耻而来,非某不用心,实是世情如此。"十娘道:"此言休使虔婆知道。郎君今夜且住,妾别有商议。"十娘自备酒肴,与公子欢饮。睡至半夜,十娘对公子道:"郎君果不能办一钱耶?妾终身之事,当如何也?"公子只是流涕,不能答一语。渐渐五更天晓,十娘道:"妾所卧絮褥内藏有碎银一百五十两,此妾私蓄,郎君可持去。三百金,妾任其半,郎君亦谋其半,庶易为力。限只四日,万勿迟误。"十娘起身将褥付公子,公子惊喜过望,唤童儿持褥而去。径到柳遇春寓中，又把夜来之情与遇春说了。将褥拆开看时，絮中都裹着零碎银子，取出兑时果是一百五十两。遇春大惊道："此妇真有心人也。既系真情，不可相负。吾当代为足下谋之。"公子道："倘得玉成，决不有负。"当下柳遇春留李公子在寓，自出头各处去借贷。两日之内，凑足一百五十两交付公子道："吾代为足下告债，非为足下，实怜杜十娘之情也。"

李甲拿了三百两银子，喜从天降，笑逐颜开，欣欣然来见十娘，刚是第九日，还不足十日。十娘问道："前日分毫难借，今日如何就有一百五十两？"公子将柳监生事情，又述了一遍。十娘以手加额道："使吾二人得遂其愿者，柳君之力也。"两个欢天喜地，又在院中过了一晚。次日，十娘早起，对李甲道："此银一交，便当随郎君去矣。舟车之类，合当预备。妾昨日于姊妹中借得白银二十两，郎君可收下为行资也。"公子正愁路费无出，但不敢开口，得银甚喜。说犹未了，鸨儿恰来敲门叫道："媺儿，今日是第十日了。"公子闻叫，启户相延道："承妈妈厚意，正欲相请。"便将银三百两放在桌上。鸨儿不料公子有银，嘿然变色，似有悔意。十娘道："儿在妈妈家中八年，所致金帛，不下数千金矣。今日从良美事，又妈妈亲口所订，三百金不欠分毫，又不曾过期。倘若妈妈失信不许，郎君持银去，儿即刻自尽。恐那时人财两失，悔之无及也。"鸨儿无词以对，腹内筹画了半晌，只得取天平兑准了银子，说道：事已如此，料留你不住了。只是你要去时，即今就去。平时穿戴衣饰之类，毫厘休想。"说罢，将公子和十娘推出房门，讨锁来就落了锁。此时九月天气，十娘才下床，尚未梳洗，随身旧衣，就拜了妈妈两拜，李公子也作了一揖。一夫一妇，离了虔婆大门。

　　　　鲤鱼脱却金钩去，摆尾摇头再不来。

公子教十娘且住片时："我去唤个小轿抬你，权往柳荣卿寓所去，再作道理。"十娘道：院中诸姊妹平昔相厚，理宜话别。况前日又承他借贷路费，不可不一谢也。"乃同公子到各姊妹处谢别，姊妹中惟谢月朗、徐素素与杜家相近，尤与十娘亲厚。十娘先到谢月朗家。月朗见十娘秃髻旧衫，惊问其故。十娘备述来因。又引李甲相见,十娘指月朗道:"前日路资,是此位姐姐所贷,郎君可致谢。"李甲连连作揖。月郎便教十娘梳洗,一面去请徐素素来家相会。十娘梳洗已毕,谢徐二美人各出所有,翠钿金钏,瑶簪宝珥,锦袖花裙,鸾带绣履,把杜十娘装扮得焕然一新,备酒作庆贺筵席。月朗让卧房与李甲杜媺二人过宿。次日,又大排筵席,遍请院中姊妹。凡十娘相厚者,无不毕集,都与他夫妇把盏称喜。吹弹歌舞,各逞其长,务要尽欢,直饮至夜分。十娘向众姊妹一一称谢。众姊妹道:"十姊为风流领袖,今从郎君去,我等相见无日。何日长行,姊妹们尚当奉送。"月朗道:"候有定期,小妹当来相报。但阿姊千里间关,同郎君远去,囊箧萧条,曾无约束,此乃吾等之事。当相与共谋之,勿令姊有穷途之虑也。"众姊妹各唯唯而散。

是晚,公子和十娘仍宿谢家。至五鼓,十娘对公子道:"吾等此去,何处安身?郎君亦曾计议有定着否?"公子道:"老父盛怒之下,若知娶妓而归,必然加以不堪,反致相累。展转寻思,尚未有万全之策。"十娘道:"父子天性,岂能终绝。既然仓卒难犯,不若与郎君于苏杭胜地,权作浮居。郎君先回,求亲友于尊大人面前劝解和顺,然后携妾于归,彼此安妥。"公子道:"此言甚当。"次日,二人起身辞了谢月朗,暂往柳监生寓中,整顿行装。杜十娘见了柳遇春,倒身下拜,谢其周全之德:"异日我夫妇必当重报。"遇春慌忙答礼道:"十娘钟情所欢,不以贫窭易心,此乃女中豪杰。仆因风吹火,谅区区何足挂齿!"三人又饮了一日酒。次早,择了出行吉日,雇倩轿马停当。十娘又遣童儿寄信,别谢月朗。临行之际,只见肩舆纷纷而至,乃谢月朗与徐素素拉众姊妹来送行。月朗道:"十姊从郎君千里间关,囊中消索,吾等甚不能忘情。今合具薄赆,十姊可检收,或长途空乏,亦可少助。"说罢,命从人挈一描金文具至前,封锁甚固,正不知什么东西在里面。十娘也不开看,也不推辞,但殷勤作谢而已。须臾,舆马齐集,仆夫催促起身。柳监生三杯别酒,和众美人送出崇文门外,各各垂泪而别。正是:

他日重逢难预必,此时分手最堪怜。

再说李公子同杜十娘行至潞河，舍陆从舟，却好有瓜洲差使船转回之便，讲定船钱，包了舱口。比及下船时，李公子囊中并无分文余剩。你道杜十娘把二十两银子与公子，如何就没了？公子在院中嫖得衣衫蓝缕，银子到手，未免在解库中取赎几件穿着，又制办了铺盖，剩来只勾轿马之费。公子正当愁闷，十娘道："郎君勿忧，众姊妹合赠，必有所济。"乃取钥开箱。公子在傍自觉惭愧，也不敢窥觑箱中虚实。只见十娘在箱里取出一个红绢袋来，掷于桌上道："郎君可开看之。"公子提在手中，觉得沉重，启而观之，皆是白银，计数整五十两。十娘仍将箱子下锁，亦不言箱中更有何物。但对公子道："承众姊妹高情，不惟途路不乏，即他日浮寓吴越间，亦可稍佐吾夫妻山水之费矣。"公子且惊且喜道："若不遇恩卿，我李甲流落他乡，死无葬身之地矣。此情此德，白头不敢忘也。"自此每谈及往事，公子必感激流涕。十娘亦曲意抚慰，一路无话。

不一日，行至瓜洲，大船停泊岸口。公子别雇了民船，安放行李。约明日侵晨，剪江而渡。其时仲冬中旬，月明如水，公子和十娘坐于舟首。公子道："自出都门，困守一舱之中，四顾有人，未得畅语。今日独据一舟，更无避忌。且已离塞北，初近江南，宜开怀畅饮，以舒向来抑郁之气，恩卿以为何如？"十娘道："妾久疏谈笑，亦有此心，郎君言及，足见同志耳。"公子乃携酒具于船首，与十娘铺毡并坐，传杯交盏。饮至半酣，公子执卮对十娘道："恩卿妙音，六院推首。某相遇之初，每闻绝调，辄不禁神魂之飞动。心事多违，彼此郁郁，鸾鸣凤奏，久矣不闻。今清江明月，深夜无人，肯为我一歌否？"十娘兴亦勃发，遂开喉顿嗓，取扇按拍，呜呜咽咽，歌出元人施君美《拜月亭》杂剧上"状元执盏与婵娟"一曲，名《小桃红》。真个：

声飞霄汉云皆驻，响入深泉鱼出游。

却说他舟有一少年，姓孙名富，字善赉，徽州新安人氏。家资巨万，积祖扬州种盐。年方二十，也是南雍中朋友。生性风流，惯向青楼买笑，红粉追欢，若嘲风弄月，到是个轻薄的头儿。事有偶然，其夜亦泊舟瓜洲渡口，独酌无聊。急听得歌声嘹亮，凤吟鸾吹，不足喻其美。起立船头，伫听半晌,方知声出邻舟。正欲相访,音响倏已寂然。乃遣仆者潜窥踪迹,访于舟人。但晓得是李相公雇的船,并不知歌者来历。孙富想道:"此歌者必非良家,怎生得他一见?"展转寻思,通宵不寐。挨至五更,忽闻江风大作。及晓,彤云密布,狂雪飞舞。怎见得,有诗为证:

千山云树灭,万径人踪绝。

扁舟蓑笠翁,独钓寒江雪。

因这风雪阻渡,舟不得开。孙富命艄公移船,泊于李家舟之傍。孙富貂帽狐裘,推窗假作看雪。值十娘梳洗方毕,纤纤玉手,揭起舟傍短帘,自泼盂中残水,粉容微露,却被孙富窥见了,果是国色天香。魂摇心荡,迎眸注目,等候再见一面,杳不可得。沉思久之,乃倚窗高吟高学士《梅花诗》二句,道:"雪满山中高士卧,月明林下美人来。"

李甲听得邻舟吟诗,舒头出舱,看是何人。只因这一看,正中了孙富之计。孙富吟诗,正要引李公子出头,他好乘机攀话。当下慌忙举手,就问:"老兄尊姓何讳?"李公子叙了姓名乡贯,少不得也问那孙富。孙富也叙过了。又叙了些太学中的闲话,渐渐亲熟。孙富便道:"风雪阻舟,乃天遣与尊兄相会,实小弟之幸也。舟次无聊,欲同尊兄上岸,就酒肆中一酌,少领清诲,万望不拒。"公子道:"萍水相逢,何当厚扰?"孙富道:"说那里话!'四海之内,皆兄弟也。'"喝教艄公打跳,童儿张伞,迎接公子过船,就于船头作揖。然后让公子先行,自己随后,各各登跳上涯。行不数步,就有个酒楼,二人上楼,拣一副洁净座头,靠窗而坐。酒保列上酒肴。孙富举杯相劝,二人赏雪饮酒。先说些斯文中套话,渐渐引入花柳之事。二人都是过来之人,志同道合,说得入港,一发成相知了。孙富屏去左右,低低问道:"昨夜尊舟清歌何人也?"李甲正要卖弄在行,遂实说道:"此乃北京名姬杜十娘也。"孙富道:"既系曲中姊妹,何以归兄?"公子遂将初遇杜十娘,如何相好,后来如何要嫁,如何借银讨他,始末根由,备细述了一遍。孙富道:"兄携丽人而归,固是快事,但不知尊府中能相容否?"公子道:"贱室不足虑。所虑者,老父性严,尚费踌躇耳!"孙富将机就机,便问道:"既是尊大人未必相容,兄所携丽人,何处安顿? 亦曾通知丽人,共作计较否?"公子攒眉而答道:"此事曾与小妾议之。"孙富欣然问道:"尊宠必有妙策。"公子道:"他意欲侨居苏杭,流连山水。使小弟先回,求亲友宛转于家君之前。俟家君回嗔作喜,然后图归,高明以为何如?"孙富沉吟半响,故作愀然之色,道:"小弟乍会之间,交浅言深,诚恐见怪。"公子道:正赖高明指教,何必谦逊?"孙富道:"尊大人位居方面,必严帷薄之嫌,平时既怪兄游非礼之地,今日岂容兄娶不节之人。况且贤亲贵友,谁不迎合尊大人之意者? 兄枉去求他,必然相拒。就有个不识时务的进言于尊大人之前,见尊大人意思不允,他就转口了。兄进不能和睦家庭,退无词以回复尊宠。即使留连山水,亦非长久之计。万一资斧困竭,岂不进退两难!"公子自知手中只有五十金,比时费去大半,说到资斧困竭,进退两难,不觉点头道是。孙富又道:"小弟还有句心腹之谈,兄肯俯听否?"公子道:"承兄过爱,更求尽言。"孙富道:"疏不间亲,还是莫说罢。"公子道:"但说何妨。"孙富道:"自古道:'妇人水性无常',况烟花之辈,少真多假。他既系六院名姝,相识定满天下;或者南边原有旧约,借兄之力,挈带而来,以为他适之地。"公子道:"这个恐未必然。"孙富道:即不然,江南子弟,最工轻薄,兄留丽人独居,难保无逾墙钻穴之事。若挈之同归,愈增尊大人之怒。为兄之计,未有善策。况父子天伦,必不可绝。若为妾而触父,因妓而弃家,海内必以兄为浮浪不经之人。异日妻不以为夫,弟不以为兄,同袍不以为友,兄何以立于天地之间? 兄今日不可不熟思也!"

公子闻言,茫然自失,移席问计:"据高明之见,何以教我?"孙富道:"仆有一计,于兄甚便。只恐兄溺枕席之爱,未必能行,使仆空费词说耳!"公子道:"兄诚有良策,使弟再睹家园之乐,乃弟之恩人也。又何惮而不言耶?"孙富道:"兄飘零岁余,严亲怀怒,闺阁离心,设身以处兄之地,诚寝食不安之时也。然尊大人所以怒兄者,不过为迷花恋柳,挥金如土,异日必为弃家荡产之人,不堪承继家业耳! 兄今日空手而归,正触其怒。兄倘能割衽席之爱,见机而作,仆愿以千金相赠。兄得千金,以报尊大人,只说在京授馆,并不曾浪费分毫,尊大人必然相信。从此家庭和睦,当无间言。

须臾之间,转祸为福。兄请三思。仆非贪丽人之色,实为兄效忠于万一也。"李甲原是没主意的人,本心惧怕老子,被孙富一席话,说透胸中之疑,起身作揖道:"闻兄大教,顿开茅塞。但小妾千里相从,义难顿绝,容归与商之。得其心肯,当奉复耳。"孙富道:"说话之间,宜放婉曲。彼既忠心为兄,必不忍使兄父子分离,定然玉成兄还乡之事矣。"二人饮了一回酒,风停雪止,天色已晚。孙富教家僮算还了酒钱,与公子携手下船。正是:

逢人且说三分话,未可全抛一片心。

却说杜十娘在舟中,摆设酒果,欲与公子小酌,竟日未回,挑灯以待。公子下船,十娘起迎,见公子颜色匆匆,似有不乐之意,乃满斟热酒劝之。公子摇首不饮,一言不发,竟自床上睡了。十娘心中不悦,乃收拾杯盘,为公子解衣就枕,问道:"今日有何见闻,而怀抱郁郁如此?"公子叹息而已,终不启口。问了三四次,公子已睡去了。十娘委决不下,坐于床头而不能寐。到夜半,公子醒来,又叹一口气。十娘道:"郎君有何难言之事,频频叹息?"公子拥被而起,欲言不语者几次,扑簌簌掉下泪来。十娘抱持公子于怀间,软言抚慰道:"妾与郎君情好,已及二载,千辛万苦,历尽艰难,得有今日。然相从数千里,未曾哀戚。今将渡江,方图百年欢笑,如何反起悲伤,必有其故。夫妇之间,死生相共,有事尽可商量,万勿讳也。"公子再被逼不过,只得含泪而言道:"仆天涯穷困,蒙恩卿不弃,委曲相从,诚乃莫大之德也。但反覆思之,老父位居方面,拘于礼法,况素性方严,恐添嗔怒,必加黜逐。你我流荡,将何底止?夫妇之欢难保,父子之伦又绝。日间蒙新安孙友邀饮,为我筹及此事,寸心如割。"十娘大惊道:"郎君意将如何?"公子道:"仆事内之人,当局而迷。孙友为我画一计颇善,但恐恩卿不从耳!"十娘道:"孙友者何人?计如果善,何不可从?"公子道:"孙友名富,新安盐商,少年风流之士也。夜间闻子清歌,因而问及。仆告以来历,并谈及难归之故,渠意欲以千金聘汝。我得千金,可藉口以见吾父母;而恩卿亦得所天。但情不能舍,是以悲泣。"说罢,泪如雨下。十娘放开两手,冷笑一声道:"为郎君画此计者,此人乃大英雄也。郎君千金之资,既得恢复,而妾归他姓,又不致为行李之累。发乎情,止乎礼,诚两便之策也。那千金在那里?"公子收泪道:"未得恩卿之诺,金尚留彼处,未曾过手。"十娘道:"明早快快应承了他,不可挫过机会。但千金重事,须得兑足交付郎君之手,妾始过舟,勿为贾竖子所欺。"

时已四鼓,十娘即起身挑灯梳洗道:"今日之妆,乃迎新送旧,非比寻常。"于是脂粉香泽,用意修饰,花钿绣袄,极其华艳,香风拂拂,光采照人。装束方完,天色已晓。孙富差家童到船头候信。十娘微窥公子,欣欣似有喜色,乃催公子快去回话,及早兑足银子。公子亲到孙富船中,回复依允。孙富道:"兑银易事,须得丽人妆台为信。"公子又回复了十娘,十娘即指描金文具道:"可便抬去。"孙富喜甚,即将白银一千两,送到公子船中。十娘亲自检看,足色足数,分毫无爽。乃手把船舷,以手招孙富。孙富一见,魂不附体。十娘启朱唇,开皓齿道:"方才箱子可暂发来,内有李郎路引一纸,可检还之也。"孙富视十娘已为瓮中之鳖,即命家童送那描金文具,安放船头之上。十娘取钥开锁,内皆抽替小箱。十娘叫公子抽第一层来看,只见翠羽明珰,瑶簪宝珥,充牣于中,约值数百金。十娘遽投之江中。李甲与孙富及两船之人,无不惊诧。又命公子再抽一箱,乃玉箫金管。又抽一箱,尽古玉紫金玩器,约值数千金。十娘尽投之于大江中。岸上之人,观者如堵。齐声道:"可惜!可惜!"正不知什么缘故。最后又抽一箱,箱中复有一匣。开匣视之,夜明之珠,约有盈把。其他祖母绿、猫儿眼,诸般异宝,目所未睹,莫能定其价之多少。众人齐声喝采,喧声如雷。十娘又欲投之于江。李甲不觉大悔,抱持十娘恸哭,那孙富也来劝解。

十娘推开公子在一边,向孙富骂道:"我与李郎备尝艰苦,不是容易到此。汝以奸淫之意,巧为谗说,一旦破人姻缘,断人恩爱,乃我之仇人。我死而有知,必当诉之神明,尚妄想枕席之欢乎!"又对李甲道:"妾风尘数年,私有所积,本为终身之计。自遇郎君,山盟海誓,白首不渝。前出都之际,假托众姊妹相赠,箱中韫藏百宝,不下万金。将润色郎君之装,归见父母,或怜妾有心,收佐中馈,得终委托,生死无憾。谁知郎君相信不深,惑于浮议,中道见弃,负妾一片真心。今日当众目之前,开箱出视,使郎君知区区千金,未为难事。妾椟中有玉,恨郎眼内无珠。命之不辰,风尘困瘁,甫得脱离,又遭弃捐。今众人各有耳目,共作证明,妾不负郎君,郎君自负妾耳!"于是众人聚观者,无不流涕,都唾骂李公子负心薄幸。公子又羞又苦,且悔且泣,方欲向十娘谢罪,十娘抱持宝匣,向江心一跳。众人急呼捞救,但见云暗江心,波涛滚滚,杳无踪影。可惜一个如花似玉的名姬,一旦葬于江鱼之腹。

> 三魂渺渺归水府,七魄悠悠入冥途。

当时旁观之人,皆咬牙切齿,争欲拳殴李甲和那孙富。慌得李孙二人,手足无措,急叫开船,分途遁去。李甲在舟中,看了千金,转忆十娘,终日愧悔,郁成狂疾,终身不痊。孙富自那日受惊,得病卧床月余,终日见杜十娘在傍诟骂,奄奄而逝。人以为江中之报也。

却说柳遇春在京坐监完满,束装回乡,停舟瓜步。偶临江净脸,失坠铜盆于水,觅渔人打捞。及至捞起,乃是个小匣儿。遇春启匣观看,内皆明珠异宝,无价之珍。遇春厚赏渔人,留于床头把玩。是夜梦见江中一女子,凌波而来,视之,乃杜十娘也。近前万福,诉以李郎薄幸之事。又道:"向承君家慷慨,以一百五十金相助,本意息肩之后,徐图报答。不意事无终始。然每怀盛情,悒悒未忘。早间曾以小匣托渔人奉致,聊表寸心,从此不复相见矣。"言讫,猛然惊醒,方知十娘已死,叹息累日。

后人评论此事,以为孙富谋夺美色,轻掷千金,固非良士。李甲不识杜十娘一片苦心,碌碌蠢才,无足道者。独谓十娘千古女侠,岂不能觅一佳侣,共跨秦楼之凤,乃错认李公子,明珠美玉,投于盲人,以致恩变为仇,万种恩情,化为流水,深可惜也!有诗叹云:

> 不会风流莫妄谈,单单情字费人参;
> 若将情字能参透,唤作风流也不惭。

The Courtesan's Jewel Box

Our story starts with the invasion of Korea by the Japanese general Hideyoshi in the twentieth year of Wan Li period (1592). When the King of Korea appealed for help, the Son of Heaven sent troops across the sea to save him; and the Board of Treasury proposed that since the grain and silver allocated to the troops were insufficient for the expedition a special tax should be raised by the sale of places in the Imperial Colleges. To this the emperor agreed.

Now this system had many advantages for those with money. In addition to having better facilities for studying and passing the examinations, the students of these colleges were assured of small official posts. Accordingly, the sons of official or wealthy families who did not want to sit for the county examination took advantage of this scheme to purchase a place in one of the Imperial Colleges. So the number of students in both the colleges in Nanjing and Beijing rose to over one thousand each.

One of these students was called Li Jia. A native of Shaoxing in Zhejiang Province, he was the oldest of three sons of a provincial treasurer. Although a licentiate, he had failed to pass the prefectural examination, he had purchased a place in the Imperial College at Beijing under the new system; and during his residence in the capital he went with a fellow-provincial and fellow-student, Liu Yuchun, to the singsong girls' quarter. Here he met a celebrated courtesan called Du Wei, who, because she was the tenth girl in the quarter, was also known as Decima.

She was sweetness and loveliness incarnate;
Her fine eyebrows were arched like distant hills;
Her eyes were as clear as autumn water;
Her face was as fresh as dew-washed lotus;
Her lips were as crimson as ripe cherries.
Ah, the pity of it! that this lovely maid
Should be cast by the roadside in the dust.

Since Decima became a courtesan she had met countless young men of rich and noble families who had not hesitated to spend all they possessed for love of her; so other singsong girls used to say:

When Decima is at the feast,
The poorest drinker drains a thousand cups;
When in our quarter Decima appears,
All other powdered faces look like ghosts.

Though Li was a gay young fellow, he had never seen such a beautiful girl. At his first meeting with Decima he was absolutely charmed by her and fell head over heels in love. And since he was not only handsome and amiable but open-handed and untiring in his pursuit of her, the attraction soon proved mutual. Realizing that her mistress was grasping and heartless, Decima had long wanted to leave her; and now that she saw how kind and devoted Li was, she wished to throw in her lot with him. Although the young man was too afraid of his father to marry her, they fell more and more deeply in love, passing whole days and nights together in pleasure and remaining as inseparable as if they were already husband and wife. They vowed solemnly never to love anyone else.

Their love was deeper than the sea,
And more sublime their faith than mountain peaks.

After Li became Decima's lover, other wealthy men who had heard of her fame tried in vain to gain access to her. At first Li spent money lavishly on her, and the procuress, all smiles and blandishments, waited on him hand and foot. But when more than a year had sped past, Li's money was nearly exhausted. He could no longer be as generous as he would have liked, and the old woman began to treat him coldly. The provincial treasurer heard that his son was frequenting the courtesans' quarter, and sent letter after letter ordering him to come home; but the young man was so enamoured of Decima's beauty that he kept postponing his return. And later, when he heard how angry his father was with him, he dared not go back.

The proverb says that friendship based on money will end once the money is spent. Decima, however, loved Li so truly that the poorer he grew the more passionately attached to him she became. Her mistress told her repeatedly to send Li about his business and, seeing that the girl refused to do so, she began to insult him in the hope that he would leave in anger. But her insults had no effect on Li, who was naturally of a mild disposition, so she could do nothing but reproach Decima every day.

"In our profession we depend on our clients for food and clothing," she said. "As we speed one guest from the front door, another should be coming in by the back. The more clients we have, the more money and silk we shall heap up. But now that this dratted Li Jia has been hanging around for more than a year, it's no use talking about new clients — even the old ones have stopped coming. We seem to have got hold of a Zhong Kui① who keeps out devils, because not a soul will come near us. There'll soon be no smoke in our chimney. What's to become of us?"

Decima, however, would not quietly submit to this. "Mr. Li did not come here empty-handed," she retorted. "Look at all the money he has spent here!"

"That was before; it's now I'm talking about. You tell him to give me a little money today for fuel and rice for the two of you. In other houses the girls are a money-tree which needs only to be shaken to shower down riches; it's just my bad luck that I've got a girl who keeps the money away. Every day I have to worry how to make ends meet, because you insist on

---

① 译者注: According to Chinese mythology, Zhong Kui was a chaser of ghosts.

supporting this pauper. Where do you think our food and clothes are coming from? Go and tell that beggar of yours that, if he's any good at all, he must give me some silver; then you can go off with him and I'll buy another girl. Wouldn't that suit us both?"

"Do you really mean it?" demanded Decima.

"Have I ever told a lie?" replied the old woman, who, knowing that Li had not a cent left and had pawned his clothes, thought it would be impossible for him to raise any money. "Of course I mean it."

"How much do you want from him?"

"If it were anyone else, I would ask for a thousand taels; but I'll ask a poor devil like him for only three hundred. With that I could buy another girl to take your place. But there's one condition: he must pay me within three days, then I shall hand you over straight away. If he hasn't paid after three days, I'll give him a good beating with my cane, the wretch, and drive him out, gentleman or no gentleman! Nobody will be able to blame me either."

"Although he is away from home and has run out of money," said Decima, "he should be able to raise three hundred taels. But three days is too little. Can't you make it ten?"

"The young fool has nothing but his bare hands," thought the procuress. "Even if I give him a hundred days, he won't be able to get the money. And when he fails to produce it, however thick-skinned he is he won't have the nerve to turn up again. Then I can get my establishment under proper control once more, and Decima will have nothing to say."

"Well, to humour you," she said, "I'll make it ten days. But if he doesn't have the money by then, don't blame me."

"If he can't find the money by then, I don't suppose he will have the face to come back," said Decima. "I am only afraid that if he does bring the three hundred taels, you may go back on your word."

"I am an old woman of fifty-one," protested the procuress. "I am worshipping Buddha and fasting ten days every month. How could I lie to you? If you don't trust me, I'll put my palm on yours to make a pledge. May

I become a dog or swine in my next life if I go back on my word!"

> *Who with a mere pint pot can gauge the sea?*
> *The bawd, for all her scheming, was a fool*
> *To think, because the scholar's purse was light,*
> *She could so easily frustrate their love.*

That night in bed Decima discussed her future with Li.

"It's not that I don't want to marry you," said the young man. "But it would cost at least a thousand taels to buy your freedom, and where can I get that now that all my money is spent?"

"I have already spoken to my mistress," replied Decima. "She wants only three hundred taels, but it must be paid within ten days. Although you have come to the end of your allowance, you must have relatives and friends in the capital from whom you can borrow. If you raise this sum, I shall be yours; and we shan't have to suffer the old woman's temper any more."

"My friends and relatives here have been cold-shouldering me because I have been spending too much time with you," said Li. "Tomorrow I'll tell them that I am packing up to leave and coming to say goodbye, then ask for money for my travelling expenses. I may be able to collect three hundred taels." So he got up, dressed and prepared to take his leave.

"Be as quick as you can!" urged Decima as he was going out. "I'll be waiting for good news." And Li promised to do his best.

On leaving the house, Li called on a number of relatives and friends, pretending that he had come to say goodbye. They were pleased to hear that he was going home, but when he mentioned that he was short of money for his journey they said nothing. As the proverb says: To speak of a loan is to put an end to friendship. They all, with good reason, considered Li as a young rake whose infatuation with a courtesan had kept him away from home for more than a year, and they knew that his father was furious with him.

"Who knows whether he is telling the truth?" they thought. "Suppose we lend him money for the journey and he spends it on girls again, when his father hears of it he will attribute the worst motives to us. Since we shall be blamed in any case, why not refuse altogether?"

"I am so sorry!" said each in turn. "I happen to be short at the moment, so I can't help you." Li received exactly the same answer from each of them, not one of his acquaintances proving generous enough to lend him even ten or twenty taels.

He called at house after house for three days without succeeding in borrowing a single cent; but he dared not tell Decima this and put her off with evasive answers. The fourth day, however, found him in such despair that he was ashamed to go back to her; but after living so long with Decima he had no other dwelling place and, having nowhere else to spend the night, he went to his fellow-provincial, Liu, and begged a bed of him. When Liu asked why he looked so worried, Li told him the whole story of how Decima wanted to marry him. Liu, however, shook his head.

"I don't believe it," he said. "Decima is the most famous courtesan in that quarter and her price must be at least ten pecks of pearls or a thousand taels of silver. Her mistress would never let her go for three hundred taels. The old woman must be annoyed because you have no money left but are monopolizing her girl without paying her; so she has thought of this trick to get rid of you. Since she has known you for a long time, she has to keep up appearances and can't drive you away outright; and, knowing that you are short of cash, she has asked for three hundred taels in order to appear generous, giving you ten days in which to raise that sum. They believe that if you can't get the money in time, you won't have the face to go back; while if you do, they will jeer at you and insult you so that you can't stay anyway. This is the kind of trick such people always play. Think it over for yourself and don't let them take you in. In my humble opinion, the sooner you sever relations with them the better."

When Li heard this he was filled with misgivings and remained silent for a long time.

"You mustn't make a wrong decision," went on Liu. "If you really want to go home and need money for the journey, your friends may be able to raise a few taels. But I doubt if you could get three hundred taels in ten months, let alone ten days, for people nowadays are simply not interested in their friends' troubles. Those women knew that you could never borrow such a sum: that's why they named this figure."

"I suppose you are right, my friend," said Li.

But, still unwilling to give up the girl, he continued to call on acquaintances to ask for a loan, no longer going back to Decima at night. He stayed with Liu for three days, until six of the ten days had passed, by which time Decima had become so anxious that she sent her little servant-boy out to look for him. The boy found Li on the main street.

"Mr. Li!" he called. "Our mistress is expecting you!"

Li, however, felt too ashamed to go back and said: "I am busy today. I will come tomorrow."

But the boy had his instructions from Decima and, taking hold of Li's coat, he would not let him go. "I was told to find you," he said. "You must come with me."

So Li, who was of course longing for his mistress, accompanied the boy to the courtesans' quarter. But when he saw Decima he was silent.

"What progress have you made?" asked Decima.

Li shed tears and said nothing.

"Are men's hearts so hard," she said, "that you cannot raise three hundred taels?"

With tears in his eyes, Li answered: "It is easier to catch a tiger in the mountain than to find a friend in need. I have been hurrying from house to house for six days, but I have not been able to borrow a cent; and it is because I was ashamed to come to you empty-handed that I have stayed away for the last few days. Today you sent for me, and I come feeling overwhelmed with shame. It is not that I haven't done my best, but people are heartless."

"Don't let the old woman hear you," said Decima. "Stay here tonight, and we'll talk it over." Then she prepared a meal and they enjoyed the food and wine together.

In the middle of the night Decima asked: "Couldn't you get any money at all? What will become of me then?"

But Li had no answer for her and could only shed tears.

Soon it was dawn and Decima said: "In my mattress I have hidden one hundred and fifty taels of silver which I have saved up, and I want you to take that. Now that I have given you half the sum, it should be easier for you to find the other half. But there are only four days left: don't lose any time." Then getting out of bed she gave the mattress to Li, who was overcome with joy.

Ordering the servant-boy to carry the mattress for him, Li went straight to Liu's lodging, where he told his friend all that had happened that night. And when they unpicked the mattress they found in the cotton padding many silver pieces which, when weighed, totalled one hundred and fifty taels. Liu was very much impressed.

"The girl must really be in love with you," he said. "Since she is so much in earnest, you mustn't let her down. I will do what I can for you."

"If you help me now," replied Li, "I shall never forget it."

Then Liu kept Li in his house, while he went round himself to all his acquaintances. In two days he borrowed one hundred and fifty taels which he gave to Li, saying: "I have done this not so much for your sake as because I am touched by the girl's devotion to you."

It was a happy Li, beaming with smiles, who came to Decima with the three hundred taels on the ninth day — one day earlier than the appointed time.

"The other day you could not borrow a cent," said Decima. "How is it that today you have got one hundred and fifty taels?" And when Li told her about his fellow-student Liu, she pressed her hands to her forehead in token of gratitude. "We must thank Mr. Liu for making our wish come true!" she cried.

They passed the night in great joy together, and the next morning Decima rose early and said to Li: "Once you have paid the money, I shall be able to leave with you. You had better decide how we are going to travel.

Yesterday I borrowed twenty taels from my friends which you can take for the journey."

Li had, in fact, been wondering where he was going to get the money for their journey, but had not liked to mention this difficulty. Now he was delighted to receive this twenty taels.

As they were talking, the mistress of the house knocked at the door.

"This is the tenth day, Decima!" she called.

When Li heard this, he opened the door to invite her in. "Thank you, aunty," he said. "I was just going to ask you over." And he placed the three hundred taels on the table.

The procuress had never thought that Li would produce the money. Her face fell and she was about to retract, when Decima said:

"I have worked here for eight years, and I must have earned several thousand taels for you in that time. This is the happy day on which I am to start a new life — you agreed to that yourself. The three hundred taels are here, not a cent less, and they have been paid on time. If you break your word, Mr. Li will take the money away and I shall immediately commit suicide. Then you will lose both the money and me, and you will be sorry."

The old woman had nothing to say to this. After long thought she finally had to fetch her balance to weigh the silver.

"Well, well," she said at last. "I suppose I can't keep you. But if you must go, go at once. And don't think you're going to take any clothes and trinkets with you." She pushed them out of the room, and called for a lock with which she padlocked the door.

It was already autumn. Decima, just risen from her bed and not yet dressed, was still wearing old clothes. She curtseyed to her mistress and Li bowed too. Then as husband and wife they left the old woman's house together.

> Like a carp escaping from a golden hook,
> They scurried off, not to return again.

"Wait while I call a sedan-chair for you," said Li to Decima. "We can go to Mr. Liu's lodging before deciding on anything." But Decima demurred.

"My friends have always been very good to me," she said, "and I ought to say goodbye to them. Besides, they were kind enough to lend us the money for our travelling expenses the other day; we ought to thank them for that." So she took Li to say goodbye to the other courtesans.

Two of these girls, Yuelang and Susu, lived nearby and were Decima's closest friends. She called first on Yuelang, who, surprised to see her dressed in old clothes and with no ornaments in her hair, asked what had happened. Decima told her and introduced Li to her. Then, pointing to Yuelang, Decima told Li:

"This is the friend who lent us the money the other day. You should thank her." And Li bowed again and again.

Presently Yuelang helped Decima to wash and comb her hair, sending at the same time for Susu. And after Decima had made her toilet, her two friends brought out all their emerald trinkets, gold bracelets, jade hairpins and ear-rings, as well as a brocade tunic and skirt, a phoenix girdle and a pair of embroidered slippers, until soon they had arrayed Decima in finery from head to foot. Then they feasted together, and Yuelang lent the lovers her bedroom for the night.

The following day they gave another big feast to which all the courtesans were invited; and not one of Decima's friends stayed away. After toasting the happy couple, they played wind and stringed instruments, and sang and danced, each doing her best to give the company pleasure. And this feast lasted till midnight, when Decima thanked each of her friends in turn.

"You were the chief among us," said the courtesans. "But now that you are leaving with your husband, we may never meet again. When you have decided on which day to set out, we shall come to see you off."

"When the date is settled, I shall let you all know," said Yuelang. "But Decima will be travelling a long way with her husband, and their resources are rather limited. We must be responsible for seeing that she doesn't have to go short on the way." The other courtesans agreed to this, then left, while Li and Decima spent the night again in Yuelang's room.

When dawn came Decima asked Li: "Where are we going from here? Have you any plan?"

"My father is already angry with me," replied Li, "and if he hears that I have married a singsong girl, not only will he make me suffer for it, but you will feel all the weight of his anger too. This has been worrying me for some time, but I have not yet thought of a way out."

"A father cannot help loving his son," said Decima, "so he won't be angry with you for ever. But perhaps, since going straight home would offend him, we had better go to some beauty spot like Suzhou or Hangzhou for the time being. You can then go home alone and ask some relatives or friends to persuade your father to forgive you. Once you have made your peace with him you can come to fetch me, and all will be well."

"That is a good idea," agreed Li.

The next morning they said goodbye to Yuelang and went to Liu's lodging to pack their baggage. When Decima saw Liu she kowtowed to him to thank him for his assistance, and promised to repay him in future.

Liu hastily bowed in return. "You must be a remarkable woman," he said, "to remain loyal to your lover even after he became poor. I merely blew upon the fire in the direction of the wind. Such a trifling service is not worth mentioning."

The three of them feasted all day, and the following morning chose an auspicious day for the journey and hired sedan-chairs and beasts. Decima also sent her boy with a letter to Yuelang to thank her and bid her farewell. When they were leaving, several sedan-chairs arrived bearing Yuelang, Susu and the other courtesans who had come to see them off.

"You are starting on a long journey with your husband and you are short of money," said Yuelang. "So we have prepared a little gift to express our love. Please accept it. If you run short on your journey, you may find it useful." She told a servant to bring over a gilt box of the type used for carrying stationery; but since this was securely locked, its contents could not be seen. Decima neither declined the gift nor opened it, but thanked them all. By now the chairs and beasts were ready, and the chair-bearers and grooms asked them to start. Liu offered the travellers three cups of wine in parting, and he and the courtesans saw them to Chongwen Gate where, wiping away tears, they all bid their friends farewell.

Uncertain whether they would meet again,
They bade farewell, with tears on either side.

In due course Li and Decima reached Luhe River where they were to take a junk. They were lucky enough to find an official despatch boat returning to Guazhou and, having settled the amount of their fare, they booked places on this junk. Once aboard, however, Li discovered that he had not a cent left. Although Decima had given him twenty taels, it was all gone! The fact was that Li had stayed in the courtesans' quarter until he had nothing but old clothes to wear; so as soon as he had money he naturally went to redeem a few of his gowns at the pawnshop and to have new bedding made. What was left of the silver was enough only for the sedan-chairs and beasts.

"Don't worry," said Decima, when she saw his anxiety. "The present that my friends gave us may prove useful." Thereupon she took a key and unlocked the box. Li, standing beside her, was too ashamed to look into the case as Decima took out a silk bag and placed it on the table.

"See what's in that," she said.

Li picked up the bag, which was quite heavy; and when he opened it he found it contained exactly fifty taels of silver. Decima meantime had locked the box again without saying what else it contained.

"How generous of the girls to give us this!" she exclaimed. "Now we have enough not only for the road but to help towards our expenses when we visit the beauty spots in Suzhou or Hangzhou."

Surprised and delighted, Li rejoined: "If not for your help, I should have died far from home without a burial place. I shall never forget how good you have been to me." After that, whenever they talked of the past Li would burst into tears of gratitude, but Decima would always comfort him tenderly.

After an uneventful journey of several days, they reached Guazhou Harbour where the junk moored. Li booked another passenger boat, had their luggage put aboard and arranged to set sail the next morning at dawn. It was midwinter and the full moon was as clear and bright as water.

"Since we left the capital," said Li to Decima as they sat together in the bow of the junk, "we have been shut up in the cabin with other passengers so that we couldn't talk freely. But today we have the whole boat to ourselves and can do as we please. Now that we are leaving North China and coming to the Yangtze River Valley, don't you think we should drink a little wine to celebrate and to cheer ourselves up?"

"Yes," said Decima. "I haven't had a chance to chat or laugh for a long time. I feel just as you do."

Li got out the wine utensils and placed them on the deck, then spread a rug on which they sat down together to drink to each other, until they were both under the spell of the wine.

"You had the loveliest voice in all your quarter," said Li, raising his cup to Decima. "The first time that I saw you and heard you sing so divinely, I lost my heart to you. But we have been upset for so long that I haven't heard your heavenly voice for many days. Now the bright moon is shining on the clear waves; it is midnight and there is no one about — won't you sing for me?"

Decima was in a happy mood, so, clearing her throat and tapping her fan on the deck to keep time, she sang. Her song was about a scholar who offered wine to a girl, and was taken from the opera *Moon Pavilion* by Shi Junmei of the Yuan Dynasty. It was set to the air known as "The Little Red Peach Blossom."

> *As her voice reached the sky, the clouds halted to listen;*
> *As her voice reached the waves, the fish frolicked for joy.*

Now on another junk nearby there was a young man called Sun Fu, who was a native of Xin'an in Huizhou. He had an estate worth millions of cash, for his family had dealt in salt in Yangzhou for generations; and now, at twenty years of age, he too had entered the Imperial College in Nanjing. This Sun was a dissolute young man who frequented the courtesans' quarters in search of amusement or to buy a smile from the singsong girls: indeed, he was one of the foremost in the pursuit of pleasure.

Sun's boat was moored at Guazhou Harbour too on this particular evening, and he was drinking alone to drown his boredom when he heard a woman singing so clearly and exquisitely that not even the song of a phoenix could compare with her voice. He stood up in the bow and listened for some time until he realized that the singing came from the next boat; but just as he was going to make inquiries, the song ended. The servant whom he sent to put discreet questions to the boatman found out that the adjacent junk had been hired by a certain Mr. Li, but was unable to learn anything about the singer.

"She must be a professional, not a respectable girl," thought Sun. "How can I contrive to see her?" Preoccupation with this problem kept him awake all night.

At the fifth watch a high wind sprang up, and by dawn the sky was filled with dark clouds. Soon a snowstorm was raging.

> *Trees on the hills are hidden by the clouds,*
> *All human tracks are blotted out below;*
> *And on the frozen river in the snow*
> *An old man fishes from his little boat.*

Since this snowstorm made it impossible to cross the river, all boats had to remain in the harbour. Sun ordered his boatman to steer closer to Li's junk; and then, having put on his sable cap and fox fur coat, he opened the window on the pretext that he was watching the snow. Thus he succeeded in catching sight of Decima, for when she had finished dressing she raised the curtain of the cabin window with one slender white hand in order to empty her basin into the river. Her more than earthly beauty made Sun's head swim, and he fastened his eyes to the spot where she had appeared, hoping to gain another glimpse of her; but he was disappointed. After some reflection, he leaned against his cabin window and chanted aloud the lines by Gao Xueshi on the plum blossom:

> *Like a hermit resting on some snow-clad hill;*
> *Like a lovely girl in some glade beneath the moon.*

When Li heard someone chanting poetry in the next boat, he leaned out to look just as Sun had hoped he would. For Sun's plan was to attract Li's attention by this means in order to draw him into conversation. Now, hastily raising his hands in greeting, Sun asked:

"What is your honourable name, sir?"

After Li introduced himself he naturally asked to know Sun's name. And, when Sun had introduced himself, they chatted about the Imperial College until very soon they were on friendly terms.

"It must be Heaven's will," said Sun, "that this snowstorm should have held up our boats in order that we should meet. I am in luck. Travelling by junk is thoroughly boring, and I would like to go ashore with you to a wineshop where I can profit by your conversation while we drink. I hope you won't refuse."

"Only meeting you by chance," replied Li, "how can I impose on you like this?"

"Oh, come," protested Sun. "Within the four seas all men are brothers."

Then he ordered his boatman to put down the gang-plank, and told his boy to hold an umbrella for Mr. Li as he came across. He bowed to Li at the bow and followed him politely ashore.

A few paces brought them to a wineshop. They went upstairs, chose a clean table by the window and sat down. When the waiter had brought wine and food, Sun asked Li to drink; and as they drank they enjoyed the sight of the snow. After they had exchanged the usual platitudes about scholarship, Sun gradually steered the conversation around to courtesans; and now that they had found a common interest — since both young men had much experience in this field — they began to talk frankly and to exchange confidences.

Presently Sun sent his servant away, and asked in a low voice: "Who was the girl who sang on your junk last night?"

Li, only too ready to boast of his conquest, announced truthfully: "That was Du Wei, the well-known courtesan of Beijing."

"If she is a courtesan, how did you manage to get hold of her?"

Then Li told him the whole story: how they had fallen in love, how Decima had wanted to marry him, and how he had borrowed money to redeem her.

"It must, no doubt, be very pleasant," said Sun, "to be taking home a beauty. But will your honourable family approve?"

"I have no anxiety on the score of my first wife," replied Li. "The only difficulty is that my father is rather strict, and I may have trouble with him."

This gave Sun the opening he had been waiting for.

"Since your respected father may disapprove, where do you intend to lodge your beauty?" he asked. "Have you discussed it with her?"

"Yes, we have discussed it," replied Li with a frown.

"And does she have a good plan?" demanded Sun eagerly.

"She wants to stay for a time in Suzhou or Hangzhou," answered Li. "And when we have visited the beauty spots there, I will return home first to ask friends or relatives to talk my father round; then, when he is no longer angry, I shall fetch her back. What do you think of this plan?"

Sun looked thoughtful for a while, pretending to be very much concerned.

"We have only just met," he said at length, "and you may take offence if a casual acquaintance advises you on such an intimate matter."

"I need your advice," protested Li. "Please don't hesitate to speak frankly."

"Well then," said Sun. "Since your father is a high provincial official, he must be very jealous of your family reputation. He has already expressed displeasure because you visited low haunts: do you think he will allow you to take a singsong girl as your wife? As for your relatives and friends, they will all take their cue from your respected father. It will be useless to ask their help; they are bound to refuse. And even if some of them are foolish enough to plead your cause to your father, once they realize that the old gentleman is against this marriage they will change their tune. So you will be causing discord in your family, and you will have no satisfactory answer to take to your mistress. Even if you enjoy the scenery in Suzhou and Hangzhou for a time, you cannot live like that indefinitely. Once your funds run low you will find yourself in a dilemma."

Only too conscious that all he possessed was fifty taels, the greater part of which was already spent, when Sun spoke of possible financial difficulties Li nodded and admitted that such, indeed, was the case.

"Now I sincerely want to give you some advice," went on Sun. "But you may not like to hear it."

"I am very much obliged to you," said Li. "Please speak frankly."

"I had better not," declared Sun. "Casual acquaintances shouldn't come between lovers."

"Never mind about that," protested Li.

"As the ancients said, women are fickle," argued Sun. "And singsong girls in particular are likely to prove untrue. Since your mistress is a well-known courtesan, she must have friends everywhere. There may be some former lover of hers in the south, and she may be making use of you for the journey here so that she can join another man."

"Oh, no, I don't think so," said Li.

"You may be right," replied Sun. "But those young southerners are notorious philanderers; and if you leave your mistress by herself, she may succumb to one of them. On the other hand, if you take her home you will make your father angrier than ever. In fact, there seems to be no way out for you.

"Now the relationship between father and son is sacred and inviolable.

If you offend your father and abandon your home for the sake of a courtesan, you will be universally condemned as a dissolute wastrel. Your wife will not consider you worthy to be her husband, your younger brother will cease to respect you as his elder, and your friends will have no more to do with you. You will find yourself a complete outcast. So I advise you to think this thing out carefully today."

This speech left Li at a complete loss. Hitching his seat nearer to Sun, he demanded earnestly. "What do you think I should do?"

"I have a scheme which would be very much to your advantage," replied Sun. "But I fear you may be too fond of your concubine to consider it, and I will have wasted my breath."

"If you have a good plan to restore me to the bosom of my family, I shall be tremendously grateful to you. Don't hesitate to speak."

"You have been away from home for more than a year, so that your father is angry and your wife displeased with you. If I were you, I would be unable to eat or sleep for remorse. But your worthy father is angry with you only because you have let yourself become infatuated with a courtesan and are spending money like water. You are showing yourself unfit to inherit his property, for if you go on in this way you are bound to bankrupt your family; so if you return home now empty-handed, the old gentleman will vent his anger on you. But if you are willing to part with your concubine and to make the best of a bad bargain, I don't mind offering you a thousand taels for her. With this sum, you can tell your father that you have been teaching in the capital instead of squandering money, and he will certainly believe you. Then peace will reign at home and you will have no more trouble; at a single stroke you will have turned calamity into good fortune. Please consider my offer carefully. It's not that I covet your courtesan's beauty. I just want to do what I can to help you out."

Li had always been a weak character who stood in great awe of his father; so Sun's argument convinced him completely and, rising from his seat, he bowed to express his thanks.

"Your excellent advice has opened my eyes," he said. "But since my concubine has come all these hundreds of miles with me, I can't sever relations with her too abruptly. I'll talk it over with her, and let you know as soon as I gain her consent."

"Break it to her gently," said Sun. "Since she is so fond of you, she can't want to estrange you from your father. I am sure she will help to restore you to your family." They went on drinking till dusk, when the wind dropped and the snow ceased. Then Sun told his servant to pay the bill, and walked hand in hand with Li back to the boat.

> *You should tell a stranger only one third of the truth;*
> *To bare your heart to him is far from wise.*

Now Decima had prepared wine and sweetmeats on the junk for Li, but he did not come back all day. At dusk she lighted the lamp to wait for him, and when he came aboard she rose to welcome him; but she noticed that he seemed flustered and upset. As she poured a cup of warm wine for him, he shook his head in refusal and went without a word to his bed. Decima was disturbed. Having put away the cups and plates and helped Li to undress, she asked:

"What has happened today to make you so sad?"

Li's only answer was a sigh. She repeated her question three or four times until he was asleep, and by then she was so uneasy that she sat on the edge of the bed unable to close her eyes. In the middle of the night the young man woke up and heaved another great sigh.

"What is preying so heavily on your mind?" asked Decima.

"Why can't you tell me?"

Li sat up, drawing the quilt around him, and tried several times to speak; but he broke off short each time and tears poured down his cheeks.

Then taking Li in her arms Decima comforted him with kind words, saying: "We have been lovers for nearly two years and won through a thousand hardships and difficulties; and you have not looked depressed once during all this long journey. Why are you so upset now when we are about to cross the Yangtze and settle down to live happily ever after? There must be a reason. As husband and wife we shall live and die together, so we should discuss our troubles together too. Please don't keep it from me."

After she had begged him several times to speak, with tears in his eyes Li said: "When I was stranded far from home you were good to me and attached yourself to me in spite of every hardship, so that I am inexpressibly grateful to you. But I have been thinking things over. My father is a high provincial official who is a stickler for convention and a very stern man. If I anger him so that he drives us out of the family, we shall be forced to wander homeless, and what will become of us then? That would mean a complete break with my father, and we could not be sure of a happy married life either. Today my friend Sun from Xin'an discussed this with me while we were drinking; and now I feel quite broken-hearted."

"What do you mean to do?" asked Decima, greatly alarmed.

"A man in trouble cannot see his way clearly," said Li. "But Mr. Sun has thought out an excellent plan for me. I am only afraid you may not agree to it."

"Who is this Mr. Sun? If his plan is good, why shouldn't I agree to it?"

"His name is Sun Fu. He is a salt merchant from Xin'an and a gallant young scholar. He heard you singing last night, so he asked about you; and when I told him our story and mentioned that we would not be able to go home, he offered a thousand taels for your hand. If I had a thousand taels, it would be easy for me to face my parents; and you would have a home too. But I can't bear to part with you. That's why I am sad." When he had said this, his tears fell like rain.

Taking her arms from his shoulders, Decima gave a strange laugh.

"He must be a fine gentleman to have thought out this plan," she said. "You will recover your thousand taels, and I shall no longer be an encumbrance to you if I can go to another man. What could be more reasonable and high-principled? This plan suits us both. Where is the silver?"

"Since I hadn't got your consent, my love," said Li, who had stopped crying, "the money is still with him. It hasn't yet changed hands."

"Mind you clinch with him first thing tomorrow," urged Decima. "You mustn't miss this opportunity. But a thousand tacls is a lot of money; be sure it is properly weighed and handed over before I cross to the other boat. Don't let that salt merchant cheat you."

It was now the fourth watch, and since dawn was approaching Decima got up and lighted the lamp to dress herself.

"Today I am dressing to usher out an old client and welcome in a new," she said. "This is an important occasion."

She applied her rouge, powder and scented oil with great care, then arrayed herself in her most splendid jewels and most magnificent embroidered gown. Her perfume scented the air and she was a dazzling sight.

By the time she had finished dressing it was already dawn and Sun had sent a servant to their junk for a reply. When Decima stole a glance at Li and saw that he looked pleased, she urged him to give a reply at once and possess himself of the silver as soon as possible. Then Li went to Sun's boat to announce that Decima was willing.

"There is no difficulty about the money," said Sun. "But I must have the lady's jewel case as a pledge."

When Li told Decima this, she pointed to her gilt box.

"Let them take that," she said.

Then Sun, in great exultation, promptly sent the thousand taels of silver to Li's boat. When Decima had looked through the packages and satisfied herself that the silver was of the finest and the amount was correct, she put one hand on the side of the boat and beckoned to Sun with the other, so that he was transported with joy.

"May I have that box back for a minute?" she asked, parting her red lips to reveal pearly teeth. "It contains Mr. Li's travel permit which I must return to him."

Satisfied that Decima could not escape him now, Sun ordered his servant to carry back her gilt box and set it down on the deck. Decima took her key and unlocked it, disclosing a series of drawers inside; and when she told Li to pull out the first drawer, he found it filled with trinkets, pearls, jade and precious stones, to the value of several hundred taels of silver. These jewels, to the consternation of Li, Sun and the others on the two boats, Decima suddenly tossed into the river.

Then she told Li to pull out a second drawer containing jade flutes and golden pipes, and a third drawer filled with curious old jade and gold ornaments worth several thousand taels. All these, too, Decima threw into the water.

By this time the bank was thronged with spectators. "What a pity!" they exclaimed.

As they were marvelling at her behaviour, she drew out the last drawer in which there was a casket. She opened the casket and they saw that it was packed with handfuls of bright pearls and other precious stones such as emeralds and cat's-eyes, the like of which they had never seen before and the value of which they could not even guess at. The onlookers cried out loudly in admiration. When Decima made as if to toss all these jewels into the river too, a remorseful Li threw his arms around her and wept bitterly, while Sun came over to plead with her also. But Decima pushed Li away and turned angrily on Sun.

"Mr. Li and I suffered many hardships to come here!" she cried. "But you, to gratify your lust, lied cunningly to him in order to break up our marriage and destroy our love. I hate you! After my death, if I become a ghost, I shall accuse you before the gods. How dare you think of enjoying me yourself!"

Then Decima turned to Li.

"I led the unhappy life of a courtesan for many years," she said, "and during that time I saved up enough to support myself in my old age. But after I met you, we swore to love each other all our lives. When we left the capital I pretended that this box was a present from my friends, whereas actually it contained jewels worth over ten thousand taels of silver with which I intended to fit you out splendidly, so that when you returned to your parents they might feel well disposed towards me and accept me as one of the family. Then I could have remained happily with you ever after. But you did not trust me and were easily swayed by lics; and now you have abandoned me midway, caring nothing for my true love. I have opened this box in front of all these people to show you that a paltry thousand taels is nothing to me. I had jewels in my casket, but you, alas, had no eyes. Fate must be against me. I escaped from the bitter lot of a courtesan only to be cast aside by you. All of you here today can be my witnesses! I have not been unfaithful to him, but he has proved untrue to me!"

Then all who were present were moved to tears. They cursed and spat at Li, accusing him of ingratitude and disloyalty; while shame, unhappiness and remorse made the young man weep bitterly. He was turning to beg Decima's forgiveness when, clasping the casket in her arms, she leapt into the river. They shouted for help, but there was a thick mist over the river and the current was strong, so she could not be found. How sad that such a beautiful and famous courtesan should fall a victim to the hungry waves!

> *The watery deep engulfed that lovely form;*
> *The river bore her from the world of men.*

Gnashing their teeth in rage, the onlookers wanted to fall upon Li and Sun; and the two young men were so alarmed that they shouted to the boatmen to cast off, escaping in opposite directions. As he stared at the thousand taels of silver, Li longed for Decima; and he sat brooding all day in shame and sorrow until he lost his reason. He remained insane all his life.

As for Sun, he fell ill with fright and kept to his bed for over a month. But he was haunted day and night by Decima's ghost, who cursed him until he died a lingering death; and all men said this was a just retribution for the crime he committed on the river.

When Liu Yuchun completed his studies in the capital and packed up to return home, his boat also moored at Guazhou; and while he was washing his face by the side of the junk, his brass basin fell into the river. He asked a fisherman to cast his net for it, but the man drew up a small casket; and when Liu opened this he found it full of priceless jewels, pearls and other treasures. Liu rewarded the fisherman well and put the casket at the head of his bed. That night he dreamed that he saw a girl coming over the waves of the river, whom he recognized as Decima. She came up to him and curtseyed, then told him how faithless Li had proved.

"You were kind enough to help me with one hundred and fifty taels," she said. "I meant to repay you after we reached our destination, and although I was unable to do so I have never forgotten your great kindness. So this morning I sent you this casket through the fisherman to express my thanks. We shall never meet again." Suddenly awaking, Liu realized that Decima was dead, and he sighed for her for several days.

Later generations, commenting on this, condemned Sun for his wickedness in plotting to obtain a beautiful girl for a thousand taels of silver. Li they considered beneath contempt because, like a fool, he failed to understand Decima's worth. As for Decima, she was a pearl among women; the pity was that instead of finding a husband worthy of her, she wasted her affection on Li. This was like casting bright pearls or rare jade before a blind man, and resulted in her great love changing to hate and all her tenderness vanishing with the flowing stream.

> *Those who have never loved had best be silent;*
> *It is no easy thing to know love's worth;*
> *And none but he who treasures constancy*
> *Deserves the name of lover on this earth.*

三

文心雕龙(五篇)[①]

神 思

古人云:"形在江海之上,心存魏阙之下。"神思之谓也。文之思也,其神远矣。故寂然凝虑,思接千载;悄焉动容,视通万里;吟咏之间,吐纳珠玉之声;眉睫之前,卷舒风云之色;其思理之致乎! 故思理为妙,神与物游。神居胸臆,而志气统其关键;物沿耳目,而辞令管其枢机。枢机方通,则物无隐貌;关键将塞,则神有遁心。

是以陶钧文思,贵在虚静,疏瀹五藏,澡雪精神。积学以储宝,酌理以富才,研阅以穷照,驯致以怿辞,然后使元解之宰,寻声律而定墨;独照之匠,窥意象而运斤:此盖驭文之首术,谋篇之大端。

夫神思方运,万涂竞萌,规矩虚位,刻镂无形。登山则情满于山,观海则意溢于海,我才之多少,将与风云而并驱矣。方其搦翰,气倍辞前,暨乎篇成,半折心始。何则? 意翻空而易奇,言征实而难巧也。是以意授于思,言授于意,密则无际,疏则千里。或理在方寸而求之域表,或义在咫尺而思隔山河。是以秉心养术,无务苦虑;含章司契,不必劳情也。

---

① 中文选自:刘勰. 文心雕龙. 龙必锟,译注. 贵阳:贵州人民出版社,1992.
英译文选自:Yang Hsien-yi & Gladys Yang. Carving a Dragon at the Core of Literature. *Chinese Literature*,1962(8):58-71.

人之禀才,迟速异分,文之制体,大小殊功。相如含笔而腐毫,扬雄辍翰而惊梦,桓谭疾感于苦思,王充气竭于思虑,张衡研《京》以十年,左思练《都》以一纪。虽有巨文,亦思之缓也。淮南崇朝而赋《骚》,枚皋应诏而成赋,子建援牍如口诵,仲宣举笔似宿构,阮瑀据案而制书,祢衡当食而草奏,虽有短篇,亦思之速也。

若夫骏发之士,心总要术,敏在虑前,应机立断;覃思之人,情饶歧路,鉴在疑后,研虑方定。机敏故造次而成功,虑疑故愈久而致绩。难易虽殊,并资博练。若学浅而空迟,才疏而徒速,以斯成器,未之前闻。是以临篇缀虑,必有二患:理郁者苦贫,辞弱者伤乱,然则博见为馈贫之粮,贯一为拯乱之药,博而能一,亦有助乎心力矣。

若情数诡杂,体变迁贸,拙辞或孕于巧义,庸事或萌于新意;视布于麻,虽云未费,杼轴献功,焕然乃珍。至于思表纤旨,文外曲致,言所不追,笔固知止。至精而后阐其妙,至变而后通其数,伊挚不能言鼎,轮扁不能语斤,其微矣乎!

赞曰:神用象通,情变所孕。物心貌求,心以理应。

刻镂声律,萌芽比兴。结虑司契,垂帷制胜。

风　骨

《诗》总"六义","风"冠其首,斯乃化感之本源,志气之符契也。是以怊怅述情,必始乎风;沈吟铺辞,莫先于骨。故辞之待骨,如体之树骸;情之含风,犹形之包气。结言端直,则文骨成焉;意气骏爽,则文风清焉。若丰藻克赡,风骨不飞,则振采失鲜,负声无力。是以缀虑裁篇,务盈守气,刚健既实,辉光乃新。其为文用,譬征鸟之使翼也。

故练于骨者,析辞必精;深乎风者,述情必显。捶字坚而难移,结响凝而不滞,此风骨之力也。若瘠义肥辞,繁杂失统,则无骨之征也。思不环周,索莫乏气,则无风之验也。昔潘勖《锡魏》,思摹经典,群才韬笔,乃其骨髓峻也;相如赋仙,气号凌云,蔚为辞宗,乃其风力遒也。能鉴斯要,可以定文,兹术或违,无务繁采。

故魏文称:"文以气为主,气之清浊有体,不可力强而致。"故其论孔融,则云"体气高妙",论徐幹,则云"时有齐气",论刘桢,则云"有逸气"。公干亦云:"孔氏卓卓,信含异气;笔墨之性,殆不可胜。"并重气之旨也。夫翟翟备色,而翾翥百步,肌丰而力沉也;鹰隼乏采,而翰飞戾天,骨劲而气猛也。文章才力,有似于此。若风骨乏采,则鸷集翰林;采乏风骨,则雉窜文囿;唯藻耀而高翔,固文笔之鸣凤也。

若夫熔铸经典之范,翔集子史之术,洞晓情变,曲昭文体,然后能孚甲新意,雕昼奇辞。昭体,故意新而不乱,晓变,故辞奇而不黩。若骨采未圆,风辞未练,而跨略旧规,驰骛新作,虽获巧意,危败亦多,岂空结奇字,纰缪而成经矣?《周书》云:"辞尚体要,弗惟好异。"盖防文滥也。然文术多门,各适所好,明者弗授,学者弗师。于是习华随侈,流遁忘反。若能确乎正式,使文明以健,则风清骨峻,篇体光华。能研诸虑,何远之有哉!

赞曰:情与气偕,辞共体并。文明以健,珪璋乃聘。

蔚彼风力,严此骨鲠。才锋峻立,符采克炳。

情　采

圣贤书辞,总称"文章",非采而何?夫水性虚而沦漪结,木体实而花萼振,文附质也。虎豹无文,则鞟同犬羊;犀兕有皮,而色资丹漆,质待文也。若乃综述性灵,敷写器象,镂心鸟迹之中,织辞鱼网之上,其为彪炳,缛采名矣。故立"文"之道,其理有三:一曰形文,五色是也;二曰声文,五音是也;三曰情文,五性是也。五色杂而成黼黻,五音比而成韶夏,五性发而为辞章,神理之数也。

《孝经》垂典,丧言不文;故知君子常言,未尝质也。《老子》疾伪,故称"美言不信",而五千精妙,则非弃美矣。庄周云,"辩雕万物",谓藻饰也。韩非云,"艳采辩说",谓绮丽也。绮丽以艳说,藻饰以辩雕,文辞之变,于斯极矣。研味《孝》、《老》,则知文质附乎性情;详览《庄》、《韩》,则见华实过乎淫侈。若择源于泾渭之流,按辔于邪正之路,亦可以驭文采矣。夫铅黛所以饰容,而盼倩生于淑姿;文采所以饰言,而辩丽本于情性。故情者文之经,辞者理之纬;经正而后纬成,理定而后辞畅:此立文之本源也。

昔诗人什篇,为情而造文;辞人赋颂,为文而造情。何以明其然?盖《风》《雅》之兴,志思蓄愤,而吟咏情性,以讽其上,此为情而造文也;诸子之徒,心非郁陶,苟驰夸饰,鬻声钓世,此为文而造情也。故为情者要约而写真,为文者淫丽而烦滥。而后之作者,采滥忽真,远弃《风》《雅》,近师辞赋,故体情之制日疏,逐文之篇愈盛。故有志深轩冕,而泛咏皋壤。心缠几务,而虚述人外。真宰弗存,翩其反矣。

夫桃李不言而成蹊,有实存也;男子树兰而不芳,无其情也。夫以草木之微,依情待实;况乎文章,述志为本,言与志反,文岂足征?

是以联辞结采,将欲明理,采滥辞诡,则心理愈翳。固知翠纶桂饵,反所以失鱼。"言隐荣华",殆谓此也。是以"衣锦褧衣",恶文太章;《贲》象穷白,贵乎反本。夫能设模以位理,拟地以置心,心定而后结音,理正而后摛藻,使文不灭质,博不溺心,正采耀乎朱蓝,间色屏于红紫,乃可谓雕琢其章,彬彬君子矣。

赞曰:言以文远,诚哉斯验。心术既形,英华乃赡。

吴锦好渝,舜英徒艳。繁采寡情,味之必厌。

夸 饰

夫形而上者谓之道,形而下者谓之器。神道难摹,精言不能追其极;形器易写,壮辞可得喻其真;才非短长,理自难易耳。故自天地以降,豫入声貌,文辞所被,夸饰恒存。虽《诗》《书》雅言,风俗训世,事必宜广,文亦过焉。是以言峻则嵩高极天,论狭则河不容舠,说多则"子孙千亿",称少则"民靡孑遗";襄陵举滔天之目,倒戈立漂杵之论;辞虽已甚,其义无害也。且夫鸮音之丑,岂有泮林而变好?荼味之苦,宁以周原而成饴?并意深褒赞,故义成矫饰。大圣所录,以垂宪章,孟轲所云,"说诗者不以文害辞，不以辞害意"也。

自宋玉、景差，夸饰始盛；相如凭风，诡滥愈甚。故《上林》之馆，奔星与宛虹入轩；从禽之盛，飞廉与鹬明俱获。及扬雄《甘泉》，酌其余波。语瑰奇则假珍于玉树；言峻极则颠坠于鬼神。至《东都》之比目，《西京》之海若，验理则理无不验，穷饰则饰犹未穷矣。又子云《羽猎》，鞭宓妃以饷屈原；张衡《羽猎》，困玄冥于朔野，娈彼洛神，既非魑魅，惟此水师，亦非魈魅；而虚用滥形，不其疏乎？此欲夸其威而饰其事，义暌剌也。

至如气貌山海，体势宫殿，嵯峨揭业，熠耀焜煌之状，光采炜炜而欲然，声貌岌岌其将动矣。莫不因夸以成状，沿饰而得奇也。于是后进之才，奖气挟声，轩翥而欲奋飞，腾掷而羞蹑步，辞人炜烨，春藻不能程其艳；言在萎绝，寒谷未足成其凋；谈欢则字与笑并，论戚则声共泣偕；信可以发蕴而飞滞，披瞽而骇聋矣。

然饰穷其要，则心声锋起；夸过其理，则名实两乖。若能酌《诗》、《书》之旷旨，翦扬、马之甚泰，使夸而有节，饰而不诬，亦可谓之懿也。

赞曰：夸饰在用，文岂循检。言必鹏运，气靡鸿渐。

倒海探珠，倾昆取琰。旷而不溢，奢而无玷。

知　音

知音其难哉！音实难知，知实难逢，逢其知音，千载其一乎！夫古来知音，多贱同而思古。所谓"日进前而不御，遥闻声而相思"也。昔《储说》始出，《子虚》初成，秦皇、汉武，恨不同时；既同时矣，则韩囚而马轻，岂不明鉴同时之贱哉！至于班固、傅毅，文在伯仲，而固嗤毅云："下笔不能自休。"及陈思论才，亦深排孔璋，敬礼请润色，叹以为美谈；季绪好诋诃，方之于田巴，意亦见矣。故魏文称"文人相轻"，非虚谈也。至如君卿唇舌，而谬欲论文，乃称"史迁著书，谘东方朔"，于是桓谭之徒，相顾嗤笑。彼实博徒，轻言负诮，况乎文士，可妄谈哉！故鉴照洞明，而贵古贱今者，二主是也；才实鸿懿，而崇己抑人者，班、曹是也；学不逮文，而信伪迷真者，楼护是也;酱瓿之议,岂多叹哉!

夫麟凤与麏雉悬绝,珠玉与砾石超殊,白日垂其照,青眸写其形。然鲁臣以麟为麏,楚人以雉为凤,魏民以夜光为怪石,宋客以燕砾为宝珠。形器易征,谬乃若是;文情难鉴,谁曰易分?夫篇章杂沓,质文交加,知多偏好,人莫圆该。慷慨者逆声而击节,酝藉者见密而高蹈;浮慧者观绮而跃心,爱奇者闻诡而惊听。会己则嗟讽,异我则沮弃,各执一隅之解,欲拟万端之变,所谓"东向而望,不见西墙"也。凡操千曲而后晓声,观千剑而后识器。故圆照之象,务先博观。阅乔岳以形培塿,酌沧波以喻畎浍。无私于轻重,不偏于憎爱,然后能平理若衡,照辞如镜矣。

是以将阅文情,先标六观:一观位体,二观置辞,三观通变,四观奇正,五观事义,六观宫商。斯术既行,则优劣见矣。夫缀文者情动而辞发,观文者披文以入情,沿波讨源,虽幽必显。世远莫见其面,觇文辄见其心。岂成篇之足深?患识照之自浅耳。夫志在山水,琴表其情,况形之笔端,理将焉匿。故心之照理,譬目之照形,目瞭则形无不分,心敏则理无不达。然而俗监之迷者,深废浅售,此庄周所以笑《折扬》,宋玉所以伤《白雪》也。昔屈平有言:"文质疏内,众不知余之异采。"见异唯知音耳。扬雄自称:"心好沉博绝丽之文。"其事浮浅,亦可知矣。夫唯深识鉴奥,必欢然内怿,譬春台之熙众人,乐饵之止过客,盖闻兰为国香,服媚弥芬;书亦国华,玩泽方美;知音君子,其垂意焉。

赞曰:洪钟万钧,夔、旷所定。良书盈箧,妙鉴乃订。

流郑淫人,无或失听。独有此律,不谬蹊径。

Carving a Dragon at the Core of Literature (Five Chapters)

On Fancy

The ancients said, "The body may be on the river or out at sea, while the heart lingers by the palace gate." This is what is meant by fancy. As for fancy in literature that goes much further. Thoughts shaped in silence can reach a thousand generations to come, while the eyes of the mind may see ten thousand *li* away. The writer with so subtle a fancy lets fall sounds like pearls or tinkling jade, while scenes unfold before his eyes like clouds shifting in the wind. The miracle of fancy lies in the human spirit's traffic with all creation. The spirit dwells in a man's breast and his will controls the lock; things come to his ears and meet his eyes, and language supplies the key. When this key serves, then nothing should remain hidden; when the lock is blocked, the spirit may disappear. So what is most needful in casting ideas into writing is the possession of a tranquil mind. A man should cleanse his heart, purify his spirit, amass knowledge to store up learning, use reason to increase his capabilities, study things carefully to improve his powers of observation, and train himself in the use of the right phrase. Then the mind, pre-eminent, can seek out rhythm to guide the pen and like a skilled craftsman give fitting form to ideas. So fancy is the prime requirement in writing, the root of any conception.

When we give rein to our fancy, innumerable paths open up ahead; we plot any course we please, inlay any invisible pattern. Would we climb a mountain? Our spirit soars above it. Survey the ocean? Our idea reach over the sea. Whatever talents we have seem to race with the wind and the clouds; we take up a pen, inspired beyond all telling, but the work when written may express only half of what was in our hearts. This is because an idea not yet formulated may easily seem striking but is hard to set down skilfully in so many words. Thoughts pass into ideas, ideas into language, sometimes corresponding so closely that no discrepancy exists, sometimes so loosely that a thousand *li* stretch between. An argument may be at hand while you seek it at the horizon; an idea may be hard by yet hid from your mind as if by mountains and rivers. So to improve his writing a man should train his mind and not count simply on cudgelling his brains. Once he knows the right way to express himself, no undue exertions are needed.

Men have different gifts: some are quick, others slow. In writing, some tasks are great and others small. Thus Ssuma Hsiang-ju① gnawed through his brush, Yang Hsiung dreamed a fearful dream after writing an essay, Huan Tan took such anxious thought that he fell ill, Wang Tsung exhausted his strength through deep meditation, Chang Heng spent ten years polishing his essay about the two capitals, and Tso Ssu worked for a dozen years on his essay on the three imperial cities. True, some of these were major works, but the writers were also slow thinkers. On the other hand, the Prince of Huainan finished his lament in one morning, Mei Kao

---

① 译者注: Ssuma Hsiang-ju (179 – 117 B. C.), famous Han dynasty writer; Yang Hsiung (53 B.C.–A. D. 18), famous Han dynasty writer and scholar who compiled the *Local Dialects*, an important lexicon in ancient China; Huan Tan (24 B.C.–A. D. 56), Han dynasty writer; Wang Tsung (A. D. 27–91), famous Han dynasty philosopher whose *Criterion of Argument* is an important philosophical work; Chang Heng (A. D. 78–139), famous Han dynasty writer; Tso Ssu, famous poet of the third century A. D.; Prince of Huainan (179–122 B. C.), well-known Han dynasty writer; and Mei Kao, Han dynasty writer.

composed essays on the spur of the moment at the imperial command, Tsao Chih① wrote as fast as if speaking, Wang Tsan② wielded his pen as if copying, Yuan Yu could dash off a letter in the saddle, Mi Heng③ could draft a report during a meal. These were shorter works, but these men were fast thinkers too. Men with quick minds readily grasp essentials and jump to rapid conclusions without much preliminary consideration, whereas men with slower minds tend to weigh all possibilities and reach a decision only after much deliberation, after first overcoming their doubts. A quick-witted man may accomplish a task in a flash, while the slower-witted takes time to achieve results. But though one way seems easy and the other hard, each depends on wide knowledge and intensive study. I have yet to hear of anything good achieved by a poor scholar working slowly, or by a dolt working fast. We face two difficulties, then, in marshalling our thoughts for writing: closed minds may result in poverty of speech, ideas that flow too freely may result in confusion. So wide knowledge is the best fare for those who lack substance, and a unifying thread of thought the best remedy for those whose ideas are confused. It follows that the combination of wide knowledge with one unifying thread of thought will aid the writer in all he undertakes.

Again, feeling may be complex and forms of expression varied. A crude expression may bring out a subtle meaning, a commonplace incident may contain the germ of new ideas. Though hemp is no different from ordinary cotton, worked up by shuttle and loom it turns into some rich and

---

① 译者注：(A. D. 192-232) son of the famous statesman Tsao Tsao, an outstanding poet at the end of the Han dynasty and a leader among contemporary poets.

② 译者注：(A. D. 177-217) famous poet at the end of the Han dynasty. He and Kung Jung (153-208), Hsu Kan (170-217), Liu Chen (?-217), Chen Lin, Yuan Yu (?-212) and Yin Yang were protégés of Tsao Tsao and his sons, and formed the most influential school of poetry at that time. They were known as the "seven writers of the Chien-an period."

③ 译者注：(A. D. 173-198) writer at the end of the Han dynasty, who was killed because he offended Tsao Tsao.

rare material. But when it comes to the finest shades of meaning or intricacies beyond the power of language to express, the writer simply has to lay down his pen. A man must grasp the essence to be able to express all its subtlety, he must grasp all the changes to understand their laws. Yet Yi Yin① could not explain his use of the cauldron nor Lun Pien② his use of the axe, for the skill of each defied description.

Epitome:

> In images is fancy dressed
> To make its changes manifest;
> When objects strike upon our view
> The mind accords due sense thereto;
> Rhythm is born and melody,
> With all the laws of prosody;
> Well-marshalled thoughts, a well-stocked mind,
> And victory is close behind!

On Sentiment and Structure

The *Book of Songs*③ has six attributes, foremost of which is sentiment. This is the source of the power to move and change men, the manifestation of human aspirations. All expression of emotion and longing must start from sentiment, while the selection of apt words and phrases must start from the structure. Language requires structure just as a body requires a skeleton; emotion must embody sentiment just as the spirit is contained in the form. Words set out in stately fashion make up structure; a vigorous spirit makes for sentiment in writing. A plethora of fine phrases without nobility of sentiment and structure is like colour drained of its brightness or a voice

---

① 译者注: Yi Yin was the adviser of King Tang who founded the Shang dynasty (1562?-1066? B.C.); Yi Yin was also supposed to be a good cook.
② 译者注: According to legend, this man was a skilful carpenter.
③ 译者注: China's earliest anthology of poetry. See *Chinese Literature* No. 3, 1962.

devoid of strength. When arranging ideas for writing we must store up ample spirit and to spare, for strength and vigour within will bring forth fresh splendour. Literature depends on spirit just as swift birds depend on their wings to fly.

One who labours over the structure will gain a fine command of language; one with deep sentiment will express emotion vividly. When language is so closely knit that no change can be made and the rhythm is controlled yet not sluggish, this is due to sentiment and structure. Poverty of thought couched in rich language, a profusion of words without a central idea, indicates the absence of structure just as a weak flow of ideas and spiritless writing indicate the absence of sentiment. When Pan Hsu[1] drafted the imperial edict appointing Tsao Tsao[2] the Duke of Wei, he took the style of old documents as his model and so noble was his structure that all other men of talent laid down their pens. When Ssuma Hsiang-ju wrote about immortals, his spirit soared to the clouds and so exalted was his sentiment that he became the father of descriptive poetry. Once we have grasped these essentials we can regulate our writing with them, while if we depart from them no amount of embellishments will serve any purpose.

Thus Emperor Wen of Wei[3] said, "In writing, the spirit is paramount. There are nobler and baser spirits in literature. Neither is the result of effort, however hard." Of Kung Jung he said, "His spirit is noble and fine." Of Hsu Kan, "Sometimes he is slow like the men of Chi." Of Liu Chen, "He has vigour." Liu Chen also said, "Kung Jung is certainly outstanding with his truly remarkable spirit and inimitable style." All these comments show the stress laid on the spirit of a writing. The pheasant, for all its variegated plumage, is too plump and heavy to fly more than a hundred paces; while drab though the eagle's colours, thanks to its strong bones and fiery spirit, it soars up to the sky. The same is true of talent in

---

①　译者注：A writer at the end of the Han dynasty.

②　译者注：(A.D. 155-220) celebrated statesman and poet in Chinese history.

③　译者注：Tsao Pei, poet, eldest son of Tsao Tsao.

literature. Sentiment and structure without colour are like vultures gathering in the world of learning, while colour without sentiment and structure is like pheasants scurrying into the field of letters. Only the clear-voiced phoenix has both splendid plumage and the power to soar high in the realm of writing.

By casting writing in classical moulds, studying the methods of philosophers and historians, delving into changes in style, and understanding the forms of literature we can give birth to new ideas and fashion striking images. Once the various forms of literature are clear, the ideas will be fresh but not confused. Once changes in styles are understood, the language will be striking but not bizarre. If before a man succeeds in combining structure and embellishments or perfecting his language to convey sentiment, he tries to bypass the old rules and hasten on to new forms, he may hit upon ingenious ideas but the likelihood of failure will be even greater. As for stringing startling phrases together, this may in time become a pernicious habit. The *Chou Documents*① says: "In language aptness ranks above novelty." This was a warning against the misuse of language. There are many ways of writing, however, and every writer has his own preference. When those who understand may not teach and those learning may not find the right masters, writers tend to seek glitter and show, flouting the rules and forgetting the right path. If men would firmly adopt the proper models to make their writing clear and vigorous, then it would possess noble sentiment, firm structure and a splendid form. When these points are grasped, the goal is not far to seek.

Epitome:

　　Spirit and feeling side by side,

　　Language and form must be allied;

　　Let lucid strength your lines pervade

　　To shine like pendents of bright jade;

---

① 译者注: Ancient historical records of the Chou dynasty, part of the *Book of Documents* which according to tradition was compiled by Confucius.

Fine sentiment should be combined
With structure vigorous and refined;
Then wit as keen as sharpest blade
Will shine with splendour of brocade.

On Feeling and Art

The works of sages and worthies are generally known as fine writing, and what is this if not "art"? Just as ripples form in water which is fluid and flowers grow from wood which is solid, so art depends on substance. Just as tigers and leopards have markings to distinguish them from dogs and sheep, while rhinoceros-hide armour is varnished red, so substance has to be adorned by art. When it comes to setting forth human nature, delineating objects, committing ideas to writing and spinning language on paper, art is needed for splendour. So there are three elements in writing: one is form, or the Five Colours; another is sound, or the Five Notes of music; the third is feeling or the Five Emotions. The Five Colours blend to make rich designs, the Five Notes combine to make enchanting music, the Five Emotions set forth in writing move men's hearts. This is the order of nature.

Since the *Book of Filial Piety*① enjoins men not to use ornate language while mourning, it appears that the customary speech of a gentleman was not plain and unadorned. Lao Tzu,② who abhorred hypocrisy, said that fair speech could not be trusted; yet even he did not repudiate beauty, for his book in five thousand words is superbly written. Chuang Tzu,③ speaking of meticulous definitions, had in mind the artifice of rhetoric. And Han Fei,④ urging the use of conceits in argument, was referring to literary

---

① 译者注：One of the Confucian canons.
② 译者注：Outstanding ancient philosopher and founder of the Taoist school, who wrote *The Way and Its Power*.
③ 译者注：(369-? B.C.) outstanding ancient philosopher of the Taoist school.
④ 译者注：(?-233 B.C.) outstanding ancient philosopher.

embellishment. Arguments adorned with embellishments and artifice in rhetoric mark writing of the highest quality.

A study of the *Book of Filial Piety* and *The Way and Its Power* shows that both art and substance depend on feeling. A careful perusal of Chuang Tzu and Han Fei reveals that over-ornateness may lead to licence. One who can distinguish the waters of confluent streams, who reins in his steed at the crossroad to choose the right way, can also check literary embellishment. Just as paint and powder may improve the appearance but beauty comes from good features, so literary adornment may improve language but splendour springs from feeling. Thus feeling is the warp of writing and language the woof of reason; only when the warp is in place can the woof be woven, and only when reason is firm can language flow freely. This is the root of writing.

The poets of old used art to vent their feelings, while later writers of descriptive poems counterfeited feeling for the sake of art. Why do I say this? Because the men who made the old folk songs sang to vent the grief and anger in their hearts and satirize those above. This is what is meant by writing to vent feeling. But Han dynasty poets, who had no sorrow in their hearts but hunted for hyperboles to dazzle the world and win a name for themselves, were counterfeiting feeling for art. Those who wrote to vent feeling were succinct and truthful; those who wrote for the sake of art were magniloquent and wearisome. Poets since that time have chosen magniloquence and discarded truth, turning their backs on the ancient songs and odes to imitate the Han descriptive poems, so that writing expressing true feeling grows daily rarer while meretricious verses are all the fashion. Thus some who hanker after official honours pay lip service to the pleasures of country life, while others whose hearts are set on power affect a desire to escape from the world of men. There is no truth in them, they have left the Way.

Peach and plum have no voice, yet because they bear fruit paths are trodden out to them. Orchids planted by a rough fellow have no fragrance, because he himself lacks feeling. If even trees and plants must have feeling and substance, how much more so must literature. The prime task of literature is to express man's will! When words run counter to true feeling, art is worthless!

Phrases are linked and colour interwoven to light up some idea; but when colour runs riot and language becomes far-fetched, the meaning is obscured. Using cassia as bait and a kingfisher's feather as fly will never catch a fish — this is what is meant by language veiled by splendour. Thus a hempen garment should be worn outside silk to avoid ostentation, and the oracle counted simplicity auspicious because it is good to return to nature. If men can take reason as their guide and keep emotion within proper bounds, once emotion is under control music can be made; once reason is in command embellishments can be adopted; for then neither will art ruin substance nor profusion of images blur the central theme, but true reds and blues will shine out while mawkish pinks and purples are set aside. Language like this, fashioned with skill, is worthy the name of fine writing.

Epitome:

> Through art words travel wide:
> This maxim is well-tried.
> Thoughts shaped within the heart
> Their radiance will impart;
> Soon soiled the rare brocade,
> Hibiscus sweet must fade;
> Empty magniloquence
> Must jar upon the sense.

On Hyperbole

Above form is the Way, below it are physical objects. The world of the spirit is so hard to grasp that not even the subtlest language can trace it to the end; but physical object are easy to describe and their true form can be expressed in forceful phrases. It is not that some writers have more talent than others, but simply that one is easier to describe. So all things in heaven or on earth find expression in sound and appearance, and to clothe them in language frequent use is made of hyperbole. Even classical works like the *Book of Songs* and the *Book of Document*, which serve as models to instruct men, inevitably cover such a wide range that recourse is often had to exaggeration. Thus height becomes "heaven-piercing peaks," narrowness "a river too small to hold a barge," a large family "millions of offspring," few inhabitants "not a soul left alive," a flood "waters surging to the sky," a defeat "the very pestles were floating in blood." This high-flown language does no violence, however, to the sense. But not even poets can make an owl's hoot melodious or transform bitter herbs into sweet. It was indeed their passion to praise that made them employ this artifice and great sages recorded these examples for future writers. Thus Mencius[①] said, "When studying the songs, do not let their music blind you to the words, nor the words blind you to the meaning."

With Sung Yu and Ching Chai,[②] hyperbole came into fashion. Ssuma Hsiang-ju followed in their steps and went to extremes. In his descriptions of the imperial forest, shooting stars and curved rainbows alight on the pavilions, while game is so plentiful that griffins and phoenixes are caught. Yang Hsiung writing of the Kanchuan Palace came under his influence and described rare plants as trees of jade, buildings as so high that even spirits must tumble down from them. As for some accounts of the east and west capitals, their reports of strange fish and sea monsters pass all bounds of credibility yet fall short of the most splendid imagery. Again, Yang Hsiung's description of an imperial hunt has the river goddess whipped to appease Chu Yuan, while Chang Heng has the God of Water besieged in the Northern Wilderness. Now the Goddess of the River Lo is no water demon, nor is the God of Water a mountain ogre. This is a slipshod use of fantastic allusions. The intention here was to heighten the effect, but the similes are too far-fetched. As for the appearance of mountains and seas or the aspect of courts

---

① 译者注:（372-289 B.C.) well-known philosopher of the Confucian school.
② 译者注: Poets of the kingdom of Chu of the third-second century B.C.

and palaces, these tower in beauty or dazzle by their splendour, so magnificent they must surely burst into flame, so steep they must surely topple down. All these depend upon exaggeration and owe their novelty to artifice. So later writers prize hyperbole. They spread their wings to soar high or leap and bound, scorning to hobble along. Do they speak of splendour? Spring flowers cannot match its brightness. Of decay? A wintry chasm is less desolate. Of joy? Words and laughter intermingle. Of sadness? Voices blend with sobs. They undoubtedly know how to release pent-up feelings, put boredom to flight, make the blind see and rouse the deaf.

However, when rhetoric oversteps the mark, discourse becomes confused; when exaggeration outstrips reason, name and reality are at variance. If we can absorb the general principles of the *Book of Songs* and *Book of Documents*, pruning the excesses of Yang Hsiung and Ssuma Hsiang-ju so as to have restraint in exaggeration and embellishment without falsification, the result will be admirable.

Epitome:

　　Employ hyperbole aright,

　　A writer has no constant law;

　　The spirit should not lag in flight,

　　Like giant roc let language soar!

　　For pearls men search the ocean bed,

　　Of jade the mountains have good store;

　　Let writing brim, not overflow,

　　Extravagant yet free from flaw.

On Discrimination

Discrimination is rare. Indeed it is hard to appreciate art, hard to find a true connoisseur — there may be only one such in a thousand years! Most critics since early times have held their own generation cheap and admired the ancients. This is known as spurning those things close at hand every day and longing for the music heard in the distance. When Han Fei's writings first appeared and Ssuma Hsiang-ju first completed his poem, the Emperor of Chin and Emperor Wu of Han wished these men were contemporaries; but once they discovered these writers were still alive, Han Fei was thrown into gaol and Ssuma Hsiang-ju treated with contempt. Is this not a clear indication that men hold contemporary writing cheap?

There was little to choose between Pan Ku① and Fu Yi② as writers, yet Pan Ku sneered at Fu Yi, saying, "He cannot lay down his pen when he starts writing." Again Tsao Chih, speaking of talent, laughed at Chen Lin; but when asked to touch up Ting Yi's③ writing Tsao Chih thought this an excellent scheme, while he compared his detractor Liu Hsiu④ to Tien Pa — all this reveals his bias. So it was not for nothing that Emperor Wen of Wei remarked that scholars despise each other.

Then there was that babbler Lou Hu⑤ who thought he could hold forth on literature and made Huan Tan and others laugh by maintaining that Ssuma Chien consulted Tungfang Shuo.⑥ If a mere playboy like Lou Hu made a fool of himself by irresponsible talk, scholars should watch their tongues much more carefully. So there are men of perception, like the two emperors, who value the ancients and despise the moderns; there are men of outstanding talent, like Pan Ku and Tsao Chih, who think highly of themselves and look down on others; and there are men lacking any knowledge of literature, like Lou Hu, who believe in what is false and are blind to the truth. No wonder, then, if some lament that writing is used as waste paper to cover a pot of sauce!

---

① 译者注：(A. D. 32-92) famous Han dynasty historian.

② 译者注：(A. D. ?-89) Han dynasty poet.

③ 译者注：A writer at the end of the Han dynasty. He asked Tsao Chih to polish his writing and said, "I know myself the merits and defects of my writing. No one in future generations will know who edited my works."

④ 译者注：Liu Hsiu, a writer at the end of the Han dynasty. He had little talent but liked to criticize people; Tien Pa, an orator in the third century B.C.

⑤ 译者注：A Han dynasty orator.

⑥ 译者注：(154-93 B.C.) a Han dynasty jester.

The unicorn and phoenix are utterly different from the stag and pheasant; pearls and jade are quite unlike pebbles and stones. Sunlight illumines them clearly for men's eyes to take in their forms, yet a subject of Lu took a unicorn for a stag, a man of Chu took a pheasant for a phoenix, a native of Wei took jade for a curious stone, a citizen of Sung took a pebble for a precious pearl. If they made such mistakes over forms like these which are easy to distinguish, of course it is difficult to distinguish between styles of writing which are hard to grasp.

Writing takes many forms, being compounded of substance and of art. Most men have certain prejudices which prevent them from seeing things in the round. The liberal may applaud a heroic strain, the thoughtful may respond to subtleties, the superficially clever may delight in show, those with a taste for the bizarre may wonder at strange tales. When the writing suits them they exclaim with pleasure, but when it is not to their taste they reject it. Each sees the infinite variety of literature from his own particular viewpoint. This is what is meant by the saying: "A man facing east cannot see the western wall."

After playing a thousand tunes a man understands music; after examining a thousand swords he understands weapons. So to gain an idea of literature as a whole we must first read widely. A view of high mountains shows the shape of hills; a dip in the ocean illustrates the shallowness of a ditch. Only a man with no prejudices great or small, no personal likes or dislikes, can weigh things up fairly and see writing as clearly as in a mirror. To examine the merits of any work of literature we must establish six criteria and consider: first, the style adopted; secondly, the language used; thirdly, the development from past traditions; fourthly, the methods of expression; fifthly, the arguments and allusions; and sixthly, the musical rhythm. After this is done, we can determine whether a work is good or bad.

The writer, aroused by feeling, is moved to expression; the reader poring over his writing enters into his feeling. If we seek the source by following the stream, we shall find it even if it lies concealed. We cannot meet the men of old face to face, but by reading their works we can see into their hearts. No writing is too deep to penetrate, the sole danger is too shallow an understanding. If a man thinking of mountains and rivers can express his feeling on the lyre, how can ideas embodied by the pen escape us? The mind grasps an idea just as the eyes perceive objects. Good eyes can distinguish between all manner of objects, and an intelligent mind can penetrate any idea. But vulgar critics may be confused, discarding what is profound to seek out what is shallow. This is why Chuang Tzu laughed at those who admired the song *Plucking the Willow*, ① and Sung Yu lamented that men could not appreciate music like *White Snow*. ② Chu Yuan once said, "Art and nature lay within me, but the crowd did not see my rare splendour. " Only a true connoisseur can discern what is finest. Yang Hsiung affirmed that he loved profound and brilliant writing, proving that he too was dissatisfied with mere show. A man of deep understanding and keen observation will have the same pleasure in his mind as a crowd of revellers on the terrace in spring or travellers stopping for good music and food. Just as the orchid, king of fragrant flowers, becomes more fragrant when worn, so books, which are sovereign flowers too, reveal their beauty when studied and analysed. Let men of discrimination ponder this!

Epitome:

> Great bells there are of weight untold,
> Their tones set true by men of old;
> And crates books are heaped up high
> Awaiting a discerning eye;
> A wanton tune leads men astray,
> Best close your ears and walk away.
> All those who hold these rules in sight
> Will never stray from what is right.

---

① 译者注: A popular air.
② 译者注: A tune enjoyed by the élite.

四

史记·项羽本纪①

　　项籍者,下相人也,字羽。初起时,年二十四。其季父项梁,梁父即楚将项燕,为秦将王翦所戮者也。项氏世世为楚将,封于项,故姓项氏。

　　项籍少时,学书不成,去学剑,又不成。项梁怒之。籍曰:"书,足以记名姓而已。剑,一人敌,不足学,学万人敌。"于是项梁乃教籍兵法,籍大喜;略知其意,又不肯竟学。项梁尝有栎阳逮,乃请蕲狱掾曹咎书,抵栎阳狱掾司马欣,以故事得已。项梁杀人,与籍避仇于吴中。吴中贤士大夫皆出项梁下。每吴中有大徭役及丧,项梁常为主办,阴以兵法部勒宾客及子弟,以是知其能。秦始皇帝游会稽,渡浙江,梁与籍俱观。籍曰:"彼可取而代也。"梁掩其口,曰:"毋妄言,族矣!"梁以此奇籍。籍长八尺余,力能扛鼎,才气过人,虽吴中子弟皆已惮籍矣。

　　秦二世元年七月,陈涉等起大泽中。其九月,会稽守通谓梁曰:"江西皆反,此亦天亡秦之时也。吾闻先即制人,后则为人所制。吾欲发兵,使公及桓楚将。"是时桓楚亡在泽中。梁曰:"桓楚亡,人莫知其处,独籍知之耳。"梁乃出,诫籍持剑居外待。梁复入,与守坐,曰:"请召籍,使受命召桓楚。"守曰:"诺。"梁召籍入。须臾,梁眴籍曰:"可行矣!"于是籍遂拔剑斩守头。项梁持守头,佩其印绶。门下大惊,扰乱,籍所击杀数十百人。一府中皆慑伏,莫敢起。梁乃召故所知豪吏,谕以所为起大事。遂举吴中

---

①　中文、英译文选自:(西汉)司马迁.史记选 I(大中华文库·汉英对照).安平秋,
　　校译.杨宪益,戴乃迭,英译.北京:外文出版社,2008.

兵。使人收下县,得精兵八千人。梁部署吴中豪杰,为校尉、候、司马。有一人不得用,自言于梁。梁曰:“前时某丧,使公主某事,不能办,以此不任用公。”众乃皆伏。于是,梁为会稽守,籍为裨将,徇下县。

广陵人召平于是为陈王徇广陵,未能下。闻陈王败走,秦兵又且至,乃渡江矫陈王命,拜梁为楚王上柱国。曰:“江东已定,急引兵西击秦!”项梁乃以八千人渡江而西。闻陈婴已下东阳,使使欲与连和俱西。陈婴者,故东阳令史,居县中,素信谨,称为长者。东阳少年杀其令,相聚数千人,欲置长,无适用,乃请陈婴。婴谢不能,遂强立婴为长,县中从者得二万人。少年欲立婴便为王,异军苍头特起。陈婴母谓婴曰:“自我为汝家妇,未尝闻汝先古之有贵者。今暴得大名,不祥。不如有所属,事成犹得封侯,事败易以亡,非世所指名也。”婴乃不敢为王。谓其军吏曰:“项氏世世将家,有名于楚,今欲举大事,将非其人不可。我倚名族,亡秦必矣。”于是众从其言,以兵属项梁。项梁渡淮,黥布、蒲将军亦以兵属焉。凡六七万人,军下邳。

当是时,秦嘉已立景驹为楚王,军彭城东,欲距项梁。项梁谓军吏曰:“陈王先首事,战不利,未闻所在。今秦嘉倍陈王而立景驹,逆无道。”乃进兵击秦嘉。秦嘉军败走,追之至胡陵。嘉还战,一日,嘉死,军降。景驹走死梁地。项梁已并秦嘉军,军胡陵,将引军而西。章邯军至栗,项梁使别将朱鸡石、余樊君与战。余樊君死,朱鸡石军败,亡走胡陵。项梁乃引兵入薛,诛鸡石。项梁前使项羽别攻襄城,襄城坚守不下。已拔,皆坑之。还报项梁。项梁闻陈王定死,召诸别将会薛计事。此时,沛公亦起沛,往焉。

居鄛人范增,年七十,素居家,好奇计。往说项梁曰:“陈胜败固当。夫秦灭六国,楚最无罪。自怀王入秦不反,楚人怜之至今,故楚南公曰:‘楚虽三户,亡秦必楚也。’今陈胜首事,不立楚后而自立,其势不长。今君起江东,楚蜂午之将皆争附君者,以君世世楚将,为能复立楚之后也。”于是项梁然其言,乃求楚怀王孙心民间,为人牧羊,立以为楚怀王,从民所望也。陈婴为楚上柱国,封五县,与怀王都盱台。项梁自号为武信君。

居数月，引兵攻亢父，与齐田荣、司马龙且军救东阿，大破秦军于东阿。田荣即引兵归，逐其王假。假亡走楚。假相田角亡走赵。角弟田间故齐将，居赵不敢归。田荣立田儋子市为齐王。项梁已破东阿下军，遂追秦军。数使使趣齐兵，欲与俱西。田荣曰："楚杀田假，赵杀田角、田间，乃发兵。"项梁曰："田假为与国之王，穷来从我，不忍杀之。"赵亦不杀田角、田间以市于齐。齐遂不肯发兵助楚。项梁使沛公及项羽别攻城阳，屠之，西破秦军濮阳东，秦兵收入濮阳。沛公、项羽乃攻定陶。定陶未下，去，西略地至雍丘，大破秦军，斩李由。还攻外黄，外黄未下。

项梁起东阿，西（北）至定陶，再破秦军，项羽等又斩李由，益轻秦，有骄色。宋义乃谏项梁曰："战胜而将骄卒惰者败。今卒少惰矣，秦兵日益，臣为君畏之。"项梁弗听。乃使宋义使于齐。道遇齐使者高陵君显，曰："公将见武信君乎？"曰："然。"曰："臣论武信君军必败。公徐行即免死，疾行则及祸。"秦果悉起兵益章邯，击楚军，大破之定陶，项梁死。沛公、项羽去外黄攻陈留，陈留坚守不能下。沛公、项羽相与谋曰："今项梁军破，士卒恐。"乃与吕臣军俱引兵而东。吕臣军彭城东，项羽军彭城西，沛公军砀。

章邯已破项梁军，则以为楚地兵不足忧，乃渡河击赵，大破之。当此时，赵歇为王，陈余为将，张耳为相，皆走入钜鹿城。章邯令王离、涉间围钜鹿，章邯军其南，筑甬道而输之粟。陈余为将，将卒数万人而军钜鹿之北，此所谓河北之军也。

楚兵已破于定陶，怀王恐，从盱台之彭城，并项羽、吕臣军自将之。以吕臣为司徒，以其父吕青为令尹。以沛公为砀郡长，封为武安侯，将砀郡兵。

初，宋义所遇齐使者高陵君显在楚军，见楚王曰："宋义论武信君之军必败，居数日，军果败。兵未战而先见败征，此可谓知兵矣。"王召宋义与计事，而大说之，因置以为上将军。项羽为鲁公为次将，范增为末将，救赵。诸别将皆属宋义，号为卿子冠军。行至安阳，留四十六日不进。项羽曰："吾闻秦军围赵王钜鹿，疾引兵渡河，楚击其外，赵应其内，破秦军必矣。"宋义曰:"不然。夫搏牛之虻不可以破虮虱。今秦攻赵,战胜则兵罢,我承其敝;不胜,则我引兵鼓行而西,必举秦矣。故不如先斗秦赵。夫被坚执锐,义不如公;坐而运策,公不如义。"因下令军中曰:"猛如虎,很如羊,贪如狼,强不可使者,皆斩之。"乃遣其子宋襄相齐,身送之至无盐,饮酒高会。天寒大雨,士卒冻饥。项羽曰:"将戮力而攻秦,久留不行。今岁饥民贫,士卒食芋菽,军无见粮,乃饮酒高会,不引兵渡河因赵食,与赵并力攻秦,乃曰'承其敝'。夫以秦之强,攻新造之赵,其势必举赵。赵举而秦强,何敝之承! 且国兵新破,王坐不安席,扫境内而专属于将军,国家安危,在此一举。今不恤士卒而徇其私,非社稷之臣。"项羽晨朝上将军宋义,即其帐中斩宋义头,出令军中曰:"宋义与齐谋反楚,楚王阴令羽诛之。"当是时,诸将皆慑服,莫敢枝梧。皆曰:"首立楚者,将军家也。今将军诛乱。"乃相与共立羽为假上将军。使人追宋义子,及之齐,杀之。使桓楚报命于怀王。怀王因使项羽为上将军,当阳君、蒲将军皆属项羽。

项羽已杀卿子冠军,威震楚国,名闻诸侯。乃遣当阳君、蒲将军将卒二万,渡河救钜鹿。战少利,陈余复请兵。项羽乃悉引兵渡河,皆沉船,破釜甑,烧庐舍,持三日粮,以示士卒必死,无一还心。于是至则围王离,与秦军遇,九战,绝其甬道,大破之,杀苏角,虏王离。涉间不降楚,自烧杀。

当是时,楚兵冠诸侯。诸侯军救钜鹿下者十余壁,莫敢纵兵。及楚击秦,诸将皆从壁上观。楚战士无不一以当十,楚兵呼声动天,诸侯军无不人人惴恐。于是已破秦军,项羽召见诸侯将,入辕门,无不膝行而前,莫敢仰视。项羽由是始为诸侯上将军,诸侯皆属焉。

章邯军棘原,项羽军漳南,相持未战。秦军数却,二世使人让章邯。章邯恐,使长史欣请事。至咸阳,留司马门三日,赵高不见,有不信之心。长史欣恐,还走其军,不敢出故道。赵高果使人追之,不及。欣至军,报曰:"赵高用事于中,下无可为者。今战能胜,高必疾妒吾功;战不能胜,不免于死。愿将军孰计之!"陈余亦遗章邯书曰:"白起为秦将,南征鄢郢,北抗马服,攻城略地,不可胜计,而竟赐死。蒙恬为秦将,北逐戎人,开榆中地数千里,竟斩阳周。何者? 功多,秦不能尽封,因以法诛之。令将军为秦将三岁矣,所亡失以十万数,而诸侯并起滋益多。彼赵高素谀日久,今事急,亦恐二世诛之,故欲以法诛将军以塞责,使人更代将军以脱其祸。夫将军居外久,多内却,有功亦诛,无功亦诛。且天之亡秦,无愚智皆知之。令将军内不能直谏,外为亡国将,孤特独立而欲常存,岂不哀哉!将军何不还兵与诸侯为从,约共攻秦,分王其地,南面称孤,此孰与身伏铁质,妻子为戮乎?"章邯狐疑,阴使候始成使项羽,欲约。约未成,项羽使蒲将军日夜引兵度三户,军漳南,与秦战,再破之。项羽悉引兵击秦军汙水上,大破之。

章邯使人见项羽,欲约。项羽召军吏谋曰:"粮少,欲听其约。"军吏皆曰:"善。"项羽乃与期洹水南殷虚上。已盟,章邯见项羽而流涕,为言赵高。项羽乃立章邯为雍王,置楚军中。使长史欣为上将军,将秦军为前行。

到新安。诸侯吏卒异时故徭使屯戍过秦中,秦中吏卒遇之多无状,及秦军降诸侯,诸侯吏卒乘胜多奴虏使之,轻折辱秦吏卒。秦吏卒多窃言曰:"章将军等诈吾属降诸侯,今能入关破秦,大善;即不能,诸侯虏吾属而东,秦必尽诛吾父母妻子。"诸将微闻其计,以告项羽。项羽乃召黥布、蒲将军计曰:"秦吏卒尚众,其心不服,至关中不听,事必危;不如击杀之,而独与章邯、长史欣、都尉翳入秦。"于是楚军夜击,坑秦卒二十余万人新安城南。

行略定秦地。函谷关有兵守关,不得入。又闻沛公已破咸阳。项羽大怒,使当阳君等击关。项羽遂入,至于戏西。沛公军霸上,未得与项羽相见。沛公左司马曹无伤使人言于项羽曰:"沛公欲王关中,使子婴为相,珍宝尽有之。"项羽大怒,曰:"旦日飨士卒,为击破沛公军!"当是时,项羽兵四十万,在新丰鸿门,沛公兵十万,在霸上。范增说项羽曰:"沛公居山东时,贪于财货,好美姬。今入关,财物无所取,妇女无所幸,此其志不在小。吾令人望其气,皆为龙虎,成五采,此天子气也。急击勿失!"

楚左尹项伯者,项羽季父也,素善留侯张良。张良是时从沛公,项伯乃夜驰之沛公军,私见张良,具告以事,欲呼张良与俱去。曰:"毋从俱死也。"张良曰:"臣为韩王送沛公,沛公今事有急,亡去不义,不可不语。"良乃入,具告沛公。沛公大惊,曰"为之奈何?"张良曰:"谁为大王为此计者?"曰:"鲰生说我曰:'距关毋内诸候,秦地可尽王也'。故听之。"良曰:"料大王士卒足以当项王乎?"沛公默然,曰:"固不如也,且为之奈何?"张良:"请往谓项伯,言沛公不敢背项王也。"沛公曰:"君安与项伯有故?"张良曰:"秦时与臣游,项伯杀人,臣活之。今事有急,故幸来告良。"沛公曰:"孰与君少长?"良曰:"长于臣。"沛公曰:"君为我呼入,吾得兄事之。"张良出,要项伯。项伯即入见沛公。沛公奉卮酒为寿,约为婚姻,曰:"吾入关,秋豪不敢有所近,籍吏民,封府库,而待将军。所以遣将守关者,备他盗之出入与非常也。日夜望将军至,岂敢反乎!愿伯具言臣之不敢倍德也。"项伯许诺。谓沛公曰:"旦日不可不蚤自来谢项王!"沛公曰:"诺。"于是项伯复夜去,至军中,具以沛公言报项王。因言曰:"沛公不先破关中,公岂敢入乎?今人有大功而击之,不义也。不如因善遇之。"项王许诺。

沛公旦日从百余骑来见项王,至鸿门,谢曰:"臣与将军戮力而攻秦,将军战河北,臣战河南,然不自意能先入关破秦,得复见将军于此。今者有小人之言,令将军与臣有隙。"项王曰:"此沛公左司马曹无伤言之;不然,籍何以至此。"项王即日因留沛公与饮。项王、项伯东向坐,亚父南向坐。亚父者,范增也。沛公北向坐,张良西向侍。范增数目项王,举所佩玉玦以示之者三。项王默然不应。范增起,出召项庄,谓曰:"君王为人不忍,若入前为寿,寿毕,请以剑舞,因击沛公于坐杀之。不者,若属皆且为所虏。"庄则入为寿。寿毕,曰:"君王与沛公饮,军中无以为乐,请以剑舞。"项王曰:"诺。"项庄拔剑起舞,项伯亦拔剑起舞,常以身翼蔽沛公,庄不得击。于是张良至军门,见樊哙。樊哙曰:"今日之事何如?"良曰:"甚急。今者项庄拔剑舞,其意常在沛公也。"哙曰:"此迫矣,臣请入,与之同命!"哙即带剑拥盾入军门。交戟之卫士欲止不内,樊哙侧其盾以撞,卫士仆地,哙遂入。披帷西向立,瞋目视项王,头发上指,目眦尽裂。项王按剑而跽曰:"客何为者?"张良曰:"沛公之参乘樊哙者也。"项王曰:"壮士,赐之卮酒。"则与斗卮酒。哙拜谢，起，立而饮之。项王曰："赐之彘肩！"则与一生彘肩。樊哙覆其盾于地，加彘肩上，拔剑切而啖之。项王曰："壮士，能复饮乎？"樊哙曰："臣死且不避，卮酒安足辞！夫秦王有虎狼之心，杀人如不能举，刑人如恐不胜，天下皆叛之。怀王与诸将约曰，'先破秦入咸阳者王之'。今沛公先破秦入咸阳，豪毛不敢有所近，封闭宫室，还军霸上，以待大王来。故遣将守关者，备他盗出入与非常也。劳苦而功高如此，未有封侯之赏，而听细说，欲诛有功之人。此亡秦之续耳，窃为大王不取也！"项王未有以应，曰："坐！"樊哙从良坐。坐须臾，沛公起如厕，因招樊哙出。

沛公已出，项王使都尉陈平召沛公。沛公曰："今者出，未辞也，为之奈何？"樊哙曰："大行不顾细谨，大礼不辞小让。如今人方为刀俎，我为鱼肉，何辞为？"于是遂去。乃令张良留谢。良问曰："大王来何操？"曰："我持白璧一双，欲献项王，玉斗一双，欲与亚父。会其怒，不敢献。公为我献之。"张良曰："谨诺。"当是时，项王军在鸿门下，沛公军在霸上，相去四十里。沛公则置车骑，脱身独骑，与樊哙、夏侯婴、靳强、纪信等四人持剑盾步走，从郦山下，道芷阳间行。沛公谓张良曰："从此道至吾军，不过二十里耳，度我至军中，公乃入。"沛公已去，间至军中，张良入谢。曰："沛公不胜杯杓，不能辞。谨使臣良奉白璧一双，再拜献大王足下；玉斗一双，再拜奉大将军足下。"项王曰："沛公安在？"良曰："闻大王有意督过之，脱身独去，已至军矣。"项王则受璧，置之坐上。亚父受玉斗，置之地，拔剑撞而破之，曰："唉！竖子不足与谋！夺项王天下者，必沛公也，吾属今为之虏矣！"沛公至军，立诛杀曹无伤。

居数日，项羽引兵西屠咸阳，杀秦降王子婴，烧秦宫室，火三月不灭；收其货宝妇女而东。人或说项王曰："关中阻山河四塞，地肥饶，可都以霸。"项王见秦宫室皆以烧残破，又心怀思欲东归，曰："富贵不归故乡，如衣绣夜行，谁知之者！"说者曰："人言楚人沐猴而冠耳，果然。"项王闻之，烹说者。

项王使人致命怀王。怀王曰："如约。"乃尊怀王为义帝。项王欲自王，先王诸将相。谓曰："天下初发难时，假立诸侯后以伐秦。然身被坚执锐首事，暴露于野三年，灭秦定天下者，皆将相诸君与籍之力也。义帝虽无功，故当分其地而王之。"诸将皆曰："善。"乃分天下，立诸将为侯王。

项王、范增疑沛公之有天下，业已讲解，又恶负约，恐诸侯叛之，乃阴谋曰："巴、蜀道险，秦之迁人皆居蜀。"乃曰："巴、蜀亦关中地也。"故立沛公为汉王，王巴、蜀、汉中，都南郑。而三分关中，王秦降将以距塞汉王。

项王乃立章邯为雍王，王咸阳以西，都废丘。长史欣者，故为栎阳狱掾，尝有德于项梁；都尉董翳者，本劝章邯降楚。故立司马欣为塞王，王咸阳以东至河，都栎阳；立董翳为翟王，王上郡，都高奴。徙魏王豹为西魏王，王河东，都平阳。瑕丘申阳者，张耳嬖臣也，先下河南，迎楚河上，故立申阳为河南王，都雒阳。韩王成因故都，都阳翟。赵将司马卬定河内，数有功，故立卬为殷王，王河内，都朝歌。徙赵王歇为代王。赵相张耳素贤，又从入关，故立耳为常山王，王赵地，都襄国。当阳君黥布为楚将，常冠军，故立布为九江王，都六。鄱君吴芮率百越佐诸侯，又从入关，故立芮为衡山王，都邾。义帝柱国共敖将兵击南郡，功多，因立敖为临江王，都江陵。徙燕王韩广为辽东王。燕将臧荼从楚救赵，因从入关，故立荼为燕王，都蓟。徙齐王田市为胶东王。齐将田都从共救赵，因从入关，故立都为齐王，都临菑。故秦所灭齐王建孙田安，项羽方渡河救赵，田安下济北数城，引其兵降项羽，故立安为济北王，都博阳。田荣者，数负项梁，又不肯将兵从楚击秦，以故不封。成安君陈余弃将印去，不从入关，然素闻其贤，有功于赵，闻其在南皮，故因环封三县。番君将梅鋗功多，故封十万户侯。项王自立为西楚霸王，王九郡，都彭城。

汉之元年四月，诸侯罢戏下，各就国。项王出之国，使人徙义帝，曰："古之帝者地方千里，必居上游。"乃使使徙义帝长沙郴县。趣义帝行，其群臣稍稍背叛之，乃阴令衡山、临江王击杀之江中。韩王成无军功，项王不使之国，与俱至彭城，废以为侯，已又杀之。臧荼之国，因逐韩广之辽东，广弗听，荼击杀广无终，并王其地。

田荣闻项羽徙齐王市胶东，而立齐将田都为齐王，乃大怒，不肯遣齐

王之胶东,因以齐反,迎击田都。田都走楚。齐王市畏项王,乃亡之胶东
就国。田荣怒,追击杀之即墨。荣因自立为齐王,而西击杀济北王田安,
并王三齐。荣与彭越将军印,令反梁地。陈余阴使张同、夏说说齐王田荣
曰:"项羽为天下宰,不平。今尽王故王于丑地,而王其群臣诸将善地,逐
其故主,赵王乃北居代,余以为不可。闻大王起兵,且不听不义,愿大王资
余兵,请以击常山,以复赵王,请以国为捍蔽。"齐王许之,因遣兵之赵。陈
余悉发三县兵,与齐并力击常山,大破之。张耳走归汉。陈余迎故赵王歇
于代,反之赵。赵王因立陈余为代王。

　　是时,汉还定三秦。项羽闻汉王皆已并关中,且东;齐、赵叛之,大怒。
乃以故吴令郑昌为韩王,以距汉;令萧公角等击彭越。彭越败萧公角等。
汉使张良徇韩,乃遗项王书曰:"汉王失职,欲得关中,如约即止,不敢东。"
又以齐、梁反书遗项王曰:"齐欲与赵并灭楚。"楚以此故,无西意,而北击
齐。征兵九江王布。布称疾不往,使将将数千人行。项王由此怨布也。
汉之二年冬,项羽遂北至城阳,田荣亦将兵会战。田荣不胜,走至平原,平
原民杀之。遂北烧夷齐城郭室屋,皆坑田荣降卒,系虏其老弱妇女。徇齐
至北海,多所残灭。齐人相聚而叛之。于是田荣弟田横收齐亡卒得数万
人,反城阳。项王因留,连战未能下。

　　春,汉王部五诸侯兵,凡五十六万人,东伐楚。项王闻之,即令诸将击
齐,而自以精兵三万人南从鲁出胡陵。四月,汉皆已入彭城,收其货宝、美
人,日置酒高会。项王乃西从萧,晨击汉军而东,至彭城,日中,大破汉军。
汉军皆走,相随入谷、泗水,杀汉卒十余万人。汉卒皆南走山,楚又追击至
灵壁东睢水上。汉军却,为楚所挤,多杀,汉卒十余万人皆入睢水,睢水为
之不流。围汉王三匝。于是大风从西北而起,折木发屋,扬沙石,窈冥昼
晦,逢迎楚军。楚军大乱,坏散,而汉王乃得与数十骑遁去。欲过沛,收家
室而西;楚亦使人追之沛,取汉王家;家皆亡,不与汉王相见。汉王道逢得
孝惠、鲁元,乃载行。楚骑追汉王,汉王急,推堕孝惠、鲁元车下,滕公常下
收载之。如是者三。曰:"虽急不可以驱,奈何弃之?"于是遂得脱。求太
公、吕后不相遇。审食其从太公、吕后间行,求汉王,反遇楚军。楚军遂与

归,报项王,项王常置军中。

是时吕后兄周吕侯为汉将兵居下邑,汉王间往从之,稍稍收其士卒。至荥阳,诸败军皆会,萧何亦发关中老弱未傅,悉诣荥阳,复大振。楚起于彭城,常乘胜逐北,与汉战荥阳南京、索间,汉败楚,楚以故不能过荥阳而西。

项王之救彭城,追汉王至荥阳,田横亦得收齐,立田荣子广为齐王。汉王之败彭城,诸侯皆复与楚而背汉。汉军荥阳,筑甬道属之河,以取敖仓粟。汉之三年,项王数侵夺汉甬道,汉王食乏,恐,请和,割荥阳以西为汉。

项王欲听之。历阳侯范增曰:"汉易与耳,今释弗取,后必悔之。"项王乃与范增急围荥阳。汉王患之,乃用陈平计,间项王。项王使者来,为太牢具,举欲进之。见使者,详惊愕曰:"吾以为亚父使者,乃反项王使者!"更持去,以恶食食项王使者。使者归报项王,项王乃疑范增与汉有私,稍夺之权。范增大怒,曰:"天下事大定矣,君王自为之。愿赐骸骨归卒伍。"项王许之。行未至彭城,疽发背而死。

汉将纪信说汉王曰:"事已急矣,请为王诳楚为王,王可以间出。"于是汉王夜出女子荥阳东门被甲二千人,楚兵四面击之。纪信乘黄屋车,傅左纛,曰:"城中食尽,汉王降。"楚军皆呼万岁。汉王亦与数十骑从城西门出,走成皋。项王见纪信,问:"汉王安在?"信曰:"汉王已出矣!"项王烧杀纪信。

汉王使御史大夫周苛、枞公、魏豹守荥阳。周苛、枞公谋曰:"反国之王,难与守城。"乃共杀魏豹。楚下荥阳城,生得周苛。项王谓周苛曰:"为我将,我以公为上将军,封三万户。"周苛骂曰:"若不趣降汉,汉今虏若,若非汉敌也。"项王怒,烹周苛,并杀枞公。

汉王之出荥阳,南走宛、叶,得九江王布,行收兵,复入保成皋。汉之四年,项王进兵围成皋,汉王逃,独与滕公出成皋北门,渡河走修武,从张耳、韩信军。诸将稍稍得出成皋,从汉王。楚遂拔成皋,欲西。汉使兵距之巩,令其不得西。

是时,彭越渡河击楚东阿,杀楚将军薛公。项王乃自东击彭越。汉王得淮阴侯兵,欲渡河南。郑忠说汉王,乃止壁河内。使刘贾将兵佐彭越,烧楚积聚。项王东击破之,走彭越。汉王则引兵渡河,复取成皋,军广武,就敖仓食。项王已定东海来,西,与汉俱临广武而军,相守数月。

当此时,彭越数反梁地,绝楚粮食,项王患之。为高俎,置太公其上,告汉王曰:"今不急下,吾烹太公。"汉王曰:"吾与项羽俱北面受命怀王,曰'约为兄弟',吾翁即若翁,必欲烹而翁,则幸分我一杯羹。"项王怒,欲杀之。项伯曰:"天下事未可知,且为天下者不顾家,虽杀之无益,只益祸耳。"项王从之。

楚、汉久相持未决,丁壮苦军旅,老弱罢转漕。项王谓汉王曰:"天下匈匈数岁者,徒以吾两人耳。愿与汉王挑战决雌雄,毋徒苦天下之民父子为也!"汉王笑谢曰:"吾宁斗智,不能斗力。"项王令壮士出挑战,汉有善骑射者楼烦,楚挑战三合,楼烦辄射杀之。项王大怒,乃自被甲持戟挑战。楼烦欲射之,项王瞋目叱之,楼烦目不敢视,手不敢发,遂走还入壁,不敢复出。汉王使人间问之,乃项王也。汉王大惊。于是项王乃即汉王相与临广武间而语。汉王数之,项王怒,欲一战。汉王不听,项王伏弩射中汉王。汉王伤,走入成皋。

项王闻淮阴侯已举河北,破齐、赵,且欲击楚,乃使龙且往击之。淮阴侯与战骑将灌婴击之,大破楚军,杀龙且。韩信因自立为齐王。项王闻龙且军破,则恐,使盱台人武涉往说淮阴侯。淮阴侯弗听。是时,彭越复反,下梁地,绝楚粮。项王乃谓海春侯大司马曹咎等曰:"谨守成皋,则汉欲挑战,慎勿与战,毋令得东而已。我十五日必诛彭越,定梁地,复从将军。"乃东行,击陈留、外黄。

外黄不下。数日,已降,项王怒,悉令男子年十五以上诣城东,欲坑之。外黄令舍人儿年十三,往说项王曰:"彭越强劫外黄,外黄恐,故且降,待大王。大王至,又皆坑之,百姓岂有归心? 从此以东,梁地十余城皆恐,莫肯下矣。"项王然其言,乃赦外黄当坑者。东至睢阳,闻之皆争下项王。

汉果数挑楚军战,楚军不出。使人辱之,五六日,大司马怒,渡兵汜水。士卒半渡,汉击之,大破楚军,尽得楚国货赂。大司马咎、长史翳、塞王欣皆自刭汜水上。大司马咎者,故蕲狱掾,长史欣亦故栎阳狱吏,两人尝有德于项梁,是以项王信任之。当是时,项王在睢阳,闻海春侯军败,则引兵还。汉军方围钟离眛于荥阳东,项王至,汉军畏楚,尽走险阻。

是时,汉兵盛食多,项王兵罢食绝。汉遣陆贾说项王,请太公,项王弗听。汉王复使侯公往说项王,项王乃与汉约,中分天下,割鸿沟以西者为汉,鸿沟而东者为楚。项王许之,即归汉王父母妻子。军皆呼万岁。汉王乃封侯公为平国君。匿弗肯复见,曰:"此天下辩士,所居倾国,故号为平国君。"项王已约,乃引兵解而东归。

汉欲西归,张良、陈平说曰:"汉有天下太半,而诸侯皆附之。楚兵罢食尽,此天亡楚之时也。不如因其机而遂取之。今释弗击,此所谓'养虎自遗患'也。"汉王听之。汉五年,汉王乃追项王至阳夏南,止军,与淮阴侯韩信、建成侯彭越期会而击楚军。至固陵,而信、越之兵不会。楚击汉军,大破之。汉王复入壁,深堑而自守。谓张子房曰:"诸侯不从约,为之奈何?"对曰:"楚兵且破,信、越未有分地,其不至固宜。君王能与共分天下,今可立致也。即不能,事未可知也。君王能自陈以东傅海,尽与韩信;睢阳以北至谷城,以与彭越。使各自为战,则楚易败也。"汉王曰:"善。"于是乃发使者告韩信、彭越曰:"并力击楚。楚破,自陈以东傅海与齐王,睢阳以北至谷城与彭相国。"使者至,韩信、彭越皆报曰:"请今进兵。"韩信乃从齐往,刘贾军从寿春并行,屠城父,至垓下。大司马周殷叛楚,以舒屠六,举九江兵,随刘贾、彭越皆会垓下,诣项王。

项王军壁垓下,兵少食尽,汉军及诸侯兵围之数重。夜闻汉军四面皆楚歌,项王乃大惊曰:"汉皆已得楚乎?是何楚人之多也!"项王则夜起,饮帐中。有美人名虞,常幸从;骏马名骓,常骑之。于是项王乃悲歌慷慨,自为诗曰:"力拔山兮气盖世,时不利兮骓不逝。骓不逝兮可奈何,虞兮虞兮奈若何!"歌数阕,美人和之。项王泣数行下,左右皆泣,莫能仰视。

于是项王乃上马骑,麾下壮士骑从者八百余人,直夜溃围南出,驰走。平明,汉军乃觉之,令骑将灌婴以五千骑追之。项王渡淮,骑能属者百余人耳。项王至阴陵，迷失道，问一田父，田父绐曰："左。"左，乃陷大泽中。以故汉追及之。项王乃复引兵而东，至东城，乃有二十八骑。汉骑追者数千人。项王自度不得脱，谓其骑曰："吾起兵至今八岁矣，身七十余战，所当者破，所击者服，未尝败北，遂霸有天下。然今卒困于此，此天之亡我，非战之罪也。今日固决死，愿为诸君快战，必三胜之，为诸君溃围，斩将，刈旗，令诸君知天亡我，非战之罪也。"乃分其骑以为四队，四向。汉军围之数重。项王谓其骑曰："吾为公取彼一将。"令四面骑驰下，期山东为三处。于是项王大呼驰下，汉军皆披靡，遂斩汉一将。是时，赤泉侯为骑将，追项王，项王瞋目而叱之，赤泉侯人马俱惊，辟易数里。与其骑会为三处，汉军不知项王所在。乃分军为三，复围之。项王乃驰，复斩汉一都尉，杀数十百人，复聚其骑，亡其两骑耳。乃谓其骑曰："何如？"骑皆伏曰："如大王言。"

于是项王乃欲东渡乌江。乌江亭长舣船待，谓项王曰："江东虽小，地方千里，众数十万人，亦足王也。愿大王急渡。今独臣有船，汉军至，无以渡。"项王笑曰："天之亡我，我何渡为！且籍与江东子弟八千人渡江而西，今无一人还，纵江东父兄怜而王我，我何面目见之！纵彼不言，籍独不愧于心乎！"乃谓亭长曰："吾知公长者，吾骑此马五岁，所当无敌，常一日行千里，不忍杀之。以赐公。"乃令骑皆下马步行，持短兵接战，独籍所杀汉军数百人。项王身亦被十余创。顾见汉骑司马吕马童，曰："若非吾故人乎？"马童面之，指王翳曰："此项王也。"项王乃曰："吾闻汉购我头千金，邑万户，吾为若德。"乃自刎而死。王翳取其头，余骑相蹂践争项王，相杀者数十人。最其后，郎中骑杨喜、骑司马吕马童、郎中吕胜、杨武各得其一体。五人共会其体，皆是。故分其地为五：封吕马童为中水侯，封王翳为杜衍侯，封杨喜为赤泉侯，封杨武为吴防侯，封吕胜为涅阳侯。

项王已死，楚地皆降汉，独鲁不下。汉乃引天下兵欲屠之，为其守礼义，为主死节，乃持项王头视鲁，鲁父兄乃降。始，楚怀王初封项籍为鲁公，及其死，鲁最后下，故以鲁公礼葬项王谷城。汉王为发哀，泣之而去。

诸项氏枝属，汉王皆不诛。乃封项伯为射阳侯。桃侯、平皋侯、玄武侯皆项氏,赐姓刘。

太史公曰:吾闻之周生曰"舜目盖重瞳子",又闻项羽亦重瞳子。羽岂其苗裔邪?何兴之暴也!夫秦失其政,陈涉首难,豪杰蜂起,相与并争,不可胜数。然羽非有尺寸,乘执起陇亩之中,三年,遂将五诸侯灭秦,分裂天下,而封王侯,政由羽出,号为"霸王"。位虽不终,近古以来未尝有也。及羽背关怀楚,放逐义帝而自立,怨王侯叛己,难矣。自矜功伐,奋其私智而不师古,谓霸王之业,欲以力征经营天下,五年卒亡其国,身死东城,尚不觉悟,而不自责,过矣。乃引"天亡我,非用兵之罪也",岂不谬哉!

Xiang Yu (Records of the Historian)

Xiang Ji, whose other name was Yu, was a man of Xiaxiang. He was twenty-four when he first rose in arms. His uncle Xiang Liang was the son of Xiang Yan, a general of Chu who was killed by the Qin general Wang Jian. For many generations the heads of the clan had been enfeoffed in Xiang as generals of Chu; hence Xiang became their family name.

As a lad Xiang Yu studied to be a scribe. Failing in this, he took up swordsmanship. When he failed in this too, Xiang Liang was angry with him, but he said:

"All scribes do is make lists of names, and swordsmen can only fight a single foe: that is not worth learning. I want to learn how to fight ten thousand foes."

Then, to his great joy, Xiang Liang taught him military strategy. But once he had a general grasp of the subject, Xiang Yu again refused to study to the end.

Xiang Liang was arrested at Yueyang, but procured a letter from Cao Jiu, gaoler of Ji, and presented this to Sima Xin, the gaoler of Yueyang, who thereupon let him go. Later Xiang Liang killed a man and fled from vengeance with Xiang Yu to Wu. As all the local figures lacked his ability, Xiang Liang generally took charge of large labour conscriptions or important funerals. And in secret he trained his followers and young men in the arts of war, to test their abilities.

When the First Emperor of Qin crossed the River Zhe on a visit to Kuaiji, Xiang Liang and Xiang Yu looked on.

"Why not take over from him?" exclaimed Xiang Yu.

"Don't talk so wildly!" said Xiang Liang, stopping his nephew's mouth. "Do you want our clan wiped out?" But this sent Xiang Yu up in his estimation.

Xiang Yu was over six feet tall and so strong that he could carry a bronze cauldron. He was more brilliant and ambitious than others, so that all the young men in the district stood in awe of him.

In the seventh month of the first year of the Second Emperor,[①] Chen She and his men rose in Daze. In the ninth month Yin Tong, governor of Kuaiji, summoned Xiang Liang and said:

"All the lower reaches of the Yangtse have revolted. Heaven is about to destroy the House of Qin. Whoever strikes first, they say, becomes a leader, while those who delay are led. I want to raise troops with you and Huan Chu as my generals."

Huan Chu was then an outlaw in the marshes.

"Huan Chu is an outlaw," replied Xiang Liang, "and no one but Xiang Yu knows where he is." He withdrew and told Xiang Yu to wait outside with his sword. Then he went back, sat down again by the governor and said, "Please summon Xiang Yu to take your orders to Huan Chu."

When the governor agreed, Xiang Liang called Xiang Yu in. After a moment he glanced at him and said, "The time has come!" Then Xiang Yu drew his sword and cut off the governor's head. Xiang Liang picked up the head and hung Yin Tong's seal and insignia on his own belt. The governor's men panicked and were thrown into confusion. Xiang Yu killed several scores of them. The whole office cowered in terror and no one dared stand against him. Then Xiang Liang summoned the chief citizens and some officers whom he knew, gave them his reasons for raising a revolt, and took command of the army of Wu. He sent officers to conscript men from the various districts and gathered a picked force of eight thousand men, appointing the best local men as his lieutenants, scouts and sergeants. One

---

① 译者注：209 B.C.

man complained that he had received no post, but Xiang Liang retorted:

"When I asked you to see to something at so-and-so's funeral, you let me down. That is why you are being passed over."

All agreed that this was just. Xiang Liang became the governor of Kuaiji with Xiang Yu as his adjutant, and they took over all the districts in that province.

Zhao Ping, a native of Guangling, attacked that city for Chen She but failed to take it. When he heard of Chen She's defeat and flight and of the Qin army's approach, he crossed the Yangtse and, pretending that he was acting on Chen She's orders, conferred on Xiang Liang the title of chief minister of Chu.

"You have conquered the land to the east," he said. "Lose no time now but lead your army west against Qin."

Xiang Liang at the head of his eight thousand men crossed the river and marched west. When he learned that Chen Ying had taken Dongyang, he sent an envoy to propose that they join forces and advance west together. Chen Ying had been secretary to the magistrate of Dongyang and was respected throughout the county for his integrity. After the young men there killed their magistrate, several thousands of men banded together and looked for a leader. Finding no one suitable, they approached Chen Ying. He declined with the excuse that he lacked ability, but they finally prevailed on him to take charge and some twenty thousand men of the county followed him. Then the young men wanted to set him up as their king and form a black-turbaned rebel force of their own.

Chen Ying's mother told him, "Since I married into your family, I have never heard that any of your ancestors ever attained noble rank. It is not safe to win fame overnight: you would do better to serve as a subordinate. Then if all goes well, you will be made a marquis; if things go badly, you can easily escape because you are not known to all."

So Chen Ying did not venture to become king. "The Xiang family has produced generals for several generations," he told his officers. "They are well known in Chu. If we want to revolt, we must have them on our side.

With the help of such a distinguished family, Qin can certainly be destroyed."

They took his advice and put their troops under Xiang Liang's command. After Xiang Liang crossed the River Huai, Ying Bu[①] and General Pu also came over to him with their men. The army, now nearly seventy thousand strong, encamped at Xiapi.

Meanwhile Qin Jia had made JingJu king of Chu and stationed his troops east of Pengcheng to block Xiang Liang's way.

"Chen She was the first to rise," said Xiang Liang to his officers. "But since his defeat we do not know what has become of him. Now Qin Jia has turned against him and made JingJu king. This is vile treachery!"

He led his men against Qin Jia and put him to flight. Xiang Liang pursued him to Huling, where Qin Jia turned to give battle. At the end of the day Qin Jia was dead and his men had surrendered. Jing Ju fled and perished in the land of Liang.

Xiang Liang took over Qin Jia's army and camped at Huling before marching west.

By now the Qin army led by Zhang Han had reached Li. Xiang Liang sent his generals Zhu Jishi and the lord of Yufan against him; but the lord of Yufan was killed and Zhu Jishi's army, routed, retreated to Huling. Xiang Liang led his men to Xue and killed Zhu Jishi. He had sent Xiang Yu to storm, Xiang Yu put all the defenders to the sword before going back to report to Xiang Liang.

When Xiang Liang heard for certain that Chen She was dead, he summoned his generals to Xue for a council. By this time Liu Bang, who had risen in Pei, had joined him.

Fan Zeng of Juchao, a man of seventy who held no public office, was a good strategist. Now he went to offer advice to Xiang Liang saying, "Chen She deserved to fall. Of the six kingdoms conquered by Qin, Chu was the most blameless. Ever since King Huai went to Qin and failed to return, the

---

① 译者注: Also known as Qing Pu.

people of Chu have never ceased to mourn him. That is why Nangong of Chu said, 'So long as three households are left in Chu, she will be the land to overthrow Qin.' But when Chen She rebelled, he set himself up as king instead of one of the House of Chu; thus his power was short-lived. Once you took up arms in the east, men of power in Chu raced to put themselves under your command, because you come of a line of generals of Chu and have it in your power to restore the royal house."

These words convinced Xiang Liang, who had a search made for the late King Huai's grandson Xin, who turned out to be herding sheep among the common people, and set him up as King Huai of Chu to satisfy popular feeling. Chen Ying was appointed his chief minister and given five counties as his fief. King Huai's capital was Xuyi. Xiang Liang himself took the title lord of Wuxin.

Some months later he led his army against Kangfu, then joined forces with Tian Rong of Qi and Marshal Sima Longju to relieve Dong'a, routing the forces of Qin there. Then Tian Rong led his troops back to Qi and drove away King Jia, who fled to Chu. His chief minister Tian Jiao fled to Zhao. Tian Jiao's younger brother Tian Jian, a former general of Qi, remained in Zhao, not daring to return. Then Tian Rong made Fu, son of Tian Dan, king of Qi. After defeating the forces of Qin at Dong'a, Xiang Liang set out in pursuit of them and sent several envoys to urge the generals of Qi to advance west with him.

Tian Rong's answer was, "We will send troops only if you kill Tian Jia and the king of Zhao kills Tian Jiao and Tian Jian."

"Tian Jia is the king of a friendly state who turned to us in time of need," objected Xiang Liang. "It would not be right to kill him." Neither would the king of Zhao kill the other two men to please Qi. So Qi sent no troops to aid Chu.

Xiang Liang dispatched Liu Bang and Xiang Yu to attack Chengyang. They slaughtered all the defenders and advanced west to defeat the Qin army east of Puyang. When the Qin forces withdrew into Puyang, Liu Bang and Xiang Yu attacked Dingtao but failed to take it. They marched west and occupied all the districts up to Yongqiu, where they inflicted another crushing defeat on the forces of Qin and beheaded Li You. They turned back to attack Waihuang, but could not take it.

Meanwhile Xiang Liang had set out from Dong'a and marched northwest to Dingtao, where once again he defeated the forces of Qin; and now that Xiang Yu and the others had beheaded Li You, he began to underestimate Qin and to grow arrogant.

Song Yi warned him, "A general who is arrogant and soldiers who slack off after a victory are sure to be defeated. Now your troops are taking it easy while the Qin army grows stronger every day. I am worried to think what will become of you."

Xiang Liang paid no attention, but sent Song Yi as his envoy to Qi. On the way Song Yi met Qi's envoy, Lord Xian of Gaoling.

"Are you going to see the lord of Wuxin (Xiang Liang)?" he asked him.

The other replied, "I am."

"I can tell you," said Song Yi, "that the lord of Wuxin is sure to be defeated. If you travel slowly, you may escape with your life. If you hurry, you will run into trouble."

All Qin's men were mobilized to reinforce Zhang Han, who attacked and routed the Chu army at Dingtao and killed Xiang Liang.

Liu Bang and Xiang Yu had left Waihuang to attack Chenliu, but the city was stubbornly defended and could not be taken. So they took counsel together. "Now that Xiang Liang's army has been routed, our men are scared," they said. They decided to go east with Lü Chen's troops. Lü Chen encamped east of Pengcheng, Xiang Yu west of Pengcheng and Liu Bang at Dang.

After defeating Xiang Liang, Zhang Han thought he had nothing to fear from the other Chu forces. He crossed the Yellow River to attack Zhao and routed its army completely. Zhao Xie, the king of Zhao, fled with his general Chen Yu and his chief minister Zhang Er to the city of Julu. Zhang Han ordered Wang Li and She Jian to besiege the city, while he stationed his own army to the south and constructed a fortified road to supply them with grain. The Zhao commander Chen Yu camped with several tens of thousands of men north of the city. This force was known as the Army North of the River.

After the defeat of the Chu army at Dingtao, King Huai of Chu took fright and moved from Xuyi to Pengcheng, where he combined the forces of Xiang Yu and Lü Chen under his own command. He appointed Lü Chen his chief commissary and his father Lü Qing prime minister. Liu Bang he made governor of Dang and marquis of Wu'an, in command of the troops of Dang.

Lord Xian of Gaoling, Qi's envoy whom Song Yi had once met and who was in the Chu army, informed King Huai, "Song Yi predicted the lord of Wuxin's defeat, and a few days later his army was indeed routed. Here is a man who understands warfare, who foresees defeat before a battle is fought."

King Huai summoned Song Yi for a talk and was so impressed that he appointed him commander-in-chief to rescue Zhao, and made Xiang Yu the duke of Lu and his second in command with Fan Zeng as third in command. All the other generals took orders from Song Yi, whose title was Lord Chief Marshal. They marched to Anyang and camped there for forty-six days without advancing.

"I hear that Qin is besieging the king of Zhao at Julu," said Xiang Yu. "If we cross the river quickly and attack from outside while the men of Zhao strike from within, we are bound to defeat the Qin army."

"No," objected Song Yi. "A gadfly which can sting a bull may not be able to kill a flea. Now Qin is attacking Zhao. If her men win they will be exhausted and we can take advantage of their weakness. If they lose we can march west with sounding drums and will certainly defeat them. Better let Qin and Zhao fight it out first. In feats of arms I am no match for you, but in strategy you are no match for me."

Then he issued this order to the troops: "Any man who is fierce as a tiger, stubborn as a sheep, greedy as a wolf, or disobedient to orders, will lose his head."

He appointed his son Song Xiang chief minister to the king of Qi and saw him to Wuyan, where he gave a banquet. The day was raw, a heavy rain was falling, and the men were hungry and cold.

Xiang Yu reflected, "Instead of hitting out hard at Qin, he has made us stay here all this time without moving. The harvest has failed, the people are destitute, and for lack of grain our men are eating taros and beans; yet he holds a great banquet! Instead of leading our troops across the river to get food from Zhao and join forces with Zhao to attack the enemy, he claims he is waiting for Qin to be exhausted. In fact, Qin is so powerful that if she attacks the newly formed state of Zhao, she is bound to defeat it. Once Zhao falls, Qin will grow even stronger. There will be no exhaustion for us to profit by. Besides, our men have recently been defeated, our king sits uneasy on his throne and has put all the resources of the kingdom at the command of Song Yi. Our whole country's future is at stake. Yet instead of caring for his troops, Song Yi attends to private affairs. He is betraying our country."

So one morning when he went to pay his respects to the marshal he entered Song Yi's tent and cut off his head. Coming out he announced to the army, "Song Yi was plotting with Qi against our state. King Huai sent me secret orders to execute him."

At this all the generals were awed into submission. "Your family first established our state," they said. "Now you have killed a traitor." They made Xiang Yu their acting commander-in-chief and sent men to Qi to capture and kill Song Yi's son. General Huan Chu was sent to report this to King Huai, who appointed Xiang Yu as commander-in-chief with the lord of Dangyang and General Pu under him.

By killing the Lord Chief Marshal Song Yi, Xiang Yu struck terror into the whole of Chu and his fame spread to other states. He sent the lord of Dangyang and General Pu across the river with twenty thousand men to raise the siege of Julu. As they met with little success, Chen Yu asked for reinforcements. Thereupon Xiang Yu led his entire force across the river.

They sank all their boats, smashed their cooking vessels, burned their huts, and carried only three day's rations with them to show their determination to fight to the death and never to turn back. They besieged Wang Li's troops, fought nine battles with the Qin army, cut its supply route and defeated it utterly. The Qin general Su Jiao was killed, Wang Li captured, and She Jian who refused to surrender perished in the fire.

By now the army of Chu outmatched all others. Ten or more armies from different states had entrenched themselves outside Julu to rescue the city, but none had dared take the field. When Chu attacked Qin, the others watched from their ramparts. Each soldier of Chu was a match for ten of the enemy. Their war-cries rent the sky, striking terror into the hearts of all who heard them. Thus when they defeated Qin and Xiang Yu summoned the other generals to his camp, they entered on their knees and none dared look up. Then Xiang Yu became commander-in-chief of the forces of these different states and their leaders took orders from him.

Zhang Han's army at Jiyuan and Xiang Yu's army south of the River Zhang confronted each other for some time without fighting. Because the Qin army had several times retreated, the Second Emperor sent an envoy to censure Zhang Han. Then the latter dispatched his secretary Sima Xin in alarm to Xianyang to ask for instructions. Three days Sima Xin waited outside the palace gate, but Zhao Gao would not see him as he did not trust him. At that Sima Xin was afraid and returned to the army by a different route. The pursuers Zhao Gao sent after him failed to overtake him.

Back with the army, Sima Xin reported, "With Zhao Gao in control there is nothing we can do. If we fight and win, he will envy our success. If we lose, he will have us killed. I hope you will think this over carefully."

Chen Yu sent Zhang Han a letter, saying:

"When Bai Qi was a general of Qin, he conquered Yan and Ying in the south and wiped out the army of the lord of Mafu in the north. He captured cities and territories past counting, yet at last he was ordered to die. Meng Tian, another general of Qin, drove away the Huns in the north and extended the territory of his state by several thousand square *li*; yet in the end his head was cut off at Yangzhou. Why was this? Because their achievements were too great for Qin to reward with fiefs large enough; hence some legal pretext was found for their execution."

"Now you have been a general of Qin for three years and lost hundreds of thousands of men, while rebellions in the different states are becoming more frequent. Zhao Gao has deceived and flattered the emperor so long that now the position is desperate he wants to make you a scapegoat to avoid being executed himself. He will take away your command to save his own skin."

"You have long been absent from the capital and have many enemies at court. You will be executed whether you win battles or not. Besides, Qin is destined to fall — wise and foolish alike can see that. Now you have no voice in the government, and if you remain at the front you will soon have no country of your own. Alone and unfriended you are, alas, doomed! Why not turn your army back and ally with the other states to attack Qin and divide the empire between you? Then you can be a king and reign supreme. This is surely better than dying by the axe and bringing destruction upon your own wife and children."

Zhang Han began to waver and secretly sent his officer Shi Cheng as an envoy to seek for some agreement with Xiang Yu. Before an agreement was reached, Xiang Yu dispatched General Pu with troops to cross Sanhu ford by night to the south bank of the River Zhang, where Pu attacked and defeated the army of Qin. Then Xiang Yu led his entire force against the Qin troops on the bank of the River Yu and completely routed them. When Zhang Han sent another envoy to seek for an agreement, Xiang Yu summoned his officers to discuss the matter.

"Our food supply is low," he said. "We had better accept his offer."

When his officers approved, Xiang Yu appointed a time to meet Zhang Han on the ruins of the old capital of Yin south of the River Huan, and there they reached an agreement. Zhang Han told Xiang Yu with tears what Zhao Gao had done, and Xiang Yu made him king of Yong and kept him in the Chu army. His secretary Sima Xin was appointed marshal of the Qin troops to lead them ahead of the main army to Xin'an.

Before this, the frontier garrisons conscripted from the eastern states had often received rough treatment at the hands of the soldiers of Qin when they passed through their territory. Now that the Qin forces had surrendered, the triumphant soldiers of the other states took their revenge by treating them as slaves and captives, humiliating and abusing them.

The men of Qin whispered among themselves, "Our commander Zhang Han tricked us into surrendering. If we enter the Pass and conquer Qin, well and good. But if we fail, they will send us east as captives and Qin will kill our parents, wives and children."

Xiang Yu's generals heard this talk and reported it, whereupon he summoned the lord of Dangyang and General Pu. "Qin's officers and men are still a large force," he said, "and in their hearts they have not submitted to us. Once inside the Pass, any disobedience would be dangerous. Before we enter Qin we had better kill them all but Zhang Han, Sima Xin his secretary, and Dong Yi his lieutenant."

So the Chu army attacked by night and massacred more than two hundred thousand Qin troops south of Xin'an.

They advanced conquering the land of Qin till they found their way barred by a force defending the Hangu Pass, which they were unable to storm. When word came that Liu Bang, lord of Pei, had already taken Xianyang, Xiang Yu flew into a passion. He made the lord of Dangyang and others storm the Pass and followed them to a place west of the River Xi.

Liu Bang's army was now at Bashang. Before he could meet with Xiang Yu, his left marshal Cao Wushang sent Xiang Yu this message: "The lord of Pei intends to be king inside the Pass, with Ziying[①] as his prime minister. He will keep all the jewels and treasures for himself."

In a rage Xiang Yu swore, "Tomorrow I shall feast my men, and then we will attack and smash Liu Bang's army!"

Xiang Yu then had four hundred thousand men encamped at Hongmen

---

① 译者注: The last ruler of Qin, who had surrendered.

near Xinfeng, and Liu Bang had one hundred thousand at Bashang.

Fan Zeng also told Xiang Yu, "When the lord of Pei was living east of the mountains, he was greedy for wealth and fond of beautiful women; but since entering the Pass he has taken neither loot nor women. This shows that he aims high. I sent men to watch the heavenly signs above his camp. They are off all colours and shaped like dragons and tigers — the signs of a Son of Heaven. You must lose no time in attacking him!"

Xiang Yu's uncle Xiang Bo, the vice-chancellor of Chu, was a friend of Zhang Liang, marquis of Liu, then in the service of Liu Bang. Xiang Bo galloped in secret to Liu Bang's camp that night to visit Zhang Liang and tell him what had happened. He urged Zhang Liang to go away with him.

"Otherwise you will perish!" he warned him.

But Zhang Liang replied, "The king of Han[①](403–230 B.C.) sent me here with the lord of Pei. It would not be right to desert him in the hour of danger. I must report this to him."

He went in and related everything to Liu Bang.

"What shall I do?" asked Liu Bang in great alarm.

"Who advised you to take this course?" inquired Zhang Liang.

"A fool of a scholar advised me to hold the Pass and not let the others in, for then I should be able to rule all Qin. I followed his plan."

"Do you think, my lord, that your troops can stand up to Xiang Yu?"

"Of course not," answered Liu Bang after a pause. "But what shall I do?"

"Let me tell Xiang Bo that the lord of Pei dares not oppose Xiang Yu."

"How do you happen to know Xiang Bo?"

"We became acquainted in the time of Qin, and I saved Xiang Bo's life once when he killed a man. Now that we are in danger, he was good enough to come and warn me."

"Which of you is the elder?"

---

① 译者注: Previously one of the Seven Warring States, now a nominal kingdom. It was Zhang Liang's native land.

"He is."

"Please ask him in. I shall treat him as I would an elder brother."

Zhang Liang brought Xiang Bo in to see Liu Bang, who offered him a goblet of wine, drank a toast to him, and pledged to link their families by marriage.

"Since I came through the Pass, I have not touched so much as a hair," he declared. "I have made a register of officials and citizens and sealed up the treasuries until the commander's arrival. I have sent officers to guard the Pass to prevent bandits going through it and to be ready for any emergency. Night and day I have been awaiting the commander. How dare I rebel against him? Please make it clear to him that I could not be so ungrateful."

Xiang Bo agreed to do so, adding, "You must come early tomorrow morning to apologize in person to Lord Xiang Yu."

This Liu Bang promised to do.

Then Xiang Bo went back by night to Xiang Yu's camp and told him all Liu Bang had said.

"If the lord of Pei had not conquered Qin, you would not have been able to enter," he pointed out. "It is wrong to attack a man who has done you so great a service. You had better treat him handsomely."

Xiang Yu agreed.

The next day Liu Bang, followed by some hundred horsemen, came to Xiang Yu's camp at Hongmen and made his apologies.

"I, your humble servant, joined with you to attack Qin," he said. "You fought north of the Yellow River while I fought south. I had not expected to be the first to enter the Pass and conquer Qin, so that we meet again here. Now some evil-minded man has been sowing doubt in your mind."

"It was your own officer Cao Wushang," replied Xiang Yu. "Otherwise such a thing would never have occurred to me."

Xiang Yu invited Liu Bang to stay for a banquet. He and Xiang Bo sat facing east, the patriarch Fan Zeng faced south; Liu Bang faced north and Zhang Liang, who was in attendance upon him, faced west. Several times

Fan Zeng shot Xiang Yu meaningful glances and three times, as a hint, raised his jade *jue*.① But Xiang Yu did not respond. Finally Fan Zeng rose and went out. Summoning Xiang Zhuang, he said:

"Our lord is too kind-hearted. Go in, drink a toast and offer to perform a sword dance. Then strike the lord of Pei down where he sits. If you don't do this, we will all end up his captives."

Xiang Zhuang went in to offer a toast, after which he said, "Our prince is drinking with the lord of Pei, but we have no entertainers in the army. May I perform a sword dance?"

"Very well," said Xiang Yu.

Xiang Zhuang drew his sword and began the dance, and Xiang Bo followed suit, shielding Liu Bang with his body so that Xiang Zhuang could not strike him.

Zhang Liang went out to the gate of the camp to see Fan Kuai, who asked, "How are things in there?"

"Touch and go," replied Zhang Liang. "Xiang Zhuang has drawn his sword to dance. He means to kill the lord of Pei."

"This is serious!" said Fan Kuai. "Let me go in and have it out with him."

Sword and shield in hand he entered the gate. Guards with crossed halberds tried to bar the way, but he charged and knocked them down with his tilted shield. Bursting into the tent, he lifted the curtain and stood facing west, glaring at Xiang Yu. His hair bristled, his eyes nearly started from his head. Xiang Yu raised himself on one knee and reached for his sword.

"Who is this stranger?" he asked.

"This is the lord of Pei's bodyguard, Fan Kuai," answered Zhang Liang.

"Stout fellow!" said Xiang Yu. "Give him a stoup of wine."

Wine was poured and presented to Fan Kuai, who bowed his thanks

---

① 译者注: An ornament in the form of a broken ring. He was hinting that Xiang Yu should break with Liu Bang.

and straightened up to drink it standing.

"Give him a leg of pork," directed Xiang Yu.

A raw leg of pork was given to Fan Kuai, who set his shield upside down on the ground, placed the pork on it, carved it with his sword and began to eat.

"Stout fellow!" cried Xiang Yu. "Can you drink any more?"

"I am not afraid of death; why should I refuse a drink?" retorted Fan Kuai. "The king of Qin had the heart of a tiger or a wolf. He killed more men than one could count and tortured others cruelly. So the whole world revolted against him. King Huai promised his generals that the first to conquer the land of Qin and enter its capital should be its king. Now the lord of Pei has conquered Qin and taken Xianyang. But he has not touched anything. He sealed up the palaces, withdrew his troops to Bashang to wait for you, and sent men to guard the Pass against bandits and other emergencies. Yet though he has laboured so hard and achieved so much, you do not reward him with noble rank but listen to worthless talk and decide to kill this hero. This is to go on in the way that led to the downfall of Qin. Please do not act like this, Your Majesty."

Xiang Yu could not answer.

"Sit down," he said.

Fan Kuai took a seat next to Zhang Liang. Presently Liu Bang got up and went out to the privy, beckoning Fan Kuai to go with him. Xiang Yu ordered his lieutenant Chen Ping to call him back.

"I've come out without taking leave," said Liu Bang. "What shall I do?"

"Where big issues are at stake you cannot trouble about trifles," said Fan Kuai. "In matters of consequence you cannot observe the minor courtesies. They are the chopper and board, we the fish and meat. Why should we take our leave?"

So Liu Bang started off, telling Zhang Liang to stay behind to make his excuses.

"What gifts did you bring with you, my lord?" asked Zhang Liang.

"A pair of white jade discs for Lord Xiang Yu, and a pair of jade wine cups for the patriarch Fan Zeng. Seeing how angry they were, I dared not present them. Will you please do so for me?"

"Very good, my lord," said Zhang Liang.

Now Xiang Yu's camp was at Hongmen and Liu Bang's at Bashang some forty *li* away. Leaving his chariot and retinue, Liu Bang rode off alone, followed on foot by Fan Kuai, Xiahou Ying, Jin Qiang and Ji Xin, who carried swords and shields. Skirting Mount Li, they took a short cut to Zhiyang.

"By this route it is only twenty *li* to my camp," Liu Bang had told Zhang Liang. "Wait until you think I have got there before you go back in."

When enough time had passed for him to reach his troops, Zhang Liang went in to apologize for him.

"The lord of Pei had too much to drink and was unable to take his leave," he said. "He asked your humble servant to present this pair of white jade discs to Your Lordship and this pair of jade wine cups to the Patriarch."

"Where is he now?" asked Xiang Yu.

"Knowing that your Lordship meant to censure him, he left alone. He must be in his camp by now."

Xiang Yu accepted the discs and placed them on his mat. But Fan Zeng put the jade cups on the ground, drew his sword and smashed them to pieces.

"Bah!" he cried. "Advice is wasted on a fool. The lord of Pei will wrest your empire from you and take us all captive."

As soon as Liu Bang reached his camp, he had Cao Wushang executed.

A few days later Xiang Yu led his troops west, massacred the citizens of Xianyang, killed Ziying, the last king of Qin who had surrendered, and set fire to the Qin palaces. The conflagration raged for three whole months. Having looted the city and seized the women there, he started east.

Someone advised him, "The region inside the Pass is surrounded by mountains and rivers which form natural barriers, and the soil is fertile.

You could make this your capital and rule supreme."

But now the Qin palaces were destroyed by fire and Xiang Yu longed to go back to his home in the east.

"What use are wealth and rank if you do not go home?" he retorted. "That is like wearing embroidered clothes at night when nobody can see you."

"They say the men of Chu are apes with hats on," observed a wit later. "It's really true."

When Xiang Yu heard this, he had the man thrown into a boiling cauldron.

Xiang Yu sent a messenger to report to King Huai.

"Let it be as we agreed," replied the king.

Then King Huai received the title of Righteous Emperor. Xiang Yu, who wished to be a king, first made the other generals and ministers kings.

"When the revolt broke out, we set up the descendants of different royal houses as a temporary measure to attack Qin," he said. "We are the ones, however, who took up arms, started the revolt and risked our lives on the battlefield for three years until Qin was overthrown and the empire pacified. The Righteous Emperor has done nothing. Let us divide up his land and make ourselves kings."

The generals agreed to this and they divided the empire, making themselves lords and kings.

Xiang Yu and Fan Zeng suspected that Liu Bang meant to seize the whole realm. But having settled their dispute with him, they hesitated to break their word for fear the other leaders might not support them. So they plotted together saying, "The lands of Ba and Shu are mountainous and impassable. That is where all the exiles used to be sent by Qin." Then, announcing that Ba and Shu were also inside the Pass, they made Liu Bang king of Han (206 B.C.-8 A.D.) to rule over Ba, Shu and Hanzhong, with his capital at Nanzheng. And Qin was divided into three kingdoms under the Qin generals who had surrendered, as buffer states against Han.

Xiang Yu made Zhang Han king of Yong to rule over the territory west of Xianyang with his capital at Feiqiu. His secreytary Sima Xin, the former gaoler of Yueyang who had helped Xiang Liang, was also made a king. So was the army commander Dong Yi, who had advised Zhang Han to surrender to Xiang Yu.

Sima Xin became king of Sai, ruling over the territory east of Xianyang as far as the Yellow River, with his capital at Yueyang. Dong Yi was made king of Di to rule Shangjun Province with his capital at Gaonu. King Bao of Wei (403–225 B. C.) was sent west to be king of West Wei, ruling over Hedong with his capital at Pingyang. ShenYang of Xiaqiu, Zhang Er's favourite who had conquered the province of Henan and surrendered to the Chu army by the river, was made king of Henan with his capital at Luoyang. King Cheng of Han (403–230 B. C.) remained where he was, with Yangzhai as his capital. Sima Ang, a general of Zhao who had conquered Henei and won several victories, was made king of Yin over Henei with his capital at Chaoge. King Xie of Zhao was transferred to be king of Dai. Zhang Er, the able chief minister of Zhao who had accompanied the Chu army through the Pass, was made king of Changshan ruling over Zhao with his capital at Xiangguo.

Ying Bu, lord of Dangyang, who had proved the bravest general of the Chu army, was made king of Jiujiang with his capital at Liu. Wu Rui, lord of Po, who had led the Bai Yue tribesmen as reinforcements to the feudal princes and followed Xiang Yu through the Pass, was made king of Hengshan with his capital at Zhu. Gong Ao, the Righteous Emperor's minister who had led troops against Nanjun and won many victories, was made king of Linjiang with his capital at Jiangling.

Han Guang, king of Yan, was transferred to be king of Liaodong. The Yan general Zang Tu, who had joined the Chu forces to rescue Zhao and accompanied Xiang Yu through the Pass, was made king of Yan with his capital at Qi. Tian Fu, king of Qi, was transferred to be king of Jiaodong. The Qi general Tian Du, who had joined the Chu forces to rescue Zhao and accompanied Xiang Yu through the Pass, was made king of Qi with his capital at Linzi.

Then there was Tian An, grandson of the former king of Qi, who was coquered by Qin. When Xiang Yu crossed the river to rescue Zhao, Tian An took several cities north of the River Ji and came over to Xiang Yu with his forces. He was therefore made king of Jibei, with his capital at Boyang.

Tian Rong, who had often disobeyed Xiang Liang's orders and refused to aid Chu against Qin, was given no title. Though Chen Yu, lord of Cheng'an, had abandoned his commander's seal and refused to follow Xiang Yu into the Pass, he was known to be a talented man who had served Zhao well. When it was learned that he was at Nanpi, he was given three adjacent counties. Mei Juan, a general under the lord of Po who had many bold deeds to his credit, received a fief of one hundred thousand households. As for Xiang Yu, he set himself up as Overlord of West Chu, with nine provinces as his kingdom and Pengcheng as his capital.

In the fourth month of the first year of Han (206 B.C.–8 A.D.),[1] the various kings withdrew their troops and returned to their own countries. When Xiang Yu reached his kingdom, he gave orders for the removal of the Righteous Emperor, saying, "In ancient times an emperor who had one thousand square *li* of territory always lived on the upper reaches of a river." His envoy told the emperor to move to the district of Chen in Changsha, and kept urging him to go till one by one the emperor's ministers left him. Then Xiang Yu secretly ordered the kings of Hengshan and Linjiang to attack and kill the emperor on the river.

As King Cheng of Han (403–230 B.C.) had won no victories, Xiang Yu prevented his return to his kingdom by taking him to Pengcheng. There, having degraded him to rank of a marquis, he killed him. When Zang Tu went to his state of Yan, he tried to drive away the former king, Han Guang, to Liaodong. As Han Guang refused to go, Zang Tu attacked and killed him at Wuzhong and annexed his territory.

When Tian Rong heard that Xiang Yu had removed the king of Qi to Jiaodong, setting up the Qi general Tian Du in his stead, he was very angry

---

① 译者注: 206 B.C.

and refused to let Tian Du take up his new position in Qi but rose in arms and attacked him. Tian Du fled to the land of Chu. Since King Wang Shi was afraid of Xiang Yu, he fled to Jiaodong, his new realm. Tian Rong pursued him in anger and killed him at Jimo. Then Tian Rong made himself king of Qi and marched west to attack and kill Tian An, king of Jibei. He now ruled over Qi, Jiaodong and Jibei. Tian Rong gave Peng Yue a commander's seal and ordered him to revolt in the land of Wei. Chen Yu also sent Zhang Tong and Xia Yue in secret to advise him.

"Xiang Yu has not divided the country fairly," they said. "He has made all the former kings rulers of poor lands, but made his generals and ministers kings of rich districts. He drove the former king of Zhao north to the land of Dai. We do not think this is right. Now we hear Your Highness has taken up arms, unable to endure this injustice. We hope you will lend us troops to attack Changshan and restore the king of Zhao. We will gladly serve as your bulwark."

Tian Rong agreed and sent troops to the land of Zhao. Chen Yu mobilized the men of his three counties and together they attacked Changshan and routed Zhang Er, who fled to Han(206 B.C.-8 A.D.). Then Chen Yu welcomed back the former king of Zhao from Dai, and the king made Chen Yu king of Dai.

At this time, the Han army turned back and conquered the three kingdoms of Yong, Sai and Di. When Xiang Yu heard that the king of Han had gained control of all the land within the Pass and was about to march east, and that Qi and Zhao had rebelled, he was very angry. He made Zheng Chang, former governor of Wu, king of Han (403–230 B.C.) to repel the king of Han's advance, and ordered Jiao the lord of Xiao and others to attack Peng Yue. But Peng Yue defeated them.

The king of Han (206 B.C.-8 A.D.) dispatched Zhang Liang to conquer Han (403–230 B.C.), and he wrote to Xiang Yu saying, "The king of Han has not received the territory promised him within the Pass. As soon as the agreement is carried out, he will halt and not advance any further east." He also sent Xiang Yu letters showing that Tian Rong and Peng Yue meant to revolt, that Qi would ally with Zhao to overthrow Chu.

Then instead of advancing west, Xiang Yu proceeded north to attack Qi. He ordered Ying Bu, the king of Jiujiang, to bring up reinforcements; but Ying Bu did not join him on the pretext of illness, merely sending a general with several thousand men. Xiang Yu hated him for this.

In the winter of the second year of Han (206 B. C.-8 A. D.), Xiang Yu went north to Chengyang, where Tian Rong joined battle with him. Tian Rong was defeated and fled to Pingyuan, to be killed by the people there. Xiang Yu advanced further north, and burned or razed to the ground all the suburbs of Qi, massacred Tian Rong's men who had surrendered, and took captive the old and infirm as well as the women. He conquered the land up to Beihai, spreading havoc and destruction. Then the men of Qi gathered together and rebelled. Tian Rong's younger brother, Tian Heng, rallied what was left of the army, numbering tens of thousands of men, and raised a revolt at Chengyang. Xiang Yu was forced to stop and launch several assaults against the city, but he failed to take it.

The following spring, the king of Han advanced east at the head of the allied troops of five states, five hundred and sixty thousand strong, to attack Chu. When Xiang Yu received word of this, he sent his generals to subdue Qi in the north, while he himself led thirty thousand picked troops south through Lu to Huling.

In the fourth month, the Han soldiers entered Pengcheng, sacked the city, seized the women, and gave all their time to carousing. Xiang Yu struck at dawn from Xiao in the west and fell upon the Han army at Pengcheng in the east. By noon the Han forces were completely routed. They fled in disorder to the Gu and Si Rivers, where more than one hundred thousand of them were drowned. The rest retreated south to the hills, but the army of Chu pursued them to the banks of the River Sui, east of Lingbi. The Han troops fell back, hard pressed by the men of Chu. Some hundred thousand soldiers of Han were cut down and their bodies, thrown into the Sui, blocked the flow of the river. The pursuers threw three cordons round the king of Han. But just then a great wind sprang up from the northwest.

It blew down trees and houses and raised swirling clouds of sand so that all grew dark and day turned into night. This storm beat against the army of Chu and threw it into confusion. Their ranks broke, enabling the king of Han to escape with several dozen horsemen.

The king of Han set out for Pei, meaning to take his family west with him. But as Xiang Yu also sent pursuers to Pei, the king's family fled and missed him. On the road he met his son, later Emperor Hui, and his daughter, later Queen Yuan of Lu, and made them ride in his carriage. When the Chu cavalry came hot on their heels, the king in desperation pushed his children out; but Xiahou Ying, lord of Teng, got down and helped them in again. This happened three times. "No matter how hard pressed we are, we cannot drive any faster," protested Xiahou Ying. "How can you abandon them?"

When they had made good their escape, the king of Han looked in vain for his father and his wife, later Empress Lü. They, escorted by Shen Yiji, were searching for him when they ran into some Chu troops instead. The men of Chu reported their capture to Xiang Yu, who kept them in his army.

At this time Empress Lü's brother, Lü Ze, was in command of the Han troops at Xiayi. There the king of Han went, rallying stragglers on the way. By the time he reached Xingyang all his defeated soldiers had reassembled. Xiao He also mobilized all the old and weak within the Pass who had not been conscripted, and sent them to Xingyang. Thus their army became a force to reckon with again.

The Chu troops, advancing from Pengcheng, followed up their victory and fought the Han army south of Xingyang between Jing and Suoting. But the men of Han defeated them there, checking their advance further west.

While Xiang Yu was relieving Pengcheng and pursuing the king of Han to Xingyang, Tian Heng was able to reconquer Qi and set up Tian Rong's son, Tian Guang, as king there. After Han's defeat at Pengcheng, all the other kings went over to Xiang Yu. The king of Han camped at Xingyang and constructed a walled road to the Yellow River to convey grain from Aocang.

In the third year of Han, Xiang Yu repeatedly cut this supply route so that the Han army ran short of food. The king of Han in alarm sued for peace, claiming only the territory west of Xingyang. Xiang Yu would have agreed, but Fan Zeng marquis of Liyang said, "The Han army is easy to crush. If you let them go, you will be sorry later." So Xiang Yu and Fan Zeng hammered at Xingyang.

In this desperate situation the king of Han adopted a plan devised by Chen Ping to sow dissension between Xiang Yu and Fan Zeng. When an envoy from Xiang Yu arrived, the king made ready a feast; but as it was being served he pretended to show great surprise on seeing who the envoy was.

"I thought you were Fan Zeng's envoy," he explained. "I see you come from Xiang Yu."

He had the feast removed and more common fare brought in.

When the envoy went back and reported this, Xiang Yu suspected Fan Zeng of being in league with Han, and little by little deprived him of his authority. Fan Zeng was very angry.

"The empire is nearly won," he said. "Your Highness can manage alone. Allow me to retire to the ranks."

Xiang Yu gave his consent. But before Fan Zeng reached Pengcheng he had an abscess on his back and died.

Then Ji Xin, a general of Han, said to the king, "We are in desperate straits, sir. Let me impersonate you to deceive the Chu army so that you may escape."

One night the king sent the women of Xingyang together with two thousand soldiers out through the east gate, and the Chu troops attacked them from all sides. Ji Xin, in the carriage with the yellow canopy and the feather pennant on the left, came out to declare, "There is no food left in the city. The king of Han surrenders."

While all the Chu soldiers were cheering, the king of Han slipped out through the west gate with a few dozen horsemen and fled to Chenggao. When Xiang Yu saw Ji Xin, he demanded: "Where is your king?"

"His Majesty had already left," was the answer.

Xiang Yu had Ji Xin burned alive.

The king of Han had entrusted the defence of Xingyang to his chief counsellor Zhou Ke, Lord Zong and Bao, once king of Wei (403-225 B.C.). Zhou Ke and Lord Zong took counsel together and said, "A rebel king can hardly be trusted to defend the city." Thereupon they killed Bao.

Then the Chu army stormed the city and captured Zhou Ke alive.

"If you will serve as my general, I will make you a chief marshal with a fief of thirty thousand families," said Xiang Yu.

But Zhou Ke swore at him, "Unless you surrender soon, the king of Han will capture you. You are no match for him."

In a rage, Xiang Yu had him thrown into the cauldron and killed Lord Zong as well.

After escaping from Xingyang, the king of Han fled south to Wan and She. He won over Ying Bu, king of Jiujiang, and raised troops to defend Chenggao.

In the fourth year of Han, Xiang Yu laid siege to Chenggao. The king fled alone with Lord Teng through the north gate, crossed the river and went to Xiuwu to join the army of Zhang Er and Han Xin. One by one his generals escaped from Chenggao and joined him. When the Chu army took Chenggao and started westwards, the king of Han sent troops to hold Gong and check their advance.

At this point Peng Yue crossed the river and attacked Dong'a in Chu, killing the Chu general Lord Xue. So Xiang Yu turned east to fight Peng Yue. Now that the king of Han had Han Xin's army, he wanted to cross the Yellow River and head south, but on Zheng Zong's advice he stayed in his positions north of the river, sending Liu Jia with troops to aid Peng Yue and burn the Chu supplies. In the east Xiang Yu defeated Peng Yue and put him to flight.

The king struck across the river and recaptured Chenggao, stationed his army on Mount Guangwu and drew supplies from Aocang. Having conquered the land in the east, Xiang Yu marched west again. He, too, stationed his army opposite Mount Guangwu, confronting the forces of Han. This stalemate lasted for some months.

Meanwhile Peng Yue continued to rebel in Liang and to intercept the Chu army's grain supply, which seriously worried Xiang Yu. He had a high scaffold built on which he set the king of Han's father.

"Surrender at once, or I shall boil your father alive!" he threatened.

"Together we received King Huai's orders and swore to be brothers," replied the king of Han. "That makes my father yours as well. If you insist on boiling your own father, do send me a bowl of the soup!"

In a great rage Xiang Yu prepared to kill the old man, but Xiang Bo reasoned with him saying, "It is not yet settled who will win the empire, and a man who aspires to be emperor will not trouble about his family. Killing him could serve no purpose but only make for trouble."

Xiang Yu listened to his advice.

For a long time Chu and Han had battled yet neither had won a decisive victory. The able-bodied men were weary of fighting while the old and weak were exhausted by grain transportation. Xiang Yu made a proposal to the king of Han.

"Because of us, the empire has been in a tumult for years. Let us settle the issue now by hand-to-hand combat instead of involving all these other men."

The king declined with a smile.

"I prefer to fight with my wits," he said, "not with brute force."

Then Xiang Yu ordered his best fighters to challenge the men of Han to single combat. In the Han army there was a skilled mounted archer named Lou Fan, who with his arrows killed each Chu warrior after a few rounds of fighting. Xiang Yu in a fury buckled on armour himself and rode out with his halberd to do battle. As Lou Fan raised his bow, Xiang Yu glared and bellowed so fiercely that the bowman dared not meet his eyes or shoot but fled back to the rampart, too terrified to take the field again. When the king of Han sent to ask the reason and found that this warrior was Xiang Yu himself, he was terrified. Xiang Yu called to the king across the lines on

Mount Guangwu. The king enumerated Xiang Yu's faults, while Xiang Yu angrily challenged him to a fight, but his challenge was not accepted. Then Xiang Yu shot him with a crossbow he had concealed, and the king fled, wounded, to Chenggao.

When Xiang Yu learned that Han Xin had conquered the land north of the Yellow River, defeated the armies of Qi and Zhao and was about to invade Chu, he sent General Long Ju to attack him. Han Xin and Guan Ying, the cavalry commander, struck back and utterly routed the Chu army, killing LongJu. Han Xin then set himself up as king of Qi.

Alarmed to hear of General Longju's defeat, Xiang Yu sent Wu She, a native of Xuyi, to win Han Xin over, but with no success.

Meanwhile Peng Yue had reconquered Liang and cut the Chu army's supply route. Xiang Yu told his high marshal Cao Jiu, marquis of Haichun, and the other generals, "See you defend Chenggao well. If the Han army challenges you, do not give battle. Simply stop them advancing eastwards. In fifteen days, when I have killed Peng Yue and retaken Liang, I shall join you again."

He marched east and attacked Chenliu and Waihuang on the way, but Waihuang held out against him for several days before it finally surrendered. In his rage he ordered all the men above fifteen to be taken to the east of the city, where he meant to have them massacred.

The thirteen-year-old son of the magistrate's steward went to him and said, "Peng Yue forced Waihuang to rebel, and because the city was afraid it submitted to him, waiting for Your Highness to come to the rescue. But now that you are here you want to butcher our men. How can you win the hearts of the people like this? East of here there are more than a dozen cities of Liang, and now they will all be afraid to surrender to you."

Xiang Yu saw the truth in what this lad said, and pardoned those who were to have been massacred. When this became known, all the cities east to Suiyang promptly surrendered.

The Han army challenged the Chu troops in Chenggao several times, but they would not be drawn. Then men were sent to insult them, until after five or six days the high marshal Cao Jiu lost his temper and started leading his men across the River Si. When half the army was across, the men of Han attacked and routed them, capturing all the treasure of the kingdom of Chu. The high marshal Cao Jiu, the secretary Dong Yi and Sima Xin, king of Sai, killed themselves by the river. Cao Jiu, former gaoler of Qi, and Sima Xin, former gaoler of Yueyang, had been trusted by Xiang Yu because of the help they had once given Xiang Liang.

At this time Xiang Yu was at Suiyang. When he learned of his army's defeat he led his troops back. The soldiers of Han were besieging Zhongli Mo east of Xingyang. At Xiang Yu's approach, they withdrew in fear to the heights.

Now the Han army was strong and had ample supplies, while Xiang Yu's troops were exhausted and had no food. The king of Han dispatched Lu Jia to ask Xiang Yu to send his father back, but Xiang Yu refused. Then the king sent Lord Hou to persuade him. This time Xiang Yu agreed to divide the empire into two. The land west of Honggou should go to Han, that east of Honggou to Chu. This agreement reached, Xiang Yu handed over the king's father and wife, while all the soldiers cheered. The king of Han called Lord Hou the Leveller of States, but would not let him appear again.

"This man is the world's greatest orator," he explained. "Wherever he goes, he causes kingdoms to fall. That is why I call him the leveller of states."

After making this agreement, Xiang Yu led his army east.

The king of Han prepared to go west, but Zhang Liang and Chen Ping advised against this saying, "You now have the greater half of the empire and the support of all the states, while the army of Chu is exhausted and has no food. Heaven has decreed Xiang Yu's downfall. You should seize this opportunity to crush him. To let Xiang Yu go now would be like bringing up a tiger — simply asking for trouble in future."

The king took their advice.

In the fifth year of Han, the king pursued Xiang Yu to south of

Yangxia and stationed his troops there, appointing a date to attack with Han Xin, marquis of Huaiyin, and Peng Yue, marquis of Jiancheng. But when he reached Guling their armies failed to appear. Xiang Yu attacked and defeated the men of Han, who retreated to their ramparts and strengthened their defences.

"The marquises have failed me. What shall I do?" the king of Han asked Zhang Liang.

"Chu is about to be crushed, but Han Xin and Peng Yue have not been given fiefs," replied Zhang Liang. "No wonder they stayed away. If you will divide the empire with them, they will come immediately. If not, the issue is by no means certain. Give Han Xin the land from Chen east to the coast, give Peng Yue the land from Suiyang north to Gucheng, so that they will be fighting for themselves. Then Chu can easily be defeated."

"Very good," said the king of Han.

He sent envoys to inform Han Xin and Peng Yue, "If you join us to attack Chu, I will give all the land between Chen and the sea to Han Xin, king of Qi, all that between Suiyang and Gucheng to Chancellor Peng Yue when Xiang Yu is defeated."

After the envoys reached them, Han Xin and Peng Yue agreed to send troops at once. Han Xin advanced from Qi while Liu Jia led his army from Shouchun, took Chengfu and wiped out its defenders. Then both forces reached Gaixia. Marshal Zhou Yin also rebelled against Xiang Yu and marched from Shu to take Liu and massacre its defenders. In addition, the army of Ying Bu, king of Jiujiang, followed the armies of Liu Jia and Peng Yue. These forces converged upon Xiang Yu at Gaixia.

Xiang Yu's army at Gaixia, with only a handful of troops and right out of supplies, was hemmed in by the men of Han and the other states. At night he heard the besiegers all about him singing Chu songs.

"Has Han already conquered Chu?" he asked in dismay. "They have so many men of Chu with them!"

He rose that night to drink in his tent. With him was the lovely Lady Yu, who followed wherever he went, and Zhui, the swift steed which he always rode. Now Xiang Yu chanted a tragic air, setting words to it himself:

> My strength uprooted mountains,
>
> My spirit overtopped the world;
>
> But the times are against me,
>
> And Zhui can gallop no more.
>
> When Zhui can gallop no more
>
> What can I do?
>
> And what is to become
>
> Of Lady Yu?

He sang this song several times and Lady Yu joined in. Tears coursed down his cheeks, while all his followers wept and bowed their heads in sorrow.

Then he mounted his horse and rode into the night with little more than eight hundred staunch followers. Breaking through the enemy lines to the south, they galloped away.

By dawn the Han army knew that he had escaped, and the cavalry officer Guan Ying was sent with five thousand horsemen in pursuit. By the time Xiang Yu crossed the River Huai, there were little more than a hundred horsemen with him. At Yinling he lost his way and asked an old man in the fields to direct him. "Bear left!" The old man deliberately deceived him, and going left he was bogged down in the marshes so that the Han cavalry came up with him.

So Xiang Yu turned back east to Dongcheng. By now only twenty-eight horsemen remained with him, while his pursuers numbered several thousand. He knew that he could not escape and told his men:

"It is eight years since I rose in arms. In that time I have fought more than seventy battles. I swept all obstacles from my path, conquered every foe I attacked, and was never defeated. That is how I won the empire. But now suddenly I am hemmed in here. This is because Heaven is against me and not because my generalship is at fault. Today I shall perish here, but for your sake I shall fight gallantly and overcome the enemy three times. For you I shall break through their lines, kill their commander and cut down their flag, so that you may know it is Heaven that has destroyed me, not my generalship that is fault."

He divided his horsemen into four groups, facing in four directions. The Han forces had surrounded them on all sides.

"Watch me kill one of their commanders for you!" he cried.

He ordered his men to gallop down in four directions and reassembled in three groups east of the hill. Then with a mighty battle-cry he charged. The Han troops scattered before him and he struck down one of their commanders. A cavalry commander named Yang Xi, the marquis of Chiquan, pursued him. But Xiang Yu glared and bellowed at him so fiercely that Yang Xi's horse bolted and fled, terrified, for several *li*.

Xiang Yu rejoined his men, who by now had reassembled in three groups. The Han forces, not knowing which group he was in, divided into three to surround them again. Once more Xiang Yu charged through their lines and killed a military tribune as well as several dozen men. When he rallied his followers again, he had lost only two of them.

"How was that?" he asked.

His men bowed and replied, "You were as good as your word, Your Majesty."

Xiang Yu now considered crossing the River Wujiang and going to the east of the Yangtse. The station master there had a boat moored and waiting. "There is not much land east of the Yangtse," he said to Xiang Yu. "But a thousand square *li* and several hundred thousand men are enough for a kingdom. You must cross quickly, Your Highness! Mine is the only boat here. When the Han army comes, they will not be able to cross."

"Heaven is against me," replied Xiang Yu with a laugh. "What use is it to cross the river? Besides, I once crossed the Yangtse and went west with eight thousand young men from the east, but now I have come back alone. Even if the elders made me king out of pity, how could I face them again? Though they said nothing, how could I hold up my head?" He turned to the station master. "I can see you are a worthy man. For five years I have ridden this horse, sweeping all before me, often galloping a thousand *li* in one day. I cannot bear to kill him. I give him to you."

He ordered his men to dismount for hand-to-hand combat. Xiang Yu alone killed several hundred men of Han and was wounded some dozen times. Then, turning to see the cavalry officer Lü Matong, he exclaimed:

"Isn't that my old friend Lü?"

Lü Matong, facing him, pointed him out to Wang Yi.

"There is Xiang Yu!"

Xiang Yu said, "I hear the king of Han has offered a reward of a thousand gold pieces and a fief of ten thousand families for my head. Let me do you a good turn!" With that he cut his own throat.

Wang Yi seized his head, while the other horsemen trampled and jostled each other for his body — several dozen of them fought and killed each other. Finally a cavalryman of the guard, Yang Xi, the cavalry marshal Lü Matong, and the knights Lü Sheng and Yang Wu secured one limb each. When the five of them fitted the limbs together, it was seen that they were indeed those of Xiang Yu, and the fief was divided among them. Lü Matong was made marquis of Zhongshui, Wang Yi marquis of Duyan, Yang Xi marquis of Chiquan, Yang Wu marquis of Wufang, and Lü Sheng marquis of Nieyang.

After Xiang Yu's death all the districts in Chu surrendered except Lu. The king of Han prepared to muster the troops of the whole country to massacre the inhabitants. But because they had proved loyal and ready to die for their master, Xiang Yu's head was displayed to them. And thereupon the elders of Lu surrendered.

As King Huai of Chu had made Xiang Yu lord of Lu and this district was the last to surrender after his death, Xiang Yu was buried at Gucheng with the rites befitting the lord of Lu. The king of Han, before leaving, conducted the funeral in person and shed tears.

Instead of punishing Xiang Yu's kinsmen, the king made Xiang Bo marquis of Yiyang. The marquises of Tao, Pinggao and Xuanwu, all of whom belonged to the Xiang clan, were given the royal surname Liu.

The Grand Historian comments: I heard from the scholar Zhou that Emperor Shun had double pupils in his eyes, and they say Xiang Yu was the same. Does this mean that he was a descendant of Shun? His rise was remarkably sudden. When the Qin government abused its power and Chen She started a rebellion, the brave men who flocked to him were too many to count. Xiang Yu had no inch of territory at the start, yet, taking this chance to rise in the countryside, within three years he commanded five states and overthrew the House of Qin. He carved up the empire and enfeoffed kings and barons. He was supreme, styling himself the Overlord, and though his rule did not endure his achievement was surely unique in recent times.

But when he gave up the land within the Pass to return to Chu, banished the Righteous Emperor and set himself up in his stead, he could hardly complain when the kings and barons turned against him. He boasted of his conquests, trusted only his personal judgement and did not follow ancient precedents. Considering himself the overlord, he tried to win the empire by military conquest, so that within five years he lost his kingdom and met his death at Dongcheng. Yet he never realized his mistake or blamed himself for his folly. What a fool he was to say that Heaven was against him and that it was not his generalship that was at fault!

五

红楼梦(第三、二十七回)^①

第三回　托内兄如海荐西宾　接外孙贾母惜孤女

却说雨村忙回头看时,不是别人,乃是当日同僚一案参革的号张如圭者。他本系此地人,革后家居,今打听得都中奏准起复旧员之信,他便四下里寻找门路,忽遇见雨村,故忙道喜。二人见了礼,张如圭便将此信告诉雨村,雨村自是欢喜,忙忙的叙了两句,遂作别各自回家。冷子兴听得此言,便忙献计,令雨村央烦林如海,转向都中去,央烦贾政。雨村领其意,作别回去,至馆中,忙寻邸报看真确了。

次日,面谋之如海。如海道:"天缘凑巧,因贱荆去世,都中家岳母念及小女无人依傍教育,前已遣了男女船只来接,因小女未曾大痊,故未及行。此刻正思向蒙训教之恩,未经酬报,遇此机会,岂有不尽心图报之理?但请放心。弟已预为筹画至此,已修下荐书一封,转托内兄,务为周旋协佐,方可稍尽弟之鄙诚,即有所费用之例,弟于内兄信中,已注明白,亦不劳尊兄多虑矣。"雨村一面打恭,谢不释口,一面又问:"不知令亲大人现居何职?只怕晚生草率,不敢遽然入都干渎。"如海笑道:"若论舍亲,与尊兄系同谱,乃荣公之孙;大内兄现袭一等将军之职,名赦,字恩侯;二内兄名

---

①　中文、英译文选自:曹雪芹,高鹗.红楼梦(大中华文库·汉英对照).杨宪益,戴乃迭译.北京:外文出版社;长沙:湖南人民出版社,1999.

政,字存周,现任工部员外郎,其为人谦恭厚道,大有祖父遗风,非膏粱轻薄仕宦之流,故弟方致书烦托。否则不但有污尊兄之清操,即弟亦不屑为矣。"雨村听了,心下方信了昨日子兴之言,于是又谢了林如海。如海乃说:"已择了正月初六日小女入都,尊兄即同路入都,岂不两便?"雨村唯唯听命,心中十分得意。如海遂打点礼物并饯行之事,雨村一一领了。

那女学生黛玉,身体方愈,原不忍弃父而往;无奈他外祖母执意要他去,且兼如海说:"汝父年将半百,再无续室之意;且汝多病,年又极小,上无亲母教育,下无姊妹兄弟扶持,今依傍外祖母,及舅氏姊妹,正好减我顾盼之忧,何反云不往?"黛玉听了,方洒泪拜别,随了奶娘,及荣府中几个老妇人登舟而去。雨村另有一只船,带二个小童,依黛玉而行。

有日到了都中,进了神京,雨村先整了衣冠,带了小童,拿着"宗侄"的名帖,至荣府的门前投了。彼时贾政已看了妹丈之书,即忙请入相会。见雨村相貌魁伟,言语不俗,且这贾政最喜读书人,礼贤下士,拯弱济危,大有祖风;况又系妹丈致意,因此优待雨村,更又不同,便竭力内中协力,题奏之日,轻轻谋了一个复职候缺,不上两个月,金陵应天府缺出,便谋补了此缺,拜辞了贾政,择日到任去了,不在话下。

且说黛玉自那日弃舟登岸时,便有荣国府打发了轿子并拉行李的车辆久候。这林黛玉常听见母亲说过,他外祖母家,与别家不同。他近日所见的这几个三等仆妇,吃穿用度,已是不凡了,何况今至其家。因此步步留心,时时在意,不肯轻易多说一句话,多行一步路,惟恐被人耻笑了他去。自上轿进入城中,从纱窗向外瞧了一瞧,其街市之繁华,人烟之阜盛,自与别处不同。又行了半日,忽见街北蹲着两个大石狮子,三间兽头大门,前列坐着十来个华冠丽服之人。正门却不开,只有东西两角门有人出入。正门上有匾,匾上大书"敕造宁国府"五个大字。黛玉想道,这必是外祖之长房了。想着,又往西行不多远,照样也是三间大门,方是荣国府了。却不进正门,只进了西角门。那轿夫抬进去,走了一箭之地,将转弯时,便歇下,退出去了。后面的婆子们已都下了轿,赶上前来;另换了三四个衣帽周全,十七八岁的小厮上来,复抬起轿子。众婆子步下围随,至一垂花门前落下。众小厮退出,众婆子上来打起轿帘,扶黛玉下了轿。林黛玉扶着婆子的手,进了垂花门,两边是抄手游廊,当中是穿堂,当地放一个紫檀架子的大理石的大插屏。转过插屏,小小三间厅,厅后就是后面的正房大院。正面五间上房,皆是雕梁画栋,两边穿山游廊厢房,挂着各色鹦鹉、画眉等鸟雀。台阶之上,坐着几个穿红着绿的丫头,一见他们来了,便忙都笑迎上来,说:"刚才老太太还念呢,可巧就来了。"于是三四人争着打起帘子,一面听得人回话说:"林姑娘到了。"

黛玉方进入房时,只见两个人搀着一位鬓发如银的老母迎上来,黛玉便知是他外祖母。方欲拜见时,早被他外祖母一把搂入怀中,心肝儿肉叫着大哭起来。当下地下侍立之人,无不掩面涕泣,黛玉也哭个不住。一时众人慢慢解劝住了,黛玉方拜见了外祖母。此即冷子兴所云之史氏太君也,贾赦、贾政之母。当下贾母一一的指与黛玉:"这是你大舅母;这是你二舅母;这是你先珠大哥的媳妇珠大嫂。"黛玉一一拜见过。贾母又说:"请姑娘们来。今日远客才来,可以不必上学去了。"众人答应了一声,便去了两个。

不一时,只见三个奶嬷嬷并五六个丫鬟,簇拥着三个姊妹来了。第一个肌肤微丰,合中身材,腮凝新荔,鼻腻鹅脂,温柔沉默,观之可亲。第二个削肩细腰,长挑身材,鸭蛋脸面,俊眼修眉,顾盼神飞,文彩精华,见之忘俗。第三个身材未足,形容尚小。其钗环裙袄,三人皆是一样的妆饰。黛玉忙起身迎上来见礼,互相厮认过,各归座了。丫鬟们斟上茶来。不过说黛玉之母如何得病,如何请医服药,如何送死发丧。不免贾母又伤感起来,因说:"我这些儿女,所疼者独有你母,今日一旦先舍我而去,连面不能一见,今见了你,我怎不伤心!"说着,搂了黛玉在怀,又呜咽起来。众人忙都宽慰解释,方略略止住。

众人见黛玉年貌虽小,其举止言谈不俗,身体面庞虽怯弱不胜,却有一段自然风流态度,便知他有不足之症。因问:"常服何药,如何不急为疗治?"黛玉笑道:"我自来是如此,从会吃饮食时,便吃药,到今未断,请了多少名医,修方配药,皆不见效。那一年,我才三岁时,听得说来了一个癞头和尚,说要化我去出家,我父母因不从他。又说:'既舍不得他,只怕他的病一生也不能好的了。若要好时,除非从此以后总不许见哭声;除父母之外,凡有外姓亲友之人,一概不见,方可平安了此一世。'疯疯癫癫,说了这些不经之谈,也没人理他。如今还是吃'人参养荣丸'。"贾母道:"这正好,我这里正配丸药呢。叫他们多配一料就是了。"

一语未了,只听后院中有人笑声,说:"我来迟了,不曾迎接远客!"黛玉纳罕道:"这些人个个皆敛声屏气,恭肃严整如此,这来者系谁,这样放诞无礼?"心下想时,只见一群媳妇丫鬟围拥着一个人,从后房进来。这个人打扮与众姑娘不同,彩绣辉煌,恍若神妃仙子:头上戴着金丝八宝攒珠髻,绾着朝阳五凤挂珠钗;项上带着赤金盘螭璎珞圈;裙边系着豆绿宫绦双鱼比目玫瑰佩;身上穿着缕金百蝶穿花大红洋缎窄褃袄,外罩五彩刻丝石青银鼠褂;下罩翡翠洒花洋绉裙。一双丹凤三角眼,两弯柳叶吊梢眉,身量苗条,体格风骚,粉面含春威不露,丹唇未启笑先闻。黛玉连忙起身接见。贾母笑道:"你不认得他,他是我们这里有名的一个泼皮破落户儿,南省俗谓作'辣子',你只叫他'凤辣子'就是了。"黛玉正不知以何称呼,只见众姊妹都忙告诉道:"这是琏嫂子。"黛玉虽不认识,曾听见母亲说过,大舅贾赦之子贾琏,娶的就是二舅母王氏之内侄女,自幼假充男儿教养的,学名王熙凤。黛玉忙陪笑见礼,以"嫂"呼之。这熙凤携着黛玉的手,上下细细的打谅了一回,仍送至贾母的身边坐下,因笑道:"天下真有这样标致人物,我今才算见了!况且这通身的气派,竟不像老祖宗的外孙女儿,竟是个嫡亲的孙女,怨不得老祖宗天天口头心头一时不忘。只可怜我这妹妹这样命苦,怎么姑妈偏就去世了!"说着,便用帕拭泪。贾母笑道:"我才好了,你倒来招我。你妹妹远客才来,身子又弱,也才劝住了,快再休提前言。"这熙凤听了,忙转悲为喜道:"正是呢!我一见妹妹,一心都在他身上了,又是喜欢,又是伤心,竟忘记了老祖宗。该打,该打!"又忙携黛玉之手,问:"妹妹几岁了?可也上过学?现吃什么药?在这里,不要想家,想要什么吃的、什么玩的,只管告诉我;丫头老婆们不好了,也只管告诉我。"

一面又问婆子们："林姑娘的行李东西可搬进来了？带了几个人来？你们赶早打扫两间下房,让他们去歇歇。"

说话时,已摆了茶果上来。熙凤亲为捧茶捧果。又见二舅母问他："月钱放完了不曾?"熙凤道："月钱已放完。才刚带着人到后楼上找缎子,找了这半日,也并没有见昨日太太说的那样,想是太太记错了。"王夫人道："有没有,什么要紧。"因又说道："该随手拿出两个来,给你这妹妹去裁衣裳的,等晚上想着,叫人再去拿罢,可别忘了。"熙凤道："这倒是我先料着了,知道妹妹不过这两日到的,我已预备下了,等太太回去,过了目,再送来。"王夫人一笑,点头不语。

当下茶果已撤,贾母命两个老嬷嬷带了黛玉去见两个舅舅。时贾赦之妻邢氏忙亦起身,笑回道："我带了外甥女过去,倒也便宜。"贾母笑道："正是呢,你也去罢,不必过来了。"邢夫人答应了一声"是"字,遂带了黛玉与王夫人作辞,大家送至穿堂前。出了垂花门,早有众小厮们拉过一辆翠幄青油车,邢夫人携了黛玉坐上,众婆子们放下车帘,方命小厮们抬起,拉至宽处,方驾上驯骡,亦出了西角门,往东过荣府正门,便入一黑油大门中,至仪门前方下来。众小厮退出,方打起车帘,邢夫人挽着黛玉手,进入院中。黛玉度其房屋院宇,必是荣府中花园隔断过来的。进入三层仪门,果见正房厢庑游廊,悉皆小巧别致,不似方才那边轩峻壮丽;且院中随处之树木山石皆有。一时进入正室,早有许多盛妆丽服之姬妾丫鬟迎着,邢夫人让黛玉坐了,一面命人到外面书房请贾赦。一时人来回说："老爷说了:'连日身子不好,见了姑娘彼此倒伤心,暂且不忍相见。劝姑娘不要伤心想家,跟着老太太和舅母,是同家里一样。姊妹们虽拙,大家一处伴着,亦可以解些烦闷。或有委屈之处,只管说得,不要外道才是。'"黛玉忙站起来,一一听了。再坐一刻,便告辞。邢夫人苦留吃过晚饭去,黛玉笑回道："舅母爱恤赐饭,原不应辞,只是还要过去拜见二舅舅,恐领了赐去不恭,异日再领,未为不可。望舅母容谅。"邢夫人听说,笑道："这倒是了。"遂令两三个嬷嬷,用方才的车,好好送了过去。于是黛玉告辞。邢夫人送至仪门前,又嘱咐了几句,眼看着车去了,方回来。

一时黛玉进入荣府,下了车。众嬷嬷引着,便往东转弯,穿过一个东西的穿堂,向南大厅之后,仪门内大院落,上房五间大正房,两边厢房鹿顶耳房钻山四通八达,轩昂壮丽,比贾母处不同。黛玉方知这便是正经正内室,一条大甬路,直接出大门的。进入堂屋中,抬头迎面,先看见一个赤金九龙青地大匾,匾上写着斗大三个大字,是"荣禧堂",后有一行小字,是"某年月日,书赐荣国公贾源",又有"万几宸翰之宝"。大紫檀雕螭案上,设着三尺来高青绿古铜鼎,悬着待漏随朝墨龙大画,一边是金蜼彝,一边是玻璃盒。地下两溜十六张楠木交椅,又有一副对联,乃乌木联牌,镶着錾银字迹,道是:

座上珠玑昭日月,堂前黼黻焕烟霞。

下面一行小字,道是:"同乡世教弟勋袭东安郡王穆莳拜手书。"

原来王夫人时常居坐宴息,亦不在正室,在东边的三间耳房内。于是老嬷嬷引黛玉进东房门来。临窗大炕上铺着猩红洋罽,正面设着大红金钱蟒靠背,石青金钱蟒引枕,秋香色金钱蟒大条褥。两边设一对梅花式洋漆小几。左边几上文王鼎匙箸香盒;右边几上汝窑美人觚,内插着时鲜花卉,并茗碗唾壶等物。地下面西一溜四张椅上,都搭着银红撒花椅披,底下四副脚踏。椅之两边,也有一对高几,几上茗碗瓶花俱备。其余陈设,自不必细说。老嬷嬷们让黛玉炕上坐,炕沿上却有两个锦褥对设,黛玉度其位次,便不上炕,只向东边椅子上坐了。本房内丫鬟忙捧上茶来。黛玉一面吃茶,一面打量这些丫鬟们,妆饰衣裙,举止行动,果亦与别家不同。

茶未吃了,只见一个穿红绫袄、青缎掐牙背心的丫鬟走来笑说道:"太太说,请林姑娘到那边坐罢。"老嬷嬷听了,于是又引黛玉出来,到了东廊三间小正房内。正房炕上横着一张炕桌,桌上堆着书籍茶具,靠东壁面西,设着青缎靠背引枕。王夫人却坐在西边下首,亦是青缎靠背坐褥。见黛玉来了,便往东让。黛玉心中料定是贾政之位。因见挨炕一溜三张椅子上,也搭着半旧弹墨椅袱,黛玉便向椅上坐了。王夫人再四携他上炕,他方挨王夫人坐了。王夫人因说:"你舅舅今日斋戒去了,再见罢。只是有一句话嘱咐你，你三个姊妹，倒都极好，以后一处念书、认字、学针线，或是偶一玩笑，都有尽让的。但我不放心的，最是一件：我有一个孽根祸胎，是这家里的'混世魔王'，今日因庙里还愿去了，尚未回来，晚间你看见便知了。你只以后不要睬他，你这些姊妹都不敢沾惹他的。"

黛玉亦常听得母亲说过，二舅母生的有个表兄，乃衔玉而诞，顽劣异常，极恶读书，最喜在内帏厮混；外祖母又极溺爱，无人敢管。今见王夫人如此说，便知说的是这表兄了。因陪笑道："舅母说的，可是衔玉所生的这位哥哥？在家时亦曾听见母亲常说，这位哥哥比我大一岁，小名就唤宝玉，虽极憨顽，在姊妹情中极好的。况我来了，自然只和姊妹一处，兄弟们自是别院另室的，岂有去沾惹之理？"王夫人笑道："你不知道原故。他与别人不同，自幼因老太太疼爱，原系同姊妹们一处娇养惯了的。若姊妹们不理他，他倒还安静些，纵然他没趣，不过出了二门，背地里拿着他两个小幺儿出气，咕唧一会子就完了。若这一日姊妹们和他多说一句话，他心里一乐，便生出多少事来。所以嘱咐你别睬他。他嘴里一时甜言蜜语，一时有天无日，一时又疯疯傻傻，只休信他。"

黛玉一一都答应着。只见一个丫鬟来回："老太太那里传晚饭了。"王夫人忙携黛玉，从后房门。由后廊往西，出了角门，是一条南北宽过道。南边是倒座三间抱厦厅，北边立着一个粉油大影壁，后有一半大门，小小一所房室。王夫人笑指向黛玉道："这是你凤姐姐的屋子，回来你好往这里找他来，少什么东西，你只管和他说就是了。"这院门上也有四五个才总角的小厮，垂手侍立。王夫人遂携黛玉，穿过一个东西穿堂，便是贾母的后院了。于是，进入后房门，已有多人在此伺候，见王夫人来了，方安桌椅。贾珠之妻李氏捧饭，熙凤安箸，王夫人进羹。贾母正面榻上独坐，两边四张空椅，熙凤忙拉了黛玉在左边第一张椅上坐了，黛玉十分推让。贾母笑道："你舅母和嫂子们不在这里吃饭。你是客，原应如此坐的。"黛玉方告了座，坐了。贾母命王夫人坐了。迎春姊妹三个告了座方上来。迎春便坐右手第一，探春左第二，惜春右第二。旁边丫鬟执着拂尘、漱盂、巾帕。李、凤二人立于案旁布让。外间伺候之媳妇丫鬟虽多，却连一声咳嗽不闻。寂然饭毕,各有丫鬟用小茶盘捧上茶来。当日林如海教女以惜福养身,云饭后务待饭粒咽完,过一时再吃茶,方不伤脾胃。今黛玉见了这里许多事情不合家中之式,不得不随的,少不得一一改过来,因而接了茶。早见人又捧过漱盂来,黛玉也照样漱了口。然后盥手毕,又捧上茶来,这方是吃的茶。贾母便说:"你们去罢,让我们自在说话儿。"王夫人听了,忙起身,又说了两句闲话,方引李、凤二人去了。贾母因问黛玉念何书,黛玉道:"只刚念了《四书》。"黛玉又问姊妹们读何书,贾母道:"读的是什么书,不过是认得两个字,不是睁眼瞎子罢了!"

一语未了,只听院外一阵脚步响,丫鬟进来笑道:"宝玉来了!"黛玉心中正疑惑着:"这个宝玉,不知是怎生个惫懒人物,懵懂顽童?倒不见那蠢物也罢了",心中正想着,忽见丫鬟话未报完,已进来了一位年轻的公子:头上戴着束发紫金冠,齐眉勒着二龙抢珠金抹额;穿一件二色金百蝶穿花大红箭袖,束着五彩丝攒花结长穗宫绦,外罩石青起花八团倭缎排穗褂;登着青缎粉底小朝靴。面若中秋之月,色如春晓之花,鬓若刀裁,眉如墨画,脸如桃瓣,睛若秋波。虽怒时而若笑,即瞋视而有情。项上金螭璎珞,又有一根五色丝绦,系着一块美玉。黛玉一见,便吃一大惊,心下想着:"好生奇怪,倒象在那里见过一般,何等眼熟到如此!"只见这宝玉向贾母请了安,贾母命:"去见你娘来。"宝玉即转身去了。一时回来,再看,已换了冠带:头上周围一转的短发,都结成了小辫,红丝结束,共攒至顶中胎发,总编一根大辫,黑亮如漆,从顶至梢,一串四颗大珠,用金八宝坠角;身上穿着银红撒花半旧大袄,仍旧带着项圈、宝玉、寄名锁、护身符等物;下面半露松花色洒花绫裤腿,锦边弹墨袜,厚底大红鞋。越显得面如敷粉,唇若施脂;转盼多情,语言常笑。天然一段风骚,全在眉梢;平生万种情思,悉堆眼角。看其外貌,最是极好,却难知其底细。后人有《西江月》二词,批宝玉极合,其词曰:

> 无故寻愁觅恨,有时似傻如狂。纵然生得好皮囊,腹内原来草莽。
> 潦倒不通世务,愚顽怕读文章。行为偏僻性乖张,那管世人诽谤!

富贵不知乐业，贫穷难耐凄凉。可怜辜负好时光，于国于家无望。

天下无能第一，古今不肖无双。寄言纨袴与膏粱，莫效此儿形状！

　　贾母因笑道："外客未见，就脱了衣裳，还不去见你妹妹！"宝玉早已看见多了一个姊妹，便料定是林姑妈之女，忙来作揖。厮见毕，归坐，细看形容，与众各别：两弯似蹙非蹙罥烟眉，一双似喜非喜含情目。态生两靥之愁，娇袭一身之病。泪光点点，娇喘微微。闲静时如姣花照水，行动处似弱柳扶风。心较比干多一窍，病如西子胜三分。宝玉看罢，因笑道："这个妹妹我曾见过的。"贾母笑道："可又是胡说，你又何曾见过他？"宝玉笑道："虽然未曾见过他，然我看着面善，心里就算是旧相识，今日只作远别重逢，亦未为不可。"贾母笑道："更好，更好，若如此，更相和睦了。"宝玉便走近黛玉身边坐下，又细细打量一番，因问："妹妹可曾读书？"黛玉道："不曾读，只上了一年学，些须认得几个字。"宝玉又道："妹妹尊名是那两字？"黛玉便说了名。宝玉又问表字。黛玉道："无字。"宝玉笑道："我送妹妹一个妙字，莫若'颦颦'二字极妙。"探春便问何出？宝玉道：《古今人物通考》上说：'西方有石名黛，可代画眉之墨。'况这林妹妹眉尖若蹙，用取这两个字，岂不两妙！"探春笑道："只恐又是你的杜撰。"宝玉笑道："除《四书》外，杜撰的太多，偏只我是杜撰不成？"又问黛玉："可也有玉无有？"众人不解其语，黛玉便忖度着因他有玉，故问我有也无，因答道："我没有那个。想来那玉，亦是件罕物，岂能人人有的。"宝玉听了，登时发作起痴狂病来，摘下那玉，就狠摔去，骂道："什么罕物，连人之高低不择，还说'通灵'不'通灵'呢！我也不要这劳什古子了！"吓的众人一拥争去拾玉。贾母急的搂了宝玉道："孽障！你生气，要打骂人容易，何苦摔那命根子！"宝玉满面泪痕哭道："家里姐姐妹妹都无有，单我有，我说无趣；如今来了一个神仙似的妹妹，也无有，可知这不是个好东西。"贾母忙哄他道："你这妹妹，原有这个来的，因你姑妈去世时，舍不得你妹妹，无法可处，遂将他的玉带了去：一则权当殉葬之礼，尽你妹妹的孝心；二则你姑妈之灵，亦可权作常得见女之意。因此他只说无有，不便自己夸张之意。你如今怎比得他？还不好生慎重带上，仔细你娘知道了。"说着，便向丫鬟手中接来，亲与他带上。宝玉听如此说，想一想，竟大有情理，也就不生别论了。

当下，奶娘来问黛玉之房舍。贾母说："今将宝玉挪出来，同我在套间暖阁里，把你林姑娘暂安碧纱橱里。等过了春天，再与他们收拾房屋，另作一番安置罢。"宝玉道："好祖宗，我就在碧纱橱外的床上很妥当，何必又出来，闹的老祖宗不得安静。"贾母想了一想说："也罢了。"每人一个奶娘，并一个丫头照管，余者在外间上夜听唤。一面早有熙凤命人送了一顶藕色花帐，并几件锦被缎褥之类。

黛玉只带了两个人来，一个是自己奶娘王嬷嬷，一个是十岁的小丫头，亦是自幼随身的，名唤雪雁。贾母见雪雁甚小，一团孩气，王嬷嬷又极老，料黛玉皆不遂心省力的，便将自己身边一个二等丫头，名唤鹦哥者，与了黛玉。外亦如迎春等例，每人除自幼乳母外，另有四个教引嬷嬷，除贴身掌管钗钏盥沐两个丫鬟外，另有五六个洒扫房屋来往使唤的小丫鬟。当下，王嬷嬷与鹦哥陪侍黛玉在碧纱橱内。宝玉之乳母李嬷嬷，并大丫鬟名唤袭人者，陪侍在外大床上。

原来这袭人亦是贾母之婢，本名珍珠。贾母因溺爱宝玉，生恐宝玉之婢无竭力尽忠之心，素喜袭人心地纯良，肯尽职任，遂与了宝玉。宝玉因知他本姓花，又曾见旧人诗句上有"花气袭人"之句，遂回明贾母，即更名袭人。这袭人亦有些痴处：伏侍贾母时，心中眼中只有一个贾母；今与了宝玉，心中眼中又只有一个宝玉。只因宝玉性情乖僻，每每规谏宝玉，宝玉不听，心中着实忧郁。

是晚，宝玉、李嬷嬷已睡了，他见里面黛玉和鹦哥犹未安歇，他自卸了妆，悄悄地进来，笑问："姑娘怎么还不安歇？"黛玉忙笑让道："姐姐请坐。"袭人在床沿上坐了。鹦哥笑道："林姑娘正在伤心，自己淌眼抹泪的，说：'今儿才来，就惹出你家哥儿的狂病来，倘或摔坏了那玉，岂不是因我之过！'因此便伤心，我好容易劝好了。"袭人道："快休如此，将来只怕比这个更奇怪的笑话儿还有呢！若为他这种行止，你多心伤感，只怕伤感不了呢。快别多心！"黛玉道："姐姐们说的，我记着就是了。究竟不知那玉是怎么个来历？上面还有字迹?"袭人道:"连一家子也不知来历,听得说,落草时从他口里掏出。上面有现成穿眼,让我拿来你看便知。"黛玉忙止道:罢了,此刻夜深了,明日再看不迟。"大家又叙了一回,方才安歇。

　　次日起来,省过贾母,因往王夫人处来,正值王夫人与熙凤在一处拆金陵来的书信看,又王夫人之兄嫂处遣了两个媳妇来说话的。黛玉虽不知原委,探春等却都晓得,是议论金陵城中所居的薛家姨母之子,姨表兄薛蟠,倚仗势力,打死人命,现在应天府案下审理。如今母舅王子腾得了信息,故遣人来告诉这边,意欲唤取进京之意。且听下回分解。

第二十七回　滴翠亭杨妃戏彩蝶　埋香冢飞燕泣残红

　　话说林黛玉正自悲泣,忽听院门响处,只见宝钗出来了,宝玉、袭人一群人送了出来。待要上去问着宝玉,又恐当着众人问羞了宝玉不便,因而闪过一旁,让宝钗去了。宝玉等进去关了门,方转过来,犹望着门洒了几点泪。自觉无味,方转身回来,无精打彩的卸了残妆。

　　紫鹃、雪雁素日知道林黛玉的情性:无事闷坐,不是愁眉,便是长叹;且好端端的不知为什么,常常的便自泪道不干的。先时还有人解劝,怕他思父母,想家乡,受了委曲,只得用话宽慰解劝。谁知后来一年一月的竟常常的如此,把这个样儿看惯,也都不理论了。所以也没人去理,由他去闷坐,只管睡觉去了。那林黛玉倚着床栏杆,两手抱着膝,眼睛含着泪,好似木雕泥塑的一般,直坐到二更多天,方才睡了。一宿无话。

　　至次日,乃是四月二十六日,原来这日未时交芒种节。尚古风俗:凡交芒种节的这日,都要设摆各色礼物,祭饯花神。言芒种一过,便是夏日了,众花皆卸,花神退位,须要饯行。然闺中更兴这件风俗,所以大观园中之人都早起来了。那些女孩子们,或用花瓣柳枝编成轿马的,或用绫锦纱罗叠成干旄旌幢的,都用彩线系了。每一棵树、每一枝花上,都系了这些物事。满园里绣带飘飘，花枝招展，更兼这些人打扮得桃羞杏让，燕妒莺惭，一时也道不尽。

　　且说宝钗、迎春、探春、惜春、李纨、凤姐等并同了大姐、香菱与众丫鬟们在园内玩耍，独不见林黛玉。迎春因说道："林妹妹怎么不见？好个懒丫头！这会子还睡觉不成？"宝钗道："你们等着，等我去闹了他来。"说着，便丢下众人，一直往潇湘馆来。正走着，只见文官等十二个女孩子也来了，上来问了好，说了一回闲话。宝钗回身指道："他们都在那里呢，你们找他们去。我叫林姑娘去就来。"说着，便逶迤往潇湘馆来。忽然抬头见宝玉进去了，宝钗便站住，低头想了一想："宝玉和林黛玉是从小儿一处长大，他兄妹间多有不避嫌疑之处，嘲笑喜怒无常；况且林黛玉素习猜忌，好弄小性儿的。此刻自己也跟了进去，一则宝玉不便，二则黛玉嫌疑。罢了，倒是回来的妙。"想毕，抽身回来。

　　刚要寻别的姊妹去，忽见前面一双玉色蝴蝶，大如团扇，一上一下迎风翩跹，十分有趣。宝钗意欲扑了来玩耍，遂向袖中取出扇子来，向草地下来扑。只见那一双蝴蝶忽起忽落，来来往往，穿花度柳，将欲过河去了。倒引的宝钗蹑手蹑脚的，一直跟到池中滴翠亭上，香汗淋漓，娇喘细细。宝钗也无心扑了，刚欲回来，只听滴翠亭里边嘁嘁喳喳有人说话。原来这亭子四面俱是游廊曲桥，盖在池中水上，四面雕镂槅子糊着纸。

　　宝钗在亭外听见说话，便煞住脚往里细听。只听说道："你瞧瞧这手帕子，果然是你丢的那块，你就拿着；要不是，就还芸二爷去。"又有一人说话："可不是我那块！拿来给我罢。"只听道："你拿什么谢我呢？难道自寻了来不成。"又答道："我既许了谢你，自然不哄你的。"又听说道："我寻了来给你，自然谢我；但只是拣的人，你就不拿什么谢他？"又回道："你别胡说。他是个爷们家，拣了我们的东西，自然该还的。我拿什么谢他呢？"又听说道："你不谢他，我怎么回他呢？况且他再三再四的和我说了，若没谢的，不许我给你呢。"半晌，又听答道：也罢，拿我这个给他，算谢他的罢。你要告诉别人呢？须说个誓来。"又听说道："我要告诉一个人，就长一个疔，日后不得好死！"又听说道：嗳呀！咱们只顾说话，看有人来悄悄在外头听见。不如把这槅子都推开了，便是人见咱们在这里，他们只当我们说玩话呢。若走到跟前，咱们也看的见，就别说了。"宝钗在外面听见这话，心中吃惊，想道："怪道从古至今那些奸淫狗盗的人，心机都不错。这一开了，见我在这里，他们岂不臊了。况才说话的语音，大似宝玉房里红儿的言语。他素昔眼空心大，是个头等刁钻古怪东西。今儿我听了他的短儿，一时人急造反，狗急跳墙，不但生事，而且我还没趣。如今便赶着躲了，料也躲不及，少不得要使个'金蝉脱壳'的法子。"犹未想完，只听"咯吱"一声，宝钗便故意放重了脚步，笑说道："颦儿，我看你往那里藏！"一面说，一面故意往前赶。那亭内的红玉、坠儿刚一推窗，只听宝钗如此说着往前赶，两个人都唬怔了。宝钗反向他二人笑道："你们把林姑娘藏在那里了？"坠儿道："何曾见林姑娘了？"宝钗道："我才在河边看着林姑娘在这里蹲着弄水儿的。我要悄悄的唬他一跳，还没有走到跟前，他倒看见我了，朝东一绕就不见了。别是藏在这里头了。"一面说，一面故意进去寻了一寻，抽身就走，口内说道："一定又钻在山子洞里去了。遇见蛇，咬一口也罢了。"一面说，一面走，心中又好笑：这件事算遮过去了，不知他二人是怎样。

谁知红玉听了宝钗的话，便信以为真。让宝钗去远，便拉坠儿道：了不得了！林姑娘蹲在这里，一定听了话去了！"坠儿听说，也半日不言语。红玉又道："这可怎么样呢？"坠儿道："便是听见了，管谁筋疼，各人干各人的就完了。"红玉道："若是宝姑娘听见，还倒罢了。林姑娘嘴里又爱刻薄人，心里又细，他一听见了，倘或走露了风声，怎么样呢？"二人正说着，只见文官、香菱、司棋、待书等上亭子来了。二人只得掩住这话，且和他们玩笑。

只见凤姐儿站在山坡上招手叫，红玉连忙弃了众人，跑至凤姐前，堆着笑问："奶奶使唤作什么事？凤姐打量了一打量，见他生的干净俏丽，说话知趣，因笑道："我的丫头今儿没跟进我来。我这会子想起一件事来，要使唤个人出去，不知你能干不能干，说的齐全不齐全？"红玉笑道："奶奶有什么话，只管吩咐我说去。若说的不齐全，误了奶奶的事，凭奶奶责罚就是了。"凤姐笑道:"你是那位小姐房里的? 我使你出去,他回来找你,我好替你说的。"红玉道:"我是宝二爷房里的。"凤姐听了,笑道:"嗳哟! 你原是宝玉房里的,怪道呢。也罢了,等他问,我替你说。你到我们家,告诉你平姐姐:外头屋里桌子上汝窑盘子架儿底下放着一卷银子,那是一百六十两,给绣匠的工价,等张材家的来要,当面称给他瞧了,再给他拿去。再里头床头间有一个小荷包拿了来。"

红玉听说,撤身去了,回来只见凤姐不在这山坡子上了。因见司棋从山洞里出来,站着系裙子,便赶上来问道:"姐姐,可知道二奶奶往那里去了? 司棋道:"没理论。"红玉听了,抽身又往四下里一看,只见那边探春、宝钗在池边看鱼。红玉上来陪笑问道:"姑娘们可知道二奶奶那去了?"探春道:"往你大奶奶院里找去。"红玉听了,才往稻香村来,顶头的只见晴雯、绮霰、碧痕、紫绡、麝月、待书、入画、莺儿等一群人来了。晴雯一见了红玉,便说道:"你只是疯罢! 院子里花儿也不浇,雀儿也不喂,茶炉子也不烧,就在外头逛。"红玉道:昨儿二爷说了,今儿不用浇花,过一日浇一回罢。我喂雀儿的时候,姐姐还睡觉呢。"碧痕道:"茶炉子呢?"红玉道:"今儿不该我烧的班儿,有茶没茶别问我。"绮霰道:"你听听他的嘴! 你们别说了,让他逛去罢。"红玉道:"你们再问问我逛了没逛? 二奶奶使唤我说话、取东西的。"说着,将荷包举给他们看,方没言语了,大家分路走开。晴雯冷笑道:"怪道呢! 原来爬上高枝儿去了,把我们不放在眼里。不知说了一句话半句话,名儿姓儿知道了不曾呢,就把他兴的这个样! 这一遭半遭儿的算不得什么,过了后儿还听得么! 有本事从今儿出了这园子,长长远远的在高枝儿上才算得。"一面说着去了。

这里红玉听说,不便分证,只得忍着气来找凤姐儿。到了李氏房中,果见凤姐儿在这里和李氏说话儿呢。红玉上来回道:"平姐姐说,奶奶刚出来了,他就把银子收了起来,才将张材家的来取,当面称了给他拿去了。"说着,将荷包递了上去。又道:"平姐姐叫我回奶奶:才旺儿进来讨奶奶的示下,好往那家去的。平姐姐就把那话按着奶奶的主意打发他去了。"凤姐笑道:"他怎么按我的主意打发去了?"红玉道:"平姐姐说:我们奶奶问这里奶奶好。原是我们二爷不在家，虽然迟了两天，只管请奶奶放心。等五奶奶好些，我们奶奶还会了五奶奶来瞧奶奶呢。五奶奶前儿打发了人来说，舅奶奶带了信来了，问奶奶好，还要和这里的姑奶奶寻两丸延年神验万全丹。若有了，奶奶打发人来，只管送在我们奶奶这里。明儿有人去，就顺路给那边舅奶奶带去。"

话未说完，李氏道："嗳哟哟！这话我就不懂了。什么'奶奶''爷爷'的一大堆。"凤姐笑道："怨不得你不懂，这是四五门子的话呢。"说着，又向红玉笑道："好孩子，难为你说的齐全。别像他们扭扭捏捏的蚊子似的。嫂子你不知道，如今除了我随手使的几个丫头、老婆之外，我就怕和别人说话，他们必定把一句话拉长了作两三截儿，咬文嚼字，拿着腔儿，哼哼唧唧的，急的我冒火，他们那里知道！先时我们平儿也是这么着，我就问着他：难道必定装蚊子哼哼就是美人了？说了几遭才好些儿了。"李宫裁笑道："都像你破落户才好。"凤姐又道："这一个丫头就好。方才两遭，说话虽不多，听那口声就简断。"说着，又向红玉笑道："你明儿伏侍我去罢。我认你作女儿，我一调理，你就出息了。"

红玉听了，"扑嗤"一笑。凤姐道："你怎么笑？你说我年轻，比你能大几岁，就作你的妈了？你还作春梦呢！你打听打听，这些人头，比你大的多的，赶着我叫妈，我不理。今儿抬举了你呢！"红玉笑道："我不是笑这个，我笑奶奶认错了辈数了。我妈是奶奶的女儿，这会子又认我作女儿。"凤姐道："谁是你妈？"李宫裁笑道："你原来不认得？他是林之孝之女。"凤姐听了十分诧异，说道："哦！原来是他的丫头。"又笑道："林之孝两口子都是锥子扎不出一声儿来的。我成日家说，他们倒是配就了的一对夫妻，一个天聋，一个地哑。那里承望养出这么样伶俐丫头来！你十几岁了？"红玉道："十七岁了。"又问名字，红玉道："原叫红玉的，因为重了宝二爷，如今只叫红儿了。"

凤姐听说，将眉一皱，把头一回，说道："讨人嫌的很！得了玉的益似的，你也玉，我也玉。"因说道："既这么着，肯跟我，我还和他妈说，'赖大家的如今事多，也不知这府里谁是谁，你替我好好的挑两个丫头我使'，他一般答应着。他饶不挑,倒把他的这女孩子送了别处去。难道跟我必定不好?"李氏笑道:"你可是又多心了。他进来在先,你说在后,怎么怨的他妈!"凤姐道:"既这么着,明儿我和宝玉说,叫他再要人,叫这丫头跟我去。可不知本人愿意不愿意?"红玉笑道:"愿意不愿意,我们也不敢说。只是跟着奶奶,我们也学些眉眼高低,出入上下,大小的事也得见识见识。"刚说着,只见王夫人的丫头来请,凤姐便辞了李宫裁去了。红玉回怡红院去,不在话下。

如今且说林黛玉因夜间失寐,次日起来迟了,闻得众姊妹都在园中作饯花会,恐人笑他痴懒,连忙梳洗了出来。刚到院中,只见宝玉进门来了,笑道:"好妹妹,你昨儿可告我了不曾? 教我悬了一夜心。"林黛玉便回头叫紫鹃道:"把屋子收拾了,下一扇纱屉;看那大燕子回来,把帘子放了下来,拿狮子倚住;烧了香,就把炉罩上。"一面说,一面直往外走。宝玉见他这样,还认作是昨日中晌的事,那知晚间的这段公案,还打恭作揖的。林黛玉正眼也不看,各自出了院门,一直找别的姊妹去了。宝玉心中纳闷,自己猜疑:看起这个光景来,不像是为昨日的事;但只昨日我回来的晚了,又没有见他,再没有冲撞了他的去处了。一面想,一面由不得随后追了来。

只见宝钗、探春正在那边看鹤舞,见黛玉去了,三个一同站着说话儿。又见宝玉来了,探春便笑道:"宝哥哥,身上好? 我整整的三天没见你了。"宝玉笑道:"妹妹身上好? 我前儿还在大嫂子跟前问你呢。"探春道:"宝哥哥,你往这里来,我和你说话。"宝玉听说,便跟了他,离了钗、玉两个,到了一棵石榴树下。探春因说道:"这几天老爷可曾叫你?"宝玉笑道:"没有叫。"探春说:"昨儿我恍惚听见说老爷叫你出去的。"宝玉笑道:"那想是别人听错了,并没叫的。"探春又笑道:"这几个月,我又攒下有十来吊钱了。你还拿了去,明儿出门逛去的时候,或是好字画,好轻巧玩意儿,替我带些来。"宝玉道:"我这么城里城外、大廊小庙的逛,也没见个新奇精致东西,左不过是那些金玉铜磁没处撂的古董,再就是绸缎、吃食、衣服了。"探春道:"谁要这些! 怎么像你上回买的那柳枝儿编的小篮子,整竹子根抠的香盒儿,胶泥垛的风炉儿,这就好了。我喜欢的什么似的,谁知他们都爱上了,都当宝贝似的抢了去了。"宝玉笑道:"原来要这个。这不值什么,拿五百钱出去给小子们,包管拉两车来。"探春道:"小厮们知道什么。你拣那朴而不俗、直而不拙者,这些东西,你多多的替我带了来。我还像上回的鞋,作一双你穿,比那双还加工夫,如何呢?"

宝玉笑道:"你提起鞋来,我想起个故事:那一回我穿着,可巧遇见了老爷,老爷就不受用,问是谁作的。我那里敢提'三妹妹'三个字,我就回说是前儿我生日,是舅母给的。老爷听了是舅母给的,才不好说什么的,半日还说:'何苦来! 虚耗人力,作践绫罗,作这样的东西。'我回来告诉了袭人,袭人说这还罢了,赵姨娘气的抱怨的了不得:'正经兄弟,鞋搭拉、袜搭拉的,没人看的见,且作这些东西!'"探春听说,登时沉下脸来,道:"这话糊涂到什么田地! 怎么我是该作鞋的人么? 环儿难道没有分例的,没有人的? 一般的衣裳是衣裳,鞋袜是鞋袜,丫头、老婆一屋子,怎么抱怨这些话! 给谁听呢! 我不过闲着没事,作一双半双,爱给那个哥哥兄弟,随我的心。谁敢管我不成! 这有什么他也气。"宝玉听了,点头笑道:"你不知道,他心里自然又有个想头了。"探春听说,益发动了气。将头一扭,说道:"连你也糊涂了! 他那想头自然是有的,不过是那阴微鄙贱的见识。他只管这么想,我只管认得老爷、太太两个人,别人我一概不管。就是姊妹弟兄跟前,谁和我好,我就和谁好。什么偏的庶的,我也不知道。论理我不该说他,但忒昏愦的不像了! 还有笑话呢:就是上回我给你那钱,替我带那玩的东西。过了两天,他见了我,也是说没钱使,怎么难,我也不理论。谁知后来丫头们出去了,他就抱怨起我来,说我攒了钱,为什么给你使,倒不给环儿使呢。我听见这话,又好笑又好气,我就出来往太太跟前去了。"正说着,只见宝钗那边笑道:"说完了,来罢。显见的是哥哥妹妹了,丢下别人,且说梯己去。我们听一句儿就使不得了!"说着,探春、宝玉二人方笑着来了。

宝玉因不见了林黛玉,便知他躲了别处去了。想了一想,越性迟两日,等他的气消一消,再去也罢了。因低头看见许多凤仙、石榴等各色落花,锦重重的落了一地,因叹道:"这里他心里生了气,也不收拾这花儿来了。待我送了去,明儿再问着他。"说着,只见宝钗约着他们往外头去。宝玉道:"我就来。"说毕,等他二人去远了,便把那花兜了起来,登山渡水,过树穿花,一直奔了那日同林黛玉葬桃花的去处来。将已到了花冢,犹未转过山坡,只听山坡那边有呜咽之声,一行数落着,哭的好不伤感。宝玉心下想道:"这不知是那房里的丫头,受了委曲,跑到这个地方来哭。"一面想,一面煞住脚步,听他哭道是:

> 花谢花飞花满天,红消香断有谁怜?
>
> 游丝软系飘春榭,落絮轻沾扑绣帘。
>
> 闺中女儿惜春暮,愁绪满怀无释处。
>
> 手把花锄出绣闺,忍踏落花来复去。
>
> 柳丝榆荚自芳菲,不管桃飘与李飞。
>
> 桃李明年能再发,明年闺中知有谁?
>
> 三月香巢已垒成,梁间燕子太无情!
>
> 明年花发虽可啄,却不道人去梁空巢也倾。
>
> 一年三百六十日,风刀霜剑严相逼。
>
> 明媚鲜妍能几时,一朝飘泊难寻觅。
>
> 花开易见落难寻,阶前闷杀葬花人。
>
> 独把花锄泪暗洒,洒上空枝见血痕。
>
> 杜鹃无语正黄昏,荷锄归去掩重门。
>
> 青灯照壁人初睡,冷雨敲窗被未温。
>
> 怪奴底事倍伤神,半为怜春半恼春。
>
> 怜春忽至恼忽去,至又无言去不闻。
>
> 昨宵庭外悲歌发,知是花魂与鸟魂?
>
> 花魂鸟魂总难留,鸟自无言花自羞。
>
> 愿奴胁下生双翼,随花飞到天尽头。
>
> 天尽头,何处有香丘?

未若锦囊收艳骨，一堆净土掩风流。

质本洁来还洁去，强于污淖陷渠沟。

尔今死去侬收葬，未卜侬身何日丧？

侬今葬花人笑痴，他年葬侬知是谁？

试看春残花渐落，便是红颜老死时。

一朝春尽红颜老，花落人亡两不知！

宝玉听了，不觉痴倒。要知端详，且听下回分解。

A Dream of Red Mansions (Chapters 3 & 27)

Chapter 3

Lin Ruhai Recommends a Tutor to His Brother-in-Law
The Lady Dowager Sends for Her Motherless Grand-Daughter

To continue. Yucun turned and saw that it was Zhang Rugui, a native of this place and his former colleague who had also been dismissed from his post for the same reason as himself, and had returned home to Yangzhou. Now there was word from the capital that a request for the reinstatement of former officials had been sanctioned, and he was busily pulling strings to find some opening. He congratulated Yucun the instant he saw him and lost no time, once greetings had been exchanged, in telling him the good news. Yucun was naturally overjoyed, but after some hurried remarks each went his own way.

Leng Zixing, who had heard everything, at once proposed asking Lin Ruhai to enlist the support of Jia Zheng in the capital. Accepting his advice, Yucun went back alone to verify the report from the *Court Gazette*.

The next day he laid his case before Lin Ruhai.

"What a lucky coincidence!" exclaimed Ruhai. "Since my wife's death my mother-in-law in the capital has been worried because my daughter has no one to bring her up. She has sent two boats with male and female attendants to fetch the child, but I delayed her departure while she was unwell. I was wondering how to repay you for your goodness in teaching her: now this gives me a chance to show my appreciation. Set your mind at rest. I foresaw this possibility and have written a letter to my brother-in-law urging him to do all he can for you as a small return for what I owe you. You mustn't worry either about any expenses that may be incurred — I've made that point clear to my brother-in-law."

Yucun bowed with profuse thanks and asked: "May I know your respected brother-in-law's position? I fear I am too uncouth to intrude on him."

Ruhai smiled. "My humble kinsmen belong to your honourable clan. They're the grandsons of the Duke of Rongguo. My elder brother-in-law Jia She, whose courtesy name is Enhou, is a hereditary general of the first rank. My second, Jia Zheng, whose courtesy name is Cunzhou, is an under-secretary in the Board of Works. He is an unassuming, generous man who takes after his grandfather. That is why I am writing to him on your behalf. If he were some purse-proud, fivolous official, I'd be dishonouring your high principles, brother, and I myself would disdain to do such a thing."

This confirmed what Zixing had said the previous day, and once more Yucun expressed his thanks.

"I've chosen the second day of next month for my daughter's departure for the capital," continued Ruhai. "It would suit both parties, surely, if you were to travel together?"

Yucun promptly agreed with the greatest satisfaction, and took the gifts and travelling expenses which Ruhai had prepared.

His pupil Daiyu, who had just got over her illness, could hardly bear to leave her father, but she had to comply with the wishes of her grandmother.

"I am nearly fifty and don't intend to marry again," Ruhai told her, "You're young and delicate, with no mother to take care of you, no sisters or brothers to look after you. If you go to stay with your grandmother and uncles' girls, that will take a great load off my mind. How can you refuse?"

So parting from him in a flood of tears, she embarked with her nurse and some elderly maid-servants from the Rong Mansion, followed by Yucun and two pages in another junk.

In due course they reached the capital and entered the city. Yucun spruced himself up and went with his pages to the gate of the Rong Mansion, where he handed in his visiting-card on which he had styled himself Jia Zheng's "nephew."

Jia Zheng, who had received his brother-in-law's letter, lost no time in asking him in. Yucun cut an impressive figure and was by no means vulgar in his conversation. Since Jia Zheng was well-disposed to scholars and, like his grandfather before him, delighted in honouring worthy men of letters and helping those in distress, and since moreover his brother-in-law had recommended Yucun, he treated him uncommonly well and did all in his power to help him. The same day that he presented a petition to the throne Yucun was rehabilitated and ordered to await an appointment. In less than two months he was sent to Jinling to fill the vacated post of prefect of Yingtian.[①] Taking leave of Jia Zheng he chose a day to proceed to his new post. But no more of this.

To return to Daiyu. When she disembarked, a sedan-chair from the Rong Mansion and carts for her luggage were waiting in readiness. She had heard a great deal from her mother about the magnificence of her grandmother's home; and during the last few days she had been impressed by the food, costumes and behaviour of the relatively low-ranking attendants escorting her. She must watch her step in her new home, she decided, be on guard every moment and weigh every word, so as not to be laughed at for any foolish blunder. As she was carried into the city she peeped out through the gauze window of the chair at the bustle in the streets and the crowds of people, the like of which she had never seen before.

After what seemed a long time they came to a street with two huge stone lions crouching on the north side, flanking a great triple gate with beast-head knockers, in front of which ten or more men in smart livery were

---

① 译者注: Another name for Nanjing.

sitting. The central gate was shut, but people were passing in and out of the smaller side gates. On a board above the main gate was written in large characters: Ningguo Mansion Built at Imperial Command.

Daiyu realized that this must be where the elder branch of her grandmother's family lived.

A little further to the west they came to another imposing triple gate. This was the Rong Mansion. Instead of going through the main gate, they entered by the smaller one on the west. The bearers carried the chair a bow-shot further, then set it down at a turning and withdrew. The maid-servants behind Daiyu had now alighted and were proceeding on foot. Three or four smartly dressed lads of seventeen or eighteen picked up the chair and, followed by the maids, carried it to a gate decorated with overhanging flowery patterns carved in wood. There the bearers withdrew, the maids raised the curtain of the chair, helped Daiyu out and supported her through the gate.

Inside, verandahs on both sides led to a three-roomed entrance hall in the middle of which stood a screen of marble in a red sandalwood frame. The hall gave access to the large court of the main building. In front were five rooms with carved beams and painted pillars, and on either side were rooms with covered passageways. Cages of brilliantly coloured parrots, thrushes and other birds hung under the eaves of the verandahs.

Several maids dressed in red and green rose from the terrace and hurried to greet them with smiles.

"The old lady was just talking about you," they cried. "And here you are."

Three or four of them ran to raise the door curtain, and a voice could be heard announcing, "Miss Lin is here."

As Daiyu entered, a silver-haired old lady supported by two maids advanced to meet her. She knew that this must be her grandmother, but before she could kowtow the old lady threw both arms around her.

"Dear heart! Flesh of my child!" she cried, and burst out sobbing.

All the attendants covered their faces and wept, and Daiyu herself could not keep back her tears. When at last the others prevailed on her to stop, Daiyu made her kowtow to her grandmother. This was the Lady Dowager from the Shi family mentioned by Leng Zixing, the mother of Jia She and Jia Zheng, who now introduced the family one by one.

"This," she said, "is your elder uncle's wife. This is your second uncle's wife. This is the wife of your late Cousin Zhu."

Daiyu greeted each in turn.

"Fetch the girls," her grandmother said. "They can be excused their lessons today in honour of our guest from far away."

Two maids went to carry out her orders. And presently the three young ladies appeared, escorted by three nurses and five or six maids.

The first was somewhat plump and of medium height. Her cheeks were the texture of newly ripened lichees, her nose as sleek as goose fat. Gentle and demure, she looked very approachable.

The second had sloping shoulders and a slender waist. She was tall and slim, with an oval face, well-defined eyebrows and lovely dancing eyes. She seemed elegant and quick-witted with an air of distinction. To look at her was to forget everything vulgar.

The third was not yet fully grown and still had the face of a child.

All three were dressed in similar tunics and skirts with the same bracelets and head ornaments.

Daiyu hastily rose to greet these cousins, and after the introductions they took seats while the maids served tea. All the talk now was of Daiyu's mother. How had she fallen ill? What medicine had the doctors prescribed? How had the funeral and mourning ceremonies been conducted? Inevitably, the Lady Dowager was most painfully affected.

"Of all my children I loved your mother best," she told Daiyu. "Now she has gone before me, and I didn't even have one last glimpse of her face. The sight of you makes me feel my heart will break!" Again she took Daiyu in her arms and wept. The others were hard put to it to comfort her.

All present had been struck by Daiyu's good breeding. For in spite of her tender years and evident delicate health, she had an air of natural distinction. Observing how frail she looked, they asked what medicine or treatment she had been having.

"I've always been like this," Daiyu said with a smile. "I've been taking medicine ever since I was weaned. Many well-known doctors have examined me, but none of their prescriptions was any use. The year I was three, I remember being told, a scabby monk came to our house and wanted to take me away to be a nun. My parents wouldn't hear of it. The monk said, 'If you can't bear to part with her she'll probably never get well. The only other remedy is to keep her from hearing weeping and from seeing any relatives apart from her father and mother. That's her only hope of having a quiet life.' No one paid any attention, of course, to such crazy talk. Now I'm still taking ginseng pills."

"That's good," approved the Lady Dowager. "We're having pills made, and I'll see they make some for you."

Just then they heard peals of laughter from the back courtyard and a voice cried:

"I'm late in greeting our guest from afar!"

Daiyu thought with surprise, "The people here are so respectful and solemn, they all seem to be holding their breath. Who can this be, so boisterous and pert?"

While she was still wondering, through the back door trooped some matrons and maids surrounding a young woman. Unlike the girls, she was richly dressed and resplendent as a fairy.

Her gold-filigree tiara was set with jewels and pearls. Her hair-clasps, in the form of five phoenixes facing the sun, had pendants of pearls. Her necklet, of red gold, was in the form of a coiled dragon studded with gems. She had double red jade pendants with pea-green tassels attached to her skirt.

Her close-fitting red satin jacket was embroidered with gold butterflies and flowers. Her turquoise cape, lined with white squirrel, was inset with designs in coloured silk. Her skirt of kingfisher-blue crepe was patterned with flowers.

She had the almond-shaped eyes of a phoenix, slanting eyebrows as long and drooping as willow leaves. Her figure was slender and her manner vivacious. The springtime charm of her powdered face gave no hint of her latent formidability. And before her crimson lips parted, her laughter rang out.

Daiyu rose quickly to greet her.

"You don't know her yet." The Lady Dowager chuckled. "She's the terror of this house. In the south they'd call her Hot Pepper. Just call her Fiery Phoenix."

Daiyu was at a loss how to address her when her cousins came to her rescue. "This is Cousin Lian's wife," they told her.

Though Daiyu had never met her, she knew from her mother that Jia Lian, the son of her first uncle Jia She, had married the niece of Lady Wang, her second uncle's wife. She had been educated like a boy and given the school-room name Xifeng.[①] Daiyu lost no time in greeting her with a smile as "cousin."

Xifeng took her hand and carefully inspected her from head to foot, then led her back to her seat by the Lady Dowager.

"Well," she cried with a laugh, "this is the first time I've set eyes on such a ravishing beauty. Her whole air is so distinguished! She doesn't take after her father, son-in-law of our Old Ancestress, but looks more like a Jia. No wonder our Old Ancestress couldn't put you out of her mind and was for ever talking or thinking about you. But poor ill-fated little cousin, losing your mother so young!" With that she dabbed her eyes with a handkerchief.

"I've only just dried my tears. Do you want to start me off again?" said the old lady playfully. "Your young cousin's had a long journey and she's delicate. We've just got her to stop crying. So don't reopen that subject."

Xifeng switched at once from grief to merriment. "Of course," she cried. "I was so carried away by joy and sorrow at sight of my little cousin, I forgot our Old Ancestress. I deserve to be caned." Taking Daiyu's hand

---

① 译者注: Splendid Phoenix.

again, she asked, "How old are you, cousin? Have you started your schooling yet? What medicine are you taking? You mustn't be home sick here. If you fancy anything special to eat or play with, don't hesitate to tell me. If the maids or old nurses aren't good to you, just let me know."

She turned then to the servants. "Have Miss Lin's luggage and things been brought in? How many attendants did she bring? Hurry up and clear out a couple of rooms where they can rest."

Meanwhile refreshments had been served. And as Xifeng handed round the tea and sweetmeats, Lady Wang asked whether she had distributed the monthly allowance.

"It's finished," was Xifeng's answer. "Just now I took some people to the upstairs storeroom at the back to look for some brocade. But though we searched for a long time we couldn't find any of the sort you described to us yesterday, madam. Could your memory have played you a trick?"

"It doesn't matter if there's none of that sort," said Lady Wang. "Just choose two lengths to make your little cousin some clothes. This evening don't forget to send for them."

"I've already done that," replied Xifeng. "Knowing my cousin would be here any day, I got everything ready. The material's waiting in your place for your inspection. If you pass it, madam, it can be sent over."

Lady Wang smiled and nodded her approval.

Now the refreshments were cleared away and the Lady Dowager ordered two nurses to take Daiyu to see her two uncles.

At once Jia She's wife, Lady Xing, rose to her feet and suggested, "Won't it be simpler if I take my niece?"

"Very well," agreed the Lady Dowager, "And there's no need for you to come back afterwards."

Lady Xing assented and then told Daiyu to take her leave of Lady Wang, after which the rest saw them to the entrance hall. Outside the ornamental gate pages were waiting beside a blue lacquered carriage with kingfisher-blue curtains, into which Lady Xing and her niece entered. Maids let down the curtains and told the bearers to start. They bore the carriage to an open space and harnessed a docile mule to it. They left by the west side gate, proceeded east past the main entrance of the Rong Mansion, entered a large black-lacquered gate and drew up in front of a ceremonial gate.

When the pages had withdrawn, the curtains were raised, and Lady Xing led Daiyu into the courtyard. It seemed to her that these buildings and grounds must be part of the Rong Mansion garden; for when they had passed three ceremonial gates she saw that the halls, side chambers and covered corridors although on a smaller scale were finely constructed. They had not the stately splendour of the other mansion, yet nothing was lacking in the way of trees, plants or artificial rockeries.

As they entered the central hall they were greeted by a crowd of heavily made-up and richly dressed concubines and maids. Lady Xing invited Daiyu to be seated while she sent a servant to the library to ask her husband to join them.

After a while the servant came back to report, "The master says he hasn't been feeling too well the last few days, and meeting the young lady would only upset them both. He isn't up to it for the time being. Miss Lin mustn't mope or be homesick here but feel at home with the old lady and her aunts. Her cousins may be silly creatures, but they'll be company for her and help to amuse her. If anyone is unkind to her, she must say so and not treat us as strangers."

Daiyu had risen to her feet to listen to this message. Shortly after this she rose again to take her leave. Lady Xing insisted that she stay for the evening meal.

"Thank you very much, aunt, you're too kind," said Daiyu. "Really I shouldn't decline. But it might look rude if I delayed in calling on my second uncle. Please excuse me and let me stay another time."

"You're quite right," said Lady Xing. She told a few elderly maids to escort her niece back in the same carriage, whereupon Daiyu took her leave. Her aunt saw her to the ceremonial gate and after giving the maids some further instructions waited to see them off.

Back in the Rong Mansion, Daiyu alighted again. The nurses led her eastwards, round a corner, through an entrance hall into a hall facing south, then passed through a ceremonial gate into a large courtyard. The northern building had five large apartments and wings on either side. This was the hub of the whole estate, more imposing by far than the Lady Dowager's quarters.

Daiyu realized that this was the main inner suite, for a broad raised avenue led straight to its gate. Once inside the hall she looked up and her eye was caught by a great blue tablet with nine gold dragons on it, on which was written in characters large as peck measures:

Hall of Glorious Felicity.

Smaller characters at the end recorded the date on which the Emperor had conferred this tablet upon Jia Yuan, the Duke of Rongguo, and it bore the Imperial seal.

On the large red sandalwood table carved with dragons an old bronze tripod, green with patina, stood about three feet high. On the wall hung a large scroll-picture of black dragons riding the waves. This was flanked by a bronze wine vessel inlaid with gold and a crystal bowl. By the walls were a row of sixteen cedar-wood armchairs; and above these hung two panels of ebony with the following couplet inset in silver:

> *Pearls on the dais outshine the sun and moon;*
> *Insignia of honour in the hall blaze like iridescent clouds.*

Small characters below recorded that this had been written by the Prince of Dungan, who signed his name Mu Shi and styled himself a fellow provincial and old family friend.

Since Lady Wang seldom sat in this main hall but used three rooms on the east side for relaxation, the nurses led Daiyu there.

The large *kang* by the window was covered with a scarlet foreign rug. In the middle were red back-rests and turquoise bolsters, both with dragon-design medallions, and a long greenish yellow mattress also with dragon medallions. At each side stood a low table of foreign lacquer in the shape of plum-blossom. On the left-hand table were a tripod, spoons, chopsticks and an incense container; on the right one, a slender-waisted porcelain vase from the Ruzhou Kiln containing flowers then in season, as well as tea-bowls and a spittoon. Below the *kang* facing the west wall were four armchairs, their covers of bright red dotted with pink flowers, and with four footstools beneath them. On either side were two tables set out with teacups and vases of flowers. The rest of the room need not be described in detail.

The nurses urged Daiyu to sit on the *kang*, on the edge of which were two brocade cushions. But feeling that this would be presumptuous, she sat instead on one of the chairs on the east side. The maids in attendance served tea, and as she sipped it she studied them, observing that their make-up, clothes and deportment were quite different from those in other families. Before she had finished her tea in came a maid wearing a red silk coat and a blue satin sleeveless jacket with silk borders. With a smile this girl announced:

"Her Ladyship asks Miss Lin to go in and take a seat over there."

At once the nurses conducted Daiyu along the eastern corridor to a small three-roomed suite facing south. On the *kang* under the window was a low table laden with books and a tea-service. Against the east wall were a none too new blue satin back-rest and a bolster.

Lady Wang was sitting in the lower place by the west wall on a none too new blue satin cover with a back-rest and a bolster. She invited her niece to take the seat on the east. But guessing that this was Jia Zheng's place, Daiyu chose one of the three chairs next to the *kang*, which had black-dotted antimacassars, looking none too new. Not until she had been pressed several times did she take a seat by her aunt.

"Your uncle's observing a fast today," said Lady Wang. "You'll see him some other time. But there's one thing I want to tell you. Your three cousins are excellent girls, and I'm sure you'll find them easy to get on with during lessons, or when you're learning embroidery or playing together. Just one thing worries me: that's my dreadful son, the bane of my life, who torments us all in this house like a real devil. He's gone to a temple today in fulfilment of a vow, but you'll see what he's like when he comes back this evening. Just pay no attention to him. None of your cousins dare to provoke him."

Daiyu's mother had often spoken of this nephew born with a piece of jade in his mouth, his wild ways, aversion to study and delight in playing about in the women's apartments. Apparently he was so spoiled by his grandmother that no one could control him. She knew Lady Wang must be referring to him.

"Does aunt mean my elder cousin with the jade in his mouth?" she asked with a smile. "Mother often spoke of him. I know he's a year older than me, his name is Baoyu, and for all his pranks he's very good to his girl cousins. But how can I provoke him? I'll be spending all my time with the other girls in a different part of the house while our boy cousins are in the outer courtyards."

"You don't understand," replied Lady Wang with a laugh. "He's not like other boys. Because the old lady's always doted on him, he's used to being spoilt with the girls. If they ignore him he keeps fairly quiet though he feels bored. He can always work off his temper by scolding some of his pages. But if the girls give him the least encouragement, he's so elated he gets up to all kinds of mischief. That's why you mustn't pay any attention to him. One moment he's all honey-sweet; the next, he's rude and recalcitrant; and in another minute he's raving like a lunatic. You can't take him seriously."

As Daiyu promised to remember this, a maid announced that dinner was to be served in the Lady Dowager's apartments. Lady Wang at once led her niece out of the back door, going west along a corridor and through a side gate to a broad road running from north to south. On the south side was a dainty three-roomed annex facing north; on the north a big screen wall painted white, behind which was a small door leading to an apartment.

"That's where your cousin Xifeng lives." Lady Wang pointed out the place. "So next time you know where to find her. If you want anything just let her know."

By the gate several young pages, their hair in tufts, stood at attention.

Lady Wang led Daiyu through an entrance hall running from east to west into the Lady Dowager's back courtyard. Stepping through the back door, they found there a crowd assembled who, as soon as they saw Lady Wang, set tables and chairs ready. Jia Zhu's widow, Li Wan, served the rice while Xifeng put out the chopsticks and Lady Wang served the soup.

The Lady Dowager was seated alone on a couch at the head of the table with two empty chairs on each side. Xifeng took Daiyu by the hand to make her sit in the first place on the left, but she persistently declined the honour.

"Your aunt and sisters-in-law don't dine here," said her grandmother with a smile. "Besides, you're a guest today. So do take that seat."

With a murmured apology, Daiyu obeyed. The Lady Dowager told Lady Wang to sit down; then Yingchun and the two other girls asked leave to be seated, Yingchun first on the right, Tanchun second on the left, and Xichun second on the right. Maids held ready dusters, bowls for rinsing the mouth and napkins, while Li Wan and Xifeng standing behind the diners plied them with food.

Although the outer room swarmed with nurses and maids, not so much as a cough was heard. The meal was eaten in silence. And immediately after, tea was brought in on small trays. Now Lin Ruhai had taught his daughter the virtue of moderation and the harm caused to the digestive system by drinking tea directly after a meal. But many customs here were different from those in her home. She would have to adapt herself to these new ways. As she took the tea, however, the rinse-bowls were proffered again, and seeing the others rinse their mouths she followed suit. After they had washed their hands tea was served once more, this time for drinking.

"You others may go," said the Lady Dowager now. "I want to have a chat with my grand-daughter."

Lady Wang promptly rose and after a few remarks led the way out, followed by Li Wan and Xifeng. Then her grandmother asked Daiyu what books she had studied.

"I've just finished the *Four Books*,"① said Daiyu. "But I'm very ignorant." Then she inquired what the other girls were reading.

"They only know a very few characters, not enough to read any books."

The words were hardly out of her mouth when they heard footsteps in the courtyard and a maid came in to announce, "Baoyu is here."

Daiyu was wondering what sort of graceless scamp or little dunce Baoyu was and feeling reluctant to meet such a stupid creature when, even as the maid announced him, in he walked.

He had on a golden coronet studded with jewels and a golden chaplet in the form of two dragons fighting for a pearl. His red archer's jacket, embroidered with golden butterflies and flowers, was tied with a coloured tasselled palace sash. Over this he wore a turquoise fringed coat of Japanese satin with a raised pattern of flowers in eight bunches. His court boots were of black satin with white soles.

His face was as radiant as the mid-autumn moon, his complexion fresh as spring flowers at dawn. The hair above his temples was as sharply outlined as if cut with a knife. His eyebrows were as black as if painted with ink, his cheeks as red as peach-blossom, his eyes bright as autumn ripples. Even when angry he seemed to smile, and there was warmth in his glance even when he frowned.

Round his neck he had a golden torque in the likeness of a dragon, and a silk cord of five colours, on which hung a beautiful piece of jade.

His appearance took Daiyu by surprise. "How very strange!" she thought. "It's as if I'd seen him somewhere before. He looks so familiar."

Baoyu paid his respects to the Lady Dowager and upon her instructions went to see his mother.

He returned before long, having changed his clothes. His short hair in small plaits tied with red silk was drawn up on the crown of his head and braided into one thick queue as black and glossy as lacquer, sporting four

---

① 译者注：Confucian classics.

large pearls attached to golden pendants in the form of the eight precious things. His coat of a flower pattern on a bright red ground was not new, and he still wore the torque, the precious jade, a lock-shaped amulet containing his Buddhistic name, and a lucky charm. Below could be glimpsed light green flowered satin trousers, black-dotted stockings with brocade borders, and thick-soled scarlet shoes.

His face looked as fair as if powdered, his lips red as rouge. His glance was full of affection, his speech interspersed with smiles. But his natural charm appeared most in his brows, for his eyes sparkled with a world of feeling. However, winning as his appearance was, it was difficult to tell what lay beneath.

Someone subsequently gave an admirable picture of Baoyu in these two verses written to the melody of *The Moon over the West River*:

> *Absurdly he courts care and melancholy*
> *And raves like any madman in his folly;*
> *For though endowed with handsome looks is he,*
> *His heart is lawless and refractory.*

> *Too dense by far to understand his duty,*
> *Too stubborn to apply himself to study,*
> *Foolhardy in his eccentricity,*
> *He's deaf to all reproach and obloquy.*

> *Left cold by riches and nobility,*
> *Unfit to bear the stings of poverty,*
> *He wastes his time and his ability,*
> *Failing his country and his family.*

> *First in this world for uselessness is he,*
> *Second to none in his deficiency.*
> *Young fops and lordlings all, be warned by me:*
> *Don't imitate this youth's perversity!*

With a smile at Baoyu, the Lady Dowager scolded, "Fancy changing your clothes before greeting our visitor. Hurry up now and pay your respects to your cousin."

Of course, Baoyu had seen this new cousin earlier on and guessed that she was the daughter of his Aunt Lin. He made haste to bow and, having greeted her, took a seat. Looking at Daiyu closely, he found her different from other girls.

Her dusky arched eyebrows were knitted and yet not frowning, her speaking eyes held both merriment and sorrow; her very frailty had charm. Her eyes sparkled with tears, her breath was soft and faint. In repose she was like a lovely flower mirrored in the water; in motion, a pliant willow swaying in the wind. She looked more sensitive than Bi Gan,[①] more delicate than Xi Shi.[②]

"I've met this cousin before," he declared at the end of his scrutiny.

"You're talking nonsense again," said his grandmother, laughing. "How could you possibly have met her?"

"Well, even if I haven't, her face looks familiar. I feel we're old friends meeting again after a long separation."

"So much the better." The Lady Dowager laughed. "That means you're bound to be good friends."

Baoyu went over to sit beside Daiyu and once more gazed fixedly at her.

"Have you done much reading, cousin?" he asked.

"No," said Daiyu. "I've only studied for a couple of years and learned a few characters."

"What's your name?"

She told him.

"And your courtesy name?"

"I have none."

---

① 译者注: A prince noted for his great intelligence at the end of the Shang Dynasty.

② 译者注: A famous beauty of the ancient Kingdom of Yue.

"I'll give you one then," he proposed with a chuckle. "What could be better than Pinpin?"①

"Where's that from?" put in Tanchun.

"*The Compendium of Men and Objects Old and New* says that in the west is a stone called *dai* which can be used instead of graphite for painting eyebrows. As Cousin Lin's eyebrows look half knit, what could be more apt than these two characters?"

"You're making that up, I'm afraid," teased Tanchun.

"Most works, apart from the *Four Books*, are made up; am I the only one who makes things up?" he retorted with a grin. Then, to the mystification of them all, he asked Daiyu if she had any jade.

Imagining that he had his own jade in mind, she answered, "No, I haven't. I suppose it's too rare for everybody to have."

This instantly threw Baoyu into one of his frenzies. Tearing off the jade he flung it on the ground.

"What's rare about it?" he stormed. "It can't even tell good people from bad. What spiritual understanding has it got? I don't want this nuisance either."

In consternation all the maids rushed forward to pick up the jade while the Lady Dowager in desperation took Baoyu in her arms.

"You wicked monster!" she scolded. "Storm at people if you're in a passion. But why should you throw away that precious thing your life depends on?"

His face stained with tears, Baoyu sobbed, "None of the girls here has one, only me. What's the fun of that? Even this newly arrived cousin who's lovely as a fairy hasn't got one either. That shows it's no good."

"She did have one once," said the old lady to soothe him. "But when your aunt was dying and was unwilling to leave her, the best she could do was to take the jade with her instead. That was like burying the living with the dead and showed your cousin's filial piety. It meant, too, that now your

---

① 译者注：Knitted Brows.

aunt's spirit can still see your cousin. That's why she said she had none, not wanting to boast about it. How can you compare with her? Now put it carefully on again lest your mother hears about this."

She took the jade from one of the maids and put it on him herself. And Baoyu, convinced by her tale, let the matter drop.

Just then a nurse came in to ask about Daiyu's quarters.

"Move Baoyu into the inner apartment of my suite," said his grandmother. "Miss Lin can stay for the time being in his Green Gauze Lodge. Once spring comes, we'll make different arrangements."

"Dear Ancestress!" coaxed Baoyu. "Let me stay outside Green Gauze Lodge. I'll do very well on that bed in the outer room. Why should I move over and disturb you?"

After a moment's reflection the Lady Dowager agreed to this. Each would be attended by a nurse and a maid, while other attendants were on night duty outside. Xifeng had already sent round a flowered lavender curtain, satin quilts and embroidered mattresses.

Daiyu had brought with her only Nanny Wang, her old wet-nurse, and ten-year-old Xueyan, who had also attended her since she was a child. Since the Lady Dowager considered Xueyan too young and childish and Nanny Wang too old to be of much service, she gave Daiyu one of her own personal attendants, a maid of the second grade called Yingge. Like Yingchun and the other young ladies, in addition to her own wet-nurse Daiyu was given four other nurses as chaperones, two personal maids to attend to her toilet and five or six girls to sweep the rooms and run errands.

Nanny Wang and Yingge accompanied Daiyu now to Green Gauze Lodge, while Baoyu's wet-nurse, Nanny Li, and his chief maid Xiren made ready the big bed for him in its outer room.

Xiren, whose original name was Zhenzhu, had been one of the Lady Dowager's maids. The old lady so doted on her grandson that she wanted to make sure he was well looked after and for this reason she gave him her favourite, Xiren, a good, conscientious girl. Baoyu knew that her surname was Hua[①] and remembered a line of poetry which ran, "the fragrance of flowers assails men." So he asked his grandmother's permission to change her name to Xiren. [②]

Xiren's strong point was devotion. Looking after the Lady Dowager she thought of no one but the Lady Dowager, and after being assigned to Baoyu she thought only of Baoyu. What worried her, though, was that he was too headstrong to listen to her advice.

That night after Baoyu and Nanny Li were asleep, Xiren noticed that Daiyu and Yingge were still up in the inner room. She tiptoed in there in her night clothes and asked:

"Why aren't you sleeping yet, miss?"

"Please sit down, sister," invited Daiyu with a smile.

Xiren sat on the edge of the bed.

"Miss Lin has been in tears all this time, she's so upset," said Yingge. "The very day of her arrival, she says, she's made our young master fly into a tantrum. If he'd smashed his jade she would have felt to blame. I've been trying to comfort her."

"Don't take it to heart," said Xiren. "I'm afraid you'll see him carrying on even more absurdly later. If you let yourself be upset by his behaviour you'll never have a moment's peace. Don't be so sensitive."

"I'll remember what you've said." promised Daiyu. "But can you tell me where that jade of his came from, and what the inscription on it is?"

Xiren told her, "Not a soul in the whole family knows where it comes from. It was found in his mouth, so we hear, when he was born, with a hole for a cord already made in it. Let me fetch it here to show you."

But Daiyu would not hear of this as it was now late. "I can look at it tomorrow," she said.

After a little more chat they went to bed.

The next morning, after paying her respects to the Lady Dowager,

---

① 译者注: Flower.
② 译者注: Literally "assails men."

Daiyu went to Lady Wang's apartments. She found her and Xifeng discussing a letter from Jinling. With them were two maid-servants who had brought a message from the house of Lady Wang's brother.

Daiyu did not understand what was going on, but Tanchun and the others knew that they were discussing Xue Pan, the son of Aunt Xue in Jinling. Presuming on his powerful connections, he had had a man beaten to death and was now to be tried in the Yingtian prefectural court. Lady Wang's brother Wang Ziteng, having been informed of this, had sent these messengers to the Rong Mansion to urge them to invite the Xue family to the capital. But more of this in the next chapter.

Chapter 27

Baochai Chases a Butterfly to Dripping Emerald Pavilion
Daiyu Weeps over Fallen Blossom by the Tomb of Flowers

As Daiyu was weeping, the gate creaked open and out came Baochai escorted by Baoyu, Xiren and other maids. Daiyu was tempted to accost Baoyu, but not wanting to embarrass him in public she stepped aside until Baochai had left and the others had gone in, when she came back and shed more tears before the closed gate. Then she went back in low spirits to her room and prepared listlessly for bed.

Zijuan and Xueyan knew their young mistress' ways. She would often sit moodily frowning or sighing over nothing or, for no apparent reason, would give way to long spells of weeping. At first they had tried to comfort her, imagining that she missed her parents and home or that someone had been unkind; but as time went by and they found this was her habit they paid little further attention. So tonight they withdrew to bed, leaving her to brood by herself.

Daiyu leaned against her bed-rail, clasping her knees. Her eyes were brimming with tears. There she stayed motionless as a statue, not lying down until after the second watch.

The next day was the twenty-sixth of the fourth month, the Festival of Grain in Ear. It was the time-honoured custom on this day to offer all manner of gifts and a farewell feast to the God of Flowers, for this festival was said to mark the beginning of summer when all the blossom had withered and the God of Flowers had to resign his throne and be seen off. As this custom is most faithfully observed by women, all the inmates of Grand View Garden rose early that day. The girls used flowers and osiers to weave small sedan-chairs and horses, or made pennants and flags of silk and gauze which they tied with gay ribbons to every tree and flower, turning the whole Garden into a blaze of colour. They decked themselves out so prettily, too, as to put the very flowers and birds to shame. But time forbids us to dwell on that splendid scene.

Now Baochai, the three Jia girls, Li Wan and Xifeng were enjoying themselves in the Garden with Xifeng's little daughter as well as Xiangling and the other maids. Only one person was missing, and that was Daiyu.

"Why isn't Cousin Lin here?" asked Yingchun. "Surely the lazy creature isn't still sleeping?"

"I'll go and rouse her," volunteered Baochai. "The rest of you wait here and I'll soon bring her."

She set off instantly for Bamboo Lodge.

On the way she met the twelve young actresses headed by Wenguan, who greeted her and chatted for a while. Then Baochai told them how to find the others and, having explained her own errand, followed the winding path towards Daiyu's quarters. As she approached Bamboo Lodge she saw Baoyu enter the courtyard. That made her pause and lower her head in thought.

"Baoyu and Daiyu grew up under one roof," she reflected. "They're so free and easy together, they don't care how they tease each other or show their feelings. And Daiyu's rather jealous and petty-minded. If I follow Baoyu in, he may not like it and she may resent it. I'd better go back."

She had started back to rejoin the other girls when a pair of jade-coloured butterflies the size of a circular fan appeared before her. They fluttered up and down most bewitchingly in the breeze. What fun it would be to catch them! Baochai drew her fan from her sleeve and ran after them over the grass. Flitting now high now low, this way and that, the butterflies led her through the flowers and willows all the way to the water's brink. By the time she neared Dripping Emerald Pavilion, panting and perspiring from all her exertions, she decided to give up the pursuit and go back. But just then she heard muffled voices from the pavilion.

Now this pavilion, which stood out in the middle of the pool, was surrounded on four sides by covered corridors with balustrades and connected with the banks by zigzag bridges. It had papered latticed windows on all four sides. Baochai stopped outside it to catch what was being said.

"Look at this handkerchief. If it's the one you lost, you can have it. If not, I'll take it back to Master Yun."

"Of course it's mine. Let me have it."

"What thanks am I going to get? You don't expect me to do this for nothing, do you?"

"Don't worry. I promised you something, I won't cheat you."

"I should hope not, after I've brought it back to you. But how are you going to thank the man who found it?"

"Don't be silly. He's a young gentleman. It's only right he should return what he finds. How could I reward him?"

"If you don't, what am I to say to him? Besides, he told me repeatedly he wouldn't let me give you this unless you offered him some reward."

A short silence followed.

"All right," came the answer at last. "Give him this from me to thank him. But swear you won't let on to a soul."

"If I do, may a boil break out in my mouth and may I die a miserable death!"

Then a note of alarm was sounded.

"Goodness! We've been so busy talking, what if someone's eavesdropping outside? We'd better open the windows. Then if people see us they'll assume we're just chatting. And if anyone comes near we'll see her and can change the subject."

Baochai could hardly believe her ears.

"No wonder they say wicked people have always been cunning!" she thought. "How they're going to blush when they open the window and see me! One of them sounded like that sly, conceited Xiaohong who works for Baoyu. She's a strange crafty creature if ever I saw one. 'Desperation drives men to rebel and a dog to jump over a wall.' If she thinks I know her secret there may be trouble, and that would be awkward for me. Well, it's too late to hide now. I must try to avoid suspicion by throwing them off the scent ..."

That same instant she heard the thud of a window opening. At once she ran forward as noisily as she could, calling out laughingly:

"Where are you hiding, Daiyu?"

Xiaohong and Zhui'er, who had just opened the window, were staggered to see her before them.

"Where have you hidden Miss Lin?" Baochai asked them merrily.

"Miss Lin? We haven't seen her," Zhui'er answered.

"Just now, from the other bank, I saw her crouching here dabbling in the water. I meant to take her by surprise but she spotted me coming and dashed off to the east. And now she's disappeared. Are you sure she's not hiding in there?"

She deliberately went in and made a search before going on.

"She must have popped into some cave in the rocks," she muttered. "If a snake bites her, serve her right."

With that she went off, laughing up her sleeve at the way she had foxed them and wondering what they were thinking.

Xiaohong, in fact, had been quite taken in. As soon as Baochai was safely out of earshot she caught Zhui'er by the arm.

"Heaven help us!" she whispered. "If Miss Lin was here she must have overheard us."

Zhui'er said nothing, and a long pause followed.

"What shall we do?" asked Xiaohong.

"What if she did hear? This is none of her business."

"It wouldn't have been so bad Miss Xue overhearing. But Miss Lin's narrow-minded and likes to make cutting remarks. If she heard, and gives us away, what shall we do?"

A stop was put to this discussion by the arrival of Wenguan with Xiangling, Siqi and Daishu. The two girls chatted with them as if nothing had happened until Xiaohong saw Xifeng beckoning from the slope. Leaving the other girls, she ran over to her.

"Can I do anything for Your Ladyship?" she asked, smiling sweetly.

Xifeng had a close look at her and was favourably impressed by her neat good looks and pleasant way of talking.

"I didn't bring my maids with me today," she said. "But now I've remembered something I want done. Do you think you could deliver a message correctly?"

Xiaohong smiled.

"Just give me your instructions, madam. If I don't get the message right and hold up your business, you can punish me."

"Tell me, which of the young ladies do you work for? Then I can explain where you are if she asks for you."

"I'm attached to Master Bao's apartments."

Xifeng chuckled.

"I see. That accounts for it. All right, if he asks, I'll let him know where you are. Now go to my house and tell your sister Pinger that she'll find a packet containing a hundred and sixty taels of silver under the stand of the *ju*-ware plate on the table in the outer room. That's for the embroiderers. When Zhang Cai's wife comes, she's to weigh it in her presence and let her take it. And there's another thing. I want you to bring me the pouch which is by the pillow on the bed in the inner room."

Xiaohong went off to carry out these orders. She returned presently to find that Xifeng had vanished. But Siqi had just emerged from a cave and stopped to fasten her skirt. Xiaohong approached her.

"Know where the Second Mistress has gone?" she asked.

"I didn't notice."

Xiaohong looked around and went to ask Tanchun and Baochai, who were watching the fish not far off.

"You'll find her with Madam Li Wan, I think," Tanchun told her.

Xiaohong promptly set off to Paddy-Sweet Cottage, but on the way met Qingwen and half a dozen other maids.

"Still prancing about!" exclaimed Qingwen as soon as she set eyes on her. "You haven't watered the flowers, fed the birds or lit the tea-stove in our courtyard, yet you gad about outside."

"Yesterday Master Bao said the flowers needn't be watered today — once every other day would do," Xiaohong retorted. "I fed the birds while you were still asleep."

"And what about the tea-stove?" demanded Bihen.

"It's not *my* turn today, so don't ask me whether there's any tea or not."

"Just listen to the way she talks," jeered Yixian. "You'd all better keep quiet and let her fool about."

"Who says I was fooling about?" snapped Xiaohong. "I've been on an errand for the Second Mistress."

With that she showed them the pouch to silence them, and they patted company.

"No wonder!" Qingwen snorted as they walked on. "Now that she's climbed to a higher branch of the tree, she won't pay any more attention to us. Our lady may have thrown her a word or two, without even knowing her name, and she's already eaten up with pride. What's so marvellous about running a little errand? We shall see if anything comes of it or not. If she's all that clever she'd better clear out of this Garden and stay perched on the top of the tree."

Xiaohong could hardly have it out with her. Swallowing her resentment she went on and found Xifeng, sure enough, chatting in Li Wan's apartment. She stepped forward to make her report.

"Sister Pinger said, madam, that as soon as Your Ladyship left she put away the money; and when Zhang Cai's wife came for it, she weighed it in her presence and gave it to her." She handed the pouch to Xifeng and continued, "Sister Pinger asked me to tell Your Ladyship: Just now Lai Wang came to ask for your instructions before setting out to the mansion where you sent him, and she sent him off after explaining Your Ladyship's wishes."

"How did she explain my wishes?" Xifeng smiled.

"She said, 'Our lady sends her compliments to Her Ladyship. Our Second Master is away from home now, so Her Ladyship shouldn't worry over a couple of days' delay. When the Fifth Mistress is better, our lady will come with her to see Her Ladyship. The Fifth Mistress sent a servant the other day to report that our lady's sister-in-law had inquired after Her Ladyship in a letter, and hoped her sister-in-law here would oblige her with two longevity pills. If Her Ladyship has any to spare, please send them to our lady, and the next person to go that way will deliver them to her sister-in-law.'"

"Mercy on us!" cut in Li Wan with a laugh. "I've lost track of all these ladies and mistresses."

"I don't blame you." Xifeng smiled. "There are five families involved." She turned to Xiaohong. "You're a good child and deliver messages clearly, not like some who mince their words or buzz like mosquitoes. You know," she turned to Li Wan, "my dear sister-in-law, I can't stand talking to most of the maids, apart from the few in my service. They don't know it, but I find it quite maddening the way they pad out a sentence and then break it down into several, the way they mince, drawl and stutter. Our Pinger used to be as bad as the rest. I asked her: Does a pretty girl have to buzz like a mosquito? And after a few scoldings she improved."

Li Wan laughed.

"Not everyone is a termagant like you."

"But I like this girl," Xifeng continued. "Admittedly, her two messages weren't long, but she spoke to the point." She smiled at Xiaohong. "You must come and work for me. I'll make you my adopted daughter and see that you turn out all right."

Xiaohong burst out laughing.

"What's so funny?" demanded Xifeng. "Do you think, because I'm not much older than you, I'm too young to be your mother? If so, you're crazy. Just ask around. There are plenty of people twice your age eager to call me mother — if only I'd let them. I'm doing you an honour."

"That wasn't why I laughed," replied Xiaohong. "I laughed because Your Ladyship has got my generation wrong. My *mother's* Your Ladyship's adopted daughter, yet now you talk of me as a daughter too."

"Who's your mother?"

"Don't you know her?" put in Li Wan with a smile. "This child is Lin Zhixiao's daughter."

"You don't say so!" exclaimed Xifeng in surprise. "Why, you can't get a word out of Lin Zhixiao and his wife, not even if you stick an awl into them. I've always said they were a well-matched couple, deaf muses the pair of them. Who could have believed they'd produce such a clever daughter? How old are you?"

"Seventeen."

Next she was asked her name.

"I was first called Hongyu," she answered. "But because of the ' yu' in Master Bao's name they call me Xiaohong now."

Xifeng frowned and tossed her head.

"Disgusting! You'd think there was something special about ' yu ', the way everybody wants that name. So in that case you can work for me. You know, sister-in-law, I told her mother, ' Lai Da's wife has her hands full, and anyway she's no idea who's who in this household. You choose a couple of good maids for me.' And she promised that's what she'd do. But instead, she sends this daughter of hers somewhere else. Did she think the girl would have a bad time with me?"

"How suspicious you are," teased Li Wan. "This child was already here by then. How can you blame her mother?"

"In that case, I'll tell Baoyu to ask for someone else and send this girl to me — if she's willing, that is."

Xiaohong smiled.

"Willing? As if that were for us to say! But if only I could work for Your Ladyship, I'd learn some manners and get more experience."

As she said this a maid came from Lady Wang to summon Xifeng, who took her leave of Li Wan. And Xiaohong went back to Happy Red Court, where we leave her.

Let us return to Daiyu, who had risen late after a sleepless night. When she heard that the other girls were farewelling the God of Flowers in the Garden, for fear of being laughed at for laziness she made haste to dress and go out. She was crossing the courtyard when Baoyu came in.

"Dear cousin, did you tell on me yesterday?" he greeted her laughingly. "You had me worrying the whole night long."

Daiyu turned away from him to Zijuan.

"When you've tidied the rooms, close the screen windows," she instructed. "As soon as the big swallows come back, you can let down the curtains. Hold them in place by moving the lions against them. And cover the censer once the incense is lit."

As she said this, she walked on.

Baoyu attributed this cold behaviour to the lines he had quoted at noon the previous day, having no idea of the incident in the evening. He bowed and raised his clasped hands in salute, but Daiyu simply ignored him, walking straight off to find the other girls.

Baoyu was puzzled.

"Surely what happened yesterday can't account for this?" he thought. "And I came back too late in the evening to see her again, so how else can I have offended her?"

With these reflections, he trailed after her.

Daiyu joined Baochai and Tanchun, who were both watching the storks dancing, and the three girls were chatting together when Baoyu arrived.

"How are you, brother?" asked Tanchun. "It's three whole days since last I saw you."

"How are you, sister?" he rejoined. "The other day I was asking our elder sister-in-law about you."

"Come over here. I want to talk to you."

The pair of them strolled aside under a pomegranate tree away from the other two.

"Has father sent for you these last few days?" asked Tanchun.

Baoyu smiled.

"No, he hasn't."

"Oh, I thought someone told me he sent for you yesterday."

"That someone must have misheard. He didn't."

Tanchun chuckled.

"These last few months I've saved a dozen strings of cash. I want you to take them. Next time you go out you can buy me some good calligraphy and paintings, or some amusing toys."

"In my strolls through the squares and temple markets inside and outside the city," Baoyu told her, "I haven't seen anything novel or really well made. Nothing but curios of gold, jade, bronze or porcelain, which would be out of place here. Or things like silk textiles, food and clothing."

"That's not what I mean. No, but things like you bought me last time: little willow baskets, incense-boxes carved out of bamboo roots, and tiny clay stoves. They were so sweet, I just loved them! But then other people fell in love with them too and grabbed them as if they were treasures."

Baoyu laughed.

"If that's what you want, those things are dirt cheap. Just give five hundred cash to the pages and they'll fetch you two cartloads."

"Those fellows have no taste. Please choose some things which are simple without being vulgar, and genuine instead of artificial. Do get me a whole lot more, and I'll make you another pair of slippers. I'll put even more work into them than last time. How's that?"

"That reminds me." Baoyu grinned. "I was wearing your slippers one day when I met father. He asked me disapprovingly who'd made them. It wouldn't have done to tell him it was you, sister; so I said they were a present from Aunt Wang on my last birthday. There wasn't much he could say to that, but after an awful silence he commented, 'What a waste of time and energy and good silk.' When I told Xiren she said: 'Never mind that, but the concubine Zhao's been complaining bitterly, "Her own younger brother Huan's shoes and socks are in holes yet she doesn't care. Instead she embroiders slippers for Baoyu.'"

Tanchun frowned.

"Did you ever hear such nonsense?" she fumed. "Is it my job to make shoes? Doesn't Huan have his fair share of clothes, shoes and socks, not to mention a whole roomful of maids and servants? What has she got to complain of? Who's she trying to impress? If I make a pair of slippers in my spare time, I can give them to any brother I choose and no one has any right to interfere. She's crazy, carrying on like that."

Baoyu nodded and smiled.

"Still, it's natural, you know, for her to see things rather differently."

This only enraged Tanchun more. She tossed her head.

"Now *you're* talking nonsense too. Of course she sees things differently with that sly, low, dirty mind of hers. Who cares what she thinks? I don't owe any duty to anyone except our parents. If my sisters, brothers and cousins are nice to me, I'll be nice to them too, regardless of which is the child of a wife or the child of a concubine. Properly speaking, I shouldn't say such things, but really that woman's the limit!

"Let me tell you another ridiculous thing too. Two days after I gave you that money to buy knick-knacks, she complained to me she was hard up. I paid no attention, of course. But after my maids left the room, she started scolding me for giving my savings to you instead of to Huan. I didn't know whether to laugh or lose my temper. So I left her and went to Her Ladyship."

But now Baochai called to them laughingly: "Haven't you talked long enough? It's clear you're brother and sister, the way you leave other people out in the cold to discuss your private affairs. Aren't we allowed to hear a single word?"

They smiled at that and joined her.

Meanwhile Daiyu had disappeared, and Baoyu knew she was avoiding him. He decided to wait a couple of days for the storm to blow over before approaching her again. Then, lowering his head, he noticed that the ground was strewn with balsam and pomegranate petals.

"She's too angry even to gather up the blossom," he sighed. "I'll take these over and try to speak to her tomorrow."

At this point Baochai urged them to take a stroll.

"I'll join you later." he said.

As soon as the other two had gone, he gathered up the fallen flowers in the skirt of his gown and made his way over a small hill, across a stream and through an orchard towards the mound where Daiyu had buried the peach-blossom. Just before rounding the hill by the flowers' grave he caught the sound of sobs on the other side. Someone was lamenting and weeping there in a heart-rending fashion.

"Some maid's been badly treated and come here to cry," he thought. "I wonder which of them it is."

He halted to listen. And this is what he heard:

> As blossoms fade and fly across the sky,
> Who pities the faded red, the scent that has been?
> Softly the gossamer floats over spring pavilions,
> Gently the willow fluff wafts to the embroidered screen.

> A girl in her chamber mourns the passing of spring,
> No relief from anxiety her poor heart knows;
> Hoe in hand she steps through her portal,
> Loath to tread on the blossoms as she comes and goes.

> Willows and elms, fresh and verdant,
> Care not if peach and plum blossom drift away;

Next year the peach and plum will bloom again,
But her chamber may stand empty on that day.

By the third month the scented nests are built,
But the swallows on the beam are heartless all;
Next year, though once again you may peck the buds,
From the beam of an empty room your nest will fall.

Each year for three hundred and sixty days
The cutting wind and biting frost contend.
How long can beauty flower fresh and fair?
In a single day wind can whirl it to its end.

Fallen, the brightest blooms are hard to find;
With aching heart their grave-digger comes now
Alone, her hoe in hand, her secret tears
Falling like drops of blood on each bare bough.

Dusk falls and the cuckoo is silent;
Her hoe brought back, the lodge is locked and still;
A green lamp lights the wall as sleep enfolds her,
Cold rain pelts the casement and her quilt is chill.

What causes my two-fold anguish?
Love for spring and resentment of spring;
For suddenly it comes and suddenly goes,
Its arrival unheralded, noiseless its departing.

Last night from the courtyard floated a sad song
Was it the soul of blossom, the soul of birds?
Hard to detain, the soul of blossom or birds,
For blossoms have no assurance, birds no words.

I long to take wing and fly
With the flowers to earth's uttermost bound;
And yet at earth's uttermost bound
Where can a fragrant burial mound be found?

Better shroud the fair petals in silk
With clean earth for their outer attire;
For pure you came and pure shall go,
Not sinking into some foul ditch or mire.

Now you are dead I come to bury you;
None has divined the day when I shall die;
Men laugh at my folly in burying fallen flowers,
But who will bury me when dead I lie?

See, when spring draws to a close and flowers fall,
This is the season when beauty must ebb and fade;
The day that spring takes wing and beauty fades
Who will care for the fallen blossom or dead maid?

Baoyu, listening, was overwhelmed with grief. To know more of this, read the next chapter.

六

燕子赋(二)①

此歌身自合，天下更无过。

雀儿和燕子，合作开元歌。

燕子实难及，能语复喽罗。一生心快健，禽里更无过。居在堂梁上，衔泥来作窠。追朋伴亲侣，滥鸟不相过。秋冬石窟隐，春夏在人间。二月来投藁，八月却皈(归)山。口衔长命草，余事且闲闲。经冬若不死，今岁重回还。游扬云中戏，宛转在空飞；还来归旧室，冬自本窠依。藁中逢一鸟，称名自雀儿，摇头径野说，语里事峥嵘。

雀儿实噆念，变弄别浮沉。知他窠窟好，乃即横来侵。问燕何山鸟？掇地作音声："徒劳来索窟，放你且收心。"

燕子语雀儿："好得辄行非！问君向者语，元本未相知。一冬来居住，温暖养妻儿，计你合惭愧，却被怨辩之！"

雀儿语燕子："恩泽莫大言，高声定无理，不假觜头喧。官司有道理，正敕见明宣。空闲石得坐，雀儿起(岂)自专。"

燕子语雀儿："好得合头痴。向吾宅里坐，却捉主人欺；如今见我索，荒(谎)语说官司。养虾蟆得痃病，报你定无疑！"

① 中文选自：王重民，王庆菽，向达，周一良，启功，曾毅公，编. 敦煌变文集. 北京：人民文学出版社，1957：262-265.

　英译文选自：Yang Xianyi & Gladys Yang. The Swallow and the Sparrow. *Chinese Literature*，1986（Summer）：153-161.

雀儿语燕子:"不由君事觜头。问君行坐处,元本住何州?宅家今括客,特敕捉浮逃;黠儿别设诮,转急且抽头。"

燕闻拍手笑:"不由事君(君事)落荒(谎)。大宅居山所,此乃是吾庄。本贯属京兆,生缘在帝乡。但知还他窟,野语不相当。纵使无籍贯,终是不关君。我得永年福,到处即安身。此言并是实,天下亦知闻;是君不信语,乞问读书人。"

雀儿语燕子:"何用苦分疏?因何得永年福?言词总是虚。精神目验在,活时解自如;功夫何处得,野语诳乡闾。头似独春鸟,身如大槛形,缘身豆汁染,脚手似针钉。恒常事皂大,径欲漫胡瓶。抚国知何道,闻我永年名。"

"昔本吾王殿,燕子作巢窟。宫人夜游戏,因便捉窠烧,当时无柱(住)处,堂梁寄一宵。其王见怜愍,愍念亦优饶。莫欺身幼小,意气极英雄。堂梁一百所,游扬在云中。水上吞浮蝱,空里接飞虫。真城无比较,曾娉海龙宫。海龙王第三女,发长七尺强,衔来腹底卧,燕岂在称扬!请读论语验,问取公冶长,当时在缧绁,缘燕免无常。"

雀儿语燕子:"侧耳用心听!如欲还君窟,且定觜头声。赤雀由称瑞,兄弟在天庭,公王共执手,朝野悉知名。一种居天地,受果不相当。麦熟我先食,禾熟在前尝。寒来及暑往,何曾别帝乡?子孙满天下,父叔遍村坊。自从能识别,慈母实心平。恒思十善业,觉悟欲无常。饥恒餐五谷,不煞一众生。怜君是远客,为此不相争。"

燕子自咨嗟:"不向雀儿夸。饥恒食九醢,渴即饮丹砂。不能别四海,心里恋洪牙。莫怪经冬隐,只为乐山家。九(久)住人憎贱,希来见喜欢;为此经冬隐,不是怕饥寒。幽岩实快乐,山野打盘珊(跚或旋),本拟将身看,却被看人看。"

"一猲虽然猛,不如众狗强;窠被夺将去,吓我作官方。空争并无益,无过见凤凰。"

雀儿被燕撮,直见鸟中王。凤凰台上坐,百鸟四边围,徘徊四顾望,见燕口衔词。"横被强夺窟,投名言雀儿。抱屈见谏诉,启奏大王知。"

　　雀儿及燕子,皆总立王前,凤凰亲处分,有理当头宣。燕子于先语:
"听臣作一言。依实说事状,发本述因缘。被侵宅舍苦,理屈岂感(敢)言。
不分黄头雀,明博结豪强。燕有宅一所,横被强夺将,理屈难缄嘿,伏乞愿
商量。日月虽耀赫,无明照覆盆,空辞元无力,谁肯入王门!"

　　凤凰嗔雀儿:"何为捉他欺! 彼此有窠窟,忽尔辄行非。"雀儿向前启:
"凤凰王今怎不知! 穷研细诸问,岂得信虚辞! 雀儿但为鸟,各自住村坊,
彼此无宅舍,到处自安身。见一空闲窟,破坏故非新;久访元无主,随便即
安身。成功不可毁,不能移改张。随便里许坐,爱护得劳藏。"

　　燕子启大王:"雀儿漫洛荒(落谎)。亦是穷奇鸟,构揆足词章。衔泥
来作窟。口里见生疮;王今不信语,乞问主人郎。"

　　凤凰当处分:"二鸟近前头。不言我早悉,事状见喽喽。薄媚黄头鸟,
便漫说缘由;急手还他窟,不得更勾留。"

　　雀儿启凤凰:"判付亦甘从。王遣还他窟,乞请且通容:雀儿是课户,
岂共外人同。燕子时来往,从坐不经冬。"

　　凤凰语雀儿:"急还燕子窟。我今已判定,雀儿不合过。朕是百鸟主,
法令不阿磨,理得合如此,不可有偏颇。"

　　燕子理得舍,欢喜复欢忻;雀儿修(羞)欲死,无处可安身。

　　燕子不求人,雀儿莫生嗔,昔问(闻)古人语,三斗始成亲。往者尧王
圣,写(摄)位二十年。郑乔事四海,对面即为婚。元百(伯)在家患,臣卿
千理期。燕王怨秦国,位马变为驎。并粮坐守死,万代得称传。百姚忆朝
廷,哽咽泪交连。断马有王义,由自不能分。午(仵)子胥罚(伐)楚,二邑
亦无言。不能攀古得(德),二人并鸟身。缘争破坏窟,徒特费精神。钱财
如粪土,人义重于山;燕今实罪过,雀儿莫生嗔。

　　雀儿语燕子:"别后不须论。室是君家室,合理不虚然。一冬来修理,
涴落悉皆然。计你合惭愧,却攘我见王身。凤凰住佛法,不拟煞伤人;忽
然责情打,几许愧金身。"

　　燕子语雀儿:"此言亦非嗔。缘君修理屋,不索价房钱。一年十二月,
月别伍百文,可中论房课,定是卖君身。"

The Swallow and the Sparrow

"The Swallow and the Sparrow" is one of the literary works discovered by chance at Dunhuang in 1900 *when double-chambered caves were opened for the first time in about one thousand years, revealing a* 20,000-*scroll library that astounded the world and remains one of the most important cultural discoveries of the* 20th *century.*

Among these manuscripts there were some works of folk literature, and the poem presented here, by an anonymous poet, was probably written in the late Tang period during the ninth or tenth century judging by the style. There are two versions, one in four-character verse and the other in five-character verse, both recounting a dispute between a swallow and a sparrow concerning a nest. The one translated here is the latter version.

The folk fu, *of which this is an example, is different from the earlier literary* fu. *It is a narrative form written in rhythmical, vernacular style.*

—The Editors

This poem stands by itself alone,
And in the world is like to none;
The swallow and the sparrow both
Together did this song bring forth.

The swallow has indeed no peer,
With diverse skill he speaks out clear;

With agile limbs he flies full fast;
All other birds he has surpassed.
Upon high rafters he doth rest,
And gathers clay to make his nest,
With friends and kinsmen doth resort,
Nor mingles with the common sort.
In stony cave from cold he hides,
In warmer days midst men abides;
In February seeks his home,
In August once again doth roam.
With herb of long life in his bill,
Delights his days of leisure fill.
If he be not in winter slain,
The next year he returns again;
He roams and sports midst clouds on high,
And whirls in flight about the sky.
But now he seeks his former home,
And to his nest again is come;
A bird he meets there unawares,
And "Sparrow" is the name he bears.

The sparrow rants, with tossing head,
Such things as should no wise be said.
All craft and skill to him belong,
And he can argue right to wrong.
He knows how good the swallow's nest,
So comes and seems like one possessed.
He asks the swallow: "From what hill
Come you, this place with noise to fill?
You come to beg a nest in vain,
But know that you may go again."

The swallow then makes this reply:
"You are a ruffian, verily;
For when your foolish words I hear
That you are ignorant is clear.
Throughout the winter here you rest,
And feed your kin in this warm nest;
I thought that shame would bow your head,
But you dispute with me instead."

The sparrow cries, in accents rude,
"Boast not to me of gratitude!
With loud words you yourself accuse;
To babble thus is of no use.
But in the judge's court are laws,
Where clearly you may read this clause:
'A vacant stone is free to all.'
You cannot me presumptuous call."

The swallow then makes this retort:
"Blackheaded fellow, all distraught,
Within my house you sit at ease,
Its master flouting as you please.
Now when you see my home I seek
You talk of courts and lying speak.
You seem a toad whom dropsies swell;
But I will pay you back full well."

The sparrow makes a new retort:
"No need to babble in this sort.
I want to ask where is your home,
And from what district are you come?
Within my house I have a guest,

Who comes all vagrants to arrest；
Then brag no more you crafty one，
But better swiftly homeward run."

The swallow laughs and claps his hand：
"I'll see you vagrant through the land.
Your house is on the mountain set，
And this my home，I much regret.
Within the capital I stay；
In royal realm I first saw day；
My nest returned is all I want；
Improper is your frenzied rant.
If I had no home anywhere，
That would be none of your affair.
Long life is mine and wealth and ease，
And I can rest me where I please.
It is the actual truth I tell，
And this all men acknowledge well；
If you still think I utter lies，
Then you can ask the scholars wise."

The sparrow says，"It is in vain
You make such efforts to explain.
How can long life belong to you?
No single word of it is true.
All creatures their own souls possess，
And while they live show liveliness；
How can such gift to you belong?
You lie to cheat the common throng.
Your head like a wood-pecker's wags，
Your body is all clothed in rags；
All stained with beans your feathers green，

Your hands and feet seem talons keen.
In boasts and brags your time you spend,
And utter nonsense without end.
Vagrant, what gift can you receive?
Talk of long life is to deceive."

"The royal court in former days
Served as the swallow's resting place;
Till palace maids one ev'ning came
And flung my nest into the flame.
Since then I had no place at all;
I lived on rafters in the hall.
My skill was noticed by the lord,
And sumptuous gifts on me he poured.
Do not despise my slender frame;
My courage is renowned to fame.
A hundred beams for rest had I,
And midst the clouds I soar on high;
I seize the gnats above the lake,
And insects from the air I take.
It is the strictest truth I tell.
In sea king's palace I did dwell;
The sea king's daughter was most fair,
And seven feet long her gleaming hair,
Whom to my breast I used to take;
It is no idle boast I make.
Go, read the Analects, I pray,
And you will find the scholar say
How he was bound in chains by foes,
Till I released him from his woes."

The sparrow interrupts him there:

"You listen to my words with care:
If you would have your nest again,
You first must cease this babbling vain.
All men red sparrows lucky call;
In heaven lived my brothers all;
To court and cottage we are known;
Princes and dukes our kinship own.
We dwell between the earth and sky,
And none there are can with us vie.
Who before us taste early wheat?
Who before us the first grains eat?
The cold succeeds the heat again,
But we leave not the King's domain.
Throughout the world our kin abound,
Our fathers in each place are found.
Since good from evil I could tell
My kindly mother trained me well;
I aim at good early and late,
And recognize the whims of Fate.
Hungry, of grain I eat my fill;
No living creature need I kill.
I pity you, vagrant and poor,
And will not argue with you more."

The swallow slowly heaves a sigh:
"Know, sparrow, that no boaster I.
Thirsty, I drink a draft divine;
Hungry, immortal fare is mine.
I wander the Four Seas among,
But for the Paradise I long.
Not strange that I in winter hide,
For well I love the mountain-side.

When long I stay, men hold me mean;
And seldom come, more rare am seen;
Thus I in winter fly from here;
Hunger and cold I do not fear.
Happy indeed the mountains still,
Where in the wilds I roam at will.
Though I would inconspicuous be,
Yet now all people look at me.
A tiger, be he ne'er so fierce,
Cannot a crowd of dogs disperse.
But now my nest in vain I seek,
While blustering of courts you speak.
Reason with you is vain I know;
Better we to the phoenix go."

The swallow and the sparrow both
To see the king of birds go forth.
The phoenix in the court presides,
And birds surround him on all sides;
He looks about him and doth see
The swallow bringing in his plea:
"My nest was seized from me by might;
I come the sparrow to indict.
Wronged, I present you with my case,
And thus appeal before Your Grace."

The swallow and the sparrow here
Before the king of birds appear.
Acting as judge the phoenix great
Bids both the birds their cases state.
Then first the swallow leads the way:
"But this, my lord, I have to say.

All that I have to speak is true;
In detail will I tell it you.
Invaded was my lawful home;
Not without reason am I come.
The yellow-headed sparrow there
Depended upon force unfair.
Though I, the swallow, own the nest,
By force he is of it possessed.
Now wronged I cannot silent stay;
That you will look to this I pray.
Although the sun and moon are bright,
A covered bowl they cannot light.
To utter empty words is nought,
And none come without cause to court."

The judge doth to the sparrow say,
"Why did you take his house away?
Houses to each of you belong;
Why should you do a thing so wrong?"

The sparrow pleads before the king:
"My lord, you do not know the thing;
But carefully the question weigh,
Nor heed what vain words he may say.
Since sparrows led a bird's life first,
Throughout each place we are dispersed.
We have no individual nest,
But where we wander there we rest.
An empty nest I did behold,
I could not find who owned the place,
That was a wretched one and old.
So rested myself there a space.

The broken parts I did repair;
Why should I have to go from there?
For there I rest myself and sleep,
And very well the place I keep."

The swallow says then to the king:
"The sparrow is a vagrant thing;
He wanders round a homeless bird,
And he is skilled in lying word.
I gathered clay this nest to fill,
And in my mouth the wounds are still;
And if of this you would have proof,
Then ask the owner of the roof."

The phoenix then makes this decree:
"Do both you birds approach to me.
Before you uttered your appeal,
The plea did well the case reveal.
You crafty bird with yellow head,
Cunning and wild was all you said.
You must return his nest today;
Nor can you any longer stay."

The sparrow then makes this reply:
"I would obey your order high;
But if I must this nest restore
I beg you to reflect once more.
Each year I pay the dues I ought;
I am not like the common sort.
The swallow comes here now and then;
In summer stays then leaves again."

The phoenix says in accents stern.
"Sparrow, this house at once return.
The judgement is already done;
The sparrow is the guilty one.
Of all the birds I am the king;
My laws admit no altering;
And this you should by reason see;
That I am biassed cannot be."

Now that the swallow wins success,
He has his fill of happiness.
The sparrow now must pine away,
Who has no more a place to stay.
"I will not claim the punishment,
So sparrow cease your discontent.
This saying in old books you find;
Three quarrels make men kinsmen kind.
Their standards we cannot attain,
Since birds we are but creatures vain;
And fighting for a broken nest,
For nought together we contest.
Wealth is but as a clod of clay;
But kind deeds as the mountains weigh.
The error then is wholly mine,
Though you do not the truth divine."

The sparrow then to him doth say,
"Let us depart and go our way.
The house should unto you belong,
And you were right and I was wrong.
But I repaired it in the cold,
And mended all the places old;

And, swallow, you should be ashamed
To have me by the phoenix blamed.
The phoenix is a judge astute,
He has no wish to execute;
But if he beat me by your claim,
My body would be full of shame."

The swallow says to him anew,
"What you just say is not quite true.
Since money for repairs you spent,
I will not ask you for the rent.
But for each month you make your stay,
Five hundred coins you ought to pay.
If rent from you I still compel,
Your body you will have to sell."

第三编

中国现当代文学英译

鲁迅作品六篇

1. 狂人日记①

　　某君昆仲，今隐其名，皆余昔日在中学时良友；分隔多年，消息渐阙。日前偶闻其一大病；适归故乡，迂道往访，则仅晤一人，言病者其弟也。劳君远道来视，然已早愈，赴某地候补矣。因大笑，出示日记二册，谓可见当日病状，不妨献诸旧友。持归阅一过，知所患盖"迫害狂"之类。语颇错杂无伦次，又多荒唐之言；亦不著月日，惟墨色字体不一，知非一时所书。间亦有略具联络者，今撮录一篇，以供医家研究。记中语误，一字不易；惟人名虽皆村人，不为世间所知，无关大体，然亦悉易去。至于书名，则本人愈后所题，不复改也。七年四月二日识。

一

　　今天晚上，很好的月光。

　　我不见他，已是三十多年；今天见了，精神分外爽快。才知道以前的三十多年，全是发昏；然而须十分小心。不然，那赵家的狗，何以看

---

①　中文选自：鲁迅. 呐喊. 上海：北新书局，1941.
　　英译文选自：Lu Hsun. *Selected Stories of Lu Hsun*. Yang Xianyi & Gladys Yang.
　　Trans. Beijing：Foreign Languages Press，1978.

我两眼呢?

我怕得有理。

<h1 style="text-align:center">二</h1>

今天全没月光,我知道不妙。早上小心出门,赵贵翁的眼色便怪:似乎怕我,似乎想害我。还有七八个人,交头接耳的议论我,张着嘴,对我笑了一笑;我便从头直冷到脚跟,晓得他们布置,都已妥当了。

我可不怕,仍旧走我的路。前面一伙小孩子,也在那里议论我;眼色也同赵贵翁一样,脸色也铁青。我想我同小孩子有什么仇,他也这样。忍不住大声说,"你告诉我!"他们可就跑了。

我想:我同赵贵翁有什么仇,同路上的人又有什么仇;只有廿年以前,把古久先生的陈年流水簿子,踹了一脚,古久先生很不高兴。赵贵翁虽然不认识他,一定也听到风声,代抱不平;约定路上的人,同我作冤对。但是小孩子呢?那时候,他们还没有出世,何以今天也睁着怪眼睛,似乎怕我,似乎想害我。这真教我怕,教我纳罕而且伤心。

我明白了。这是他们娘老子教的!

<h1 style="text-align:center">三</h1>

晚上总是睡不着。凡事须得研究,才会明白。

他们——也有给知县打枷过的,也有给绅士掌过嘴的,也有衙役占了他妻子的,也有老子娘被债主逼死的;他们那时候的脸色,全没有昨天这么怕,也没有这么凶。

最奇怪的是昨天街上的那个女人,打他儿子,嘴里说道,"老子呀!我要咬你几口才出气!"他眼睛却看着我。我出了一惊,遮掩不住;那青面獠牙的一伙人,便都哄笑起来。陈老五赶上前,硬把我拖回家中了。

拖我回家,家里的人都装作不认识我;他们的脸色,也全同别人一样。进了书房,便反扣上门,宛然是关了一只鸡鸭。这一件事,越教我猜不出底细。

前几天，狼子村的佃户来告荒，对我大哥说，他们村里的一个大恶人，给大家打死了；几个人便挖出他的心肝来，用油煎炒了吃，可以壮壮胆子。我插了一句嘴，佃户和大哥便都看我几眼。今天才晓得他们的眼光，全同外面的那伙人一模一样。

想起来，我从顶上直冷到脚跟。

他们会吃人，就未必不会吃我。

你看那女人"咬你几口"的话，和一伙青面獠牙人的笑，和前天佃户的话，明明是暗号。我看出他话中全是毒，笑中全是刀。他们的牙齿，全是白厉厉的排着，这就是吃人的家伙。

照我自己想，虽然不是恶人，自从踹了古家的簿子，可就难说了。他们似乎别有心思，我全猜不出。况且他们一翻脸，便说人是恶人。我还记得大哥教我做论，无论怎样好人，翻他几句，他便打上几个圈；原谅坏人几句，他便说"翻天妙手，与众不同"。我那里猜得到他们的心思，究竟怎样；况且是要吃的时候。

凡事总须研究，才会明白。古来时常吃人，我也还记得，可是不甚清楚。我翻开历史一查，这历史没有年代，歪歪斜斜的每叶上都写着"仁义道德"几个字。我横竖睡不着，仔细看了半夜，才从字缝里看出字来，满本都写着两个字是"吃人"！

书上写着这许多字，佃户说了这许多话，却都笑吟吟的睁着怪眼看我。

我也是人，他们想要吃我了！

四

早上，我静坐了一会儿。陈老五送进饭来，一碗菜，一碗蒸鱼；这鱼的眼睛，白而且硬，张着嘴，同那一伙想吃人的人一样。吃了几筷，滑溜溜的不知是鱼是人，便把他兜肚连肠的吐出。

我说"老五，对大哥说，我闷得慌，想到园里走走。"老五不答应，走了；停一会，可就来开了门。

我也不动,研究他们如何摆布我;知道他们一定不肯放松。果然!我大哥引了一个老头子,慢慢走来;他满眼凶光,怕我看出,只是低头向着地,从眼镜横边暗暗看我。大哥说,"今天你仿佛很好。"我说"是的。"大哥说,"今天请何先生来,给你诊一诊。"我说"可以!"其实我岂不知道这老头子是刽子手扮的!无非借了看脉这名目,揣一揣肥瘠:因这功劳,也分一片肉吃。我也不怕;虽然不吃人,胆子却比他们还壮。伸出两个拳头,看他如何下手。老头子坐着,闭了眼睛,摸了好一会,呆了好一会;便张开他鬼眼睛说,"不要乱想。静静的养几天,就好了。"

不要乱想,静静的养!养肥了,他们是自然可以多吃;我有什么好处,怎么会"好了"?他们这群人,又想吃人,又是鬼鬼祟祟,想法子遮掩,不敢直截下手,真要令我笑死。我忍不住,便放声大笑起来,十分快活。自己晓得这笑声里面,有的是义勇和正气。老头子和大哥,都失了色,被我这勇气正气镇压住了。

但是我有勇气,他们便越想吃我,沾光一点这勇气。老头子跨出门,走不多远,便低声对大哥说道,"赶紧吃罢!"大哥点点头。原来也有你!这一件大发见,虽似意外,也在意中:合伙吃我的人,便是我的哥哥!

吃人的是我哥哥!

我是吃人的人的兄弟!

我自己被人吃了,可仍然是吃人的人的兄弟!

五

这几天是退一步想:假使那老头子不是刽子手扮的,真是医生,也仍然是吃人的人。他们的祖师李时珍做的"本草什么"上,明明写着人肉可以煎吃;他还能说自己不吃人么?

至于我家大哥,也毫不冤枉他。他对我讲书的时候,亲口说过可以"易子而食";又一回偶然议论起一个不好的人,他便说不但该杀,还当"食肉寝皮"。我那时年纪还小,心跳了好半天。前天狼子村佃户来说吃心肝的事,他也毫不奇怪,不住的点头。可见心思是同从前一样狠。既然可以

"易子而食"，便什么都易得，什么人都吃得。我从前单听他讲道理，也胡涂过去；现在晓得他讲道理的时候，不但唇边还抹着人油，而且心里满装着吃人的意思。

六

黑漆漆的，不知是日是夜。赵家的狗又叫起来了。

狮子似的凶心，兔子的怯弱，狐狸的狡猾，……

七

我晓得他们的方法，直捷杀了，是不肯的，而且也不敢，怕有祸祟。所以他们大家连络，布满了罗网，逼我自戕。试看前几天街上男女的样子，和这几天我大哥的作为，便足可悟出八九分了。最好是解下腰带，挂在梁上，自己紧紧勒死；他们没有杀人的罪名，又偿了心愿，自然都欢天喜地的发出一种呜呜咽咽的笑声。否则惊吓忧愁死了，虽则略瘦，也还可以首肯几下。

他们是只会吃死肉的！——记得什么书上说，有一种东西，叫"海乙那"的，眼光和样子都很难看；时常吃死肉，连极大的骨头，都细细嚼烂，咽下肚子去，想起来也教人害怕。"海乙那"是狼的亲眷，狼是狗的本家。前天赵家的狗，看我几眼，可见他也同谋，早已接洽。老头子眼看着地，岂能瞒得我过。

最可怜的是我的大哥，他也是人，何以毫不害怕；而且合伙吃我呢？还是历来惯了，不以为非呢？还是丧了良心，明知故犯呢？

我诅咒吃人的人，先从他起头；要劝转吃人的人，也先从他下手。

八

其实这种道理，到了现在，他们也该早已懂得，……

忽然来了一个人；年纪不过二十左右，相貌是不很看得清楚，满面笑容，对了我点头，他的笑也不像真笑。我便问他，"吃人的事，对么？"他仍然笑着说，"不是荒年，怎么会吃人。"我立刻就晓得，他也是一伙，喜欢吃人的；便自勇气百倍，偏要问他。

"对么?"

"这等事问他什么。你真会……说笑话。……今天天气很好。"

天气是好，月色也很亮了。可是我要问你，"对么?"

他不以为然了。含含胡胡的答道，"不……"

"不对? 他们何以竟吃?!"

"没有的事……"

"没有的事? 狼子村现吃；还有书上都写着，通红斩新!"

他便变了脸，铁一般青。睁着眼说，"有许有的，这是从来如此……"

"从来如此，便对么?"

"我不同你讲这些道理；总之你不该说，你说便是你错!"

我直跳起来，张开眼，这人便不见了。全身出了一大片汗。他的年纪，比我大哥小得远，居然也是一伙；这一定是他娘老子先教的。还怕已经教给他儿子了；所以连小孩子，也都恶狠狠的看我。

九

自己想吃人，又怕被别人吃了，都用着疑心极深的眼光，面面相觑。……

去了这心思，放心做事走路吃饭睡觉，何等舒服。这只是一条门槛，一个关头。他们可是父子兄弟夫妇朋友师生仇敌和各不相识的人，都结成一伙，互相劝勉，互相牵掣，死也不肯跨过这一步。

十

大清早，去寻我大哥；他立在堂门外看天，我便走到他背后，拦住门，格外沉静，格外和气的对他说，

"大哥，我有话告诉你。"

"你说就是，"他赶紧回过脸来，点点头。

"我只有几句话，可是说不出来。大哥，大约当初野蛮的人，都吃过一点人。后来因为心思不同，有的不吃人了，一味要好，便变了人，变了真的人。有的却还吃，——也同虫子一样，有的变了鱼鸟猴子，一直变到人。有的不要好，至今还是虫子。这吃人的人比不吃人的人，何等惭愧。怕比虫子的惭愧猴子，还差得很远很远。

"易牙蒸了他儿子，给桀纣吃，还是一直从前的事。谁晓得从盘古开辟天地以后，一直吃到易牙的儿子；从易牙的儿子，一直吃到徐锡林；从徐锡林，又一直吃到狼子村捉住的人。去年城里杀了犯人，还有一个生痨病的人，用馒头蘸血舐。

"他们要吃我，你一个人，原也无法可想；然而又何必去入伙。吃人的人，什么事做不出；他们会吃我，也会吃你，一伙里面，也会自吃。但只要转一步，只要立刻改了，也就是人人太平。虽然从来如此，我们今天也可以格外要好，说是不能！大哥，我相信你能说，前天佃户要减租，你说过不能。"

当初，他还只是冷笑，随后眼光便凶狠起来，一到说破他们的隐情，那就满脸都变成青色了。大门外立着一伙人，赵贵翁和他的狗，也在里面，都探头探脑的挨进来。有的是看不出面貌，似乎用布蒙着；有的是仍旧青面獠牙，抿着嘴笑。我认识他们是一伙，都是吃人的人。可是也晓得他们心思很不一样，一种是以为从来如此，应该吃的；一种是知道不该吃，可是仍然要吃，又怕别人说破他，所以听了我的话，越发气愤不过，可是抿着嘴冷笑。

这时候，大哥也忽然显出凶相，高声喝道，

"都出去！疯子有什么好看！"

这时候，我又懂得一件他们的巧妙了。他们岂但不肯改，而且早已布置；预备下一个疯子的名目罩上我。将来吃了，不但太平无事，怕还会有人见情。佃户说的大家吃了一个恶人，正是这方法。这是他们的老谱！

陈老五也气愤愤的直走进来。如何按得住我的口，我偏要对这伙人说，

"你们可以改了,从真心改起! 要晓得将来容不得吃人的人,活在世上。"

"你们要不改,自己也会吃尽。即使生得多,也会给真的人除灭了,同猎人打完狼子一样! ——同虫子一样!"

那一伙人,都被陈老五赶走了。大哥也不知那里去了。陈老五劝我回屋子里去。屋里面全是黑沉沉的。横梁和椽子都在头上发抖;抖了一会,就大起来,堆在我身上。

万分沉重,动弹不得;他的意思是要我死。我晓得他的沉重是假的,便挣扎出来,出了一身汗。可是偏要说,

"你们立刻改了,从真心改起! 你们要晓得将来是容不得吃人的人,……"

十一

太阳也不出,门也不开,日日是两顿饭。

我捏起筷子,便想起我大哥;晓得妹子死掉的缘故,也全在他。那时我妹子才五岁,可爱可怜的样子,还在眼前。母亲哭个不住,他却劝母亲不要哭;大约因为自己吃了,哭起来不免有点过意不去。如果还能过意不去,……

妹子是被大哥吃了,母亲知道没有,我可不得而知。

母亲想也知道;不过哭的时候,却并没有说明,大约也以为应当的了。记得我四五岁时,坐在堂前乘凉,大哥说爷娘生病,做儿子的须割下一片肉来,煮熟了请他吃,才算好人;母亲也没有说不行。一片吃得,整个的自然也吃得。但是那天的哭法,现在想起来,实在还教人伤心,这真是奇极的事!

十二

不能想了。

四千年来时时吃人的地方,今天才明白,我也在其中混了多年;大哥

正管着家务，妹子恰恰死了，他未必不和在饭菜里，暗暗给我们吃。

我未必无意之中，不吃了我妹子的几片肉，现在也轮到我自己，……

有了四千年吃人履历的我，当初虽然不知道，现在明白，难见真的人！

十三

没有吃过人的孩子，或者还有？

救救孩子……

一九一八年四月

A Madman's Diary

Two brothers, whose names I need not mention here, were both good friends of mine in high school; but after a separation of many years we gradually lost touch. Some time ago I happened to hear that one of them was seriously ill, and since I was going back to my old home I broke my journey to call on them, I saw only one, however, who told me that the invalid was his younger brother.

"I appreciate your coming such a long way to see us," he said, "but my brother recovered some time ago and has gone elsewhere to take up an official post." Then, laughing, he produced two volumes of his brother's diary, saying that from these the nature of his past illness could be seen, and that there was no harm in showing them to an old friend. I took the diary away, read it through, and found that he had suffered from a form of persecution complex. The writing was most confused and incoherent, and he had made many wild statements; moreover he had omitted to give any dates, so that only by the colour of the ink and the differences in the writing could one tell that it was not written at one time. Certain sections, however, were not altogether disconnected, and I have copied out a part to serve as a subject for medical research. I have not altered a single illogicality in the diary and have changed only the names, even though the people referred to are all country folk, unknown to the world and of no consequence. As for the title, it was chosen by the diarist himself after his recovery, and I did not change it.

I

Tonight the moon is very bright.

I have not seen it for over thirty years, so today when I saw it I felt in unusually high spirits. I begin to realize that during the past thirty-odd years I have been in the dark; but now I must be extremely careful. Otherwise why should that dog at the Chao house have looked at me twice?

I have reason for my fear.

II

Tonight there is no moon at all, I know that this bodes ill. This morning when I went out cautiously, Mr. Chao had a strange look in his eyes, as if he were afraid of me, as if he wanted to murder me. There were seven or eight others, who discussed me in a whisper. And they were afraid of my seeing them. All the people I passed were like that. The fiercest among them grinned at me; whereupon I shivered from head to foot, knowing that their preparations were complete.

I was not afraid, however, but continued on my way. A group of children in front were also discussing me, and the look in their eyes was just like that in Mr. Chao's while their faces too were ghastly pale. I wondered what grudge these children could have against me to make them behave like this. I could not help calling out: "Tell me!" But then they ran away.

I wonder what grudge Mr. Chao can have against me, what grudge the people on the road can have against me. I can think of nothing except that twenty years ago I trod on Mr. Ku Chiu's[①] account sheets for many years past, and Mr. Ku was very displeased. Although Mr. Chao does not know him, he must have heard talk of this and decided to avenge him, so he is conspiring against me with the people on the road, But then what of the children? At that time they were not yet born, so why should they eye me so strangely today, as if they were afraid of me, as if they wanted to murder me? This really frightens me, it is so bewildering and upsetting.

I know. They must have learned this from their parents!

III

I can't sleep at night. Everything requires careful consideration if one is

---

①　译者注: Ku Chiu means "Ancient Times". Lu Hsun had in mind the long history of feudal oppression in China.

to understand it.

Those people, some of whom have been pilloried by the magistrate, slapped in the face by the local gentry, had their wives taken away by bailiffs, or their parents driven to suicide by creditors, never looked as frightened and as fierce then as they did yesterday.

The most extraordinary thing was that woman on the street yesterday who spanked her son and said, "Little devil! I'd like to bite several mouthfuls out of you to work off my feelings!" Yet all the time she looked at me. I gave a start, unable to control myself; then all those green-faced, long-toothed people began to laugh derisively. Old Chen hurried forward and dragged me home.

He dragged me home. The folk at home all pretended not to know me; they had the same look in their eyes as all the others. When I went into the study, they locked the door outside as if cooping up a chicken or a duck. This incident left me even more bewildered.

A few days ago a tenant of ours from Wolf Cub Village came to report the failure of the crops, and told my elder brother that a notorious character in their village had been beaten to death; then some people had taken out his heart and liver, fried them in oil and eaten them, as a means of increasing their courage. When I interrupted, the tenant and my brother both stared at me. Only today have I realized that they had exactly the same look in their eyes as those people outside.

Just to think of it sets me shivering from the crown of my head to the soles of my feet.

They eat human beings, so they may eat me.

I see that woman's "bite several mouthfuls out of you," the laughter of those green-faced, long-toothed people and the tenant's story the other day are obviously secret signs. I realize all the poison in their speech, all the daggers in their laughter. Their teeth are white and glistening: they are all man-eaters.

It seems to me, although I am not a bad man, ever since I trod on Mr. Ku's accounts it has been touch-and-go. They seem to have secrets which I cannot guess, and once they are angry they will call anyone a bad character. I remember when my elder brother taught me to write compositions, no matter how good a man was, if I produced arguments to the contrary he would mark that passage to show his approval; while if I excused evil-doers, he would say: "Good for you, that shows originality." How can I possibly guess their secret thoughts — especially when they are ready to eat people?

Everything requires careful consideration if one is to understand it. In ancient times, as I recollect, people often ate human beings, but I am rather hazy about it. I tried to look this up, but my history has no chronology, and scrawled all over each page are the words: "Virtue and Morality". Since I could not sleep anyway, I read intently half the night, until I began to see words between the lines, the whole book being filled with the two words — "Eat people".

All these words written in the book, all the words spoken by our tenant, gaze at me strangely with an enigmatic smile.

I too am a man, and they want to eat me!

IV

In the morning I sat quietly for some time. Old Chen brought lunch in: one bowl of vegetables, one bowl of steamed fish. The eyes of the fish were white and hard, and its mouth was open just like those people who want to eat human beings. After a few mouthfuls I could not tell whether the slippery morsels were fish or human flesh, so I brought it all up.

I said, "Old Chen, tell my brother that I feel quite suffocated, and want to have a stroll in the garden." Old Chen said nothing but went out, and presently he came back and opened the gate.

I did not move, but watched to see how they would treat me, feeling certain that they would not let me go. Sure enough! My elder brother came slowly out, leading an old man. There was a murderous gleam in his eyes, and fearing that I would see it he lowered his head, stealing glances at me from the side of his spectacles.

"You seem to be very well today," said my brother.

"Yes," said I.

"I have invited Mr. Ho here today," said my brother, "to examine you."

"All right," said I. Actually I knew quite well that this old man was the executioner in disguise! He simply used the pretext of feeling my pulse to see how fat I was; for by so doing he would receive a share of my flesh. Still I was not afraid. Although I do not eat men, my courage is greater than theirs. I held out my two fists, to see what he would do. The old man sat down, closed his eyes, fumbled for some time and remained still for some time; then he opened his shifty eyes and said, "Don't let your imagination run away with you. Rest quietly for a few days, and you will be all right."

Don't let your imagination run away with you! Rest quietly for a few days! When I have grown fat, naturally they will have more to eat; but what good will it do me, or how can it be "all right"? All these people wanting to eat human flesh and at the same time stealthily trying to keep up appearances, not daring to act promptly, really made me nearly die of laughter. I could not help roaring with laughter, I was so amused. I knew that in this laughter were courage and integrity. Both the old man and my brother turned pale, awed by my courage and integrity.

But just because I am brave they are the more eager to eat me, in order to acquire some of my courage. The old man went out of the gate, but before he had gone far he said to my brother in a low voice, "To be eaten at once!" And my brother nodded. So you are in it too! This stupendous discovery, although it came as a shock, is yet no more than I had expected: the accomplice in eating me is my elder brother!

The eater of human flesh is my elder brother!

I am the younger brother of an eater of human flesh!

I myself will be eaten by others, but none the less I am the younger brother of an eater of human flesh!

V

These few days I have been thinking again: suppose that old man were not an executioner in disguise, but a real doctor; he would be none the less an eater of human flesh. In that book on herbs, written by his predecessor Li Shih-chen[①], it is clearly stated that men's flesh can he boiled and eaten; so can he still say that he does not eat men?

As for my elder brother, I have also good reason to suspect him. When he was teaching me, he said with his own lips, "People exchange their sons to eat." And once in discussing a bad man, he said that not only did he deserve to be killed, he should "have his flesh eaten and his hide slept on."[②] I was still young then, and my heart beat faster for some time, he was not at all surprised by the story that our tenant from Wolf Cub Village told us the other day about eating a man's heart and liver, but kept nodding his head. He is evidently just as cruel as before. Since it is possible to "exchange sons to eat," then anything can be exchanged, anyone can be eaten. In the past I simply listened to his explanations, and let it go at that; now I know that when he explained it to me, not only was there human fat at the corner of his lips, but his whole heart was set on eating men.

VI

Pitch dark. I don't know whether it is day or night. The Chao family dog has started barking again.

The fierceness of a lion, the timidity of a rabbit, the craftiness of a fox ...

VII

I know their way; they are not willing to kill anyone outright, nor do they dare, for fear of the consequences. Instead they have banded together and set traps everywhere, to force me to kill myself. The behaviour of the men and women in the street a few days ago, and my elder brother's attitude

---

① 译者注: A famous pharmacologist (1518 – 1593), author of *Ben-cao-gang-mu*, the *Materia Medica*.

② 译者注: These are quotations from the old classic *Zuo Zhuan*.

these last few days, make it quite obvious. What they like best is for a man to take off his belt, and hang himself from a beam; for then they can enjoy their heart's desire without being blamed for murder. Naturally that sets them roaring with delighted laughter. On the other hand, if a man is frightened or worried to death, although that makes him rather thin, they still nod in approval.

They only eat dead flesh! I remember reading somewhere of a hideous beast, with an ugly look in its eye, called "hyena" which often eats dead flesh. Even the largest bones it grinds into fragments and swallows: the mere thought of this is enough to terrify one. Hyenas are related to wolves, and wolves belong to the canine species. The other day the dog in the Chao house looked at me several times; obviously it is in the plot too and has become their accomplice. The old man's eyes were cast down, but that did not deceive me!

The most deplorable is my elder brother. He is also a man, so why is he not afraid, why is he plotting with others to eat me? Is it that when one is used to it he no longer thinks it a crime? Or is it that he has hardened his heart to do something he knows is wrong?

In cursing man-eaters, I shall start with my brother, and in dissuading man-eaters, I shall start with him too.

VIII

Actually, such arguments should have convinced them long ago ...

Suddenly someone came in. He was only about twenty years old and I did not see his features very clearly. His face was wreathed in smiles, but when he nodded to me his smile did not seem genuine. I asked him "Is it right to eat human beings?"

Still smiling, he replied, "When there is no famine how can one eat human beings?"

I realized at once, he was one of them; but still I summoned up courage to repeat my question:

"Is it right?"

"What makes you ask such a thing? You really are ... fond of a joke ... It is very fine today."

"It is fine, and the moon is very bright. But I want to ask you: Is it right?"

He looked disconcerted, and muttered: "No ..."

"No? Then why do they still do it?"

"What are you talking about?"

"What am I talking about? They are eating men now in Wolf Cub Village, and you can see it written all over the books, in fresh red ink."

His expression changed, and he grew ghastly pale. "It may be so," he said, staring at me. "It has always been like that ..."

"Is it right because it has always been like that?"

"I refuse to discuss these things with you. Anyway, you shouldn't talk about it. Whoever talks about it is in the wrong!"

I leaped up and opened my eyes wide, but the man had vanished. I was soaked with perspiration. He was much younger than my elder brother, but even so he was in it. He must have been taught by his parents. And I am afraid he has already taught his son: that is why even the children look at me so fiercely.

IX

Wanting to eat men, at the same time afraid of being eaten themselves, they all look at each other with the deepest suspicion ...

How comfortable life would be for them if they could rid themselves of such obsessions and go to work, walk, eat and sleep at ease. They have only this one step to take. Yet fathers and sons, husbands and wives, brothers, friends, teachers and students, sworn enemies and even strangers, have all joined in this conspiracy, discouraging and preventing each other from taking this step.

X

Early this morning I went to look for my elder brother. He was standing outside the hall door looking at the sky, when I walked up behind him, stood between him and the door, and with exceptional poise and politeness said to him:

"Brother, I have something to say to you."

"Well, what is it?" he asked, quickly turning towards me and nodding.

"It is very little, but I find it difficult to say. Brother, probably all primitive people ate a little human flesh to begin with. Later, because their outlook changed, some of them stopped, and because they tried to be good they changed into men, changed into real men. But some are still eating — just like reptiles. Some have changed into fish, birds, monkeys and finally men; but some do not try to be good and remain reptiles still. When those who eat men compare themselves with those who do not, how ashamed they must be. Probably much more ashamed than the reptiles are before monkeys.

"In ancient times Yi Ya boiled his son for Chieh and Chou to eat; that is the old story. ① But actually since the creation of heaven and earth by Pan Ku men have been eating each other, from the time of Yi Ya's son to the time of Hsu Hsi-lin, ② and from the time of Hsu Hsi-lin down to the man caught in Wolf Cub Village. Last year they executed a criminal in the city, and a consumptive soaked a piece of bread in his blood and sucked it.

"They want to eat me, and of course you can do nothing about it single-handed; but why should you join them? As man-eaters they are capable of anything. If they eat me, they can eat you as well; members of the same group can still eat each other. But if you will just change your ways immediately, then everyone will have peace. Although this has been going on since time immemorial, today we could make a special effort to be good,

---

① 译者注: According to ancient records, Yi Ya cooked his son and presented him to Duke Huan of Chi who reigned from 685 to 643 B.C. Chieh and Chou were tyrants of an earlier age. The madman has made a mistake here.

② 译者注: A revolutionary at the end of the Ching dynasty (1644–1911), Hsu Hsi-lin was executed in 1907 for assassinating a Ching official. His heart and liver were eaten.

and say this is not to be done! I'm sure you can say so, brother. The other day when the tenant wanted the rent reduced, you said it couldn't be done."

At first he only smiled cynically, then a murderous gleam came into his eyes, and when I spoke of their secret his face turned pale. Outside the gate stood a group of people, including Mr. Chao and his dog, all craning their necks to peer in. I could not see all their faces, for they seemed to be masked in cloths; some of them looked pale and ghastly still, concealing their laughter. I knew they were one band, all eaters of human flesh. But I also knew that they did not all think alike by any means. Some of them thought that since it had always been so, men should be eaten. Some of them knew that they should not eat men, but still wanted to; and they were afraid people might discover their secret; thus when they heard me they became angry, but they still smiled their cynical, tight-lipped smile.

Suddenly my brother looked furious, and shouted in a loud voice:

"Get out of here, all of you! What is the point of looking at a madman?"

Then I realized part of their cunning. They would never be willing to change their stand, and their plans were all laid; they had stigmatized me as a madman. In future when I was eaten, not only would there be no trouble, but people would probably be grateful to them. When our tenant spoke of the villagers eating a bad character, it was exactly the same device. This is their old trick.

Old Chen came in too, in a great temper, but they could not stop my mouth, I had to speak to those people:

"You should change, change from the bottom of your hearts!" I said. "You most know that in future there will be no place for man-eaters in the world.

"If you don't change, you may all be eaten by each other. Although so many are born, they will be wiped out by the real men, just like wolves killed by hunters. Just like reptiles!"

Old Chen drove everybody away. My brother had disappeared. Old Chen advised me to go back to my room. The room was pitch dark. The beams and rafters shook above my head. After shaking for some time they grew larger. They piled on top of me.

The weight was so great, I could not move. They meant that I should die. I knew that the weight was false, so I struggled out, covered in perspiration. But I had to say:

"You should change at once, change from the bottom of your hearts! You must know that in future there will be no place for man-eaters in the world ..."

XI

The sun does not shine, the door is not opened, every day two meals.

I took up my chopsticks, then thought of my elder brother; I know now how my little sister died: it was all through him. My sister was only five at the time. I can still remember how lovable and pathetic she looked. Mother cried and cried, but he begged her not to cry, probably because he had eaten her himself, and so her crying made him feel ashamed. If he had any sense of shame ...

My sister was eaten by my brother, but I don't know whether mother realized it or not.

I think mother must have known, but when she cried she did not say so outright, probably because she thought it proper too. I remember when I was four or five years old, sitting in the cool of the hall, my brother told me that if a man's parents were ill, he should cut off a piece of his flesh and boil it for them if he wanted to be considered a good son; and mother did not contradict him. If one piece could be eaten, obviously so could the whole. And yet just to think of the mourning then still makes my heart bleed; that is the extraordinary thing about it!

XII

I can't bear to think of it.

I have only just realized that I have been living all these years in a place where for four thousand years they have been eating human flesh. My brother had just taken over the charge of the house when our sister died, and he may well have used her flesh in our rice and dishes, making us eat it unwittingly.

It is possible that I ate several pieces of my sister's flesh unwittingly, and now it is my turn, ...

How can a man like myself, after four thousand years of man-caring history — even though I knew nothing about it at first — ever hope to face real men?

XIII

Perhaps there are still children who have not eaten men? Save the children ...

April 1918

2. 孔乙己①

鲁镇的酒店的格局,是和别处不同的:都是当街一个曲尺形的大柜台,柜里面预备着热水,可以随时温酒。做工的人,傍午傍晚散了工,每每花四文铜钱,买一碗酒,——这是二十多年前的事,现在每碗要涨到十文,——靠柜外站着,热热的喝了休息;倘肯多花一文,便可以买一碟盐煮笋,或者茴香豆,做下酒物了,如果出到十几文,那就能买一样荤菜,但这些顾客,多是短衣帮,大抵没有这样阔绰。只有穿长衫的,才踱进店面隔壁的房子里,要酒要菜,慢慢地坐喝。

我从十二岁起,便在镇口的咸亨酒店里当伙计,掌柜说,样子太傻,怕侍候不了长衫主顾,就在外面做点事罢。外面的短衣主顾,虽然容易说话,但唠唠叨叨缠夹不清的也很不少。他们往往要亲眼看着黄酒从坛子里舀出,看过壶子底里有水没有,又亲看将壶子放在热水里,然后放心:在这严重兼督下,羼水也很为难。所以过了几天,掌柜又说我干不了这事。幸亏荐头的情面大,辞退不得,便改为专管温酒的一种无聊职务了。

我从此便整天的站在柜台里,专管我的职务。虽然没有什么失职,但总觉得有些单调,有些无聊。掌柜是一副凶脸孔,主顾也没有好声气,教人活泼不得;只有孔乙己到店,才可以笑几声,所以至今还记得。

孔乙己是站着喝酒而穿长衫的唯一的人。他身材很高大;青白脸色,皱纹间时常夹些伤痕;一部乱蓬蓬的花白的胡子。穿的虽然是长衫,可是又脏又破,似乎十多年没有补,也没有洗。他对人说话,总是满口之乎者也,教人半懂不懂的。因为他姓孔,别人便从描红纸上的"上大人孔乙己"这半懂不懂的话里,替他取下一个绰号,叫作孔乙己。孔乙己一到店,所

---

① 中文选自:鲁迅. 呐喊. 上海:北新书局,1941.
英译文选自:Lu Hsun. *Selected Stories of Lu Hsun*. Yang Xianyi & Gladys Yang. Trans. Beijing:Foreign Languages Press,1978.

有喝酒的人便都看着他笑，有的叫道，"孔乙己，你脸上又添上新伤疤了！"他不回答，对柜里说，"温两碗酒，要一碟茴香豆。"便排出九文大钱。他们又故意的高声嚷道，"你一定又偷了人家的东西了！"孔乙己睁大眼睛说，"你怎么这样凭空污人清白……""什么清白？我前天亲眼见你偷了何家的书，吊着打。"孔乙己便涨红了脸，额上的青筋条条绽出，争辩道，"窃书不能算偷……窃书！……读书人的事，能算偷么？"接连便是难懂的话，什么"君子固穷"，什么"者乎"之类，引得众人都哄笑起来：店内外充满了快活的空气。

听人家背地里谈论，孔乙己原来也读过书，但终于没有进学，又不会营生；于是愈过愈穷，弄到将要讨饭了。幸而写得一笔好字，便替人家钞钞书，换一碗饭吃。可惜他又有一样坏脾气，便是好吃懒做。坐不到几天，便连人和书籍纸张笔砚，一齐失踪。如是几次，叫他钞书的人也没有了。孔乙己没有法，便免不了偶然做些偷窃的事。但他在我们店里，品行却比别人都好，就是从不拖欠；虽然间或没有现钱，暂时记在粉板上，但不出一月，定然还清，从粉板上拭去了孔乙己的名字。

孔乙己喝过半碗酒，涨红的脸色渐渐复了原，旁人便又问道，"孔乙己，你当真认识字么？"孔乙己看着问他的人，显出不屑置辩的神气。他们便接着说道，"你怎的连半个秀才也捞不到呢？"孔乙己立刻显出颓唐不安模样，脸上笼上了一层灰色，嘴里说些话；这回可是全是之乎者也之类，一些不懂了。在这时候，众人也都哄笑起来：店内外充满了快活的空气。

在这些时候，我可以附和着笑，掌柜是决不责备的。而且掌柜见了孔乙己，也每每这样问他，引人发笑。孔乙己自己知道不能和他们谈天，便只好向孩子说话。有一回对我说道，"你读过书么？"我略略点一点头。他说，"读过书，……我便考你一考。茴香豆的茴字，怎样写的？"我想，讨饭一样的人，也配考我么？便回过脸去，不再理会。孔乙己等了许久，很恳切的说道，"不能写罢？……我教给你，记着！这些字应该记着。将来做掌柜的时候，写账要用。"我暗想我和掌柜的等级还很远呢，而且我们掌柜也从不将茴香豆上账；又好笑，又不耐烦，懒懒的答他道，"谁要你教，不是草头底下一个来回的回字么?"孔乙己显出极高兴的样子,将两个指头的长指甲敲着柜台,点头说,"对呀对呀! ……回字有四样写法,你知道么?"我愈不耐烦了,努着嘴走远。孔乙己刚用指甲蘸了酒,想在柜上写字,见我毫不热心,便又叹一口气,显出极惋惜的样子。

有几回,邻居孩子听得笑声,也赶热闹,围住了孔乙己。他便给他们茴香豆吃,一人一颗。孩子吃完豆,仍然不散,眼睛都望着碟子。孔乙己着了慌,伸开五指将碟子罩住,弯腰下去说道,"不多了,我已经不多了。"直起身又看一看豆,自己摇头说,"不多不多! 多乎哉? 不多也。"于是这一群孩子都在笑声里走散了。

孔乙己是这样的使人快活,可是没有他,别人也便这么过。

有一天,大约是中秋前的两三天,掌柜正在慢慢的结账,取下粉板,忽然说,"孔乙己长久没有来了。还欠十九个钱呢!"我才也觉得他的确长久没有来了。一个喝酒的人说道,"他怎么会来? ……他打折了腿了。"掌柜说,"哦!""他总仍旧是偷。这一回,是自己发昏,竟偷到丁举人家里去了。他家的东西,偷得的么?""后来怎么样?""怎么样? 先写服辩,后来是打,打了大半夜,再打折了腿。""后来呢?""后来打折了腿了。""打折了怎样呢?""怎样? ……谁晓得? 许是死了。"掌柜也不再问,仍然慢慢的算他的账。

中秋之后,秋风是一天凉比一天,看看将近初冬;我整天的靠着火,也须穿上棉袄了。一天的下半天,没有一个顾客,我正合了眼坐着。忽然间听得一个声音,"温一碗酒。"这声音虽然极低,却很耳熟。看时又全没有人。站起来向外一望,那孔乙己便在柜台下对了门槛坐着。他脸上黑而且瘦,已经不成样子;穿一件破夹袄,盘着两腿,下面垫一个蒲包,用草绳在肩上挂住;见了我,又说道,"温一碗酒。"掌柜也伸出头去,一面说,"孔乙己么? 你还欠十九个钱呢!"孔乙己很颓唐的仰面答道,"这……下回还清罢。这一回是现钱,酒要好。"掌柜仍然同平常一样,笑着对他说,"孔乙己,你又偷了东西了!"但他这回却不十分分辩,单说了一句"不要取笑!""取笑? 要是不偷,怎么会打断腿?"孔乙己低声说道,"跌断,跌,跌……"

他的眼色,很像恳求掌柜,不要再提。此时已经聚集了几个人,便和掌柜都笑了。我温了酒,端出去,放在门槛上。他从破衣袋里摸出四文大钱,放在我手里,见他满手是泥,原来他便用这手走来的。不一会,他喝完酒,便又在旁人的说笑声中,坐着用这手慢慢走去了。

自此以后,又长久没有看见孔乙己。到了年关,掌柜取下粉板说,"孔乙己还欠十九个钱呢!"到第二年的端午,又说"孔乙己还欠十九个钱呢!"到中秋可是没有说,再到年关也没有看见他。

我到现在终于没有见——大约孔乙己的确死了。

一九一九年三月

Kung I-chi

The wine shops in Luchen are not like those in other parts of China. They all have a right-angled counter facing the street, where hot water is kept ready for warming wine. When men come off work at midday and in the evening they buy a bowl of wine; it cost four coppers twenty years ago, but now it costs ten. Standing beside the counter, they drink it warm, and relax. Another copper will buy a plate of salted bamboo shoots or peas flavoured with aniseed, to go with the wine; while for a dozen coppers you can buy a meat dish. But most of these customers belong to the short-coated class, few of whom can afford this. Only those in long gowns enter the adjacent room to order wine and dishes, and sit and drink at leisure.

At the age of twelve I started work as a waiter in Prosperity Tavern, at the entrance to the town. The tavern keeper said I looked too foolish to serve the long-gowned customers, so I was given work in the outer room. Although the short-coated customers there were more easily pleased, there were quite a few trouble-makers among them too. They would insist on watching with their own eyes as the yellow wine was ladled from the keg, looking to see if there were any water at the bottom of the wine pot, and inspecting for themselves the immersion of the pot in hot water. Under such keen scrutiny, it was very difficult to dilute the wine. So after a few days my employer decided I was not suited for this work. Fortunately I had been recommended by someone influential, so he could not dismiss me, and I was transferred to the dull work of warming wine.

Thenceforward I stood all day behind the counter, fully engaged with my duties. Although I gave satisfaction at this work, I found it monotonous and futile. Our employer was a fierce-looking individual, and the customers were a morose lot, so that it was impossible to be gay. Only when Kung I-chi came to the tavern could I laugh a little. That is why I still remember him.

Kung was the only long-gowned customer to drink his wine standing.

He was a big man, strangely pallid, with scars that often showed among the wrinkles of his face. He had a large, unkempt beard, streaked with white. Although he wore a long gown, it was dirty and tattered, and looked as if it had not been washed or mended for over ten years. He used so many archaisms in his speech, it was impossible to understand half he said. As his surname was Kung, he was nicknamed "Kung I-chi," the first three characters in a children's copybook. Whenever he came into the shop, everyone would look at him and chuckle. And someone would call out:

"Kung I-chi! There are some fresh scars on your face!"

Ignoring this remark, Kung would come to the counter to order two bowls of heated wine and a dish of peas flavoured with aniseed. For this he produced nine coppers. Someone else would call out, in deliberately loud tones:

"You must have been stealing again!"

"Why ruin a man's good name groundlessly?" he would ask, opening his eyes wide.

"Pooh, good name indeed! The day before yesterday I saw you with my own eyes being hung up and beaten for stealing books from the Ho family!"

Then Kung would flush, the veins on his forehead standing out as he remonstrated: "Taking a book can't be considered stealing, ... Taking a book, the affair of a scholar, can't be considered stealing!" Then followed quotations from the classics, [1] like "A gentleman keeps his integrity even in poverty," and a jumble of archaic expressions till everybody was roaring with laughter and the whole tavern was gay.

From gossip I heard, Kung I-chi had studied the classics but had never passed the official examination. With no way of making a living, he grew poorer and poorer, until he was practically reduced to beggary. Happily, he was a good calligrapher, and could get enough copying work to support himself. Unfortunately he had failings: he liked drinking and was lazy. So after a few days he would invariably disappear, taking books, paper,

①　译者注：From *The Analects of Confucius*.

brushes and inkstone with him. After this had happened several times, nobody wanted to employ him as a copyist again. Then there was no alternative for him but to take to occasional pilfering. In our tavern his behaviour was exemplary. He never failed to pay up, although sometimes, when he had no ready money, his name would appear on the board where we listed debtors. However, in less than a month he would always settle, and his name would be wiped off the board again.

After drinking half a howl of wine, Kung would regain his composure. But then someone would ask:

"Kung I-chi, do you really know how to read?"

When Kung looked as if such a question were beneath contempt, they would continue: "How is it you never passed even the lowest official examination?"

At that Kung would look disconsolate and ill at ease. His face would turn pale and his lips move, but only to utter those unintelligible classical expressions. Then everybody would laugh heartily again, and the whole tavern would be merry.

At such times, I could join in the laughter without being scolded by my master. In fact he often put such questions to Kung himself, to evoke laughter. Knowing it was no use talking to them, Kung would chat to us children. Once he asked me:

"Have you had any schooling?"

When I nodded, he said, "Well then, I'll test you. How do you write the character *hui* in *hui-xiang* (aniseed — *Translator*) peas?"

I thought, "I'm not going to be tested by a beggar!" So I turned away and ignored him. After waiting for some time, he said very earnestly:

"You can't write it? I'll show you how. Mind you remember! You ought to remember such characters, because later when you have a shop of your own, you'll need them to make up your accounts."

It seemed to me I was still very far from owning a shop; besides, our employer never entered *hui-xiang* peas in the account book. Amused yet exasperated, I answered listlessly: "Who wants you as a teacher? Isn't it the character *hui* with the grass radical?"

Kung was delighted, and tapped two long fingernails on the counter. "Right, right!" he said, nodding. "Only there are four different ways of writing *hui*. Do you know them?" My patience exhausted, I scowled and made off. Kung I-chi had dipped his finger in wine, in order to trace the characters on the counter; but when he saw how indifferent I was, he sighed and looked most disappointed.

Sometimes children in the neighbourhood, hearing laughter, came to join in the fun, and surrounded Kung I-chi Then he would give them peas flavoured with aniseed, one apiece. After eating the peas, the children would still hang round, their eyes on the dish. Flustered, he would cover the dish with his hand and, bending forward from the waist, would say: "There isn't much. I haven't much as it is." Then straightening up to look at the peas again, he would shake his head. "Not much! Verily, not much, forsooth!" Then the children would scamper off, with shouts of laughter.

Kung I-chi was very good company, but we got along all right without him too.

One day, a few days before the Mid-Autumn Festival, the tavern keeper was laboriously making out his accounts. Taking down the board from the wall, he suddenly said: "Kung I-chi hasn't been in for a long time. He still owes nineteen coppers!" That made me realize how long it was since we had seen him.

"How could he come?" one of the customers said. "His legs were broken in that last beating."

"Ah!"

"He was stealing again. This time he was fool enough to steal from Mr. Ting, the provincial scholar! As if anybody could get away with that!"

"What then?"

"What then? First he had to write a confession, then he was beaten. The beating lasted nearly all night, until his legs were broken."

"And then?"

"Well, his legs were broken."

"Yes, but after that?"

"After? ... Who knows? He may be dead."

The tavern keeper did not pursue his questions, but went on slowly making up his accounts.

After the Mid-Autumn Festival the wind grew colder every day, as winter came on. Even though I spent all my time by the stove, I had to wear my padded jacket. One afternoon, when the shop was empty, I was sitting with my eyes closed when I heard a voice:

"Warm a bowl of wine."

The voice was very low, yet familiar. But when I looked up, there was no one in sight. I stood up and looked towards the door, and there, facing the threshold, beneath the counter, sat Kung I-chi. His face was haggard and lean, and he looked in a terrible condition. He had on a ragged lined jacket, and was sitting cross-legged on a mat which was attached to his shoulders by a straw rope. When he saw me, he repeated:

"Warm a bowl of wine."

At this point my employer leaned over the counter and said: "Is that Kung I-chi? You still owe nineteen coppers!"

"That ... I'll settle next time," replied Kung, looking up disconsolately. "Here's ready money; the wine must be good."

The tavern keeper, just as in the past, chuckled and said:

"Kung I-chi, you've been stealing again!"

But instead of protesting vigorously, the other simply said:

"You like your joke."

"Joke? If you didn't steal, why did they break your legs?"

"I fell," said Kung in a low voice. "I broke them in a fall." His eyes pleaded with the tavern keeper to let the matter drop. By now several people had gathered round, and they all laughed. I warmed the wine, carried it over, and set it on the threshold. He produced four coppers from his ragged coat pocket, and placed them in my hand. As he did so I saw that his hands were covered with mud — he must have crawled here on them. Presently he finished the wine and, amid the laughter and comments of the others, slowly dragged himself off by his hands.

A long time went by after that without our seeing Kung again. At the end of the year, when the tavern keeper took down the board, he said, "Kung I-chi still owes nineteen coppers!" At the Dragon Boat Festival the next year, he said the same thing again. But when the Mid-Autumn Festival came, he did not mention it. And another New Year came round without our seeing any more of him.

Nor have I ever seen him since — probably Kung I-chi is really dead.

March 1919

3. 故 乡[①]

我冒了严寒,回到相隔二千余里,别了二十余年的故乡去。

时候既然是深冬;渐近故乡时,天气又阴晦了,冷风吹进船舱中,呜呜的响,从蓬隙向外一望,苍黄的天底下,远近横着几个萧索的荒村,没有一些活气。我的心禁不住悲凉起来了。

啊!这不是我二十年来时时记得的故乡?

我所记得的故乡全不如此。我的故乡好得多了。但要我记起他的美丽,说出他的佳处来,却又没有影像,没有言辞了。仿佛也就如此。于是我自己解释说:故乡本也如此,——虽然没有进步,也未必有如我所感的悲凉,这只是我自己心情的改变罢了,因为我这次回乡,本没有什么好心绪。

我这次是专为了别他而来的。我们多年聚族而居的老屋,已经公同卖给别姓了,交屋的期限,只在本年,所以必须赶在正月初一以前,永别了熟识的老屋,而且远离了熟识的故乡,搬家到我在谋食的异地去。

第二日清早晨我到了我家的门口了。瓦楞上许多枯草的断茎当风抖着,正在说明这老屋难免易主的原因。几房的本家大约已经搬走了,所以很寂静。我到了自家的房外,我的母亲早已迎着出来了,接着便飞出了八岁的侄儿宏儿。

我的母亲很高兴,但也藏着许多凄凉的神情,教我坐下,歇息,喝茶,且不谈搬家的事。宏儿没有见过我,远远的对面站着只是看。

但我们终于谈到搬家的事。我说外间的寓所已经租定了,又买了几件家具,此外须将家里所有的木器卖去,再去增添。母亲也说好,而且行

---

① 中文选自:鲁迅.呐喊.上海:北新书局,1941.
英译文选自:Lu Hsun. *Selected Stories of Lu Hsun*. Yang Xianyi & Gladys Yang.
Trans. Beijing:Foreign Languages Press,1978.

李也略已齐集,木器不便搬运的,也小半卖去了,只是收不起钱来。

"你休息一两天,去拜望亲戚本家一回,我们便可以走了。"母亲说。

"是的。"

"还有闰土,他每到我家来时,总问起你,很想见你一回面。我已经将你到家的大约日期通知他,他也许就要来了。"

这时候,我的脑里忽然闪出一幅神异的图画来:深蓝的天空中挂着一轮金黄的圆月,下面是海边的沙地,都种着一望无际的碧绿的西瓜,其间有一个十一二岁的少年,项带银圈,手捏一柄钢叉,向一匹猹尽力的刺去,那猹却将身一扭,反从他的胯下逃走了。

这少年便是闰土。我认识他时,也不过十多岁,离现在将有三十年了;那时我的父亲还在世,家景也好,我正是一个少爷。那一年,我家是一件大祭祀的值年。这祭祀,说是三十多年才能轮到一回,所以很郑重;正月里供祖像,供品很多,祭器很讲究,拜的人也很多,祭器也很要防偷去。我家只有一个忙月(我们这里给人做工的分三种:整年给一定人家做工的叫长工;按日给人做工的叫短工;自己也种地,只在过年过节以及收租时候来给一定人家做工的称忙月),忙不过来,他便对父亲说,可以叫他的儿子闰土来管祭器的。

我的父亲允许了;我也很高兴,因为我早听到闰土这名字,而且知道他和我仿佛年纪,闰月生的,五行缺土,所以他的父亲叫他闰土。他是能装弶捉小鸟雀的。

我于是日日盼望新年,新年到,闰土也就到了。好容易到了年末,有一日,母亲告诉我,闰土来了,我便飞跑的去看。他正在厨房里,紫色的圆脸,头戴一顶小毡帽,颈上套一个明晃晃的银项圈,这可见他的父亲十分爱他,怕他死去,所以在神佛面前许下愿心,用圈子将他套住了。他见人很怕羞,只是不怕我,没有旁人的时候,便和我说话,于是不到半日,我们便熟识了。

我们那时候不知道谈些什么,只记得闰土很高兴,说是上城之后,见了许多没有见过的东西。

第二日,我便要他捕鸟。他说:

"这不能。须大雪下了才好。我们沙地上,下了雪,我扫出一块空地来,用短棒支起一个大竹匾,撒下秕谷,看鸟雀来吃时,我远远地将缚在棒上的绳子只一拉,那鸟雀就罩在竹匾下了。什么都有:稻鸡,角鸡,鹁鸪,蓝背……"

我于是又很盼望下雪。

闰土又对我说:

"现在太冷,你夏天到我们这里来。我们日里到海边捡贝壳去,红的绿的都有,鬼见怕也有,观音手也有。晚上我和爹管西瓜去,你也去。"

"管贼么?"

"不是。走路的人口渴了摘一个瓜吃,我们这里是不算偷的。要管的是獾猪,刺猬,猹。月亮底下,你听,啦啦的响了,猹在咬瓜了。你便捏了胡叉,轻轻地走去……"

我那时并不知道这所谓猹的是怎么一件东西——便是现在也没有知道——只是无端的觉得状如小狗而很凶猛。

"他不咬人么?"

"有胡叉呢。走到了,看见猹了,你便刺。这畜生很伶俐,倒向你奔来,反从胯下窜了。他的皮毛是油一般的滑……"

我素不知道天下有这许多新鲜事:海边有如许五色的贝壳;西瓜有这样危险的经历,我先前单知道他在水果店里出卖罢了。

"我们沙地里,潮汛要来的时候,就有许多跳鱼儿只是跳,都有青蛙似的两个脚……"

阿!闰土的心里有无穷无尽的希奇的事,都是我往常的朋友所不知道的。他们不知道一些事,闰土在海边时,他们都和我一样只看见院子里高墙上的四角的天空。

可惜正月过去了,闰土须回家里去,我急得大哭,他也躲到厨房里,哭着不肯出门,但终于被他父亲带走了。他后来还托他的父亲带给我一包贝壳和几支很好看的鸟毛,我也曾送他一两次东西,但从此没有再见面。

　　现在我的母亲提起了他,我这儿时的记忆,忽而全都闪电似的苏生过来,似乎看到了我的美丽的故乡了。我应声说:

　　"这好极!他,——怎样?……"

　　"他?……他景况也很不如意……"母亲说着,便向房外看,"这些人又来了。说是买木器,顺手也就随便拿走的,我得去看看。"

　　母亲站起身,出去了。门外有几个女人的声音。我便招宏儿走近面前,和他闲话:问他可会写字,可愿意出门。

　　"我们坐火车去么?"

　　"我们坐火车去。"

　　"船呢?"

　　"先坐船,……"

　　"哈!这模样了!胡子这么长了!"一种尖利的怪声突然大叫起来。

　　我吃了一吓,赶忙抬起头,却见一个凸颧骨,薄嘴唇,五十岁上下的女人站在我面前,两手搭在髀间,没有系裙,张着两脚,正像一个画图仪器里细脚伶仃的圆规。

　　我愕然了。

　　"不认识了么?我还抱过你咧!"

　　我愈加愕然了。幸而我的母亲也就进来,从旁说:

　　"他多年出门,统忘却了。你该记得罢,"便向着我说,"这是斜对门的杨二嫂,……开豆腐店的。"

　　哦,我记得了。我孩子时候,在斜对门的豆腐店里确乎终日坐着一个杨二嫂,人都叫伊"豆腐西施"。但是擦着白粉,颧骨没有这么高,嘴唇也没有这么薄,而且终日坐着,我也从没有见过这圆规式的姿势。那时人说:因为伊,这豆腐店的买卖非常好。但这大约因为年龄的关系,我却并未蒙着一毫感化,所以竟完全忘却了。然而圆规很不平,显出鄙夷的神色,仿佛嗤笑法国人不知道拿破仑,美国人不知道华盛顿似的,冷笑说:

　　"忘了?这真是贵人眼高……"

　　"那有这事……我……"我惶恐着,站起来说。

"那么,我对你说。迅哥儿,你阔了,搬动又笨重,你还要什么这些破烂木器,让我拿去罢。我们小户人家,用得着。"

"我并没有阔哩。我须卖了这些,再去……"

"阿呀呀,你放了道台了,还说不阔?你现在有三房姨太太;出门便是八抬的大轿,还说不阔?吓,什么都瞒不过我。"

我知道无话可说了,便闭了口,默默的站着。

"阿呀阿呀,真是愈有钱,便愈是一毫不肯放松,愈是一毫不肯放松,便愈有钱……"圆规一面愤愤的回转身,一面絮絮的说,慢慢向外走,顺便将我母亲的一副手套塞在裤腰里,出去了。

此后又有近处的本家和亲戚来访问我。我一面应酬,偷空便收拾些行李,这样的过了三四天。

一日是天气很冷的午后,我吃过午饭,坐着喝茶,觉得外面有人进来了,便回头去看。我看时,不由的非常出惊,慌忙站起身,迎着走去。

这来的便是闰土。虽然我一见便知道是闰土,但又不是我这记忆上的闰土了。他身材增加了一倍;先前的紫色的圆脸,已经变作灰黄,而且加上了很深的皱纹;眼睛也像他父亲一样,周围都肿得通红,这我知道,在海边种地的人,终日吹着海风,大抵是这样的。他头上是一顶破毡帽,身上只一件极薄的棉衣,浑身瑟索着;手里提着一个纸包和一支长烟管,那手也不是我所记得的红活圆实的手,却又粗又笨而且开裂,像是松树皮了。

我这时很兴奋,但不知道怎么说才好,只是说:

"阿!闰土哥,——你来了?……"

我接着便有许多话,想要连珠一般涌出:角鸡,跳鱼儿,贝壳,猹,……但又总觉得被什么挡着似的,单在脑里面回旋,吐不出口外去。

他站住了,脸上现出欢喜和凄凉的神情;动着嘴唇,却没有作声。他的态度终于恭敬起来了,分明的叫道:

"老爷!……"

我似乎打了一个寒噤;我就知道,我们之间已经隔了一层可悲的厚障壁了。我也说不出话。

他回过头去说，"水生，给老爷磕头。"便拖出躲在背后的孩子来，这正是一个廿年前的闰土，只是黄瘦些，颈子上没有银圈罢了。"这是第五个孩子，没有见过世面，躲躲闪闪……"

母亲和宏儿下楼来了，他们大约也听到了声音。

"老太太。信是早收到了。我实在喜欢的不得了，知道老爷回来……"闰土说。

"阿，你怎的这样客气起来。你们先前不是哥弟称呼么？还是照旧：迅哥儿。"母亲高兴的说。

"阿呀，老太太真是……这成什么规矩。那时是孩子，不懂事……"闰土说着，又叫水生上来打拱，那孩子却害羞，紧紧的只贴在他背后。

"他就是水生？第五个？都是生人，怕生也难怪的；还是宏儿和他去走走。"母亲说。

宏儿听得这话，便来招水生，水生却松松爽爽同他一路出去了。母亲叫闰土坐，他迟疑了一回，终于就了坐，将长烟管靠在桌旁，递过纸包来，说：

"冬天没有什么东西了。这一点干青豆倒是自家晒在那里的，请老爷……"

我问问他的景况。他只是摇头。

"非常难。第六个孩子也会帮忙了，却总是吃不够……又不太平……什么地方都要钱，没有规定……收成又坏。种出东西来，挑去卖，总要捐几回钱，折了本；不去卖，又只能烂掉……"

他只是摇头；脸上虽然刻着许多皱纹，却全然不动，仿佛石像一般。他大约只是觉得苦，却又形容不出，沉默了片时，便拿起烟管来默默的吸烟了。

母亲问他，知道他的家里事务忙，明天便得回去；又没有吃过午饭，便叫他自己到厨下炒饭吃去。

他出去了；母亲和我都叹息他的景况：多子，饥荒，苛税，兵，匪，官，绅,都苦得他像一个木偶人了。母亲对我说,凡是不必搬走的东西,尽可以送他,可以听他自己去拣择。

下午,他拣好了几件东西:两条长桌,四个椅子,一副香炉和烛台,一杆抬秤。他又要所有的草灰(我们这里煮饭是烧稻草的,那灰,可以做沙地的肥料),待我们启程的时候,他用船来载去。

夜间,我们又谈些闲天,都是无关紧要的话;第二天早晨,他就领了水生回去了。

又过了九日,是我们启程的日期。闰土早晨便到了,水生没有同来,却只带着一个五岁的女儿管船只。我们终日很忙碌,再没有谈天的工夫。来客也不少,有送行的,有拿东西的,有送行兼拿东西的。待到傍晚我们上船的时候,这老屋里的所有破旧大小粗细东西,已经一扫而空了。

我们的船向前走,两岸的青山在黄昏中,都装成了深黛颜色,连着退向船后梢去。

宏儿和我靠着船窗,同看外面模糊的风景,他忽然问道:

"大伯! 我们什么时候回来?"

"回来? 你怎么还没有走就想回来了。"

"可是,水生约我到他家玩去咧……"他睁着大的黑眼睛,痴痴的想。

我和母亲也都有些惘然,于是又提起闰土来。母亲说,那豆腐西施的杨二嫂,自从我家收拾行李以来,本是每日必到的,前天伊在灰堆里,掏出十多个碗碟来,议论之后,便定说是闰土埋着的,他可以在运灰的时候,一齐搬回家里去;杨二嫂发见了这件事,自己很以为功,便拿了那狗气杀(这是我们这里养鸡的器具,木盘上面有着栅栏,内盛食料,鸡可以伸进颈子去啄,狗却不能,只能看着气死),飞也似的跑了,亏伊装着这么高低的小脚,竟跑得这样快。

老屋离我愈远了;故乡的山水也都渐渐远离了我,但我却并不感到怎样的留恋。我只觉得我四面有看不见的高墙,将我隔成孤身,使我非常气闷;那西瓜地上的银项圈的小英雄的影像,我本来十分清楚,现在却忽地模糊了,又使我非常的悲哀。

母亲和宏儿都睡着了。

我躺着,听船底潺潺的水声,知道我在走我的路。我想:我竟与闰土隔绝到这地步了,但我们的后辈还是一气,宏儿不是正在想念水生么。我希望他们不再像我,又大家隔膜起来……然而我又不愿意他们因为要一气,都如我的辛苦展转而生活,也不愿意他们都如闰土的辛苦麻木而生活,也不愿意都如别人的辛苦恣睢而生活。他们应该有新的生活,为我们所未经生活过的。

我想到希望,忽然害怕起来了。闰土要香炉和烛台的时候,我还暗地里笑他,以为他总是崇拜偶像,什么时候都不忘却。现在我所谓希望,不也是我自己手制的偶像么?只是他的愿望切近,我的愿望茫远罢了。

我在朦胧中,眼前展开一片海边碧绿的沙地来,上面深蓝的天空中挂着一轮金黄的圆月。我想:希望本是无所谓有,无所谓无的。这正如地上的路;其实地上本没有路,走的人多了,也便成了路。

一九二一年一月

My Old Home

Braving the bitter cold, I travelled more than seven hundred miles back to the old home I had left over twenty years before.

It was late winter. As we drew near my former home the day became overcast and a cold wind blew into the cabin of our boat, while all one could see through the chinks in our bamboo awning were a few desolate villages, void of any sign of life, scattered far and near under the sombre yellow sky. I could not help feeling depressed.

Ah! Surely this was not the old home I had remembered for the past twenty years?

The old home I remembered was nor in the least like this. My old home was much better. But if you asked me to recall its peculiar charm or describe its beauties, I had no clear impression, no words to describe it. And now it seemed this was all there was to it. Then I rationalized the matter to myself, saying: Home was always like this, and although it has not improved, still it is not so depressing as I imagine; it is only my mood that has changed, because I am coming back to the country this time with no illusions.

This time I had come with the sole object of saying goodbye. The old house our clan had lived in for so many years had already been sold to another family, and was to change hands before the end of the year. I had to hurry there before New Year's Day to say goodbye for ever to the familiar old house, and to move my family to another place where I was working, far from my old home town.

At dawn on the second day I reached the gateway of my home. Broken stems of withered grass on the roof, trembling in the wind, made very clear the reason why this old house could not avoid changing hands. Several branches of our clan had probably already moved away, so it was unusually quiet. By the time I reached the house my mother was already at the door to welcome me, and my eight-year-old nephew, Hung-erh, rushed out after her.

Though mother was delighted, she was also trying to hide a certain feeling of sadness. She told me to sit down and rest and have some tea, letting the removal wait for the time being. Hung-erh, who had never seen me before, stood watching me at a distance.

But finally we had to talk about the removal. I said that rooms had already been rented elsewhere, and I had bought a little furniture; in addition it would be necessary to sell all the furniture in the house in order to buy more things. Mother agreed, saying that the luggage was nearly all packed, and about half the furniture that could not easily be moved had already been sold. Only it was difficult to get people to pay up.

"You must rest for a day or two, and call on our relatives, and then we can go," said mother.

"Yes."

"Then there is Jun-tu. Each time he comes here he always asks after you, and wants very much to see you again. I told him the probable date of your return home, and he may be coming any time."

At this point a strange picture suddenly flashed into my mind: a golden moon suspended in a deep blue sky and beneath it the seashore, planted as far as the eye could see with jade-green watermelons, while in their midst a boy of eleven or twelve, wearing a silver necklet and grasping a steel pitchfork in his hand, was thrusting with all his might at a *zha* which dodged the blow and escaped between his legs.

This boy was Jun-tu. When I first met him he was just over ten — that was thirty years ago, and at that time my father was still alive and the family well off, so I was really a spoilt child. That year it was our family's turn to take charge of a big ancestral sacrifice, which came round only once in thirty years, and hence was an important one. In the first month the ancestral images were presented and offerings made, and since the sacrificial vessels were very fine and there was such a crowd of worshippers, it was necessary to guard against theft. Our family had only one part-time labourer. (In our district we divide labourers into three classes: those who work all the year for one family are called full-timers; those who are hired by the day are called dailies; and those who farm their own land and only work for one family at New Year, during festivals or when rents are being collected are called part-timers.) And since there was so much to be done, he told my father that he would send for his son Jun-tu to look after the sacrificial vessels.

When my father gave his consent I was overjoyed, because I had long since heard of Jun-tu and knew that he was about my own age, born in the intercalary month,① and when his horoscope was told it was found that of the five elements that of earth was lacking, so his father called him Jun-tu (Intercalary Earth). He could set traps and catch small birds.

I looked forward every day to New Year, for New Year would bring Jun-tu. At last, when the end of the year came, one day mother told me that Jun-tu had come, and I flew to see him. He was standing in the kitchen. He had a round, crimson face and wore a small felt cap on his head and a gleaming silver necklet round his neck, showing that his father doted on him and, fearing he might die, had made a pledge with the gods and buddhas, using the necklet as a talisman. He was very shy, and I was the only person he was not afraid of. When there was no one else there, he would talk with me, so in a few hours we were fast friends.

I don't know what we talked of then, but I remember that Jun-tu was in high spirits, saying that since he had come to town he had seen many new things.

The next day I wanted him to catch birds.

"Can't be done," he said. "It's only possible after a heavy snowfall. On our sands, after it snows, I sweep clear a patch of ground, prop up a big threshing basket with a short stick, and scatter husks of grain beneath. When the birds come there to eat, I tug a string tied to the stick, and the birds are caught in the basket. There are all kinds: wild pheasants,

---

① 译者注: The Chinese lunar calendar reckons 360 days to a year, and each month comprises 29 or 30 days, never 31. Hence every few years a 13th, or intercalary, month is inserted in the calendar.

woodcocks, wood-pigeons, 'blue-backs' ..."

Accordingly I looked forward very eagerly to snow.

"Just now it is too cold," said Jun-tu another time, "but you must come to our place in summer. In the daytime we'll go to the seashore to look for shells, there are green ones and red ones, besides 'scare-devil' shells and 'buddha's hands.' In the evening when dad and I go to see to the watermelons, you shall come too."

"Is it to look out for thieves?"

"No. If passers-by are thirsty and pick a watermelon, folk down our way don't consider it as stealing. What we have to look out for are badgers, hedgehogs and *zha*. When under the moonlight you hear the crunching sound made by the *zha* when it bites the melons, then you take your pitchfork and creep stealthily over ..."

I had no idea then what this thing called *zha* was — and I am not much clearer now for that matter — but somehow I felt it was something like a small dog, and very fierce.

"Don't they bite people?"

"You have a pitchfork. You go across, and when you see it you strike. It's a very cunning creature and will rush towards you and get away between your legs. Its fur is as slippery as oil ..."

I had never known that all these strange things existed: at the seashore there were shells all colours of the rainbow; watermelons were exposed to such danger, yet all I had known of them before was that they were sold in the greengrocer's.

"On our shore, when the tide comes in, there are lots of jumping fish, each with two legs like a frog ..."

Jun-tu's mind was a treasure-house of such strange lore, all of it outside the ken of my former friends. They were ignorant of all these things and, while Jun-tu lived by the sea, they like me could see only the four corners of the sky above the high courtyard wall.

Unfortunately, a month after New Year Jun-tu had to go home. I burst into teats and he took refuge in the kitchen, crying and refusing to come out, until finally his father carried him off. Later he sent me by his father a packet of shells and a few very beautiful feathers, and I sent him presents once or twice, but we never saw each other again.

Now that my mother mentioned him, this childhood memory sprang into life like a flash of lightning, and I seemed to see my beautiful old home. So I answered:

"Fine! And he — how is he?"

He's not at all well off either," said mother. And then, looking out of the door: "Here come those people again. They say they want to buy our furniture; but actually they just want to see what they can pick up. I must go and watch them."

Mother stood up and went out. The voices of several women could he heard outside. I called Hung-erh to me and started talking to him, asking him whether he could write, and whether he would be glad to leave.

"Shall we be going by train?"

"Yes, we shall go by train."

"And boat?"

"We shall take a boat first."

"Oh! Like this! With such a long moustache!" A strange shrill voice suddenly rang out.

I looked up with a start, and saw a woman of about fifty with prominent cheekbones and thin lips. With her hands on her hips, not wearing a skirt but with her trousered legs apart, she stood in front of me just like the compass in a box of geometrical instruments.

I was flabbergasted.

"Don't you know me? Why, I have held you in my arms!"

I felt even more flabbergasted. Fortunately my mother came in just then and said:

"He has been away so long, you must excuse him for forgetting. You should remember," she said to me, "this is Mrs. Yang from across the road ... She has a beancurd shop."

Then, to be sure, I remembered. When I was a child there was a Mrs. Yang who used to sit nearly all day long in the beancurd shop across the road, and everybody used to call her Beancurd Beauty. She used to powder herself, and her cheekbones were not so prominent then nor her lips so thin; moreover she remained seated all the time, so that I had never noticed this resemblance to a compass. In those days people said that, thanks to her, that beancurd shop did very good business. But, probably on account of my age, she had made no impression on me, so that later I forgot her entirely. However, the Compass was extremely indignant and looked at me most contemptuously, just as one might look at a Frenchman who had never heard of Napoleon or an American who had never heard of Washington, and smiling sarcastically she said:

"You had forgotten? Naturally I am beneath your notice ..."

"Certainly not ... I ..." I answered nervously, getting to my feet.

"Then you listen to me, Master Hsun. You have grown rich, and they are too heavy to move, so you can't possibly want these old pieces of furniture any more. You had better let me take them away. Poor people like us can do with them."

"I haven't grown rich. I must sell these in order to buy ..."

"Oh, come now, you have been made the intendant of a circuit, how can you still say you're not rich? You have three concubines now, and whenever you go out it is in a big sedan-chair with eight bearers. Do you still say you're not rich? Hah! You can't hide anything from me."

Knowing there was nothing I could say, I remained silent.

"Come now, really, the more money people have the more miserly they get, and the more miserly they are the more money they get ..." remarked the Compass, turning indignantly away and walking slowly off, casually picking up a pair of mother's gloves and stuffing them into her pocket as she went out.

After this a number of relatives in the neighbourhood came to call.

In the intervals between entertaining them I did some packing, and so three or four days passed.

One very cold afternoon, I sat drinking tea after lunch when I was aware of someone coming in, and turned my head to see who it was. At the first glance I gave an involuntary start, hastily stood up and went over to welcome him.

The newcomer was Jun-tu. But although I knew at a glance that this was Jun-tu, it was not the Jun-tu I remembered. He had grown to twice his former size. His round face, once crimson, had become sallow, and acquired deep lines and wrinkles; his eyes too had become like his father's, the rims swollen and red, a feature common to most peasants who work by the sea and are exposed all day to the wind from the ocean. He wore a shabby felt cap and just one very thin padded jacket, with the result that he was shivering from head to foot. He carried a paper package and a long pipe, nor was his hand the plump red hand I remembered, but coarse and clumsy and chapped, like the bark of a pine tree.

Delighted as I was, I did not know how to express myself, and could only say:

"Oh! Jun-tu — so it's you? ..."

After this there were so many things I wanted to talk about, they should have poured out like a string of beads: woodcocks, jumping fish, shells, *zha* .... But I was tongue-tied, unable to put all I was thinking into words.

He stood there, mixed joy and sadness showing on his face. His lips moved, but not a sound did he utter. Finally, assuming a respectful attitude, he said clearly:

"Master! ..."

I felt a shiver run through me; for I knew then what a lamentably thick wall had grown up between us. Yet I could not say anything.

He turned his head to call:

"Shui-sheng, bow to the master." Then he pulled forward a boy who had been hiding behind his back, and this was just the Jun-tu of twenty years before, only a little paler and thinner, and he had no silver necklet.

"This is my fifth," he said. "He's not used to company, so he's shy and awkward."

Mother came downstairs with Hung-erh, probably after hearing our voices.

"I got your letter some time ago, madam," said Jun-tu. "I was really so pleased to know the master was coming back ..."

"Now, why are you so polite? Weren't you playmates together in the past?" said mother gaily. "You had better still call him Brother Hsun as before."

"Oh, you are really too ... What bad manners that would be. I was a child then and didn't understand." As he was speaking Jun-tu motioned Shui-sheng to come and bow, but the child was shy, and stood stock-still behind his father.

"So he is Shui-sheng? Your fifth?" asked mother. "We are all strangers, you can't blame him for feeling shy. Hung-erh had better take him out to play."

When Hung-erh heard this he went over to Shui-sheng, and Shui-sheng went out with him, entirely at his ease. Mother asked Jun-tu to sit down, and after a little hesitation he did so; then leaning his long pipe against the table he handed over the paper package, saying:

"In winter there is nothing worth bringing; but these few beans we dried ourselves, if you will excuse the liberty, sir."

When I asked him how things were with him, he just shook his head.

"In a very bad way. Even my sixth can do a little work, but still we haven't enough to eat ... and then there is no security ... all sorts of people want money, there is no fixed rule ... and the harvests are bad. You grow things, and when you take them to sell you always have to pay several taxes and lose money, while if you don't try to sell, the things may go bad ..."

He kept shaking his head; yet, although his face was lined with wrinkles, not one of them moved, just as if he were a stone statue. No doubt he felt intensely bitter, but could not express himself. After a pause he took up his pipe and began to smoke in silence.

From her chat with him, mother learned that he was busy at home and had to go back the next day; and since he had had no lunch, she told him to go to the kitchen and fry some rice for himself.

After he had gone out, mother and I both shook our heads over his hard life: many children, famines, taxes, soldiers, bandits, officials and landed gentry, all had squeezed him as dry as a mummy. Mother said that we should offer him all the things we were not going to take away, letting him choose for himself.

That afternoon he picked out a number of things: two long tables, four chairs, an incense burner and candlesticks, and one balance. He also asked for all the ashes from the stove (in our part we cook over straw, and the ashes can be used to fertilize sandy soil), saying that when we left he would come to take them away by boat.

That night we talked again, but not of anything serious; and the next morning he went away with Shui-sheng.

After another nine days it was time for us to leave. Jun-tu came in the morning. Shui-sheng did not come with him — he had just brought a little girl of five to watch the boat. We were very busy all day, and had no time to talk. We also had quite a number of visitors, some to see us off, some to fetch things, and some to do both. It was nearly evening when we left by boat, and by that time everything in the house, however old or shabby, large or small, fine or coarse, had been cleared away.

As we set off, in the dusk, the green mountains on either side of the river became deep blue, receding towards the stern of the boat.

Hung-erh and I, leaning against the cabin window, were looking out together at the indistinct scene outside, when suddenly he asked:

"Uncle, when shall we go back?"

"Go back? Do you mean that before you've left you want to go back?"

"Well, Shui-sheng has invited me to his home ..."

He opened wide his black eyes in anxious thought.

Mother and I both felt rather sad, and so Jun-tu's name came up again. Mother said that ever since our family started packing up, Mrs. Yang from the beancurd shop had come over every day, and the day before in the ash-heap she had unearthed a dozen bowls and plates, which after some discussion she insisted must have been buried there by Jun-tu, so that when he came to remove the ashes he could take them home at the same rime. After making this discovery Mrs. Yang was very pleased with herself, and flew off raking the dog-teaser with her. (The dog-teaser is used by poultry keepers in our parts. It is a wooden cage inside which food is put, so that hens can stretch their necks in to eat but dogs can only look on furiously.) And it was a marvel, considering the size of her feet, how fast she could run.

I was leaving the old house farther and farther behind, while the hills and rivers of my old home were also receding gradually ever farther in the distance. But I felt no regret. I only felt that all round me was an invisible high wall, cutting me off from my fellows, and this depressed me thoroughly. The vision of that small hero with the silver necklet among the watermelons had formerly been as clear as day, but now it suddenly blurred, adding to my depression.

Mother and Hung-erh fell asleep.

I lay down, listening to the water rippling beneath the boat, and knew that I was going my way. I thought: although there is such a barrier between Jun-tu and myself, the children still have much in common, for wasn't Hung-erh thinking of Shui-sheng just now? I hope they will not be like us, that they will not allow a barrier to grow up between them. But again I would not like them, because they want to be akin, all to have a treadmill existence like mine, nor to suffer like Jun-ru until they become stupefied, nor yet, like others, to devote all their energies to dissipation. They should have a new life, a life we have never experienced.

The access of hope made me suddenly afraid. When Jun-tu asked for the incense burner and candlesticks I had laughed up my sleeve at him, to think that he still worshipped idols and could not put them out of his mind. Yet what I now called hope was no more than an idol I had created myself. The only difference was that what he desired was close at hand, while what I desired was less easily realized.

As I dozed, a stretch of jade-green seashore spread itself before my eyes, and above a round golden moon hung in a deep blue sky. I thought: hope cannot be said to exist, nor can it be said not to exist. It is just like roads across the earth. For actually the earth had no roads to begin with, but when many men pass one way, a road is made.

January 1921

4. 社　戏[①]

　　我在倒数上去的二十年中，只看过两回中国戏，前十年是绝不看，因为没有看戏的意思和机会，那两回全在后十年，然而都没有看出什么来就走了。

　　第一回是民国元年我初到北京的时候，当时一个朋友对我说，北京戏最好，你不去见见世面么？我想，看戏是有味的，而况在北京呢。于是都兴致勃勃的跑到什么园，戏文已经开场了，在外面也早听到冬冬地响。我们挨进门，几个红的绿的在我的眼前一闪烁，便又看见戏台下满是许多头，再定神四面看，却见中间也还有几个空座，挤过去要坐时，又有人对我发议论，我因为耳朵已经嗅的响着了，用了心，才听到他是说"有人，不行!"

　　我们退到后面，一个辫子很光的却来领我们到了侧面，指出一个地位来。这所谓地位者，原来是一条长凳，然而他那坐板比我的上腿要狭到四分之三，他的脚比我的下腿要长过三分之二。我先是没有爬上去的勇气，接着便联想到私刑拷打的刑具，不由的毛骨悚然的走出了。

　　走了许多路，忽听得我的朋友的声音道，"究竟怎的?"我回过脸去，原来他也被我带出来了。他很诧异的说，"怎么总是走，不答应?"我说，"朋友，对不起，我耳朵只在冬冬喤喤的响，并没有听到你的话。"

　　后来我每一想到，便很以为奇怪，似乎这戏太不好，——否则便是我近来在戏台下不适于生存了。

　　第二回忘记了那一年，总之是募集湖北水灾捐而谭叫天还没有死。捐法是两元钱买一张戏票，可以到第一舞台去看戏，扮演的多是名角，其

――――――――――

①　中文选自：鲁迅. 呐喊. 上海：北新书局，1941.

　　英译文选自：Lu Hsun. *Selected Stories of Lu Hsun*. Yang Xianyi & Gladys Yang. Trans. Beijing：Foreign Languages Press，1978.

一就是小叫天。我买了一张票,本是对于劝募人聊以塞责的,然而似乎又有好事家乘机对我说了些叫天不可不看的大法要了。我于是忘了前几年的冬冬喤喤之灾,竟到第一舞台去了,但大约一半也因为重价购来的宝票,总得使用了才舒服。我打听得叫天出台是迟的,而第一舞台却是新式构造,用不着争座位,便放了心,延宕到九点钟才去,谁料照例,人都满了,连立足也难,我只得挤在远处的人丛中看一个老旦在台上唱。那老旦嘴边插着两个点火的纸捻子,旁边有一个鬼卒,我费尽思量,才疑心他或者是目连的母亲,因为后来又出来了一个和尚。然而我又不知道那名角是谁,就去问挤小在我的左边的一位胖绅士。他很看不起似的斜瞥了我一眼,说道,"龚云甫!"我深愧浅陋而且粗疏,脸上一热,同时脑里也制出了决不再问的定章,于是看小旦唱,看花旦唱,看老生唱,看不知什么角色唱,看一大班人乱打,看两三个人互打,从九点多到十点,从十点到十一点,从十一点到十一点半,从十一点半到十二点,——然而叫天竟还没有来。

我向来没有这样忍耐的等待过什么事物,而况这身边的胖绅士的吁吁的喘气,这台上的冬冬喤喤的敲打,红红绿绿的晃荡,加之以十二点,忽而使我省误到在这里不适于生存了。我同时便机械的拧转身子,用力往外只一挤,觉得背后便已满满的,大约那弹性的胖绅士早在我的空处胖开了他的右半身了。我后无回路,自然挤而又挤,终于出了大门。街上除了专等看客的车辆之外,几乎没有什么行人了,大门口却还有十几个人昂着头看戏目,别有一堆人站着并不看什么,我想:他们大概是看散戏之后出来的女人们的,而叫天却还没有来……

然而夜气很清爽,真所谓"沁人心脾",我在北京遇着这样的好空气,仿佛这是第一遭了。

这一夜,就是我对于中国戏告了别的一夜,此后再没有想到他,即使偶而经过戏园,我们也漠不相关,精神上早已一在天之南一在地之北了。

但是前几天,我忽在无意之中看到一本日本文的书,可惜忘记了书名和著者,总之是关于中国戏的。其中有一篇,大意仿佛说,中国戏是大敲,大叫,大跳,使看客头昏脑眩,很不适于剧场,但若在野外散漫的所在,远远的看起来,也自有他的风致。我当时觉着这正是说了在我意中而未曾想到的话,因为我确记得在野外看过很好的戏,到北京以后的连进两回戏园去,也许还是受了那时的影响哩。可惜我不知道怎么一来,竟将书名忘却了。

至于我看好戏的时候,却实在已经是"远哉遥遥"的了,其时恐怕我还不过十一二岁。我们鲁镇的习惯,本来是凡有出嫁的女儿,倘自己还未当家,夏间便大抵回到母家去消夏。那时我的祖母虽然还康建,但母亲也已分担了些家务,所以夏期便不能多日的归省了,只得在扫墓完毕之后,抽空去住几天,这时我便每年跟了我的母亲住在外祖母的家里。那地方叫平桥村,是一个离海边不远,极偏僻的,临河的小村庄;住户不满三十家,都种田,打鱼,只有一家很小的杂货店。但在我是乐土:因为我在这里不但得到优待,又可以免念"秩秩斯干幽幽南山"了。和我一同玩的是许多小朋友,因为有了远客,他们也都从父母那里得了减少工作的许可,伴我来游戏。在小村里,一家的客,几乎也就是公共的。我们年纪都相仿,但论起行辈来,却至少是叔子,有几个还是太公,因为他们合村都同姓,是本家。然而我们是朋友,即使偶而吵闹起来,打了太公,一村的老老少少,也决没有一个会想出"犯上"这两个字来,而他们也百分之九十九不识字。

我们每天的事情大概是掘蚯蚓,掘来穿在铜丝做的小钩上,伏在河沿上去钓虾。虾是水世界里的呆子,决不惮用了自己的两个钳捧着钩尖送到嘴里去的,所以不半天便可以钓到一大碗。这虾照例是归我吃的。其次便是一同去放牛,但或者因为高等动物了的缘故罢,黄牛水牛都欺生,敢于欺侮我,因此我也总不敢走近身,只好远远地跟着,站着。这时候,小朋友们便不再原谅我会读"秩秩斯干",却全都嘲笑起来了。

至于我在那里所第一盼望的,却在到赵庄去看戏。赵庄是离平桥村五里的较大的村庄;平桥村太小,自己演不起戏,每年总付给赵庄多少钱,算作合做的。当时我并不想到他们为什么年年要演戏。现在想,那或者是春赛,是社戏了。

就在我十一二岁时候的这一年,这日期也看看等到了。不料这一年真可惜,在早上就叫不到船。平桥村只有一只早出晚归的航船是大船,决没有留用的道理。其余的都是小船,不合用;央人到邻村去问,也没有,早都给别人定下了。外祖母很气恼,怪家里的人不早定,絮叨起来。母亲便宽慰伊,说我们鲁镇的戏比小村里的好得多,一年看几回,今天就算了。只有我急得要哭,母亲却竭力的嘱咐我,说万不能装模装样,怕又招外祖母生气,又不准和别人一同去,说是怕外祖母要担心。

总之,是完了。到下午,我的朋友都去了,戏已经开场了,我似乎听到锣鼓的声音,而且知道他们在戏台下买豆浆喝。

这一天我不钓虾,东西也少吃。母亲很为难,没有法子想。到晚饭时候,外祖母也终于觉察了,并且说我应当不高兴,他们太怠慢,是待客的礼数里从来没有的。吃饭之后,看过戏的少年们也都聚拢来了,高高兴兴的来讲戏。只有我不开口;他们都叹息而且表同情。忽然间,一个最聪明的双喜大悟似的提议了,他说,"大船? 八叔的航船不是回来了么?"十几个别的少年也大悟,立刻撺掇起来,说可以坐了这航船和我一同去。我高兴了。然而外祖母又怕都是孩子,不可靠;母亲又说是若叫大人一同去,他们白天全有工作,要他熬夜,是不合情理的。在这迟疑之中,双喜可又看出底细来了,便又大声的说道,"我写包票! 船又大;迅哥儿向来不乱跑;我们又都是识水性的!"

诚然! 这十多个少年,委实没有一个不会凫水的,而且两三个还是弄潮的好手。

外祖母和母亲也相信,便不再驳回,都微笑了。我们立刻一哄的出了门。我的很重的心忽而轻松了,身体也似乎舒展到说不出的大。一出门,便望见月下的平桥内泊着一只白篷的航船,大家跳下船,双喜拔前篙,阿发拔后篙,年幼的都陪我坐在舱中,较大的聚在船尾。母亲送出来吩咐"要小心"的时候,我们已经点开船,在桥石上一磕,退后几尺,即又上前出了桥。于是架起两支橹,一支两人,一里一换,有说笑的,有嚷的,夹着潺潺的船头激水的声音,在左右都是碧绿的豆麦田地的河流中,飞一般径向赵庄前进了。

两岸的豆麦和河底的水草所发散出来的清香,夹杂在水气中扑面的吹来;月色便朦胧在这水气里。淡黑的起伏的连山,仿佛是踊跃的铁的兽脊似的,都远远的向船尾跑去了,但我却还以为船慢。他们换了四回手,渐望见依稀的赵庄,而且似乎听到歌吹了,还有几点火,料想便是戏台,但或者也许是渔火。

那声音大概是横笛,宛转,悠扬,使我的心也沉静,然而又自失起来,觉得要和他弥散在含着豆麦蕴藻之香的夜气里。

那火接近了,果然是渔火;我才记得先前望见的也不是赵庄。那是正对船头的一丛松柏林,我去年也曾经去游玩过,还看见破的石马倒在地下,一个石羊蹲在草里呢。过了那林,船便弯进了叉港,于是赵庄便真在眼前了。

最惹眼的是屹立在庄外临河的空地上的一座戏台,模胡在远处的月夜中,和空间几乎分不出界限,我疑心画上见过的仙境,就在这里出现了。这时船走得更快,不多时,在台上显出人物来,红红绿绿的动,近台的河里一望乌黑的是看戏的人家的船篷。

"近台没有什么空了,我们远远的看罢。"阿发说。

这时船慢了,不久就到,果然近不得台旁,大家只能下了篙,比那正对戏台的神棚还要远。其实我们这白篷的航船,本也不愿意和乌篷的船在一处,而况没有空地呢……

在停船的匆忙中,看见台上有一个黑的长胡子的背上插着四张旗,捏着长枪,和一群赤膊的人正打仗。双喜说,那就是有名的铁头老生,能连翻八十四个筋斗,他日里亲自数过的。

我们便都挤在船头上看打仗,但那铁头老生却又并不翻筋斗,只有几个赤膊的人翻,翻了一阵,都进去了,接着走出一个小旦来,咿咿呀呀的唱。双喜说,"晚上看客少,铁头老生也懈了,谁肯显本领给白地看呢?"我相信这话对,因为其时台下已经不很有人,乡下人为了明天的工作,熬不得夜,早都睡觉去了,疏疏朗朗的站着的不过是几十个本村和邻村的闲汉。乌篷船里的那些土财主的家眷固然在,然而他们也不在乎看戏,多半是专到戏台下来吃糕饼水果和瓜子的。所以简直可以算白地。

然而我的意思却也并不在乎看翻筋斗。我最愿意看的是一个人蒙了白布,两手在头上捧着一支棒似的蛇头的蛇精,其次是套了黄布衣跳老虎。但是等了许多时都不见,小旦虽然进去了,立刻又出来了一个很老的小生。我有些疲倦了,托桂生买豆浆去。他去了一刻,回来说,"没有。卖豆浆的聋子也回去了。日里倒有,我还喝了两碗呢。现在去舀一瓢水来给你喝罢。"

我不喝水,支撑着仍然看,也说不出见了些什么,只觉得戏子的脸都渐渐的有些稀奇了,那五官渐不明显,似乎融成一片的再没有什么高低。年纪小的几个多打呵欠了,大的也各管自己谈话。忽而一个红衫的小丑被绑在台柱子上,给一个花白胡子的用马鞭打起来了,大家才又振作精神的笑着看。在这一夜里,我以为这实在要算是最好的一折。

然而老旦终于出台了。老旦本来是我所最怕的东西,尤其是怕他坐下了唱。这时候,看见大家也都很扫兴,才知道他们的意见是和我一致的。那老旦当初还只是踱来踱去的唱,后来竟在中间的一把交椅上坐下了。我很担心;双喜他们却就破口喃喃的骂。我忍耐的等着,许多工夫,只见那老旦将手一抬,我以为就要站起来了,不料他却又慢慢的放下在原地方,仍旧唱。全船里几个人不住的吁气,其余的也打起哈欠来。双喜终于熬不住了,说道,怕他会唱到天明还不完,还是我们走的好罢。

大家立刻都赞成,和开船时候一样踊跃,三四人径奔船尾,拔了篙,点退几丈,回转船头,驾起橹,骂着老旦,又向那松柏林前进了。

月还没有落,仿佛看戏也并不很久似的,而一离赵庄,月光又显得格外的皎洁。回望戏台在灯火光中,却又如初来未到时候一般,又漂渺得像一座仙山楼阁,满被红霞罩着了。吹到耳边来的又是横笛,很悠扬;我疑心老旦已经进去了,但也不好意思说再回去看。

不多久,松柏林早在船后了,船行也并不慢,但周围的黑暗只是浓,可知已经到了深夜。他们一面议论着戏子，或骂，或笑，一面加紧的摇船。这一次船头的激水声更其响亮了，那航船，就像一条大白鱼背着一群孩子在浪花里蹿，连夜渔的几个老渔父，也停了艇子看着喝采起来。

离平桥村还有一里模样，船行却慢了，摇船的都说很疲乏，因为太用力，而且许久没有东西吃。这回想出来的是桂生，说是罗汉豆正旺相，柴火又现成，我们可以偷一点来煮吃。大家都赞成，立刻近岸停了船；岸上的田里，乌油油的都是结实的罗汉豆。

"阿阿，阿发，这边是你家的，这边是老六一家的，我们偷那一边的呢？"双喜先跳下去了，在岸上说。

我们也都跳上岸。阿发一面跳，一面说道，"且慢，让我来看一看罢，"他于是往来的摸了一回，直起身来说道，"偷我们的罢，我们的大得多呢。"一声答应，大家便散开在阿发家的豆田里，各摘了一大捧，抛入船舱中。双喜以为再多偷，倘给阿发的娘知道是要哭骂的，于是各人便到六一公公的田里又各偷了一大捧。

我们中间几个年长的仍然慢慢的摇着船，几个到后舱去生火，年幼的和我都剥豆。不久豆熟了，便任凭航船浮在水面上，都围起来用手撮着吃。吃完豆，又开船，一面洗器具，豆荚豆壳全抛在河水里，什么痕迹也没有了。双喜所虑的是用了八公公船上的盐和柴，这老头子很细心，一定要知道，会骂的。然而大家议论之后，归结是不怕。他如果骂，我们便要他归还去年在岸边拾去的一枝枯柏树，而且当面叫他"八癞子"。

"都回来了！那里会错。我原说过写包票的！"双喜在船头上忽而大声的说。

我向船头一望，前面已经是平桥。桥脚上站着一个人，却是我的母亲，双喜便是对伊说着话。我走出前舱去，船也就进了平桥了，停了船，我们纷纷都上岸。母亲颇有些生气，说是过了三更了，怎么回来得这样迟，但也就高兴了，笑着邀大家去吃炒米。

大家都说已经吃了点心，又渴睡，不如及早睡的好，各自回去了。

第二天，我向午才起来，并没有听到什么关系八公公盐柴事件的纠葛,下午仍然去钓虾。

"双喜,你们这班小鬼,昨天偷了我的豆了罢?又不肯好好的摘,踏坏了不少。"我抬头看时,是六一公公棹着小船,卖了豆回来了,船肚里还有剩下的一堆豆。

"是的。我们请客。我们当初还不要你的呢。你看,你把我的虾吓跑了!"双喜说。

六一公公看见我,便停了楫,笑道,"请客?——这是应该的。"于是对我说,

"迅哥儿,昨天的戏可好么?"

我点一点头,说道,"好。"

"豆可中吃呢?"

我又点一点头,说道,"很好。"

不料六一公公竟非常感激起来,将大拇指一翘,得意的说道,"这真是大市镇里出来的读过书的人才识货!我的豆种是粒粒挑选过的,乡下人不识好歹,还说我的豆比不上别人的呢。我今天也要送些给我们的姑奶奶尝尝去……"他于是打着楫子过去了。

待到母亲叫我回去吃晚饭的时候,桌上便有一大碗煮熟了的罗汉豆,就是六一公公送给母亲和我吃的。听说他还对母亲极口夸奖我,说"小小年纪便有见识,将来一定要中状元。姑奶奶,你的福气是可以写包票的了。"但我吃了豆,却并没有昨夜的豆那么好。

真的,一直到现在,我实在再没有吃到那夜似的好豆,——也不再看到那夜似的好戏了。

一九二二年十月

Village Opera

During the past twenty years I have been to the Chinese opera only twice. During the first ten years I never went, having neither the desire nor the opportunity. The two occasions on which I went were in the past ten years, but each time I left without seeing anything in it.

The first time was in 1912 when I was new to Peking. A friend told me Peking had the best opera and that seeing it was an experience I shouldn't miss. I thought it might be interesting to see an opera, especially in Peking, and hurried in high spirits to some theatre, the name of which I have forgotten. The performance had already started. Even outside I could hear the beat of the drums. As we squeezed in, bright colours flashed in view, and I saw many heads in the auditorium; as I scanned the theatre I saw a few seats in the middle still empty. But when I squeezed in to sit down, someone spoke up. There was such a throbbing in my ears I had to listen attentively to catch what he was saying — "Sorry, these seats are taken!"

We went to the back, but then a man with a glossy queue led us to a side aisle, and indicated an unoccupied place. This was a bench only three-quarters the width of my thighs, but with legs nearly twice as long as mine. To begin with I hadn't the courage to get up there, and then it reminded me of some instrument of torture, and with an involuntary shudder I fled.

I had gone some distance, when I heard my friend's voice, asking: "Well, what's the matter?" Looking over my shoulder I saw he had followed me out. He seemed very surprised. "Why do you march along without a word?" he demanded.

"I'm sorry," I told him. "There's such a pounding in my ears, I couldn't hear you."

Whenever I thought back on the incident, it struck me as very strange, and I supposed that the opera had been a very poor one — or else a theatre was no place for me.

I forget in what year I made the second venture, but funds were being raised for flood victims in Hupeh, and Tan Hsin-pei[①] was still alive. By paying two dollars for a ticket, you contributed money and could go to the Number One Theatre to see an opera with a cast made up for the most part of famous actors, one being Tan Hsin-pei himself. I bought a ticket primarily to satisfy the collector, but then some busy-body seized the opportunity to tell me why Tan Hsin-pei simply had to be seen. At that, I forgot the disastrous din and crash of a few years before, and went to the theatre — probably half because I had paid so much for that precious ticket that I wouldn't feel comfortable if I didn't use it. I learned that Tan Hsin-pei made his appearance late in the evening, and Number One Theatre was a modern one where you didn't have to fight for your seat. That reassured me, and I waited till nine o'clock before setting out. To my surprise, just as before, it was full. There was hardly any standing room and I had to squeeze into the crowd at the rear to watch an actor singing an old woman's part. He had a paper spill burning at each corner of his mouth and there was a devil-soldier beside him. I racked my brains and guessed that this might be Maudgalyayana's mother,[②] because the next to come on was a monk. Not recognizing the actor, I asked a fat gentleman who was squeezed in on my left. "Kung Yun-fu!"[③] he said, throwing me a withering look from the corner of his eye. My face burned with shame for my ignorant blunder, and I mentally resolved that at all costs I would ask no more questions. Then I watched a heroine and her maid sing, next an old man and some other characters I couldn't identify. After that, I watched a whole group fight a free-for-all, and after that, two or three people fighting together — from after nine till ten, from ten till eleven, from eleven till eleven thirty, from eleven thirty till twelve: but there was no sign of Tan Hsin-pei.

Never in my life have I waited for anything so patiently. But the

---

① 译者注: A famous actor in Peking opera.

② 译者注: Maudgalyayana was a disciple of Buddha. Legend has it that his mother went to hell for her sins, and he rescued her.

③ 译者注: Another famous actor in Peking opera, who played old women's roles.

wheezes of the fat gentleman next to me, the clanging, tinkling, drumming and gonging on the stage, the whirl of bright colours and the lateness of the hour suddenly made me realize that this was no place for me. Mechanically I turned round, and tried with might and main to shove my way out. I felt the place behind me fill up at once — no doubt the elastic fat gentleman had expanded his right side into my empty place. With my retreat cut off, naturally there was nothing to do but push and push till at last I was out of the door. Apart from the rickshaws waiting for the playgoers, there was practically no one walking outside, but there were still a dozen people by the gate looking up at the programme, and another group not looking at anything, who must, I thought, be waiting to watch the women come out after the show was over. There was no sign of Tan Hsin-pei ...

But the night air was so brisk, it went right through me. This seemed to be the first time I had known such good air in Peking.

I said goodbye to Chinese opera that night. I never thought about it again, and, if by any chance I passed a theatre, it meant nothing to me for in spirit we were poles apart.

A few days ago, however, I happened to read a Japanese book — unfortunately I have forgotten the title and author, but it was about the Chinese opera. One chapter made the point that Chinese opera is so full of gongs and cymbals, shouting and jumping, that it makes the onlookers' heads swim. It is quite unsuited for presentation in a theatre but, if performed in the open air and watched from a distance, it has its charm. I felt this put into words what had remained unformulated in my mind, because as a matter of fact I clearly remembered seeing a really good opera in the country, and it was under its influence, perhaps, that after coming to Peking, I went twice to the theatre. It's a pity that, somehow or other, I've forgotten the name of that book.

As to when I saw that good opera, it was really "long, long ago," and I could not have been much more than eleven or twelve. It was the custom in Luchen where we lived for married women who were not yet in charge of the household to go back to their parents' home for the summer. Although my father's mother was then still quite strong, my mother had quite a few household duties. She could not spend many days at her own home during the summer. She could take a few days only after visiting the ancestral graves. At such times I always went with her to stay in her parents' house. It was in a place called Pingchao Village, not far from the sea, a very out-of-the-way little village on a river, with less than thirty households, peasants and fishermen, and just one tiny grocery. In my eyes, however, it was heaven, for not only was I treated as a guest of honour, but I could skip reading the *Book of Songs*.①

There were many children for me to play with. For with the arrival of a visitor from such a distance they got permission from their parents to do less work in order to play with me. In a small village the guest of one family is virtually the guest of the whole community. We were all about the same age, but when it came to determining seniority, many were at least my uncles or grand-uncles, since everybody in the village had the same family name and belonged to one clan. But we were all good friends, and if by some chance we fell out and I hit one of my grand-uncles, it never occurred to any child or grown-up in the village to call it "disrespect to elders." Ninety-nine out of a hundred of them could neither read nor write.

We spent most of our days digging up worms, putting them on little hooks made of copper wire, and lying on the river bank to catch shrimps. Shrimps are the silliest water creatures: they willingly use their own pincers to push the point of the hook into their mouths; so in a few hours we could catch a big bowlful. It became the custom to give these shrimps to me. Another thing we did was to take the buffaloes out together, but, maybe because they are animals of a higher species, oxen and buffaloes are hostile to strangers, and they treated me with contempt so that I never dared get too close to them. I could only follow at a distance and stand there. At such times my small friends were no longer impressed by the fact that I could recite classical poetry, but would hoot with laughter.

---

① 译者注: The earliest anthology of poetry in China.

What I looked forward to most was going to Chaochuang to see the opera. Chaochuang was a slightly larger village about two miles away. Since Pingchiao was too small to afford to put on operas, every year it contributed some money for a performance at Chaochuang. At the time, I wasn't curious why they should have operas every year. Thinking about it now, I dare say it may have been for the late spring festival or for the village sacrifice.

That year when I was eleven or twelve, the long-awaited day arrived. But as ill luck would have it, there was no boat for hire that morning. Pingchiao Village had only one sailing boat, which left in the morning and came back in the evening. This was a large boat which it was out of the question to hire; and all the other boats were unsuitable because they were too small. Someone was sent round to the neighbouring villages to ask if they had boats, but no — they had all been hired already. My grandmother was very upset, blamed my cousins for not hiring one earlier, and began to complain. Mother tried to comfort her by saying the operas at Luchen were much better than in these little villages, and there were several every year, so there was no need to go today. But I was nearly in tears from disappointment, and mother did her best to impress on me that no matter what, I must not make a scene, because it would upset my grandmother; and I mustn't go with other people either, for then grandmother would be worried.

In a word, it had fallen through. After lunch, when all my friends had left and the opera had started, I imagined I could hear the sound of gongs and drums, and saw them, with my mind's eye, in front of the stage buying soya-bean milk.

I didn't catch shrimps that day, and didn't eat much either. Mother was very upset, but there was nothing she could do. By supper time grandmother realized how I felt, and said I was quite right to be angry, they had been too negligent, and never before had guests been treated so badly. After the meal, youngsters who had come back from the opera gathered round and gaily described it all for us. I was the only one silent; they all sighed and said how sorry they were for me. Suddenly one of the brightest, called Shuang-hsi, had an inspiration, and said: "A big boat — hasn't Eighth Grand-uncle's boat come back?" A dozen other boys picked up the idea in a flash, and at once started agitating to take the boat and go with me. I cheered up. But grandmother was nervous, thinking we were all children and undependable. And mother said that since the grown-ups all had to work the next day, it wouldn't be fair to ask them to go with us and stay up all night. While our fate hung in the balance, Shuang-hsi went to the root of the question and declared loudly: "I give my word it'll be all right! It's a big boat, Brother Hsun never jumps around, and we can all swim!"

It was true. There wasn't one boy in the dozen who wasn't a fish in water, and two or three of them were first-rate swimmers.

Grandmother and mother were convinced and did not raise any more objections. They both smiled, and we immediately rushed out.

My heavy heart suddenly became light, and I felt as though I were floating on air. When we got outside, I saw in the moonlight a boat with a white awning moored at the bridge. We jumped aboard, Shuang-hsi seized the front pole and Ah-fa the back one; the younger boys sat down with me in the middle of the boat, while the older ones went to the stern. By the time mother followed us out to say "Be careful!" we had already cast off. We pushed off from the bridge, floated back a few feet, then moved forward under the bridge. Two oars were set up, each manned by two boys who changed shifts every third of a mile. Chatter, laughter and shouts mingled with the lapping of the water against the bow of our boat; to our right and left, as we flew forward towards Chaochuang, were emerald green fields of beans and wheat.

The mist hung over the water, the scent of beans, wheat and river weeds wafted towards us, and the moonlight shone faintly through the mist. In the distance, grey hills, undulating like the backs of some leaping iron beasts, seemed to be racing past the stern of our boat; but still I felt our progress was slow. When the oarsmen had changed shifts four times, it was just possible to see the faint outline of Chaochuang, and catch the sound of singing. There were several lights too, which we guessed must be on the stage, unless they were fishermen's lights.

The music we heard was probably flutes. Eddying round and round and up and down, it soothed me and set me dreaming at the same time, till I felt as though I were about to drift far away with it through the night air heavy with the scent of beans and wheat and river weeds.

As we approached the lights, we found they were fishermen's lights after all, and I realized I hadn't been looking at Chaochuang at all. Directly ahead of us was a pine wood where I had played the year before, and seen the broken stone horse that had fallen on its side, and a stone sheep couched in the grass. When we passed the wood, the boat rounded a bend into a cove, and Chaochuang was really before us.

Our eyes were drawn to the stage standing in a plot of empty ground by the river outside the village, hazy in the distant moonlight, barely distinguishable from its surroundings. It seemed that the fairyland I had seen in pictures had come alive here. The boat was moving faster now, and presently we could make out figures on the stage and a blaze of bright colours, and the river close to the stage was black with the boat awnings of people who had come to watch the play.

"There's no room near the stage, let's watch from a distance," suggested Ah-fa,

The boat had slowed down now, and soon we arrived. True enough, it was impossible to get close to the stage. We had to make our boat fast even further from the stage than the shrine opposite it. We did not regret it, though, for we did not want our boat with its white awning to mix with those common black boats; and there was no room for us anyway ...

While we hastily moored, there appeared on the stage a man with a long black beard who had four pennons fixed to his back. With a spear he fought a whole group of bare-armed men. Shuang-hsi told us this was a famous acrobat who could turn eighty-four somersaults, one after the other. He had counted for himself earlier in the day.

We all crowded to the bow to watch the fighting, but the acrobat didn't turn any somersaults. Some of the bare-armed men turned head over heels a few times, then trooped off. Then a girl came out, and sang in a long drawn-out voice. "There aren't many people in the evening," said Shuang-hsi, "and the acrobat's taking it easy. Nobody wants to show his skill without an audience." That was common sense, because by then there really weren't many people left to watch. The country folk had work the next day, and couldn't stay up all night, so they had all gone to bed. Just a score or so of idlers from Chaochuang and the villages around remained sprinkled about. The families of the local rich were still there in the boats with black awnings, but they weren't really interested in the opera. Most of them had gone to the foot of the stage to eat cakes, fruit or melon seeds. So it didn't really amount to an audience.

As a matter of fact, I wasn't keen on the somersaults. What I wanted to see most was a snake spirit swathed in white, its two hands clasping on its head a wand-like snake's head. My second choice was a leaping tiger dressed in yellow. But though I waited a long time, they didn't appear. The girl was followed at once by a very old man acting the part of a young man. I was rather tired and asked Kuei-sheng to buy me some soya-bean milk. He came back in a little while to say: "There isn't any. The deaf man who sells it has gone. There was some in the daytime, I drank two bowls then. I'll get you a dipperful of water to drink."

I didn't drink the water, but stuck it out as best I could. I can't say what I saw, but it seemed that the faces of the players gradually became very strange, the features blurred as though they had melted into one flat surface. Most of the younger boys yawned, while the older ones chatted among themselves. It was only when a clown in a red shirt was fastened to a pillar on the stage, and a greybeard started horsewhipping him that we all roused ourselves to watch again and laughed. I really think that was the best scene of the evening.

But then the old woman came out. This was the character I most dreaded, especially when she sat down to sing. Now I saw by everybody's disappointment that they felt as I did. In the beginning, the old woman just walked to and fro singing, then she sat on a chair in the middle of the stage. I was really distressed, and Shuang-hsi and the others started swearing. I waited patiently until, after a long time, the old woman raised her hand, and I thought she was going to stand up. But despite my hopes she lowered her hand slowly to its original position, and went on singing just as before. Some of the boys in the boat couldn't help groaning, and the rest began to yawn again. Finally Shuang-hsi couldn't stand it any longer. He said he was afraid the old woman would go on singing till dawn, and we had better leave. We all promptly agreed, and became as eager as when we had set out. Three or four boys ran to the stern, seized the poles to punt back several yards, and headed the boat around. Cursing the old singer, they set up the oars, and started back for the pine wood.

Judging from the position of the moon, we had not been watching very long, and once we left Chaochuang the moonlight seemed unusually bright. When we turned back to see the lantern-lit stage, it looked just as it had when we came, hazy as a fairy pavilion, covered in a rosy mist. Once again the flutes piped melodiously in our ears. I thought the old woman must have finished, but couldn't very well suggest going back again to see.

Soon the pine wood was behind us. Our boat was moving rather fast, but there was such thick darkness all around you could tell it was very late. As they discussed the players, laughing and swearing, the towers pulled faster on the oars. Now the plash of water against our bow was even more distinct. The boat seemed like a great white fish carrying a freight of children on its back through the foam. Some old fishermen who fished all night stopped their punts to cheer at the sight.

We were still about a third of a mile from Pingchiao when our boat slowed down, and the oarsmen said they were tired after rowing so hard. We'd had nothing to eat for hours. It was Kuei-sheng who had a brilliant idea this time. He said the lohan beans were ripe, and we had fuel on the boat — we could use a little to cook the beans. Everybody agreed, and we immediately headed towards the bank. The pitch-black fields were filled with succulent beans.

"Hey! Ah-fa! It's your family's over here, and Old Liu Yi's over there. Which shall we take?" Shuang-hsi had been the first to leap ashore, and was calling from the bank.

As we all jumped ashore too, Ah-fa said: "Wait a minute and I'll take a look." He walked up and down feeling the beans, then straightened up to say: "Take ours, they're much bigger." With a shout we scattered through the bean field of Ah-fa's family, each picking a big handful of beans and throwing them into the boat. Shuang-hsi thought that if we took any more and Ah-fa's mother found out, there would be trouble, so we all went to Old Liu Yi's field to pick another handful each.

Then a few of the older boys started rowing slowly again, while others lit a fire in the stern, and the younger boys and I shelled the beans. Soon they were cooked, and we let the boat drift while we gathered round and ate them with our fingers. When we had finished eating we went on again, washing the pot and throwing the pods into the river, to destroy all traces. Shuang-hsi was uneasy because we had used the salt and firewood on Eighth Grand-uncle's boat, and the old man was so sharp he would be sure to find out and scold us. But after some discussion we decided there was nothing to fear. If he did scold us we would ask him to return the pine branch he had taken the previous year from the river bank, and call him "Old Scabby" to his face.

"We're all back! How could anything have happened? Didn't I guarantee it would be all right!" Shuang-hsi's voice suddenly rang out from the bow.

Looking past him, I saw we were already at Pingchiao, and someone was standing at the foot of the bridge — it was mother. It was to her that Shuang-hsi had called. As I walked up to the bow the boat passed under the bridge, then stopped, and we all went ashore. Mother was rather annoyed, and asked why we had come back so late — it was after midnight. But she was soon in a good humour again, and smiled as she invited everybody to come back and have some puffed rice.

They told her we had all eaten something, and were sleepy, so they had better get to bed at once, and off we all went to our own homes.

I didn't get up till noon the next day, and there was no word of any trouble with Eighth Grand-uncle over the salt or firewood. In the afternoon we went to catch shrimps as usual.

"Shuang-hsi, you young rascals stole my beans yesterday! And you didn't pick them properly, you trampled down quite a few." I looked up and saw Old Liu Yi on a punt, coming back from selling beans. There was still a heap of left-over beans at the bottom of the punt.

"Yes. We were treating a visitor. We didn't mean to take yours to begin with," said Shuang-hsi. "Look! You've frightened away my shrimp!"

When the old man saw me, he stopped punting, and chuckled. "Treating a visitor? So you should." Then he asked me: "Was yesterday's opera good?"

"Yes." I nodded.

"Did you enjoy the beans?"

"Very much." I nodded again.

To my surprise, the old man was greatly pleased. He stuck up a thumb, and declared with satisfaction: "People from big towns who have studied really know what's good. I select my bean seeds one by one. Country folk can't tell good from bad, and say my beans aren't as good as other people's. I'll give some to your mother today for her to try ..." Then he punted off.

When mother called me home for supper, there was a large bowl of boiled beans on the table, which Old Liu Yi had brought for her and me to eat. I heard he had praised me highly to mother, saying, "He's so young, yet he knows what's what. He's sure to pass all the official examinations in future. Your fortune's as good as made." But when I ate the beans, they didn't taste as good as the ones we'd eaten the night before.

It's a fact, right up till now, I've really never eaten such good beans, or seen such a good opera, as I did that night.

October 1922

5. 祝 福①

旧历的年底毕竟最像年底,村镇上不必说,就在天空中也显出将到新年的气象来。灰白色的沉重的晚云中间时时发出闪光,接着一声钝响,是送灶的爆竹;近处燃放的可就更强烈了,震耳的大音还没有息,空气里已经散满了幽微的火药香。我是正在这一夜回到我的故乡鲁镇的。虽说故乡,然而已没有家,所以只得暂寓在鲁四老爷的宅子里。他是我的本家,比我长一辈,应该称之曰"四叔",是一个讲理学的老监生。他比先前并没有什么大改变,单是老了些,但也还未留胡子,一见面是寒暄,寒暄之后说我"胖了",说我"胖了"之后即大骂其新党。但我知道,这并非借题在骂我:因为他所骂的还是康有为。但是,谈话是总不投机的了,于是不多久,我便一个人剩在书房里。

第二天我起得很迟,午饭之后,出去看了几个本家和朋友;第三天也照样。他们也都没有什么大改变,单是老了些;家中却一律忙,都在准备着"祝福"。这是鲁镇年终的大典,致敬尽礼,迎接福神,拜求来年一年中的好运气的。杀鸡,宰鹅,买猪肉,用心细细的洗,女人的臂膊都在水里浸得通红,有的还带着绞丝银镯子。煮熟之后,横七竖八的插些筷子在这类东西上,可就称为"福礼"了,五更天陈列起来,并且点上香烛,恭请福神们来享用,拜的却只限于男人,拜完自然仍然是放爆竹。年年如此,家家如此,——只要买得起福礼和爆竹之类的——今年自然也如此。天色愈阴暗了,下午竟下起雪来,雪花大的有梅花那么大,满天飞舞,夹着烟霭和忙碌的气色,将鲁镇乱成一团糟。我回到四叔的书房里时,瓦楞上已经雪白,房里也映得较光明,极分明的显出壁上挂着的朱拓的大"壽"字,陈抟

---

① 中文选自:鲁迅. 彷徨.北京:人民文学出版社,1956.
英译文选自:Lu Hsun. *Selected Stories of Lu Hsun*. Yang Xianyi & Gladys Yang. Trans. Beijing:Foreign Languages Press,1978.

老祖写的;一边的对联已经脱落,松松的卷了放在长桌上,一边的还在,道是"事理通达心气和平"。我又无聊赖的到窗下的案头去一翻,只见一堆似乎未必完全的《康熙字典》,一部《近思录集注》和一部《四书衬》。无论如何,我明天决计要走了。

况且,一直到昨天遇见祥林嫂的事,也就使我不能安住。那是下午,我到镇的东头访过一个朋友,走出来,就在河边遇见她;而且见她瞪着的眼睛的视线,就知道明明是向我走来的。我这回在鲁镇所见的人们中,改变之大,可以说无过于她的了:五年前的花白的头发,即今已经全白,全不像四十上下的人;脸上瘦削不堪,黄中带黑,而且消尽了先前悲哀的神色,仿佛是木刻似的;只有那眼珠间或一轮,还可以表示她是一个活物。她一手提着竹篮,内中一个破碗,空的;一手拄着一支比她更长的竹竿,下端开了裂:她分明已经纯乎是一个乞丐了。

我就站住,豫备她来讨钱。

"你回来了?"她先这样问。

"是的。"

"这正好。你是识字的,又是出门人,见识得多。我正要问你一件事——"她那没有精采的眼睛忽然发光了。

我万料不到她却说出这样的话来,诧异的站着。

"就是——"她走近两步,放低了声音,极秘密似的切切的说,"一个人死了之后,究竟有没有魂灵的?"

我很悚然,一见她的眼钉着我的,背上也就遭了芒刺一般,比在学校里遇到不及豫防的临时考,教师又偏是站在身旁的时候,惶急得多了。对于魂灵的有无,我自己是向来毫不介意的;但在此刻,怎样回答她好呢?我在极短期的踌蹰中,想,这里的人照例相信鬼,然而她,却疑惑了,——或者不如说希望:希望其有,又希望其无……,人何必增添末路的人的苦恼,一为她起见,不如说有罢。

"也许有罢,——我想。"我于是吞吞吐吐的说。

"那么,也就有地狱了?"

"阿！地狱？"我很吃惊，只得支吾着，"地狱？——论理，就该也有。——然而也未必，……谁来管这等事……。"

"那么，死掉的一家的人，都能见面的？"

"唉唉，见面不见面呢？……"这时我已知道自己也还是完全一个愚人，什么踌蹰，什么计画，都挡不住三句问，我即刻胆怯起来了，便想全翻过先前的话来，"那是，……实在，我说不清……。其实，究竟有没有魂灵，我也说不清。"

我乘她不再紧接的问，迈开步便走，匆匆的逃回四叔的家中，心里很觉得不安逸。自己想，我这答话怕于她有些危险。她大约因为在别人的祝福时候，感到自身的寂寞了，然而会不会含有别的什么意思的呢？——或者是有了什么豫感了？倘有别的意思，又因此发生别的事，则我的答话委实该负若干的责任……。但随后也就自笑，觉得偶尔的事，本没有什么深意义，而我偏要细细推敲，正无怪教育家要说是生着神经病；而况明明说过"说不清"，已经推翻了答话的全局，即使发生什么事，于我也毫无关系了。

"说不清"是一句极有用的话。不更事的勇敢的少年，往往敢于给人解决疑问，选定医生，万一结果不佳，大抵反成了怨府，然而一用这说不清来作结束，便事事逍遥自在了。我在这时，更感到这一句话的必要，即使和讨饭的女人说话，也是万不可省的。

但是我总觉得不安，过了一夜，也仍然时时记忆起来，仿佛怀着什么不祥的豫感；在阴沉的雪天里，在无聊的书房里，这不安愈加强烈了。不如走罢，明天进城去。福兴楼的清燉鱼翅，一元一大盘，价廉物美，现在不知增价了否？往日同游的朋友，虽然已经云散，然而鱼翅是不可不吃的，即使只有我一个……。无论如何，我明天决计要走了。

我因为常见些但愿不如所料，以为未毕竟如所料的事，却每每恰如所料的起来，所以很恐怕这事也一律。果然，特别的情形开始了。傍晚，我竟听到有些人聚在内室里谈话，仿佛议论什么事似的，但不一会，说话声也就止了，只有四叔且走而且高声的说：

"不早不迟,偏偏要在这时候——这就可见是一个谬种!"

我先是诧异,接着是很不安,似乎这话于我有关系。试望门外,谁也没有。好容易待到晚饭前他们的短工来冲茶,我才得了打听消息的机会。

"刚才,四老爷和谁生气呢?"我问。

"还不是和祥林嫂?"那短工简捷的说。

"祥林嫂? 怎么了?"我又赶紧的问。

"老了。"

"死了?"我的心突然紧缩,几乎跳起来,脸上大约也变了色。但他始终没有抬头,所以全不觉。我也就镇定了自己,接着问:

"什么时候死的?"

"什么时候? ——昨天夜里,或者就是今天罢。——我说不清。"

"怎么死的?"

"怎么死的? ——还不是穷死的?"他淡然的回答,仍然没有抬头向我看,出去了。

然而我的惊惶却不过暂时的事,随着就觉得要来的事,已经过去,并不必仰仗我自己的"说不清"和他之所谓"穷死的"的宽慰,心地已经渐渐轻松;不过偶然之间,还似乎有些负疚。晚饭摆出来了,四叔俨然的陪着。我也还想打听些关于祥林嫂的消息,但知道他虽然读过"鬼神者二气之良能也",而忌讳仍然极多,当临近祝福时候,是万不可提起死亡疾病之类的话的;倘不得已,就该用一种替代的隐语,可惜我又不知道,因此屡次想问,而终于中止了。我从他俨然的脸色上,又忽而疑他正以为我不早不迟,偏要在这时候来打搅他,也是一个谬种,便立刻告诉他明天要离开鲁镇,进城去,趁早放宽了他的心。他也不很留。这样闷闷的吃完了一餐饭。

冬季日短,又是雪天,夜色早已笼罩了全市镇。人们都在灯下匆忙,但窗外很寂静。雪花落在积得厚厚的雪褥上面,听去似乎瑟瑟有声,使人更加感得沉寂。我独坐在发出黄光的菜油灯下,想,这百无聊赖的祥林嫂,被人们弃在尘芥堆中的,看得厌倦了的陈旧的玩物,先前还将形骸露在尘芥里,从活得有趣的人们看来,恐怕要怪讶她何以还要存在,现在总算被无常打扫得干干净净了。魂灵的有无,我不知道;然而在现世,则无聊生者不生,即使厌见者不见,为人为己,也还都不错。我静听着窗外似乎瑟瑟作响的雪花声,一面想,反而渐渐的舒畅起来。

然而先前所见所闻的她的半生事迹的断片,至此也联成一片了。

她不是鲁镇人。有一年的冬初,四叔家里要换女工,做中人的卫老婆子带她进来了,头上扎着白头绳,乌裙,蓝夹袄,月白背心,年纪大约二十六七,脸色青黄,但两颊却还是红的。卫老婆子叫她祥林嫂,说是自己母家的邻舍,死了当家人,所以出来做工了。四叔皱了皱眉,四婶已经知道了他的意思,是在讨厌她是一个寡妇。但看她模样还周正,手脚都壮大,又只是顺着眼,不开一句口,很像一个安分耐劳的人,便不管四叔的皱眉,将她留下了。试工期内,她整天的做,似乎闲着就无聊,又有力,简直抵得过一个男子,所以第三天就定局,每月工钱五百文。

大家都叫她祥林嫂;没问她姓什么,但中人是卫家山人,既说是邻居,那大概也就姓卫了。她不很爱说话,别人问了才回答,答的也不多。直到十几天之后,这才陆续的知道她家里还有严厉的婆婆;一个小叔子,十多岁,能打柴了;她是春天没了丈夫的;他本来也打柴为生,比她小十岁:大家所知道的就只是这一点。

日子很快的过去了,她的做工却毫没有懈,食物不论,力气是不惜的。人们都说鲁四老爷家里雇着了女工,实在比勤快的男人还勤快。到年底,扫尘,洗地,杀鸡,宰鹅,彻夜的煮福礼,全是一人担当,竟没有添短工。然而她反满足,口角边渐渐的有了笑影,脸上也白胖了。

新年才过,她从河边淘米回来时,忽而失了色,说刚才远远地看见一个男人在对岸徘徊,很像夫家的堂伯,恐怕是正在寻她而来的。四婶很惊疑,打听底细,她又不说。四叔一知道,就皱一皱眉,道:

"这不好。恐怕她是逃出来的。"

她诚然是逃出来的,不多久,这推想就证实了。

此后大约十几天,大家正已渐渐忘却了先前的事,卫老婆子忽而带了一个三十多岁的女人进来了,说那是祥林嫂的婆婆。那女人虽是山里人模样,然而应酬很从容,说话也能干,寒暄之后,就赔罪,说她特来叫她的儿媳回家去,因为开春事务忙,而家中只有老的和小的,人手不够了。

"既是她的婆婆要她回去,那有什么话可说呢。"四叔说。

于是算清了工钱,一共一千七百五十文,她全存在主人家,一文也还没有用,便都交给她的婆婆。那女人又取了衣服,道过谢,出去了。其时已经是正午。

"阿呀,米呢?祥林嫂不是去淘米的么?……"好一会,四婶这才惊叫起来。她大约有些饿,记得午饭了。

于是大家分头寻淘箩。她先到厨下,次到堂前,后到卧房,全不见淘箩的影子。四叔踱出门外,也不见,一直到河边,才见平平正正的放在岸上,旁边还有一株菜。

看见的人报告说,河里面上午就泊了一只白篷船,篷是全盖起来的,不知道什么人在里面,但事前也没有人去理会他。待到祥林嫂出来淘米,刚刚要跪下去,那船里便突然跳出两个男人来,像是山里人,一个抱住她,一个帮着,拖进船去了。祥林嫂还哭喊了几声,此后便再没有什么声息,大约给用什么堵住了罢。接着就走上两个女人来,一个不认识,一个就是卫婆子。窥探舱里,不很分明,她像是捆了躺在船板上。

"可恶!然而……"四叔说。

这一天是四婶自己煮中饭;他们的儿子阿牛烧火。

午饭之后,卫老婆子又来了。

"可恶!"四叔说。

"你是什么意思?亏你还会再来见我们。"四婶洗着碗,一见面就愤愤的说,"你自己荐她来,又合伙劫她去,闹得沸反盈天的,大家看了成个什么样子?你拿我们家里开玩笑么?"

"阿呀阿呀,我真上当。我这回,就是为此特地来说说清楚的。她来求我荐地方,我那里料得到是瞒着她的婆婆的呢。对不起,四老爷,四太太。总是我老发昏不小心,对不起主顾。幸而府上是向来宽洪大量,不肯和小人计较的。这回我一定荐一个好的来折罪……。"

"然而……。"四叔说。

于是祥林嫂事件便告终结,不久也就忘却了。

只有四婶,因为后来雇用的女工,大抵非懒即馋,或者馋而且懒,左右不如意,所以也还提起祥林嫂。每当这些时候,她往往自言自语的说,"她现在不知道怎么样了?"意思是希望她再来。但到第二年的新正,她也就绝了望。

新正将尽,卫老婆子来拜年了,已经喝得醉醺醺的,自说因为回了一趟卫家山的娘家,住下几天,所以来得迟了。她们问答之间,自然就谈到祥林嫂。

"她么?"卫老婆子高兴的说,"现在是交了好运了。她婆婆来抓她回去的时候,是早已许给了贺家墺的贺老六的,所以回家之后不几天,也就装在花轿里抬去了。"

"阿呀,这样的婆婆! ……"四婶惊奇的说。

"阿呀,我的太太! 你真是大户人家的太太的话。我们山里人,小户人家,这算得什么? 她有小叔子,也得娶老婆。不嫁了她,那有这一注钱来做聘礼? 他的婆婆倒是精明强干的女人呵,很有打算,所以就将地嫁到里山去。倘许给本村人,财礼就不多;惟独肯嫁进深山野墺里去的女人少,所以她就到手了八十千。现在第二个儿子的媳妇也娶进了,财礼花了五十,除去办喜事的费用,还剩十多千。吓,你看,这多么好打算? ……"

"祥林嫂竟肯依? ……"

"这有什么依不依。——闹是谁也总要闹一闹的,只要用绳子一捆,塞在花轿里,抬到男家,捺上花冠,拜堂,关上房门,就完事了。可是祥林嫂真出格,听说那时实在闹得利害,大家还都说大约因为在念书人家做过事,所以与众不同呢。太太,我们见得多了:回头人出嫁,哭喊的也有,说要寻死觅活的也有,抬到男家闹得拜不成天地的也有,连花烛都砸了的也有。祥林嫂可是异乎寻常,他们说她一路只是嚎,骂,抬到贺家墺,喉咙已经全哑了。拉出轿来，两个男人和她的小叔子使劲的擒住她也还拜不成天地。他们一不小心，一松手，阿呀，阿弥陀佛，她就一头撞在香案角上，头上碰了一个大窟窿，鲜血直流，用了两把香灰，包上两块红布还止不住血呢。直到七手八脚的将她和男人反关在新房里，还是骂，阿呀呀，这真是……。"她摇一摇头，顺下眼睛，不说了。

"后来怎么样呢？"四婶还问。

"听说第二天也没有起来。"她抬起眼来说。

"后来呢？"

"后来？——起来了。她到年底就生了一个孩子，男的，新年就两岁了。我在娘家这几天，就有人到贺家墺去，回来说看见他们娘儿俩，母亲也胖，儿子也胖；上头又没有婆婆，男人所有的是力气，会做活；房子是自家的。——唉唉，她真是交了好运了。"

从此之后，四婶也就不再提起祥林嫂。

但有一年的秋季，大约是得到祥林嫂好运的消息之后的又过了两个新年，她竟又站在四叔家的堂前了。桌上放着一个荸荠式的圆篮，檐下一个小铺盖。她仍然头上扎着白头绳，乌裙，蓝夹袄，月白背心，脸色青黄，只是两颊上已经消失了血色，顺着眼，眼角上带些泪痕，眼光也没有先前那样精神了。而且仍然是卫老婆子领着，显出慈悲模样，絮絮的对四婶说：

"……这实在是叫作'天有不测风云'，她的男人是坚实人，谁知道年纪青青，就会断送在伤寒上？本来已经好了的，吃了一碗冷饭，复发了。幸亏有儿子；她又能做，打柴摘茶养蚕都来得，本来还可以守着，谁知道那孩子又会给狼衔去的呢？春天快完了，村上倒反来了狼，谁料到？现在她只剩了一个光身了。大伯来收屋，又赶她。她真是走投无路了，只好来求老主人。好在她现在已经再没有什么牵挂，太太家里又凑巧要换人，所以我就领她来。——我想，熟门熟路，比生手实在好得多……。"

"我真傻，真的，"祥林嫂抬起她没有神采的眼睛来，接着说。"我单知道下雪的时候野兽在山墺里没有食吃,会到村里来;我不知道春天也会有。我一清早起来就开了门,拿小篮盛了一篮豆,叫我们的阿毛坐在门槛上剥豆去。他是很听话的,我的话句句听;他出去了。我就在屋后劈柴,淘米,米下了锅,要蒸豆。我叫阿毛,没有应,出去口看,只见豆撒得一地,没有我们的阿毛了。他是不到别家去玩的;各处去一问,果然没有。我急了,央人出去寻。直到下半天,寻来寻去寻到山墺里,看见刺柴上挂着一只他的小鞋。大家都说,糟了,怕是遭了狼了。再进去;他果然躺在草窠里,肚里的五脏已经都给吃空了,手上还紧紧的捏着那只小篮呢。……"她接着但是呜咽,说不出成句的话来。

四婶起刻还踌蹰,待到听完她自己的话,眼圈就有些红了。她想了一想,便教拿圆篮和铺盖到下房去。卫老婆子仿佛卸了一肩重担似的嘘一口气,祥林嫂比初来时候神气舒畅些,不待指引,自己驯熟的安放了铺盖。她从此又在鲁镇做女工了。

大家仍然叫她祥林嫂。

然而这一回,她的境遇却改变得非常大。上工之后的两三天,主人们就觉得她手脚已没有先前一样灵活,记性也坏得多,死尸似的脸上又整日没有笑影,四婶的口气上,已颇有些不满了。当她初到的时候,四叔虽然照例皱过眉,但鉴于向来雇用女工之难,也就并不大反对,只是暗暗地告诫四婶说,这种人虽然似乎很可怜,但是败坏风俗的,用她帮忙还可以,祭祀时候可用不着她沾手,一切饭菜,只好自己做,否则,不干不净,祖宗是不吃的。

四叔家里最重大的事件是祭祀,祥林嫂先前最忙的时候也就是祭祀,这回她却清闲了。桌子放在堂中央,系上桌帏,她还记得照旧的去分配酒杯和筷子。

"祥林嫂,你放着罢! 我来摆。"四婶慌忙的说。

她讪讪的缩了手,又去取烛台。

"祥林嫂,你放着罢! 我来拿。"四婶又慌忙的说。

她转了几个圆圈,终于没有事情做,只得疑惑的走开。她在这一天可做的事是不过坐在灶下烧火。

镇上的人们也仍然叫她祥林嫂,但音调和先前很不同;也还和她讲话,但笑容却冷冷的了。她全不理会那些事,只是直着眼睛,和大家讲她自己日夜不忘的故事:

"我真傻,真的,"她说,"我单知道雪天是野兽在深山里没有食吃,会到村里来;我不知道春天也会有。我一大早起来就开了门,拿小篮盛了一篮豆,叫我们的阿毛坐在门槛上剥豆去。他是很听话的孩子,我的话句句听;他就出去了。我就在屋后劈柴,淘米,米下了锅,打算蒸豆。我叫,'阿毛'! 没有应。出去一看,只见豆撒得满地,没有我们的阿毛了。各处去一问,都没有。我急了,央人去寻去。直到下半天,几个人寻到山墺里,看见刺柴上挂着一只他的小鞋。大家都说,完了,怕是遭了狼了;再进去;果然,他躺在草窠里,肚里的五脏已经都给吃空了,可怜他手里还紧紧的捏着那只小篮呢。……"她于是淌下眼泪来,声音也呜咽了。

这故事倒颇有效,男人听到这里,往往敛起笑容,没趣的走了开去;女人们却不独宽恕了她似的,脸上立刻改换了鄙薄的神气,还要陪出许多眼泪来。有些老女人没有在街头听到她的话,便特意寻来,要听她这一段悲惨的故事。直到她说到呜咽,她们也就一齐流下那停在眼角上的眼泪,叹息一番,满足的去了,一面还纷纷的评论着。

她就只是反复的向人说她悲惨的故事,常常引住了三五个人来听她。但不久,大家也都听得纯熟了,便是最慈悲的念佛的老太太们,眼里也再不见有一点泪的痕迹。后来全镇的人们几乎都能背诵她的话,一听到就烦厌得头痛。

"我真傻,真的,"她开首说。

"是的,你是单知道雪天野兽在深山里没有食吃,才会到村里来的。"他们立即打断她的话,走开去了。

她张着口怔怔的站着,直着眼睛看他们,接着也就走了,似乎自己也觉得没趣。但她还妄想,希图从别的事,如小篮,豆,别人的孩子上,引出她的阿毛的故事来。倘一看见两三岁的小孩子,她就说:

"唉唉,我们的阿毛如果还在,也就有这么大了。……"

孩子看见她的眼光就吃惊,牵着母亲的衣襟催她走。于是又只剩下她一个,终于没趣的也走了,后来大家又都知道了她的脾气,只要有孩子在眼前,便似笑非笑的先问她,道:

"祥林嫂,你们的阿毛如果还在,不是也就有这么大了么?"

她未必知道她的悲哀经大家咀嚼赏鉴了许多天,早已成为渣滓,只值得烦厌和唾弃;但从人们的笑影上,也仿佛觉得这又冷又尖,自己再没有开口的必要了。她单是一瞥他们,并不回答一句话。

鲁镇永远是过新年,腊月二十以后就火起来了。四叔家里这回须雇男短工,还是忙不过来,另叫柳妈做帮手,杀鸡,宰鹅;然而柳妈是善女人,吃素,不杀生的,只肯洗器皿。祥林嫂除烧火之外,没有别的事,却闲着了,坐着只看柳妈洗器皿。微雪点点的下来了。

"唉唉,我真傻,"祥林嫂看了天空,叹息着,独语似的说。

"祥林嫂,你又来了。"柳妈不耐烦的看着她的脸,说。"我问你:你额角上的伤痕,不就是那时撞坏的么?"

"唔唔。"她含胡的回答。

"我问你:你那时怎么后来竟依了呢?"

"我么?……"

"你呀。我想:这总是你自己愿意了,不然……。"

"阿阿,你不知道他力气多么大呀。"

"我不信。我不信你这么大的力气,真会拗他不过。你后来一定是自己肯了,倒推说他力气大。"

"阿阿,你……你倒自己试试着。"她笑了。

柳妈的打皱的脸也笑起来,使她蹙缩得像一个核桃;干枯的小眼睛一看祥林嫂的额角,又钉住她的眼。祥林嫂似很局促了,立刻敛了笑容,旋转眼光,自去看雪花。

"祥林嫂,你实在不合算。"柳妈诡秘的说。"再一强,或者索性撞一个死,就好了。现在呢,你和你的第二个男人过活不到两年,倒落了一件大罪名。你想,你将来到阴司去,那两个死鬼的男人还要争,你给了谁好呢?阎罗大王只好把你锯开来,分给他们。我想,这真是。"

她脸上就显出恐怖的神色来,这是在山村里所未曾知道的。

"我想,你不如及早抵当。你到土地庙里去捐一条门槛,当作你的替身,给千人踏,万人跨,赎了这一世的罪名,免得死了去受苦。"

她当时并不回答什么话,但大约非常苦闷了,第二天早上起来的时候,两眼上便都围着大黑圈。早饭之后,她便到镇的西头的土地庙里去求捐门槛。庙祝起初执意不允许,直到她急得流泪,才勉强答应了。价目是大钱十二千。

她久已不和人们交口,因为阿毛的故事是早被大家厌弃了的;但自从和柳妈谈了天,似乎又即传扬开去,许多人都发生了新趣味,又来逗她说话了。至于题目,那自然是换了一个新样,专在她额上的伤疤。

"祥林嫂,我问你:你那时怎么竟肯了?"一个说。

"唉,可惜,白撞了这一下。"一个看着她的疤,应和道。

她大约从他们的笑容和声调上,也知道是在嘲笑她,所以总是瞪着眼睛,不说一句话,后来连头也不回了。她整日紧闭了嘴唇,头上带着大家以为耻辱的记号的那伤痕,默默的跑街,扫地,洗菜,淘米。快够一年,她才从四婶手里支取了历来积存的工钱,换算了十二元鹰洋,请假到镇的西头去。但不到一顿饭时候,她便回来,神气很舒畅,眼光也分外有神,高兴似的对四婶说,自己已经在土地庙捐了门槛了。

冬至的祭祖时节,她做得更出力,看四婶装好祭品,和阿牛将桌子抬到堂屋中央,她便坦然的去拿酒杯和筷子。

"你放着罢,祥林嫂!"四婶慌忙大声说。

她像是受了炮烙似的缩手,脸色同时变作灰黑,也不再去取烛台,只是失神的站着。直到四叔上香的时候,教她走开,她才走开。这一回她的变化非常大,第二天,不但眼睛窈陷下去,连精神也更不济了。而且很胆怯,不独怕暗夜,怕黑影,即使看见人,虽是自己的主人,也总惴惴的,有如在白天出穴游行的小鼠;否则呆坐着,直是一个木偶人。不半年,头发也花白起来了,记性尤其坏,甚而至于常常忘却了去淘米。

"祥林嫂怎么这样了?倒不如那时不留她。"四婶有时当面就这样说,似乎是警告她。

然而她总如此,全不见有怜悧起来的希望。他们于是想打发她走了,教她回到卫老婆子那里去。但当我还在鲁镇的时候,不过单是这样说;看现在的情状,可见后来终于实行了。然而她是从四叔家出去就成了乞丐的呢,还是先到卫老婆子家然后再成乞丐的呢?那我可不知道。

我给那些因为在近旁而极响的爆竹声惊醒,看见豆一般大的黄色的灯火光,接着又听得毕毕剥剥的鞭炮,是四叔家正在"祝福"了;知道已是五更将近时候。我在蒙胧中,又隐约听到远处的爆竹声联绵不断,似乎合成一天音响的浓云,夹着团团飞舞的雪花,拥抱了全市镇。我在这繁响的拥抱中,也懒散而且舒适,从白天以至初夜的疑虑,全给祝福的空气一扫而空了,只觉得天地圣众歆享了牲醴和香烟,都醉醺醺的在空中蹒跚,豫备给鲁镇的人们以无限的幸福。

一九二四年二月七日

The New Year's Sacrifice

New Year's Eve of the old calendar[①] seems after all more like the real New Year's Eve; for, to say nothing of the villages and towns, even in the air there is a feeling that New Year is coming. From the pale, lowering evening clouds issue frequent flashes of lightning, followed by a rumbling sound of firecrackers celebrating the departure of the Hearth God; while, nearer by, the firecrackers explode even more violently, and before the deafening report dies away the air is filled with a faint smell of powder. It was on such a night that I returned to Luchen, my native place. Although I call it my native place, I had had no home there for some time, so I had to put up temporarily with a certain Mr. Lu, the fourth son of his family. He is a member of our clan, and belongs to the generation before mine, so I ought to call him "Fourth Uncle." An old student of the imperial college[②] who went in for Neo-Confucianism, I found him very little changed in any way, simply slightly older, but without any moustache as yet. When we met, after exchanging a few polite remarks he said I was fatter, and after saying that immediately started a violent attack on the revolutionaries. I knew this was not meant personally, because the object of the attack was still Kang Yu-wei.[③] Nevertheless, conversation proved difficult, so that in a short time I found myself alone in the study.

The next day I got up very late, and after lunch went out to see some relatives and friends. The day after I did the same. None of them was greatly changed, simply slightly older; but every family was busy preparing for "the sacrifice." This is the great end-of-year ceremony in Luchen, when people reverently welcome the God of Fortune and solicit good fortune for

---

① 译者注：The Chinese lunar calendar.
② 译者注：The highest institute of learning in the Ching dynasty.
③ 译者注：A famous reformist who lived from 1858 to 1927 and advocated constitutional monarchy.

the coming year. They kill chickens and geese and buy pork, scouring and scrubbing until all the women's arms turn red in the water. Some of them still wear twisted silver bracelets. After the meat is cooked some chopsticks are thrust into it at random, and this is called the "offering." It is set out at dawn when incense and candles are lit, and they reverently invite the God of Fortune to come and partake of the offering. Only men can be worshippers, and after the sacrifice they naturally continue to let off firecrackers as before. This happens every year, in every family, provided they can afford to buy the offering and firecrackers; and this year they naturally followed the old custom.

The day grew overcast. In the afternoon it actually started to snow, the biggest snow-flakes as large as plum blossom petals fluttered about the sky; and this, combined with the smoke and air of activity, made Luchen appear in a ferment. When I returned to my uncle's study the roof of the house was already white with snow. The room also appeared brighter, the great red rubbing hanging on the wall showing up very clearly the character for Longevity written by the Taoist saint Chen Tuan. [1] One of a pair of scrolls had fallen down and was lying loosely rolled up on the long table, but the other was still hanging there, bearing the words: "By understanding reason we achieve tranquillity of mind." Idly, I went to turn over the books on the table beneath the window, but all I could find was a pile of what looked like an incomplete set of *Kang Hsi's Dictionary*, [2] a volume of *Chiang Yung's Notes to Chu Hsi's Philosophical Writings* and a volume of *Commentaries on the Four Books*. [3] At all events, I made up my mind to leave the next day.

Besides, the very thought of my meeting with Hsiang Lin's Wife the day before made me uncomfortable. It happened in the afternoon. I had been visiting a friend in the eastern part of the town. As I came out I met

---

① 译者注：A hermit at the beginning of the tenth century.

② 译者注：A Chinese dictionary compiled under the auspices of Emperor Kang Hsi who reigned from 1662 to 1722.

③ 译者注：Confucian classics.

her by the river, and seeing the way she fastened her eyes on me I knew very well she meant to speak to me. Of all the people I had seen this time at Luchen none had changed as much as she: her hair, which had been streaked with white five years before, was now completely white, quite unlike someone in her forties. Her face was fearfully thin and dark in its sallowness, and had moreover lost its former expression of sadness, looking as if carved out of wood. Only an occasional flicker of her eyes showed she was still a living creature. In one hand she carried a wicker basket, in which was a broken bowl, empty; in the other she held a bamboo pole longer than herself, split at the bottom: it was clear she had become a beggar.

I stood still, waiting for her to come and ask for money.

"You have come back?" she asked me first.

"Yes."

"That is very good. You are a scholar, and have travelled too and seen a lot. I just want to ask you something." Her lustreless eyes suddenly gleamed.

I never guessed she would talk to me like this. I stood there taken by surprise.

"It is this." She drew two paces nearer, and whispered very confidentially: "After a person dies, does he turn into a ghost or not?"

As she fixed her eyes on me I was seized with foreboding. A shiver ran down my spine and I felt more nervous than during an unexpected examination at school, when unfortunately the teacher stands by one's side. Personally, I had never given the least thought to the question of the existence of spirits. In this emergency how should I answer her? Hesitating for a moment, I reflected: "It is the tradition here to believe in spirits, yet she seems to be sceptical — perhaps it would be better to say she hopes: hopes that there is immortality and yet hopes that there is not. Why increase the sufferings of the wretched? To give her something to look forward to, it would be better to say there is."

"There may be, I think," I told her hesitantly.

"Then, there must also be a Hell?"

"What, Hell?" Greatly startled, I could only try to evade the question. "Hell? According to reason there should be one too — but not necessarily. Who cares about it anyway? ..."

"Then will all the people of one family who have died see each other again?"

"Well, as to whether they will see each other again or not ..." I realized now that I was a complete fool; for all my hesitation and reflection I had been unable to answer her three questions. Immediately I lost confidence and wanted to say the exact opposite of what I had previously said. "In this case ... as a matter of fact, I am not sure ... Actually, regarding the question of ghosts, I am not sure either."

In order to avoid further importunate questions, I walked off, and beat a hasty retreat to my uncle's house, feeling exceedingly uncomfortable. I thought to myself: "I am afraid my answer will prove dangerous to her. Probably it is just that when other people are celebrating she feels lonely by herself, but could there be another reason? Could she have had some premonition? If there is another reason, and as a result something happens, then, through my answer, I shall be held responsible to a certain extent." Finally, however, I ended by laughing at myself, thinking that such a chance meeting could have no great significance, and yet I was taking it so to heart; no wonder certain educationalists called me a neurotic. Moreover I had distinctly said, "I am not sure," contradicting my previous answer; so that even if anything did happen, it would have nothing at all to do with me.

"I am not sure" is a most useful phrase.

Inexperienced and rash young men often take it upon themselves to solve people's problems for them or choose doctors for them, and if by any chance things turn out badly, they are probably held to blame; but by simply concluding with this phrase "I am not sure," one can free oneself of all responsibility. At this time I felt even more strongly the necessity for such a phrase, since even in speaking with a beggar woman there was no dispensing with it.

However, I continued to feel uncomfortable, and even after a night's rest my mind kept running on this, as if I had a premonition of some untoward development. In that oppressive snowy weather, in the gloomy study, this discomfort increased. It would be better to leave: I should go back to town the next day. The boiled shark's fins in the Fu Hsing Restaurant used to cost a dollar for a large portion, and I wondered if this cheap and delicious dish had increased in price or not. Although the friends who had accompanied me in the old days had scattered, even if I was alone the shark's fins still had to be tasted. At all events, I made up my mind to leave the next day.

After experiencing many times that things which I hoped would not happen and felt should not happen invariably did happen, I was desperately afraid this would prove another such case. And, indeed, strange things did begin to happen. Towards evening I heard talking — it sounded like a discussion — in the inner room; but soon the conversation ended, and all I heard was my uncle saying loudly as he walked out: "Not earlier nor later, but just at this time — sure sign of a bad character!"

At first I felt astonished, then very uncomfortable, thinking these words must refer to me. I looked outside the door, but no one was there. I contained myself with difficulty till their servant came in before dinner to brew a pot of tea, when at last I had a chance to make some enquiries.

"With whom was Mr. Lu angry just now?" I asked.

"Why, still with Hsiang Lin's Wife," he replied briefly.

"Hsiang Lin's Wife? How was that?" I asked again.

"She's dead."

"Dead?" My heart suddenly missed a beat. I started, and probably changed colour too. But since he did not raise his head, he was probably quite unaware of how I felt. Then I controlled myself, and asked:

"When did she die?"

"When? Last night, or else today, I'm not sure."

"How did she die?"

"How did she die? Why, of poverty of course." He answered placidly and, still without having raised his head to look at me, went out.

However, my agitation was only short-lived, for now that something I had felt imminent had already taken place, I no longer had to take refuge in my "I'm not sure," or the servant's expression "dying of poverty" for comfort. My heart already felt lighter. Only from time to time something still seemed to weigh on it. Dinner was served, and my uncle solemnly accompanied me. I wanted to ask about Hsiang Lin's Wife, but knew that although he had read, "Ghosts and spirits are properties of Nature,"[①] he had retained many superstitions, and on the eve of this sacrifice it was out of the question to mention anything like death or illness. In case of necessity one could use veiled allusions, but unfortunately I did not know how to, so although questions kept rising to the tip of my tongue, I had to bite them back. From his solemn expression I suddenly suspected that he looked on me as choosing not earlier nor later but just this time to come and trouble him, and that I was also a bad character; therefore to set his mind at rest I told him at once that I intended to leave Luchen the next day and go back to the city. He did not press me greatly to stay. So we quietly finished the meal.

In winter the days are short and, now that it was snowing, darkness already enveloped the whole town. Everybody was busy beneath the lamplight, but outside the windows it was very quiet. Snow-flakes fell on the thickly piled snow, as if they were whispering, making me feel even more lonely. I sat by myself under the yellow gleam of the vegetable oil lamp and thought, "This poor woman, abandoned by people in the dust as a tiresome and worn-out toy, once left her own imprint in the dust, and those who enjoy life must have wondered at her for wishing to prolong her existence; but now at least she has been swept clear by eternity. Whether spirits exist or not I do not know; but in the present world when a meaningless existence ends, so that someone whom others are tired of seeing is no longer seen, it is just as well, both for the individual concerned and for others." I listened quietly to see if I could hear the snow falling outside the window, still

---

① 译者注: A Confucian saying.

pursuing this train of thought, until gradually I felt less ill at ease.

Fragments of her life, seen or heard before, now combined to form one whole.

She did not belong to Luchen. One year at the beginning of winter, when my uncle's family wanted to change their maidservant, Old Mrs. Wei brought her in and introduced her. Her hair was tied with white bands, she wore a black skirt, blue jacket and pale green bodice, and was about twenty-six, with a pale skin but rosy cheeks. Old Mrs. Wei called her Hsiang Lin's Wife, and said that she was a neighbour of her mother's family, and because her husband was dead she wanted to go out to work. My uncle knitted his brows and my aunt immediately understood that he disapproved of her because she was a widow. She looked very suitable, though, with big strong feet and hands, and a meek expression; and she had said nothing but showed every sign of being tractable and hard-working. So my aunt paid no attention to my uncle's frown, but kept her. During the period of probation she worked from morning till night, as if she found resting dull, and she was so strong that she could do a man's work; accordingly on the third day it was settled, and each month she was to be paid five hundred cash.

Everybody called her Hsiang Lin's Wife. They did not ask her her own name; but since she was introduced by someone from Wei Village who said she was a neighbour, presumably her name was also Wei. She was not very talkative, only answering when other people spoke to her, and her answers were brief. It was not until a dozen days or so had passed that they learned little by little that she still had a severe mother-in-law at home and a younger brother-in-law more than ten years old, who could cut wood. Her husband, who had been a woodcutter too, had died in the spring. He had been ten years younger than she. [1] This little was all that people learned from her.

The days passed quickly. She worked as hard as ever; she would eat

---

[1] 译者注: In old China it used to be common in country districts for young women to be married to boys of ten or eleven. The bride's labour could then be exploited by her husband's family.

anything, and did not spare herself. Everybody agreed that the Lu family had found a very good maidservant, who really got through more work than a hard-working man. At the end of the year she swept, mopped, killed chickens and geese and sat up to boil the sacrificial meat, single-handed, so the family did not have to hire extra help. Nevertheless she, on her side, was satisfied; gradually the trace of a smile appeared at the corner of her mouth. She became plumper and her skin whiter.

New Year was scarcely over when she came back from washing rice by the river looking pale, and said that in the distance she had just seen a man wandering on the opposite bank who looked very like her husband's cousin, and probably he had come to look for her. My aunt, much alarmed, made detailed enquiries, but failed to get any further information. As soon as my uncle learned of it he frowned and said, "This is bad. She must have run away from her husband's family."

Before long this inference that she had run away was confirmed.

About a fortnight later, just as everybody was beginning to forget what had happened, Old Mrs. Wei suddenly called, bringing with her a woman in her thirties who, she said, was the maidservant's mother-in-law. Although the woman looked like a villager, she behaved with great self-possession and had a ready tongue in her head. After the usual polite remarks she apologized for coming to take her daughter-in-law home, saying there was a great deal to be done at the beginning of spring, and since there were only old people and children at home they were short-handed. "Since it is her mother-in-law who wants her to go back, what is there to be said?" was my uncle's comment.

Thereupon her wages were reckoned up. They amounted to one thousand seven hundred and fifty cash, all of which she had left with her mistress without using a single coin. My aunt gave the entire amount to her mother-in-law. The latter also took her clothes, thanked Mr. and Mrs. Lu and went out. By this time it was already noon.

"Oh, the rice! Didn't Hsiang Lin's Wife go to wash the rice?" my aunt exclaimed some time later. Probably she was rather hungry, so that she remembered lunch.

Thereupon everybody set about looking for the rice basket. My aunt went first to the kitchen, then to the hall, then to the bedroom; but not a trace of it was to be seen anywhere. My uncle went outside, but could not find it either; only when he went right down to the riverside did he see it, set down fair and square on the bank, with a bundle of vegetables beside it.

Some people there told him that a boat with a white awning had moored there in the morning, but since the awning covered the boat completely they did not know who was inside, and before this incident no one had paid any attention to it. But when Hsiang Lin's Wife came to wash rice, two men looking like country people jumped off the boat just as she was kneeling down and seizing hold of her carried her on board. After several shouts and cries, Hsiang Lin's Wife became silent: they had probably stopped her mouth. Then two women walked up, one of them a stranger and the other Old Mrs. Wei. When the people who told this story tried to peep into the boat they could not see very clearly, but Hsiang Lin's Wife seemed to be lying bound on the floor of the boat.

"Disgraceful! Still ..." said my uncle.

That day my aunt cooked the midday meal herself, and my cousin Ah Niu lit the fire.

After lunch Old Mrs. Wei came again.

"Disgraceful!" said my uncle.

"What is the meaning of this? How dare you come here again!" My aunt, who was washing dishes, started scolding as soon as she saw her. "You recommended her yourself, and then plotted to have her carried off, causing all this stir. What will people think? Are you trying to make a laughing-stock of our family?"

"Aiya, I was really taken in! Now I have come specially to clear up this business. When she asked me to find her work, how was I to know that she had left home without her mother-in-law's consent? I am very sorry, Mr. Lu, Mrs. Lu. Because I am so old and foolish and careless, I have offended my patrons. However, it is lucky for me that your family is always so generous and kind, and unwilling to be hard on your inferiors. This time I promise to find you someone good to make up for my mistake."

"Still …" said my uncle.

Thereupon the business of Hsiang Lin's Wife was concluded, and before long it was also forgotten.

Only my aunt, because the maidservants taken on afterwards were all lazy or fond of stealing food, or else both lazy and fond of stealing food, with not a good one in the lot, still often spoke of Hsiang Lin's Wife. On such occasions she would always say to herself, "I wonder what has become of her now?" meaning that she would like to have her back. But by the following New Year she too gave up hope.

The New Year's holiday was nearly over when Old Mrs. Wei, already half tipsy, came to pay her respects, and said it was because she had been back to Wei Village to visit her mother's family and stayed a few days that she had come late. During the course of conversation they naturally came to speak of Hsiang Lin's Wife.

"She?" said Mrs. Wei cheerfully. "She is in luck now. When her mother-in-law dragged her home, she had already promised her to the sixth son of the Ho family in Ho Village. Not long after she reached home they put her in the bridal chair and sent her off."

"Aiya! What a mother-in-law!" exclaimed my aunt in amazement.

"Ah, madam, you really talk like a great lady! We country folk, poor women, think nothing of that. She still had a younger brother-in-law who had to be married. And if they hadn't found her a husband, where would they have found the money for his wedding? But her mother-in-law is a clever and capable woman, who knows how to drive a good bargain, so she married her off into the mountains. If she had married her to someone in the same village, she wouldn't have got so much money; but since very few women are willing to marry someone living deep in the mountains, she got eighty thousand cash. Now the second son is married, the presents only cost her fifty thousand, and after paying the wedding expenses she still has over ten thousand left. Just think, doesn't this show she knows how to drive a good bargain? ..."

"But was Hsiang Lin's Wife willing?"

"It wasn't a question of being willing or not. Of course anyone would have protested. They just tied her up with a rope, stuffed her into the bridal chair, carried her to the man's house, put on the bridal headdress, performed the ceremony in the hall and locked them in their room; and that was that. But Hsiang Lin's Wife is quite a character. I heard she really put up a great struggle, and everybody said she was different from other people because she had worked in a scholar's family. We go-betweens, madam, see a great deal. When widows remarry, some cry and shout, some threaten to commit suicide, some when they have been carried to the man's house won't go through the ceremony, and some even smash the wedding candlesticks. But Hsiang Lin's Wife was different from the rest. They said she shouted and cursed all the way, so that by the time they had carried her to Ho Village she was completely hoarse. When they dragged her out of the chair, although the two chairbearers and her young brother-in-law used all their strength, they couldn't force her to go through the ceremony. The moment they were careless enough to loosen their grip — gracious Buddha! — she threw herself against a corner of the table and knocked a big hole in her head. The blood poured out; and although they used two handfuls of incense ashes and bandaged her with two pieces of red cloth, they still couldn't stop the bleeding. Finally it took all of them together to get her shut up with her husband in the bridal chamber, where she went on cursing. Oh, it was really dreadful!" She shook her head, cast down her eyes and said no more.

"And after that what happened?" asked my aunt.

"They said the next day she still didn't get up," said Old Mrs. Wei, raising her eyes.

"And after?"

"After? She got up. At the end of the year she had a baby, a boy, who was two this New Year. ① These few days when I was at home some people went to Ho Village, and when they came back they said they had seen her and her son, and that both mother and baby are fat. There is no mother-in-law over her, the man is a strong fellow who can earn a living, and the house is their own. Well, well, she is really in luck."

After this even my aunt gave up talking of Hsiang Lin's Wife.

But one autumn, two New Years after they heard how lucky Hsiang Lin's Wife had been, she actually reappeared on the threshold of my uncle's house. On the table she placed a round bulb-shaped basket, and under the eaves a small roll of bedding. Her hair was still wrapped in white bands, and she wore a black skirt, blue jacket and pale green bodice. But her skin was sallow and her cheeks had lost their colour; she kept her eyes downcast, and her eyes, with their tear-stained rims, were no longer bright. Just as before, it was Old Mrs. Wei, looking very benevolent, who brought her in, and who explained at length to my aunt:

"It was really a bolt from the blue. Her husband was so strong, nobody could have guessed that a young fellow like that would die of typhoid fever. First he seemed better, but then he ate a bowl of cold rice and the sickness came back. Luckily she had the boy, and she can work, whether it is chopping wood, picking tea-leaves or raising silkworms; so at first she was able to carry on. Then who could believe that the child, too, would be carried off by a wolf? Although it was nearly the end of spring, still wolves came to the village — how could anyone have guessed that? Now she is all on her own. Her brother-in-law came to take the house, and turned her out; so she has really no way open to her but to come and ask help from her former mistress. Luckily this time there is nobody to stop her, and you happen to be wanting a new servant, so I have brought her here. I think someone who is used to your ways is much better than a new hand ...."

---

① 译者注: It was the custom in China to reckon a child as one year old at birth, and to add another year to his age as New Year.

"I was really stupid, really ..." Hsiang Lin's Wife raised her listless eyes to say. "I only knew that when it snows the wild beasts in the glen have nothing to eat and may come to the villages; I didn't know that in spring they came too. I got up at dawn and opened the door, filled a small basket with beans and called our Ah Mao to go and sit on the threshold and shell the beans. He was very obedient and always did as I told him: he went out. Then I chopped wood at the back of the house and washed the rice, and when the rice was in the pan and I wanted to boil the beans I called Ah Mao, but there was no answer; and when I went out to look, all I could see was beans scattered on the ground, but no Ah Mao. He never went to other families to play; and in fact at each place where I went to ask, there was no sign of him. I became desperate, and begged people to go to look for him. Only in the afternoon, after looking everywhere else, did they go to look in the glen and see one of his little shoes caught on a bramble. 'That's bad,' they said, 'he must have met a wolf.' And sure enough when they went further in there he was, lying in the wolf's lair, with all his entrails eaten away, his hand still tightly clutching that little basket ..." At this point she started crying, and was unable to complete the sentence.

My aunt had been undecided at first, but by the end of this story the rims of her eyes were rather red. After thinking for a moment she told her to take the round basket and bedding into the servants' quarters. Old Mrs. Wei heaved a long sigh as if relieved of a great burden. Hsiang Lin's Wife looked a little more at ease than when she first came and, without having to be told the way, quietly took away her bedding. From this time on she worked again as a maidservant in Luchen.

Everybody still called her Hsiang Lin's Wife.

However, she had changed a great deal. She had not been there more than three days before her master and mistress realized that she was not as quick as before. Since her memory was much worse, and her impassive face never showed the least trace of a smile, my aunt already expressed herself very far from satisfied. When the woman first arrived, although my uncle frowned as before, because they invariably had such difficulty in finding servants he did not object very strongly, only secretly warned my aunt that while such people may seem very pitiful they exert a bad moral influence. Thus although it would be all right for her to do ordinary work she must not join in the preparations for sacrifice; they would have to prepare all the dishes themselves, for otherwise they would be unclean and the ancestors would not accept them.

The most important event in my uncle's household was the ancestral sacrifice, and formerly this had been the busiest time for Hsiang Lin's Wife; but now she had very little to do. When the table was placed in the centre of the hall and the curtain fastened, she still remembered how to set out the winecups and chopsticks in the old way.

"Hsiang Lin's Wife, put those down!" said my aunt hastily.

She sheepishly withdrew her hand and went to get the candlesticks.

"Hsiang Lin's Wife, put those down!" cried my aunt hastily again. "I'll fetch them."

After walking round several times without finding anything to do, Hsiang Lin's Wife could only go hesitantly away. All she did that day was to sit by the stove and feed the fire.

The people in the town still called her Hsiang Lin's Wife, but in a different tone from before; and although they talked to her still, their manner was colder. She did not mind this in the least, only, looking straight in front of her, she would tell everybody her story, which night or day was never out of her mind.

"I was really stupid, really," she would say. "I only knew that when it snows the wild beasts in the glen have nothing to eat and may come to the villages; I didn't know that in spring they came too. I got up at dawn and opened the door, filled a small basket with beans and called our Ah Mao to go and sit on the threshold and shell them. He was very obedient and always did as I told him: he went out. Then I chopped wood at the back of the house and washed the rice, and when the rice was in the pan and I wanted to boil the beans I called Ah Mao, but there was no answer; and when I went out to look, all I could see was beans scattered on the ground, but no Ah

Mao. He never went to other families to play; and in fact at each place where I went to ask, there was no sign of him. I became desperate, and begged people to go to look for him. Only in the afternoon, after looking everywhere else, did they go to look in the glen and see one of his little shoes caught on a bramble. 'That's bad,' they said, 'he must have met a wolf.' And sure enough when they went further in there he was, lying in the wolf's lair, with all his entrails eaten away, his hand still tightly clutching that small basket ..." At this point she would start crying and her voice would trail away.

This story was rather effective, and when men heard it they often stopped smiling and walked away disconcerted, while the women not only seemed to forgive her but their faces immediately lost their contemptuous look and they added their tears to hers. There were some old women who had not heard her speaking in the street, who went specially to look for her, to hear her sad tale. When her voice trailed away and she started to cry, they joined in, shedding the tears which had gathered in their eyes. Then they sighed, and went away satisfied, exchanging comments.

She asked nothing better than to tell her sad story over and over again, often gathering three or four hearers. But before long everybody knew it by heart, until even in the eyes of the most kindly, Buddha fearing old ladies not a trace of tears could be seen. In the end, almost everyone in the town could recite her tale, and it bored and exasperated them to hear it.

"I was really stupid, really ..." she would begin.

"Yes, you only knew that in snowy weather the wild beasts in the mountains had nothing to eat and might come down to the villages." Promptly cutting short her recital, they walked away.

She would stand there open-mouthed, looking at them with a dazed expression, and then go away too, as if she also felt disconcerted. But she still brooded over it, hoping from other topics such as small baskets, beans and other people's children, to lead up to the story of her Ah Mao. If she saw a child of two or three, she would say, "Oh dear, if my Ah Mao were still alive, he would be just as big ..."

Children seeing the look in her eyes would take fright and, clutching the hems of their mothers' clothes, try to tug them away. Thereupon she would be left by herself again, and finally walk away disconcerted. Later everybody knew what she was like, and it only needed a child present for them to ask her with an artificial smile, "Hsiang Lin's Wife, if your Ah Mao were alive, wouldn't he be just as big as that?"

She probably did not realize that her story, after having been turned over and tasted by people for so many days, had long since become stale, only exciting disgust and contempt; but from the way people smiled she seemed to know that they were cold and sarcastic, and that there was no need for her to say any more. She would simply look at them, not answering a word.

In Luchen people celebrate New Year in a big way: preparations start from the twentieth day of the twelfth month onwards. That year my uncle's household found it necessary to hire a temporary manservant, but since there was still a great deal to do they also called in another maidservant, Liu Ma, to help. Chickens and geese had to be killed; but Liu Ma was a devout woman who abstained from meat, did not kill living things, and would only wash the sacrificial dishes. Hsiang Lin's Wife had nothing to do but feed the fire. She sat there, resting, watching Liu Ma as she washed the sacrificial dishes. A light snow began to fall.

"Dear me, I was really stupid," began Hsiang Lin's Wife, as if to herself, looking at the sky and sighing.

"Hsiang Lin's Wife, there you go again," said Liu Ma, looking at her impatiently. "I ask you: that wound on your forehead, wasn't it then you got it?"

"Uh, huh," she answered vaguely.

"Let me ask you: what made you willing after all?"

"Me?"

"Yes. What I think is, you must have been willing; otherwise ..."

"Oh dear, you don't know how strong he was.

"I don't believe it. I don't believe he was so strong that you really couldn't keep him off. You must have been willing, only you put the blame on his being so strong."

"Oh dear, you ... you try for yourself and see." She smiled.

Liu Ma's lined face broke into a smile too, making it wrinkled like a walnut; her small beady eyes swept Hsiang Lin's Wife's forehead and fastened on her eyes. As if rather embarrassed, Hsiang Lin's Wife immediately stopped smiling, averted her eyes and looked at the snow-flakes.

"Hsiang Lin's Wife, that was really a bad bargain," continued Liu Ma mysteriously. "If you had held out longer or knocked yourself to death, it would have been better. As it is, after living with your second husband for less than two years, you are guilty of a great crime. Just think: when you go down to the lower world in future, these two men's ghosts will fight over you. To which will you go? The King of Hell will have no choice but to cut you in two and divide you between them. I think, really ..."

Then terror showed in her face. This was something she had never heard in the mountains.

"I think you had better take precautions beforehand. Go to the Tutelary God's Temple and buy a threshold to be your substitute, so that thousands of people can walk over it and trample on it, in order to atone for your sins in this life and avoid torment after death."

At the time Hsiang Lin's Wife said nothing, but she must have taken this to heart, for the next morning when she got up there were dark circles beneath her eyes. After breakfast she went to the Tutelary God's Temple at the west end of the village, and asked to buy a threshold. The temple priests would not agree at first, and only when she shed tears did they give a grudging consent. The price was twelve thousand cash.

She had long since given up talking to people, because Ah Mao's story was received with such contempt; but news of her conversation with Liu Ma that day spread, and many people took a fresh interest in her and came again to tease her into talking. As for the subject, that had naturally changed to deal with the wound on her forehead.

"Hsiang Lin's Wife, I ask you: what made you willing after all that time?" one would cry.

"Oh, what a pity, to have had this knock for nothing," another looking at her scar would agree.

Probably she knew from their smiles and tone of voice that they were making fun of her, for she always looked steadily at them without saying a word, and finally did not even turn her head. All day long she kept her lips tightly closed, bearing on her head the scar which everyone considered a mark of shame, silently shopping, sweeping the floor, washing vegetables, preparing rice. Only after nearly a year did she take from my aunt her wages which had accumulated. She changed them for twelve silver dollars, and asking for leave went to the west end of the town. In less time than it takes for a meal she was back again, looking much comforted, and with an unaccustomed light in her eyes. She told my aunt happily that she had bought a threshold in the Tutelary God's Temple.

When the time came for the ancestral sacrifice at the winter equinox, she worked harder than ever, and seeing my aunt take out the sacrificial utensils and with Ah Niu carry the table into the middle of the hall, she went confidently to fetch the winecups and chopsticks.

"Put those down, Hsiang Lin's Wife!" my aunt called out hastily.

She withdrew her hand as if scorched, her face turned ashen-grey, and instead of fetching the candlesticks she just stood there dazed. Only when my uncle came to burn incense and told her to go, did she walk away. This time the change in her was very great, for the next day not only were her eyes sunken, but even her spirit seemed broken. Moreover she became very timid, not only afraid of the dark and shadows, but also of the sight of anyone. Even her own master or mistress made her look as frightened as a little mouse that has come out of its hole in the daytime. For the rest, she would sit stupidly, like a wooden statue. In less than half a year her hair began to turn grey, and her memory became much worse, reaching a point when she was constantly forgetting to go and prepare the rice.

"What has come over Hsiang Lin's Wife? It would really have been better not to have kept her that time." My aunt would sometimes speak like this in front of her, as if to warn her.

However, she remained this way, so that it was impossible to see any hope of her improving. They finally decided to get rid of her and tell her to go back to Old Mrs. Wei. While I was at Luchen they were still only talking of this; but judging by what happened later, it is evident that this was what they must have done. Whether after leaving my uncle's household she became a beggar, or whether she went first to Old Mrs. Wei's house and later became a beggar, I do not know.

I was woken up by firecrackers exploding noisily close at hand, saw the glow of the yellow oil lamp as large as a bean, and heard the splutter of fireworks as my uncle's household celebrated the sacrifice. I knew that it was nearly dawn. I felt bewildered, hearing as in a dream the confused continuous sound of distant crackers which seemed to form one dense cloud of noise in the sky, joining the whirling snow-flakes to envelop the whole town. Wrapped in this medley of sound, relaxed and at ease, the doubt which had preyed on me from dawn to early night was swept clean away by the atmosphere of celebration, and I felt only that the saints of heaven and earth had accepted the sacrifice and incense and were all reeling with intoxication in the sky, preparing to give the people of Luchen boundless good fortune.

February 7, 1924

6. 无声的中国

——二月十六日在香港青年会讲①

以我这样没有什么可听的无聊的讲演,又在这样大雨的时候,竟还有这许多来听的诸君,我首先应当声明我的郑重的感谢。

我现在所讲的题目是:《无声的中国》。

现在,浙江,陕西,都在打仗,那里的人民哭着呢还是笑着呢,我们不知道。香港似乎很太平,住在这里的中国人,舒服呢还是不很舒服呢,别人也不知道。

发表自己的思想,感情给大家知道的是要用文章的,然而拿文章来达意,现在一般的中国人还做不到。这也怪不得我们;因为那文字,先就是我们的祖先留传给我们的可怕的遗产。人们费了多年的工夫,还是难于运用。因为难,许多人便不理它了,甚至于连自己的姓也写不清是张还是章,或者简直不会写,或者说道:Chang。虽然能说话,而只有几个人听到,远处的人们便不知道,结果也等于无声。又因为难,有些人便当作宝贝,像玩把戏似的,之乎者也,只有几个人懂,——其实是不知道可真懂,而大多数的人们却不懂得,结果也等于无声。

文明人和野蛮人的分别,其一,是文明人有文字,能够把他们的思想,感情,借此传给大众,传给将来。中国虽然有文字,现在却已经和大家不相干,用的是难懂的古文,讲的是陈旧的古意思,所有的声音,都是过去的,都就是只等于零的。所以,大家不能互相了解,正像一大盘散沙。

将文章当作古董,以不能使人认识,使人懂得为好,也许是有趣的事罢。但是,结果怎样呢? 是我们已经不能将我们想说的话说出来。我们受了损害,受了侮辱,总是不能说出些应说的话。拿最近的事情来说,如

---

① 中文、英译文选自:鲁迅. 鲁迅杂文选. 杨宪益,戴乃迭,译. 南京:译林出版社,2009.

中日战争，"拳匪"事件，民元革命这些大事件，一直到现在，我们可有一部像样的著作？民国以来，也还是谁也不作声。反而在外国，倒常有说起中国的，但那都不是中国人自己的声音，是别人的声音。

这不能说话的毛病，在明朝是还没有这样厉害的；他们还比较地能够说些要说的话。待到满洲人以异族侵入中国，讲历史的，尤其是讲宋末的事情的人被杀害了，讲时事的自然也被杀害了。所以，到乾隆年间，人民大家便更不敢用文章来说话了。所谓读书人，便只好躲起来读经，校刊古书，做些古时的文章，和当时毫无关系的文章。有些新意，也还是不行的；不是学韩，便是学苏。韩愈苏轼他们，用他们自己的文章来说当时要说的话，那当然可以的。我们却并非唐宋时人，怎么做和我们毫无关系的时候的文章呢。即使做得像，也是唐宋时代的声音，韩愈苏轼的声音，而不是我们现代的声音。然而直到现在，中国人却还耍着这样的旧戏法。人是有的，没有声音，寂寞得很。——人会没有声音的么？没有，可以说：是死了。倘要说得客气一点，那就是：已经哑了。

要恢复这多年无声的中国，是不容易的，正如命令一个死掉的人道："你活过来！"我虽然并不懂得宗教，但我以为正如想出现一个宗教上之所谓"奇迹"一样。

首先来尝试这工作的是"五四运动"前一年，胡适之先生所提倡的"文学革命"。"革命"这两个字，在这里不知道可害怕，有些地方是一听到就害怕的。但这和文学两字连起来的"革命"，却没有法国革命的"革命"那么可怕，不过是革新，改换一个字，就很平和了，我们就称为"文学革新"罢，中国文字上，这样的花样是很多的。那大意也并不可怕，不过说：我们不必再去费尽心机，学说古代的死人的话，要说现代的活人的话；不要将文章看作古董，要做容易懂得的白话的文章。然而，单是文学革新是不够的，因为腐败思想，能用古文做，也能用白话做。所以后来就有人提倡思想革新。思想革新的结果，是发生社会革新运动。这运动一发生，自然一面就发生反动，于是便酿成战斗……

但是，在中国，刚刚提起文学革新，就有反动了。不过白话文却渐渐风行起来,不大受阻碍。这是怎么一回事呢?就因为当时又有钱玄同先生提倡废止汉字,用罗马字母来替代。这本也不过是一种文字革新,很平常的,但被不喜欢改革的中国人听见,就大不得了了,于是便放过了比较的平和的文学革命,而竭力来骂钱玄同。白话乘了这一个机会,居然减去了许多敌人,反而没有阻碍,能够流行了。

中国人的性情是总喜欢调和,折中的。譬如你说,这屋子太暗,须在这里开一个窗,大家一定不允许的。但如果你主张拆掉屋顶,他们就会来调和,愿意开窗了。没有更激烈的主张,他们总连平和的改革也不肯行。那时白话文之得以通行,就因为有废掉中国字而用罗马字母的议论的缘故。

其实,文言和白话的优劣的讨论,本该早已过去了,但中国是总不肯早早解决的,到现在还有许多无谓的议论。例如,有的说:古文各省人都能懂,白话就各处不同,反而不能互相了解了。殊不知这只要教育普及和交通发达就好,那时就人人都能懂较为易解的白话文;至于古文,何尝各省人都能懂,便是一省里,也没有许多人懂得的。有的说:如果都用白话文,人们便不能看古书,中国的文化就灭亡了。其实呢,现在的人们大可以不必看古书,即使古书里真有好东西,也可以用白话来译出的,用不着那么心惊胆战。他们又有人说,外国尚且译中国书,足见其好,我们自己倒不看么?殊不知埃及的古书,外国人也译,非洲黑人的神话,外国人也译,他们别有用意,即使译出,也算不了怎样光荣的事的。

近来还有一种说法,是思想革新紧要,文字改革倒在其次,所以不如用浅显的文言来作新思想的文章,可以少招一重反对。这话似乎也有理。然而我们知道,连他长指甲都不肯剪去的人,是决不肯剪去他的辫子的。

因为我们说着古代的话,说着大家不明白,不听见的话,已经弄得像一盘散沙,痛痒不相关了。我们要活过来,首先就须由青年们不再说孔子孟子和韩愈柳宗元们的话。时代不同,情形也两样,孔子时代的香港不这样,孔子口调的"香港论"是无从做起的,"吁嗟阔哉香港也",不过是笑话。

我们要说现代的,自己的话;用活着的白话,将自己的思想,感情直白地说出来。但是,这也要受前辈先生非笑的。他们说白话文卑鄙,没有价值;他们说年青人作品幼稚,贻笑大方。我们中国能做文言的有多少呢,其余的都只能说白话,难道这许多中国人,就都是卑鄙,没有价值的么?至于幼稚,尤其没有什么可羞,正如孩子对于老人,毫没有什么可羞一样。幼稚是会生长,会成熟的,只不要衰老,腐败,就好。倘说待到纯熟了才可以动手,那是虽是村妇也不至于这样蠢。她的孩子学走路,即使跌倒了,她决不至于叫孩子从此躺在床上,待到学会了走法再下地面来的。

青年们先可以将中国变成一个有声的中国。大胆地说话,勇敢地进行,忘掉了一切利害,推开了古人,将自己的真心的话发表出来。——真,自然是不容易的。譬如态度,就不容易真,讲演时候就不是我的真态度,因为我对朋友,孩子说话时候的态度是不这样的。——但总可以说些较真的话,发些较真的声音。只有真的声音,才能感动中国的人和世界的人;必须有了真的声音,才能和世界的人同在世界上生活。

我们试想现在没有声音的民族是那几种民族。我们可听到埃及人的声音? 可听到安南,朝鲜的声音? 印度除了泰戈尔,别的声音可还有?

我们此后实在只有两条路:一是抱着古文而死掉,一是舍掉古文而生存。

Silent China

—A Talk Given at the Hongkong Y.M.C.A. on February the Sixteenth

First of all, I want to express my respectful appreciation to all of you who have come through this pelting rain to hear one of my empty and futile talks.

My subject today is Silent China.

There is fighting now in Chekiang and Shensi, but we do not know whether folk there are laughing or crying. Hongkong seems very quiet, but outsiders do not know whether the Chinese who live here are comfortable or not.

Men communicate their thoughts and feelings through writing, yet most Chinese nowadays are still unable to express themselves this way. This is not our fault, for our written language is a fearful legacy left us by our forbears. Even after years of effort, it is hard to write. And because it is hard, many people simply ignore it. A man may not be sure which character *chang* his name is, or may not be able to write his name at all, only to say it. Although he can speak, not many can hear him; so those at a distance are left in ignorance, and this is tantamount to silence. Again, because it is hard, some regard it as a treasure and amuse themselves by using erudite terms which only a small minority understands. We cannot be sure, indeed, that even this minority understands; and since the great majority certainly does not, this too is tantamount to silence.

One of the differences between civilized men and savages is that civilized men have writing to convey their thoughts and feelings to the rest of the world and to posterity. China also has writing, but a writing quite divorced from the mass of the people. Couched in crabbed, archaic language, it describes outmoded, archaic sentiments. All its utterances belong to the past, and therefore amount to nothing. Hence our people, unable to understand each other, are like a great dish of loose sand.

It may be amusing to treat writing as a curio — the fewer who know and understand it the better. But what is the result? Already we are unable to express our feelings. Injured or insulted, we cannot retort as we should. Consider, for instance, such recent happenings in China as the Sino-Japanese War, the Boxer Rebellion and the 1911 Revolution. All these were major events, yet so far not one good work on them has appeared. Nor has anyone spoken out since the Republic was founded. Abroad, on the other hand, references are constantly being made to China — but by foreigners, not by Chinese.

This dumbness was not so serious during the Ming dynasty, when Chinese expressed themselves comparatively better. But when the alien Manchus invaded our country they killed all who talked about history — especially late Sung history — and those, of course, who talked about current events. Thus by the reign of Chien Lung, men no longer dared express themselves in writing. So-called scholars took refuge in studying the classics, collating and reprinting old books, and writing a little in the ancient style on subjects quite unrelated to their own time. New ideas were taboo: you wrote like either Han Yu or Su Tung-po. These men were quite all right in their own way — they said what needed to be said about their own time. But how can we, who are not living in the Tang or Sung dynasty, write in the style of an age so far removed from our own? Even if the imitation is convincing, the voice is from the Tang or Sung dynasty, the voice of Han Yu or Su Tung-po, not the voice of our generation. But Chinese today are still playing this same old game. We have men but no voices, and how lonely that is! Can men be silent? No, not unless they are dead, or — to put it more politely — when they are dumb.

To restore speech to this China which has been silent for centuries is not an easy matter. It is like ordering a dead man to live again. Though I know nothing of religion, I fancy this approximates to what believers call a "miracle."

The first to attempt this was Dr. Hu Shih, who a year before the May the Fourth Movement advocated a "literary revolution." I do not know if you are frightened of the word "revolution" here, but in some places people are terrified of it. However, this literary "revolution" is not as fearful as the French Revolution. It simply means a reform, and once we substitute the word "reform", it sounds quite inoffensive. So let us do that. The Chinese language is very ingenious this way. All we want is this: instead of overtaxing our brains to learn the speech of men long since dead, we should speak that of living men. Instead of treating language as a curio, we should write in the easily understood vernacular. A simple literary reform is not enough, though, for corrupt ideas can be conveyed in the vernacular just as well as in classical Chinese. This is why a reform of ideas was later proposed. And this led to a movement for social reform. As soon as this started, opposition sprang up, and a battle began to rage.

In China, the mere mention of literary reform is enough to arouse opposition. Still, the vernacular gradually made up leeway, and met with fewer obstacles. How was this? It was because Mr. Chien Hsuan-tung was at the same time proposing to abolish Chinese ideographs and romanize the language. This would have been merely a normal language reform, but when our die-hard Chinese heard of it, they thought the end of the world had come, and hastily passed the relatively inoffensive literary reform in order to devote all their energies to abusing Chien Hsuan-tung. The vernacular took advantage of this to spread, since it now had far fewer opponents and less obstacles in its way.

By temperament the Chinese love compromise and a happy mean. For instance, if you say this room is too dark and a window should be made, everyone is sure to disagree. But if you propose taking off the roof, they will compromise and be glad to make a window. In the absence of more drastic proposals, they will never agree to the most inoffensive reforms. The vernacular was able to spread only because of the proposal to abolish Chinese characters and use a Romanized alphabet.

The fact is, the time has long since passed for canvassing the respective merits of the classical language and the vernacular, but China abhors quick decisions, and many futile debates are still going on. Some, for instance, say: Classical Chinese is comprehensible in every province, whereas the vernacular varies from place to place and cannot be understood throughout the country. But, as everyone knows, once we have universal education and better communications, the whole country will understand the more intelligible vernacular. As for the classical language, it is not comprehensible to everyone in every province, but only to a few. Others argue that if everyone uses the vernacular, we shall not be able to read the classics, and Chinese culture will perish. The fact is, we of this generation had much better not read the classics. There is no need to be alarmed — if the classics really contain anything of value, they can be translated into the vernacular. Yet others urge that since foreigners have translated our classics, thus proving their worth, we ought to read them ourselves. But, as everyone knows, foreigners have also translated the hieroglyphic texts of the Egyptians and the myths of the African Negroes. They do so from ulterior motives, and to be translated by them is no great honour.

Recently others have argued that since thought reform is what matters, while language reform is secondary, it is better to use clear, simple classical language to convey the new ideas, to arouse less opposition. This sounds like sense. But we know that the men unwilling to cut their long fingernails will never cut their queues.

Because we use the language of the ancients, which the people cannot understand and do not hear, we are like a dish of loose sand — oblivious to each other's sufferings. The first necessity, if we want to come to life, is for our young people to stop speaking the language of Confucius and Mencius, Han Yu and Liu Tsung-yuan. This is a different era, and times have changed. Hongkong was not like this in the time of Confucius, and we cannot use the old sage's language to write on Hongkong. Such phrases as "Hongkong, how great thou art!" are simply nonsense.

We must speak our own language, the language of today, using the living vernacular to give clear expression to our thoughts and feelings. Of course, we shall be jeered at for this by our elders and betters, who consider the vernacular vulgar and worthless, and say young writers are childish and will make fools of themselves. But how many in China can write the classical language? The rest can only use the vernacular. Do you mean to say that all these Chinese are vulgar and worthless? As for childishness, that is nothing to be ashamed of, any more than children need be ashamed of comparison with grown-ups. The childish can grow and mature; and as long as they do not become decrepit and corrupt, all will be well. As for waiting till you are mature before making a move, not even a country woman would be so foolish. If her child falls down while learning to walk, she does not order him to stay in bed until he has mastered the art of walking.

First our young people must turn China into an articulate country. Speak out boldly, advance fearlessly, with no thought of personal gain, brushing aside the ancients, and expressing your true thoughts. Of course, to be truthful is far from easy. It is not easy to be truly oneself, for instance. When I make a speech I am not truly myself — for I talk differently to children or to my friends. Still, we can talk in a relatively truthful way and express relatively truthful ideas. And only then shall we be able to move the people of China and the world. Only then shall we be able to live in the world with all the other nations.

Let us think which are the nations today which are silent. Can we hear the voice of the Egyptian people? Can we hear the Annamese or the Koreans? Is there any voice raised in India but that of Tagore?

There are only two paths open to us. One is to cling to our classical language and die; the other is to cast that language aside and live.

二

太阳照在桑干河上(第四十六、四十七节)①

四十六　解放

　　程仁跟着大伙儿走回家去,显得特别沉默,人家高声说话,笑谑,人家互相打闹,碰在他身上时,他也只悄悄地让开。他无法说明他自己,开始他觉得他为难,慢慢成了一种委屈,后来倒成为十分退缩了。仿佛自己犯了罪似的,自己做了对不起人的事,抬不起头来了。这是以前从没有过的感觉。他听章品说了很多,好像句句都向着自己,他第一次发觉了自己的丑恶,这丑恶却为章品看得那样清楚。本来他是一个老实人,从不欺骗人,但如今他觉得自己不诚实,他骗了他自己。他发现自己从来说不娶黑妮只是一句假话,他只不过为的怕人批评才勉强的逃避着她。他疏远她,只不过为着骗人,并非对她的伯父,对村上一个最坏的人,对人人痛恨的人有什么仇恨。他从前总是扪心无愧,以为没有袒护过他,实际他从来也没有反对过他呀!他为了他侄女把他的一切都宽恕了呀!他看不见他过去给大伙儿的糟害,他忘了自己在他家的受苦和剥削了。他要别人去算账,去要红契,可是自己就没有勇气去算账!他不是种着他八亩旱地二亩

---

　　①　中文选自:丁玲. 太阳照在桑干河上. 北京:人民文学出版社,1979.
　　英译文选自:Ding Ling. *The Sun Rises over the Sanggan River*. Yang Xianyi &
Gladys Yang. Trans. Beijing:Foreign Languages Press,1984.

水地么！章品说不应当忘本，他可不是忘了本！他什么地方是为穷人打算的呢？他只替自己打算，生怕自己把一个地主的侄女儿，一个坏蛋的侄女得罪了。他曾经瞧不起张正典。张正典为了一个老婆，为了某些生活上的小便宜，一天天往丈人那里凑过去，脱离了自己兄弟伙子的同志，脱离了庄户主，村上人谁也瞧不起他。可是他自己呢，他没有娶人家闺女，也没有去他们家，他只放在心里悄悄地维护着她，也就是维护了他们，维护了地主阶层的利益，这还说他没有忘本，他什么地方比张正典好呢？

他的步子越走越慢，这一些模糊的感觉，此起彼伏地在他脑子中翻腾，他落在大伙儿的后面了。小巷子有一家门开了，呀的一声，听见走出来一个人，在黑处小便，一会又进去了，把门砰的关上。程仁无力地茫然望着暗处，他该怎么办呢？

不远就到了他的家，他住在一个大杂院里。门虚掩着，他轻轻地走了进去，院子里都睡静了，听到上屋的房东的鼾声。对面那家养的几只鸡，也不安地在它们的小笼子里转侧，和低低地喀喀喀地叫着。

从他的屋子里露出一些微弱的光亮。他忘记他母亲已不在家，她到他姐姐家去了，去陪伴刚刚坐月子的姐姐。因此他对于那光亮毫没有感到惊诧。他懒洋洋的跨进门去。

一星星小火残留在豆油灯的灯捻上，那种不透明的灰沉沉的微光比黑暗更显得阴沉。当他进屋后，在靠炕的那个黑角角里便慢慢移动出一个黑影。他没有理会它，只觉得这阴影同自己隔了很远似的。偶然那么想道——娘还没睡么？却仍旧自管自地往炕这头坐上去。

这个黑影果然是个女人，她靠近他了，他还没有躺下去，却忽然意识到他娘已经几天不在家了。而这个女人却又不像他娘，他不觉发出一种突然受惊后的厉声问道："你是谁？"

那女人也猛地一下把他的臂膀按住，连声道："是咱！是你表妗子。"

他缩回了手，把背靠紧了壁，直直地望着这个鬼魅的人影。

她迅速地递给他一个布包，做出一副和缓的，实际是尴尬的声音，要笑又笑不出来，低低地说道："给你，是咱黑妮给你的。黑妮还要自个来，她有话要给你说,她发誓赌咒要跟你一辈子。咱说仁子! 你可别没良心啦……"

他本能地想挥动自己的手,把这个女人,把这个布包,把这些话都挥开去。可是他没有那样做,他手举不起来,罪恶和羞耻压住了他。他想骂她,舌头却像吃了什么怪药一样只感到麻木。

那个老妇人,便又接下去道:"她伯父啥也答应她了。人也给你,地也给你,这一共是十八亩,连菜园子的全在这里哪。仁子! 咱黑妮就靠定了你啦。"

一阵寒噤通过程仁的全身,他觉得有许多眼睛在顶棚上,在墙缝隙里望着他,向他嘲笑。

钱文贵的老婆把脸更凑近了过来,嘴放在他耳边,清清楚楚地说道:"她伯父说也不能让你为难,你是农会主任嘛,还能不闹斗争,只要你心里明白,嗯,到底咱们是一家子啦! ……"她发出鹭鸶一样的声音笑了,那样的无耻,使人恐惧。

程仁不能忍受了。他抖动一下自己,像把背上的重负用力抖掉一样。一个很难听的声音冲出了喉咙:"你走! 你出去!"

老女人被他的声音震动了,退了一步,吃吃的还想说什么,一时又说不出来。

他顺手把那个小布包也甩了过去,被羞辱的感觉更增加他的愤怒,他嚷道:"咱瞧不起你这几亩臭地,你来收买咱,不行! 拿回去,咱们有算账的那天!"

女人像跟着那个甩下来的布包往外滚,两只小脚像踩不到平地似的,身子乱摇晃。好容易才站住脚,她一手扶着门,喘了口气,停了停,又往前凑过去,她战战兢兢地说:"咱黑妮……"

"不准你说这个名字,咱不要听!"程仁陡地跳下来,恶狠狠地站到她面前,她害怕他拿拳头打她,便把头偏下去,却又不敢喊出来。

微微的灯光照在她可怕的脸上,头发蓬着,惊惶的眼睛睁得大大的,嘴歪扭在一面,露出里面的黄牙。程仁感到有一种报复的适意,不觉狞笑道:"你还不走,你们那个老头子已经扣起来了,关在许有武的后院子里,你回家哭去吧。准备准备木料。"

那个影子缩小了下去,慢慢地离开他,她退到了院子。他再跟到大门上,她又忽然往前看了看他,便哇地一声哭了起来,直冲出门外去了。哭声也渐渐消灭在黑暗里。

程仁突然像从噩梦惊醒,又像站在四野荒漠的平原上。他摇了摇头慢慢踱到院子里来,抬头望了望秋凉的天空,星儿在那里悠闲地眨着眼。上屋里已经没有鼾声,只听见四围的墙脚下热闹的虫鸣,而那对面鸡笼里的鸡,却在那黑暗的狭笼里抖动着翅膀,使劲高啼了。

"不要落在群众运动的尾巴上,不要落在群众的后面,不要忘记自己从哪里来。"这些话又在程仁的脑中轰起,但他已不再为那些无形中捆绑着他的绳索而苦恼了,他也抖动两肩,轻松地回到了房里。

四十七　决战之前

这家的人跑到那家,老头子找老头子,青年人找青年人,妇女找妇女,人们见着时只用一个会意的眼光,便凑拢到一起了。他告诉他这件事,他也告诉他这件事,他们先用一种不相信的口气来谈,甚至用一种惊骇的声调,互相问询。他们去问那些靠近干部的人,去问民兵,有的就去问干部。消息证实了,可是消息也增多了。有人说当张正国去到钱文贵家的时候,已经找不着他了,后来是在圈牲口屋里的草堆里拉出来的。有的说他还躺在炕上,看见张正国时只说:"啊!你来了!咱老早就等着你的。"又有人说民兵都不敢动手,张正国捆了他一绳子。还有人说他走的时候,把一双新洋纱袜子也穿上了,还披了件青呢大衫,怕半夜冷哩,嗯,说不定是怕捞不到一件像样的衣服回老家咧。

年老的女人们还坐在灶头烧早饭,可是年轻的人连吃饭也没有心肠,一群群的绕到许有武的门口去瞧。门口有个放哨的民兵不准他们进去,他们说找人,硬闯进去了。他们钻进那几户人家,问他们,他们说也没见着咧，只知天还没亮就有人闹起来，人是关在后边的一个较远较小的僻院子里。那里只有一大间柴房，如今柴也没有，只有一个土炕，一些烂木料。他们还要往里去，小院的门关得紧紧的。里外都有民兵，他们只得退回来。还有人以为在门缝里瞧见了钱文贵，说他很悠然地在摇着扇子。

有些知道的人便说："昨天县里的老章下来了，别看人长得嫩，到底是拿枪杆出身，在咱们地区混了不少时候，经过场面。办这些事，文绉绉就不行。"

街上像赶集一样的人来人往，黑板报前挤满了人，前边的人念着，后边的人听着，念着听着的人都笑了。他们站到合作社卖东西的木窗前，伸着头往里望，看见有干部在里边走动，便扯长耳朵想听到些什么。

那个顾长生的娘饭也顾不上烧，把她稀薄的顶发抿了抿，又站在街头了。她女儿时时跑出来叫她回去，她也不回，她一望着有人过路就问："咱村子昨晚上扣下了人，你知道么？"

人们知道她话多，不爱理她，马马虎虎答应她一句便走过去了。也有人会因为高兴，便忘记了她的脾气，她便凑过来说道："嗯！这可见了青天啦！要是咱村子上不把这个旗杆扳掉，共产党再贤明太阳也照不到的。从前咱长生他爹，赶冬里闲空点，有时卖个花生饼子，他说咱们赚了钱，没有孝敬他，在年里把他爹的篮子收了。他爹没法，送给他十斤花生，一斤白糖。这可反把他臊了，把送去的东西倒了一地，说咱们看扁了他，硬加上咱们一个违法的罪名，要把他爹送到大乡里去惩办。他爹是个老实人，没有法，叩头，赔钱，总算没送去。后来又要把咱长生送到铁红山去当苦力，铁红山谁不知道，有去路，没回路的，咱们又把一只猪卖了。嗯！咱总得要回咱这只猪来的，总有七八十斤啦……"

那些积极分子，像郭富贵，王新田，侯忠全的儿子侯清槐都更挤到合作社来，跟在张裕民，李昌他们后边往韩老汉家里跑。他们愿意找那些工作人员，从他们那里得到更多的启示。

民兵也好像多了，川流不息，有时几个人一串串地跑，像发生了重大事件一样。人家问他们什么，他们也一本正经的不说。

侯殿魁也走出来了,仍旧悄悄地坐在墙根前,天时还早,太阳只照到墙头上,他还披了一件夹衫,装晒太阳呢。他趁着大伙儿不注意的时候,偷听几句,放在心里捉摸。侯清槐偏爱往这里走过,每走过总露出一副得意的样子,有时就高声向旁人说:"咱们要一个一个的来收拾!"

刚刚在昨天把儿子关在屋里的侯忠全,一早就听到那个羊倌老婆跑来叽叽咕咕,他平日看不上这个女人,嫌她爱说话,爱管闲事,赶忙走到屋子外边去。但他仍旧听到她们所说的内容了,他舍不得不听下去,站在窗外拨弄挂在廊上的几根火绒,不走开,他不敢相信有这回事。羊倌老婆走了,他老婆也像看赛会的那么高兴的出去了。儿子女儿不在家。他忍不住站在门口望望,一会儿他侄子李之祥走来了,李之祥别话都不说,只说:"姑爹!咱看你那个皇历使不得了,如今真的换了朝代啦。"他也只说:"怎么?真的?""对,扣起来了,要大家告状咧!""该个什么罪?""咱说该个死罪!"老头子不说了。禁不住有些惊惶,好像一个船客突然见着大风浪来了似的那种说不清的心悸。又觉得喜欢,这种喜欢还只能深深地藏在心里,好像一下看见了连梦想也不敢去想想的东西实现了,东西就放在手边,却还要隐饰自己的感情,不愿动手去拿,惟恐把这东西骇跑,现实仍旧又变成一个幻影,他只能用怀疑的心情,反复地问自己:怎么搞的?真有这回事么?但最后他扔给了自己一个满意的答复:坏人,终有坏报,因果报应是逃不脱的!后来他也忍不住跑出去,装做并不打听什么的样子走到大街上去,他朝人多的方向走,慢慢便也蹓到戏台的场子跟前了。他看见人太多便背转身,躲到一边去敲他的火镰,却在这一敲的时候,他看见坐在墙角落里像个老乞丐的侯殿魁,他还看见那个一贯道正在悄悄看他咧。他觉得像被打了一样,那悄悄投过来的责罚的眼光,反使他抬不起头,他赶忙把两手垂下,弯着腰,逃走了。

小学生也不上学,站在学校门口观望,有些人又跑到学校里面去,看不见什么又退出来了,别的人也跟着去看看。两个教员都不知忙什么,一个跑进,一个跑出。人们还抓着任国忠问呢。任国忠心慌得很,想回家去,看见民兵太多又不敢,他想骗自己:"你怕什么?你又不是地主,又不是汉奸,又不是'方块'①,又不是这村的人,教书还有错,不怕,他妈的钱文贵扣起来了,活该,与你有什么相干?"但心总是不安,为什么章品昨天叮嘱他要等着他呢?他有什么鬼事要找他,这会儿还有好事!他的确没有办法可以离开这个村子。那个老吴就像知道他的心事似的老在他前前后后转,他走到什么地方都看得见那个红鼻子在眼前晃。

后来章品也出现了,他还是穿了那件没领的衬衫,光着头,没穿袜子,用根绳把鞋子系上,衫子薄,看见腰上有件东西鼓了出来,下边还露出了一块蓝绸子,人们都围了上去,七嘴八舌,他不知听谁的好。

"老章!你把咱们村搞完了走吧。"

"你们要把钱文贵怎样啦?"

"什么时候闹斗争呀?"

"早就该扣他了的。"

"哼!不扣起来,谁敢讲话?"

"这一下可是毛主席给咱做主啦……"

章品看见人们这样高兴,也禁不住愉快地笑着,两片嘴唇笑开了就合不拢来,又拿手不住地去摸那伸长在外边的脖项,便说道:"你们看吧,还是谁的力量大,只要老百姓乐意怎样,就能怎样,如今可得大家紧紧地团结着,只有团结起来才能推倒旧势力,才能翻身!你们村上头一个尖已经扣下来了,你们有冤伸冤,有仇报仇,把头一尖扳倒了,就不怕了,有什么,说什么,告下状来好办他,咱们县上给你们撑腰,腰壮着咧,不怕,嘿……"

章品走到了学校,学校外边围了很多人,张裕民也跟着进去了,门上站一个民兵,有些人猜着了,有些人莫名其妙,都在外边等着瞧。只见老吴跑过去了,又跑回来。一会刘教员也走了过去,看了看外边,没说什么。不久章品和张裕民都出来了,小学教员任国忠跟在他旁边。他背了个小铺盖卷,结结巴巴地不知在说些什么,章品看见很多人围着,便向那个民兵说:"你陪任教员先走一段,慢慢走,咱随后就来。"

---

①　作者注:指国民党特务。

任国忠只得装出若无其事的样子，跟跟跄跄地走了出去，有些人也跟去看，跟了一段路又踅回来了。

群众中有人说："咱早就说这家伙不是好人，鬼鬼祟祟尽在有钱人屁股后边跑，也不知忙些什么？"

又有人问："把他扣到县上去？"

章品只笑着问："你们看这人怎么样？"

大家答："谁还看不出，他把墨水吃到肚子里去了，一身透黑。"

"年轻人嘛！咱们想法教育，还教不过来？咱带他回县上入教员训练班去，把他脑子改造好再给你们送回来，这才免得误了你们的子弟。"章品说完便往外走。

大家又说："这可对着啦，好好给管教管教。"

人们跟上来又说："老章！你就走啦，你走了咱们怎么搞呀！"

章品一边走一边道："过两天咱再来，咱还有事啦。这里有文同志他们，你们有意见就去找他们。找张裕民也行。"

张裕民一直送他往外走，他们又说了半天，到村口章品才说："你回去吧。一切事看老百姓的意见，就容易办，你看今早这情况，人都胆壮了，不怕斗不起来，不过，唉——"他迟疑了半天没有说下去。

张裕民又望望他，他也对他望望，两个人都明白了是个什么问题梗着，半天，章品不得不说："人千万别打死。"

"那么交给你们吧。"

章品又沉思起来，他想不出一个好办法，他经常在村子里工作，懂得农民的心理，要末不斗争，要斗就往死里斗。他们不愿经过法律的手续，他们怕经过法律的手续，把他们认为应该枪毙的却只判了徒刑。他们常常觉得八路军太宽大了，他们还没具有较远大的眼光，他们要求报复，要求痛快。有些村的农民常常会不管三七二十一，一阵子拳头先打死再说。区村干部都往老百姓身上推，老百姓人多着呢，也不知是谁。章品也知道村干部就同老百姓一样的思想，他们总担心着将来的报复，一不做，二不休。一时要说通很多人，却实在不容易。

"交给我们,那倒不必,县上一下子也不能解决许多人,还是在村上解决。"

"唉,"张裕民也感觉得太为难了,说道:"你还有什么不知道的? 老百姓有劲没劲全在这里。"

"你也有这种想法么?"章品问。

"干部里边有这种想法的可多着呢。"

"这是一种变天思想,咱们要纠正它,随便打死人影响是不好的。咱们可以搜集他的罪状交给法院,死人不经过法院是不对的。咱们今天斗争是在政治上打垮他,要他向人民低头,还不一定要消灭他的肉体。你得说服大家。"

"嗯。"张裕民只得答应他。

"事情办着再看,咱到县上先把情况汇报了后大家再商量,如果老百姓一定要他死,罪也该死,那时咱们再派人来吧。我一个人也做不得主,你是明白的,——听,打锣了,暂时就这样吧:要往死里斗,却把人留着;要在斗争里看出人民团结的力量,要在斗争里消灭变天思想。"

当张裕民走回村子时,老吴已经把锣打向南街去了,锣声特别响亮,许多人吆喝着,跟在他后边。只听见:

"铛……铛铛"锣声一住,他的沙嗓子便愉快地大声唱了起来:"活捉五通神,快乐赛新年,赶快来开会,告状把身翻。"

The Sun Shines over the Sanggan River (Chapters 46 & 47)

46

WALKING home with the crowd Young Cheng was unusually silent, while the others talked and joked loudly and indulged in horseplay together. Whenever anyone bumped into him he just gave way quietly. He could not explain himself. To begin with he had felt embarrassed, then wronged, and finally rather timid. It was as if he had committed some crime or injured somebody, so that he could not hold up his head. Such a feeling he had never experienced before. Listening to all that Comrade Pin said it seemed as if every sentence was aimed at him, and he became conscious for the first time of his own vile conduct. Pin had seen it clearly. Young Cheng had been a straightforward fellow who never deceived people, but now he felt he was dishonest, he had deceived himself. He realized it had simply been a pretence when he said he would not marry Heini. It was only because he was afraid of criticism that he had forced himself to avoid her and keep her at a distance. It was only to deceive people, not because he had any hatred for her uncle, the worst man in the village, whom everyone detested. Hitherto he had always had a clear conscience, thinking he had not sided with Schemer Qian, whereas in fact he had never opposed him! For his niece's sake he had forgiven him everything! He had overlooked the injuries

Schemer Qian had done to everyone in the past, had forgotten how he himself had suffered and been exploited in his house. He wanted others to go to settle accounts and ask for the title deeds, while he himself was not brave enough to settle accounts. Had he not cultivated eight *mu* of dry and two *mu* of irrigated land of his? Pin said they must not forget their origin, but he had forgotten. In what way had he been thinking of the poor? He had been thinking only of himself, mortally afraid of offending the niece of a landlord, the niece of a rogue. He had looked down on Security Officer Zhang because the latter, for the sake of his wife and some small conveniences, grew every day closer to his father-in-law, drifting away from the comrades in the group who were his brothers, and from the peasants, until all the villagers despised him. But in his own case, although he had not married Schemer Qian's niece or been to their house, only secretly protecting her in his heart, it was equivalent to protecting them all, to upholding the privileges of the landowning class — how could he claim not to have forgotten his origin or to be better in any way than Zhang?

His steps grew slower and slower as these thoughts flashed through his mind, and he fell behind the crowd. A door in the lane opened with a creak, and he heard someone step outside for a moment, then go in again closing the door behind him. Listlessly Young Cheng gazed blankly into the darkness — what ought he to do?

Presently he reached his home, which was in a courtyard where several families lived together. The door was not bolted and he walked quietly in. Everybody was asleep and he could hear snores from the north room. The hens kept by the family opposite stirred restlessly in their small coop, and gave a few soft squawks.

A faint light showed from his room. He had forgotten that his mother was no longer at home, having gone to stay with her sister to keep her company during her lying-in. So he was not surprised by the light, as he stepped apathetically over the threshold.

A tiny point of flame hovered on the wick of the oil lamp, and the faint light seemed more gloomy than complete darkness. As he went in, a shadow detached itself slowly from the black corner by the *kang*. He paid no attention, feeling as if this shadow had nothing to do with him. It just occurred to him to think, "Hasn't Ma gone to bed yet?" However, still immersed in his own affairs he went and sat down on one end of the *kang*.

Sure enough the black shadow was a woman. She came over to him before he had lain down, and he suddenly remembered that his mother had been away for several days. Besides, this woman did not look like his mother. Involuntarily, in his surprise he asked sharply: "Who are you?"

The woman made a sudden clutch at his arm, and said: "It's me! Aunty."

He withdrew his hand, backed up against the wall, and looked fixedly at this ghostly shadow.

She immediately gave him a cloth bundle, and in a tone meant to be kindly but actually embarrassed, wanting to laugh but unable to do so, said softly: "Here you are. It's a present from Heini. She wanted to come herself because she has something to say to you. She solemnly swears she wants to be your wife. Cheng! Don't let her down!"

He wanted to send this woman with her bundle and her talk packing, but he did not do it. He could not raise his hand. Guilt and shame pinned it down. He wanted to curse her, but his tongue was numb as if he had taken some strange drug.

"Her uncle will do anything for her," Mrs. Qian went on. "You can have her, you can have the land, eighteen *mu* altogether including the vegetable garden. Cheng! Our Heini's counting on you!"

Young Cheng shuddered from head to foot. He felt there were countless eyes in the ceiling and in the cracks of the wall smiling sarcastically at him.

Qian's wife thrust her face closer to his, her mouth by his ear, and said distinctly: "Her uncle says we mustn't put you in an awkward position. You're chairman of the peasants' association. Of course you have to say things. Just so long as you understand at heart. Well, after all we are one family! ... " She squawked like an egret and laughed with appalling shamelessness.

Young Cheng could stand it no longer. He shook himself, as if using all his might to dislodge a heavy load from his back. "Go away!" The words burst harshly from his throat. "Get out of here!"

Shaken by his tone, Mrs. Qian recoiled a step. She moved her lips, but for the moment could not speak.

Picking up the cloth bundle he threw it at her, his sense of insult increasing his fury, and shouted: "I don't give a damn for your stinking land! You've come to buy me, but it's no use! Take it back. A day will come when we'll settle accounts."

She seemed to roll outside with the bundle that had been thrown down, her small feet scarcely touching the ground, as she rocked from side to side. Regaining her balance with difficulty, she clutched the door post with one hand and paused, panting, then darted forward again, saying tremulously: "Our Heini ..."

"Don't you use that name again. I don't want to hear it!" Young Cheng leapt forward to confront her furiously. Fearing he would strike her she lowered her head but dared not cry out.

The feeble rays of the light lit up her fearful expression, her hair dishevelled, her wild eyes staring wide, her lips awry disclosing the yellow teeth. Young Cheng tasted the gratification of revenge. With a ghastly smile he said: "Are you still not going? Your old man has already been arrested and shut up in Landlord Xu's backyard. You'd better go home to cry. Get some wood ready for the coffin."

The shadow contracted, receding slowly from him as she retreated into the courtyard. He followed her to the gate where she suddenly came forward again to look at him, then burst out wailing and hurried outside. The sound of her cries gradually died away in the darkness.

Young Cheng felt as if he had suddenly woken up from a bad dream or as if he were standing on a wild plain. Shaking his head he walked slowly back into the courtyard, looking up at the autumn sky where the stars were twinkling quietly. No more snores were coming from the north room. The lively chirrups of insects could be heard from the four corners of the wall, while the fowls in the hen-coop opposite shook and stretched their wings in the dark narrow coop, and crowed stridently.

"Don't fall behind the mass movement. Don't fall behind the masses. Don't forget your own origin." These words started milling through his head again. But he no longer felt distressed by the invisible bonds that had bound him. He shook himself and went, relaxed and with a light heart, into the house.

47

PEOPLE from different families called on each other, old men sought out their cronies, youngsters their pals, women other women. When people saw each other they exchanged significant glances, then put their heads together. They told each other of what had happened, first speaking rather sceptically or even in a shocked tone, and after questioning each other they would go to ask those who were close to the cadres, or the militia, while some of them went to see the cadres. The news was confirmed, but it grew in the telling. Some people said that by the time Swarthy Guo went to look for Schemer Qian he was not to be found, and finally was dragged out from under the hay in the stable. Others said that he was lying on the *kang* and on Guo's arrival all he said was, "So you've come. I've been expecting this a long time." Still others said the militia dared not lift their hands against him, and it was Guo who tied him up. Others again said that before leaving he put on a new pair of socks as well as a green woollen gown, saying it was cold in the middle of the night. Maybe it was because he was afraid he would have no decent clothes to die in!

Old women were still sitting on the end of the *kang* cooking breakfast, but the young people had lost interest even in food. Group after group made its way to Landlord Xu's gate to have a look. A militiaman on guard at the gate forbade them to go in, but they said they were looking for someone and forced their way in. Pushing their way among the families who lived there they questioned them, but they said they had seen nothing. All they knew was that while it was still dark there had been a commotion, and Qian was shut up in a rather out-of-the-way little courtyard at the back. There was just a big room for firewood there. Now there was no firewood left, only an earthen *kang* and some broken boards. When they still wanted to go in and look they found the gate to the small courtyard firmly fastened. There were militiamen within and without, so they had to leave. But some of them thought they could see Schemer Qian through a crack in the door, fanning himself most unconcernedly.

Those in the know said: "Yesterday Comrade Pin from the county government arrived. He may look soft, but after all he did grow up with a gun in his hand. He's knocked around our district for quite a time, and been through a lot. In a business like this it's no use being cultured and refined."

The streets were filled with people as if it were market-day. There was a crowd in front of the blackboard news, the people in front reading and the ones at the back listening, all of them smiling. Others stood in front of the sales window of the co-operative and craned their necks to look inside, and when they saw cadres moving about inside they strained their ears to hear what was being said.

Sheng's mother could not be bothered to cook. She fastened up her skimpy hair and went out into the street. Her daughter kept coming out to call her home, but she refused to go. Whenever anyone crossed the road she would ask: "Do you know someone was arrested in out village last night?"

Everybody knew she was a gossip, and did not pay much attention, giving a careless answer and passing on. But some, because they were in a good humour, forgot her temper. Then she dashed forward and said: "Ah! At long last the sky is clear! If our village doesn't overthrow that flagpole, no matter how capable and just the Communists are, the sun won't reach us. In the old days Sheng's dad when he had a little spare time in winter would sometimes sell peanut cakes, but Schemer Qian said we had earned money and didn't give him presents, and at New Year confiscated his basket. There was nothing my man could do except give him ten catties of peanuts and a catty of sugar. But that brought shame on Qian and he threw all the presents on the ground. He said we had taken him wrong and insisted we had broken the law, wanting to send my husband to be tried in the *xiang*court. My husband was a simple fellow. He didn't know what to do, and after kowtowing and paying him money he got off being sent. Later Qian wanted to send my Sheng to Hongshan as a coolie. Everybody knew that people who went to Hongshan never came back, so then we had to sell a pig. Ah! I mean to get that pig back. It was at least seventy or eighty catties ..."

Enthusiasts like Young Guo, Wang and Tenant Hou's son all crowded into the co-operative, then hurried after Yumin, Freckles Li and the others to Old Han's house, wanting to find the members of the work team to get more information from them.

There seemed to be an unending stream of militiamen too, sometimes several running in a row as if something tremendous had happened. But if questioned they maintained a wooden silence.

Landlord Hou came out too and sat down stealthily as usual at the foot of the wall. Since it was still early and the sun had only reached the top of the wall he was wearing a lined jacket. As he pretended to be sunning himself, he took advantage of the times they overlooked him to try to catch a few sentences to file in his mind for future reference. Young Hou kept on walking in Landlord Hou's direction, wearing a look of complacence, sometimes saying loudly to bystanders: "We must clean them up!"

Tenant Hou, who only yesterday had locked his son in the house, had heard the shepherd's wife talking to his wife as soon as he woke up. Since he usually despised the woman, thinking her a gossip and busybody, he went out at once. However he could not help hearing what they were talking about and had to go on listening, standing outside the window playing with some thread hanging on the porch, unwilling to leave. He could not believe his ears. After the shepherd's wife had left, his wife went out in high spirits as if she were going to the fair. His son and daughter were out. He could not resist standing in the doorway looking out, and presently his nephew Vineyard Li came over and said: "Uncle! Seems to me that calendar of yours is out of date. Now we've really changed dynasties."

"What? Really?" was all he said.

"Yes, he's been arrested, everybody's asked to accuse him!"

"What should his punishment be?"

"I should say death!"

The old man said nothing. He could not overcome a feeling of panic, anxious as a boatman who suddenly sees a storm approaching. He was happy too, but this happiness could only be hidden deep in his heart. It was as if he had suddenly seen something he dared not hope for even in his dreams realized, already at hand, but he still wanted to conceal his feelings. He dared not stretch out his hand for fear of frightening it away, for fear that the actuality would once more change into an illusion. He could only ask himself sceptically again, "How did it happen? Can it be true?" However, finally he gave himself a satisfactory answer — bad people must always come to a bad end; men reap what they sow! Finally he went out too, walking to the main street pretending he was not looking for news. He headed for where the crowd was thickest, and presently arrived at the front of the stage. Seeing that there were too many people, he turned round and withdrew to one side to strike his flint. But while he was striking it he saw Landlord Hou sitting like an old beggar at the corner of the wall looking furtively at him. He felt as if he had been whipped. That stealthy glance of reproach made him hang his head, and immediately letting his hands fall he hurried off with bent back.

The school children were not having lessons either, but standing and looking out from the school gate. Some people rushed into the school, but finding nothing came out again, followed by others. The two teachers were both busy, hurrying in and out. Some people seized Teacher Ren to question him. Ren was completely panic-stricken and wanted to go home, but dared not because there were so many militiamen about. He tried to deceive himself: "What are you afraid of? You're not a landlord or a traitor or a spy. You don't even belong to the village. Just teaching, how can you go wrong? Don't be afraid. That bastard Qian has been arrested, and it serves him right. What's it got to do with you?" Still he could not allay his fears. Why had Comrade Pin told him to wait for him yesterday? What the devil did he want to see him about? It couldn't be anything good now! There was no way for him to leave the village. Red-nosed Wu, as if he knew what was in his mind, was always at his heels. Wherever he went he could see that red nose glistening.

Finally Pin appeared, still wearing the same collarless shirt, bareheaded, without socks on, his shoes tied with string. His shirt was thin, with a bulge showed at his waist where he carried a gun. People crowded round him, all talking at once, so that he didn't know whom to listen to.

"Pin! Don't go till you've cleared up our village."

"What are you going to do with Schemer Qian?"

"When's the trial going to be?"

"Should have been arrested long ago."

"Ah, before he was arrested who dared say anything?"

"This time Chairman Mao's answered our wishes ..."

Seeing how happy they all were, Pin could not help laughing with pleasure. Rubbing his neck repeatedly he said: "You see who's stronger after all. The people can do whatever they want, only now the thing is to get everyone to unite closely. Only by uniting closely can the old powers be overthrown and we stand on our own feet! The chief racketeer in your village has already been arrested. Those with grievances should speak up, those who want vengeance state their cases. Now that the Number One Racketeer's overthrown, there's no need to be afraid. You can say what you like. Bring your charges against him so that we can deal with him. We in the county are behind you. With our backing don't be afraid!"

A crowd surrounded the school when Pin went there. Yumin followed him in, and a militiaman stood guard at the door. Some people guessed what was happening while some were in the dark, but they all waited outside to see. They saw Red-nosed Wu hurry to and fro. Presently Teacher Liu came over too and looked outside without saying anything. Soon Pin and Yumin came out with Teacher Ren at their side carrying a roll of bedding on his back, mumbling incoherently. Seeing all the people outside Pin said to the militiaman: "You escort Mr. Ren some of the way. Walk slowly, I'll catch up with you presently."

Trying to look unconcerned, Ren walked shakily out. Some villagers followed him out of curiosity, but turned back after a short distance.

Someone in the crowd said: "I said long ago that fellow was no good. All the time sneakily making up the rich. Wonder what he was up to?"

"Is he being taken to the county?" asked another.

"What's your opinion of him?" asked Pin, smiling.

"Who doesn't know?" they all said. "He's drunk so much ink he's turned black."

"He's young! We must try to reform him and he'll be all right. I'm going to take him back to the county to join the teachers' training class. When his mind's been remoulded you shall have him back. This way he won't spoil your children!" Having said this Pin walked out.

"That's fair enough, said the crowd. "Have him well taught."

Some caught up and said: "Comrade Pin, are you going? If you go how shall we manage?"

"I'll be back in a couple of days," said Pin as he walked on. "I have things to attend to. Comrade Wen and the others are here. If you've any ideas go and see them. Or see Yumin."

Yumin escorted Pin right out of the village, and as they walked they had another long talk. By the village gate Pin said: "You go back. Consult the people's opinion in everything, and it will be easy. Look how things are this morning — everybody's bold, no need to fear they won't attack. Only — well — " He paused for a minute, but did not finish the sentence.

Yumin looked at him and he looked at Yumin, both realizing what the problem was, and after a long interval Pin had to say: "Whatever happens, don't let him be killed."

"In that case we'd better hand him over to you."

Pin started thinking hard again. He could not think of a good solution. He was used to working in villages and understood the psychology of peasants: either don't attack or attack to kill. They did not like going through legal procedure, fearing that, if they did so, someone they thought deserved death might only be imprisoned. They often felt the Eighth Route Army was too lenient. They were not yet able to take a longer view, but clamoured for revenge, for a clean sweep. The peasants in some villages just killed their hated oppressors under a rain of fists. The district and village cadres all put the blame on the masses, but there were so many people it was impossible to say who was responsible. Pin knew too that the village cadres, just like the masses, worried lest the tables should be turned in future, and were therefore eager to do the job thoroughly. To persuade many people at short notice was far from easy.

"No need to hand him over to us. The county government can't settle so many cases all at once. Better settle it in the village."

"Uh huh." Yumin realized the difficulty too. He was rather at a loss and said: "You understand the whole situation, don't you? Whether the people will be enthusiastic or not depends entirely on this."

"Is that the way you feel too?" asked Pin.

"Most of the cadres feel that way."

"That means you fear the reactionaries may come back. We ought to correct that outlook. Killing people at will isn't good. We can collect statements of his crimes to give the court. Execution ought to be legally carried out. In agitating nowadays we defeat landlords on political grounds, wanting them to bow to the people, not necessarily wanting to kill them. You'll have to talk the villagers round."

"Um." Yumin had to agree.

"See how you get on, and after I've reported the situation at the county government we'll all discuss it again. If the people really want him killed, and his crimes deserve death, then we'll send cadres over. I can't settle the matter by myself, you know that ... Listen, the gong's being sounded. We'll leave it at that for the time being. You must organize people to be thorough, but have him kept alive. During the struggle we want to see the united strength of the masses, and do away with that fear that the reactionaries may return."

By the time Yumin was back in the village Red-nosed Wu had already sounded the gong down to the south street. The gong was unusually loud, and many people were following him, shouting. All one could hear was "Dong ... dong, dong." When the gong stopped, his hoarse voice started chanting cheerfully: "The Demon's caught alive! We're happy as at New Year! Hurry to the meeting! Accuse him without fear!"

三

王贵与李香香(第二部)①

一　闹革命

三边没树石头少，

庄户人的日子过不了。

天上无云地下旱，

过不了日子另打算。

羊群走路靠头羊，

陕北起了共产党，

头名老刘二名高岗，

红旗插到半天上。

草堆上落火星大火烧，

红旗一展穷人都红了。

千里的雷声万里的闪，

快里马撒②红了个遍。

紫红犍牛自带耧，

① 中文选自：李季．王贵与李香香．北京：人民文学出版社，1953．
英译文选自：Li Chi. *Wang Kuei and Li Hsiang-hsiang*. Yang Xianyi & Gladys Yang. Trans. Beijing：Foreign Languages Press，1954．

② 作者注："快里马撒"，即很快很快的意思。

闹革命的心思人人有。

前半晌还是个庄稼汉，

到黑里①背枪打营盘。

打开寨子分粮食，

土地牛羊分个光。

少先队来赤卫军，

净是些十八九的年轻人。

女人们走路一阵风，

长头发剪成短缨缨。

上河里涨水下河里混，

王贵暗里参加了赤卫军。

白天到滩里去放羊，

黑夜里开会闹革命；

开罢会来鸡子叫，

十几里路往回跑。

白天放羊一整天，

黑夜不眨一眨眼。

身子劳碌精神好，

闹革命的心劲一满高。

手指头五个不一般长，

王贵的心思和人不一样。

别人的仇恨像座山，

王贵的仇恨比天高：

活活打死老父亲，

迩刻又要抢心上的人！

牛马当了整五年，

_____

① 作者注："黑里"，即夜里。

崔二爷没给过一个工钱。

崔二爷来胡日弄①，

修寨子买马又招兵。

地主豪绅个个凶，

崔二爷是个大坏髹！

庄户人个个想吃他的肉，

狗儿见他也哼几哼。

众人向游击队长提意见，

早早的打下死羊湾。

心急等不得豆煮烂，

定下个日子腊月二十三。

半夜先捉定崔二爷，

到天明大队开进死羊湾。

定下计划人忙乱，

——后天就是二十三。

二 太阳会从西边出来吗？

打着了狐子兔子搬家，

听见闹革命崔二爷心害怕。

白天夜晚不瞌睡，

一垛墙想堵黄河水。

明里查来暗里访，

打听谁个随了共产党。

听说王贵暗里闹革命，

---

① 作者注："胡日弄"，即胡作乱为。

崔二爷头上冒火星！

放羊回来刚进门，

两条麻绳捆上身。

顺着捆来横着绑，

五花大绑吊在二梁上。

全庄的男女都叫上，

都来看闹革命的啥下场！

连着打断了两根红柳棍，

昏死过去又拿凉水喷。

麻油点灯灯花亮，

王贵浑身扒了个光；

两根麻绳捆着胳膊腿，

捆成个鸭子倒浮水；

满脸浑身血道道，

活像个剥了皮的牛不老①。

崔二爷来气凶凶，

打一皮鞭问一声：

"癞虾蟆想吃天鹅肉，

穷鬼们还想闹成个大事情？

"撒泡尿来照照你的影，

毡眉鼠眼还会成了精！

"五黄六月会飘雪花？

太阳会从西边出来吗？"

"老狗入你不要耍威风，

不过三天要你狗命！

————————

① 编者注："牛不老"，方言，小犊，小牛。

"我一个死了不要紧，
千万个穷汉后面跟！"
"王贵你不要说大话，
说来话去咱们是一家。
"姓崔的没有亏待过你，
猴娃娃养成大后生。
"过罢河来你拆了桥，
翅膀硬了你忘了恩。
"马无毛病成了龙，
该是你一时糊涂没想通？
"浪子回头金不换，
放下杀猪刀成神仙。
"千错万错我不怪你，
年轻人没把握我知道哩。"
"老王八你不要灌米汤，
又软又硬我不上你的当；
"世上没良心的就数你，
打死我亲大把我当牲畜；
"苦死苦活一年到头干，
整整五年没见你半个钱；
"五更半夜牲口正吃草，
老狗入你就把我吼叫起来了；
"没有衣裳没有被，
五年穿你两件老羊皮；
你吃的大米和白面，
我吃顿黄米当过年；
"一句话来三瞪眼，
三天两头挨皮鞭；

"姓崔的你是娘老子养，
我王贵娘肚里也怀了十个月胎！
"你是人来我也是个人，
为啥你这样没良心?!
"我王贵虽穷心眼亮，
自己的事情有主张；
"闹革命成功我翻了身，
不闹革命我也活不长；
"跳蚤不死一股劲的跳，
管他死活就是我这命一条；
"要杀要刮由你挑，
你的鬼心眼我知道：
"硬办法不成软办法来，
想叫我顺了你把良心坏，
"趁早收起你那鬼算盘，
想叫我当狗难上难。"
崔二爷气的像疯狗，
撕破了老脸一跳三尺高。
"狗咬巴屎你不是人敬的，
好话不听你还骂人哩！"
说个"打"字皮鞭如雨下，
痛的王贵紧咬着牙。
一阵阵黄风一阵阵沙，
香香看着心上如刀扎！
一阵阵打颤一阵阵麻，
打王贵就像打着了她！
脸皮发红又发白，
眼泪珠噙着不敢滴下来；

两耳发烧浑身麻，

活像一个死娃娃。

为救亲人想的办法好，

偷偷的跑出了大门道，

一边走来一边想：

"王贵的命儿就在今晚上；

"他常到刘家圪崂去开会，

那里该住着游击队。

"快走快跑把信送，

迟一步亲人就难活命！"

三　红旗插到死羊湾

队长的哨子呼呼响，

挂枪上马人人忙。

听说王贵受苦刑，

半夜三更传命令：

"王贵是咱好同志，

再怎么也不能叫他把命送！"

二十匹马队前边走，

赤卫军、少先队紧跟上。

马蹄落地嚓嚓响，

长枪、短枪、红缨枪；

人有精神马有劲，

麻麻亮时开了枪。

白生生的蔓菁一条根，

庄户人和游击队是一条心。

听见枪声齐下手，

菜刀、鸟枪、打狗棍；

里应外合一起干，

死羊湾闹的翻了天。

枪声乱响鸡狗乱叫唤，

游击队打进了死羊湾。

崔二爷在炕上睡大觉，

听见枪声往起跳。

打罢王贵发了瘾，

大烟抽得正起劲；

黄铜烟灯玻璃罩，

银镶的烟葫芦不能解心焦；

大小老婆两三个，

那个也没有香香好！

肥羊肉掉在狗嘴里头，

三抢两抢夺不到手。

王贵这一回再也活不成，

小香香就成了我的了。

越想越甜赛沙糖，

涎水流在下巴上。

烟灯旁边做了一个梦，

把香香抱在怀当中；

又酸又甜好梦做不长，

"噼啪""噼啪"枪声响。

头一枪惊醒坐起来，

第二枪响时跳下炕。

连忙叫起狗腿子：

"关着大门快上房！

"那边过来那边打，

一人赏你们十块响洋。"

人马多枪声稠不一样，

二爷心里改了主张；

太阳没出满天韶，

崔二爷从后门溜跑了；

太阳出来天大亮，

红旗插在崄畔上；

太阳出来一朵花，

游击队和咱穷汉们是一家。

滚滚的米汤热腾腾的馍，

招待咱游击队好吃喝。

救下王贵松开了绳，

游击队的同志们个个眼圈红。

把王贵痛的直昏过，

香香哭着叫"哥哥"！

"你要死了我也不得活，

睁一睁眼睛看一看我！"

四 自由结婚

太阳出来遍地红，

革命带来了好光景。

崔二爷在时就像大黑天，

十有九家没吃穿。

穷人翻身赶跑崔二爷，

死羊湾变成活羊湾。

灯盏里没油灯不明，

庄户人没地种就像没油的灯；

有了土地灯花亮，

人人脸上发红光。

吃一嘴黄连吃一嘴糖，

王贵娶了李香香。

男女自由都平等，

自由结婚新时样。

唐僧取经过了七十二个洞，

王贵和香香受的折磨数不清。

千难万难心不变，

患难夫妻实在甜。

俊鸟投窝叫喳喳，

香香进洞房泪如麻。

清泉里淌水水不断，

滴湿了王贵的新布衫。

"半夜里就等着公鸡叫，

为这个日子把人盼死了。"

香香想哭又想笑，

不知道怎么说着好。

王贵笑的说不出来话，

看着香香还想她！

双双拉着香香的手，

难说难笑难开口：

"不是闹革命穷人翻不了身，

不是闹革命咱俩也结不了婚！

"革命救了你和我，

革命救了咱们庄户人。

"一杆红旗要大家扛，
红旗倒了大家都遭殃。
"快马上路牛耕地，
闹革命是咱们自己的事。
"天上下雨地下滑，
自己跌倒自己爬。
"太阳出来一股劲的红，
我打算长远闹革命。"
过门三天安了家，
游击队上报名啦。
羊肚子手巾缠头上，
肩膀上背着无烟钢。
十天半月有空了，
请假回来看香香。
看罢香香归队去，
香香送到沟底里。
沟湾里胶泥黄又多，
挖块胶泥捏咱两个；
捏一个你来捏一个我，
捏的就像活人托；
摔碎了泥人再重和，
再捏一个你来再捏一个我；
哥哥身上有妹妹，
妹妹身上也有哥哥。
捏完了泥人叫："哥哥，
再等几天你来看我。"

Wang Kuei and Li Hsiang-hsiang (Part Two)

The Revolution

No trees and few stones had Sanpien,

The peasants' lot was bitter then.

No clouds above, below a drought,

They had to think of some way out.

A flock of goats follows the goat at the head,

Through northern Shensi the Communists spread.

With Liu Chih-tan[①] to lead them, high

They raised the Red flag to the sky.

From a spark in the hay a big fire can spread,

Soon as the Red flag appeared the poor turned Red.

Thunder's heard and lightning seen for miles around,

Quick as thought Communism covered the ground.

Willingly his plough a roan ox draws,

And all folk support a revolutionary cause.

---

① 译者注: Liu Chih-tan, organizer and leader of the Communist Party and the Red Army in northern Shensi during the Second Revolutionary Civil War Period (1927–1936). In 1936, he fell in battle while resisting the Kuomintang forces who were attempting to prevent the Red Army from fighting the Japanese aggressors.

Still common peasants in broad daylight,

They take guns to storm the garrison at night.

When the forts are opened, they divide the grain;

Land, sheep, cattle, are all disposed of then.

The Youth Corps, and the Red Guard so keen,

Consist of youngsters of eighteen or nineteen.

Women on the road are like a gust of wind,

Their long hair cut in a bob behind.

The lower stream is muddied when the upper stream runs high,

Wang Kuei joined the Red Guard secretly.

Leading his cattle to the marsh when it was light,

To revolutionary meetings he went at night.

He would stay at the meeting until the cock crowed,

And then hurry miles back along the homeward road.

During the day his goats he had to keep,

During the night not a wink of sleep.

Tired as he was, his spirits were high,

For the revolution he was ready to die.

The fingers of one hand are not the same length,

And Wang Kuei's longing surpassed the rest in strength;

Other people's hatred was like a mountain high,

But Wang Kuei's hatred was higher than the sky.

Tsui had had his father beaten till he died,

And now he wished to steal Wang Kuei's bride!

Five years like a beast Wang had toiled away,

Not paid a single cent by Landlord Tsui.

Nothing was too crooked for Landlord Tsui to do,

He built forts, bought horses, hired soldiers too.

The landlords and gentry were vicious every one,

But Landlord Tsui had the rest outdone!

Peasants felt that his flesh they'd like to bite,

Even the dogs barked at his sight.

To the guerillas the people used to say,
"Hurry up and capture Dead Goat Bay."
Though beans are still raw, hungry people can't wait;
They fixed the twenty-third of December as the date.
At midnight they would arrest Landlord Tsui,
At dawn troops would enter Dead Goat Bay.
When the plan was made, they all felt stirred;
Only two more days to the twenty-third!

Can the Sun Rise in the Western Sky?

When a fox is hunted, the rabbits run away;
News of revolution struck fear in Landlord Tsui.
He dared not sleep either early or late,
As if one wall could stop the river's spate.
Openly and on the sly he investigated
To find out who were with the Communists related.
When he heard Wang Kuei was working underground,
The landlord's heart with rage began to pound!
When Wang left his flock and came inside,
With two thick ropes of hemp he was tied.
The landlord had him trussed and slung,
Then from the rafter he was hung.
All the villagers were summoned straight,
To witness a revolutionary's fate.
Two red willow canes on his back were broken;
When he fainted, with cold water he was awoken.
When we burn oil, a bright light is made;
Wang Kuei's clothes from his body were flayed.
He was tied by two ropes from thigh to throat,
Trussed like a duck in a pond to float,

All his face and body with blood overlaid,

Like an ox that's living flayed.

Landlord Tsui seemed with rage about to choke,

And shouted at Wang between each stroke:

"Dirty frogs want to feed on crane;

You poor scum hope for great happenings in vain.

Look at yourself in some dirty water, do!

What great deeds can be done by dogs like you?

Can snow fall in mid-July?

Can the sun rise in the western sky?"

"No need, old dog, to swagger about,

The wind will blow your oil lamp out.

What does death matter in my case?

Millions of others will take my place!"

"Wang Kuei, don't talk so recklessly;

You and I are the same family.

What injustice to you have I ever done?

I brought up a foundling like my own son.

You tear down the bridge once the river is crossed,

Your feathers grown, your gratitude lost.

A horse without blemish may be a dragon yet;

Are you so stupid this fact to forget?

A penitent prodigal's prized above gold,

And butchers can turn into gods, we're told.

Still, to forgive all your faults I'm ready;

Young men, I know, are very unsteady."

"No use, old turtle, your turning sweet;

You'll find this customer hard to cheat.

In all the world's no greater knave;

You killed my dad, made me a slave.

The whole year round I sweated away,

But for five years I haven't had a cent of pay.

Cattle eat hay at the dead of night,

But you called me up, old dog, out of spite;

I've had no clothes, no bedding in the cold,

In these five years only two sheepskins old.

The whole year round you had good cheer,

While I ate coarse grain at New Year.

A glare always followed what you had to say,

And I got the whip every other day;

You had parents to care for you,

D'you think I didn't have a mother too?

If you're human so am I,

But you show no sign of humanity.

I may be poor, but I'm not quite blind;

It's not so hard to make up my mind.

If we succeed, my position will be strong;

And without a revolution I shan't live long.

Long as they live, fleas jump, and so shall I;

I've only the one life, and I'm not afraid to die.

Kill me or skin me as you feel inclined;

Well I know your devilish mind.

When bullying fails, you try soft-soap,

You want me to sell my soul — what a hope!

You'd better abandon, your devilish scheme,

To make me your slave is harder than you dream."

Tsui's loss of face was so complete,

Like a mad dog he jumped three feet.

"Dirty dog, beneath contempt, utterly perverse!

When you're spoken kindly to, you only curse!"

Once more the whip showered blows like rain,

And Wang Kuei gritted his teeth with pain.

A gust of wind, a gust of sand,

Hsiang-hsiang felt it was more than she could stand!

She shook and trembled, weak in every limb,
Tortured by the blows that fell on him!
Her face turned white and then turned red,
Tears gathered in her eyes that she dared not shed;
Her head was swimming, numb her body grown,
Like a living creature turned to stone.
Then to save her lover she hit upon a plan,
And out of the front gate secretly she ran,
Thinking to herself as she hurried away:
"Wang Kuei may not last another day.
He often went to meetings at Liu Fair,
There surely must be guerillas there.
I must go to tell them, just as fast as I can;
If I'm too late, my lover's a dead man."

The Red Flag Is Planted in Dead Goat Bay

Loud on his whistle the sergeant blew,
To fetch rifles, mount horses, everyone flew.
When news was received of Wang Kuei's cruel plight,
An order went round in the third watch at night:
"A loyal comrade and true is Wang Kuei,
His life must at no cost be thrown away!"
Out set the Red Guard and the Youth Corps,
With a troop of twenty horsemen before.
Cloppety-clop! the horse hooves rung,
On the men's shoulders rifles were slung.
With steeds so swift, men so high-hearted,
Before daybreak the fight had started.
Only one root has the turnip white,
With the guerillas the peasants unite;

When they hear shooting, out they all run,

Some with a stick or chopper, some a shot-gun.

Those within and those without together pound away,

And so the revolution came to Dead Goat Bay.

Shots sounded, dogs barked madly, roosters crowed,

As into Dead Goat Bay the guerillas rode.

Landlord Tsui was sleeping soundly in his bed,

But at the sound of shooting up he leapt in dread;

Having worked off his anger by beating Wang Kuei,

A pipe of opium had made him quite gay.

But the copper lamp with its glass shade by him,

And silver-plated pipe did not satisfy him.

He'd two or three wives, both old and young, there;

But none of them could with Hsiang-hsiang compare!

In a dog's jaws fat mutton sometimes lands,

Yet Tsui had failed to get her into his hands.

"This will be the death of Wang Kuei, the swine;

And then little Hsiang-hsiang will surely be mine."

Sweeter than brown sugar the prospect appeared,

His ugly mouth watered and he dribbled on his beard.

So he dreamt, the opium lamp beside him placed,

How in his arms Hsiang-hsiang he had embraced.

Not for long, however, did this sweet dream last,

For Bang! Bang! Bang! the gun shots rang out fast.

Startled from his sleep at the very first shot,

Down from his bed at the second he got.

He shouted for his thugs in a fearful flurry:

"Bar the gate, and get on to the roof! Now hurry!

Wherever they come from, shoot them dead!

I'll give you ten silver dollars a head!"

But more men came, shot followed shot;

Tsui felt things were getting a little too hot.

And before the sun had risen that day,

Through the back gate he slipped away.

When the bright sun on high did ride,

The Red flag was planted on the hillside.

Like a great blossom blazed the sun,

Guerillas and peasants rejoiced as one.

"Here's thick rice gruel, bubbling hot!"

They fed the guerillas on the spot.

Wang Kuei was helped down, his ropes untied,

But at sight of him they nearly cried.

The pain had made him faint away,

And Hsiang-hsiang wept as she called Wang Kuei.

"I shall die too if you die," she cries.

"Look at me, love! Open your eyes!"

Free Marriage

Red is the earth beneath the sun's blaze,

For revolution has brought better days.

In the time of Landlord Tsui everything looked black,

Nine peasants out of ten had no clothes on their back.

When the poor revolted, they drove away Tsui;

And Dead Goat Bay became Live Goat Bay.

When a lamp lacks oil, it cannot burn bright;

Peasants without land are like an unreplenished light.

Once given land, a bright light they spread;

Everybody's face with joy looks red.

After eating gentian, sugar tastes so sweet!

Wang Kuei and Hsiang-hsiang married, and their joy was complete.

Today men and women are equal and free,

Free marriage is the fashion in the new society.

Like the poor pilgrim in his progress of old,

Both of them had suffered hardships untold.

Through a thousand troubles they did not despair,

Sweet it is to see such a well-tried pair.

Like the bird chirping as to its nest it flies,

Tears on her wedding night poured from Hsiang-hsiang's eyes.

Water from a fountain flows forever down,

And with her tears she wet Wang Kuei's new gown.

"All night I waited to hear the cock crow;

I nearly went mad," said he. "Time seemed so slow!"

Hsiang-hsiang wants both to laugh and to cry;

She cannot speak, she feels too shy.

Wang Kuei, smiling, remains tongue-tied,

Thinking only of Hsiang-hsiang his bride!

Tightly he clutches Hsiang-hsiang's hands,

Hard to speak, hard to smile, speechless he stands.

"By the revolution the rich we overthrew,

Without the revolution I could not have married you!

It was the revolution that saved you and me,

It was the revolution that made us peasants free.

To keep the Red flag flying is up to us all;

We all shall be lost if the flag should fall.

Quickly let horses fly, oxen drive the plough;

To spread revolution is our duty now.

The earth is slippery after heavy rain;

But if we tumble, we can rise again.

Now the sun is shining so red and gay,

I'm with the revolution till my dying day."

When they settled down, and three days had gone,

As a guerilla Wang Kuei signed on.

On his head he wrapped a cloth to keep off the sun,

And over his shoulder carried a gun.

Ev'ry week or fortnight, when he was free,

He would ask leave to go home Hsiang-hsiang to see.

And she'd see him off to the end of the glen,

When he went back to his corps again.

Rich brown mud in the valley lay.

"Let's make two figures out of the clay.

Make one of you and make one of me,

Make them as lifelike as they can be.

Break them and mix them and make them anew,

A figure of me and a figure of you.

Then I'll have something of you in me,

And something of me in you there'll be."

When the figures are finished, Hsiang-hsiang says,

"Come back, love, to see me in a few days."

四

屈原(第二幕)①

楚宫内廷。

正面四大圆柱并列,中为明堂内室,左右有房,房前各有阶,右为宾阶,左为阼阶。室后壁有奇古之壁画。左右房与室之间及前侧二面均垂帘幕,可透视,房之后壁正中有门,门上有金兽含环,门及壁上均有彩画。(此在南面,柱用深红色,帘幕用黄色。)

右翼为总章内室之右房,亦有阶有柱有帘有壁画等事,与正面同。(此在正西面,柱色同,帘幕用白色。)

左翼为青阳内室之左房,布置同。(此在正东面,柱色同,帘幕用青色。)

正前隙地为中霤。正中及左右建构不相衔接,其间有侧道可通中霤。

明堂内室中设有王位,较高大,左右两侧各设一位。

幕开,南后郑袖立正中阶上指挥女史数人在室中布置。于王位面以虎皮,其前亦以虎皮席地。于左右位面以豹皮,其前亦以豹皮席地。另有女史数人在左右房中拂拭编钟编磬琴瑟等陈设。

南后年三十四五,美艳而矫健。俟布置停当后,略加巡视,表示满意。

① 中文选自:郭沫若. 屈原. 北京:人民出版社,1953.
英译文选自:Kuo Mo-jo. *Chu Yuan*. Yang Xianyi & Gladys Yang. Trans. Beijing:Foreign Languages Press,1978.

后： 你们倒还敏捷。我还怕你们来不及啦，现在算好，一切都停当了。

女甲： 启禀南后，那前面两房的帘幕，是不是就揭开来？

后： 不，那等开筵之后再行揭开。歌舞的人都已经准备停当了吧？

女乙： 都早已准备停当了，西边是准备唱歌的，东边是准备跳舞的。

后： 那很好，还要叫他们注意一下，不要耽误了时刻，不要弄乱了次序。

女等： 是，我们一定要严格地督率着他们。

后： 我看，你们应该把职守分一下才好。（指女史甲）你管堂上奏乐和行酒的事。（指女史乙）你管堂下歌舞的事。你们两个各自选几个得力的人做帮手。今天的事情假使办得很好，我一定要赏你们的。假使办得不好，那你们可晓得我的脾气！

女等：（表示惶恐，但亦显得光耀）是，我们一定要尽我们的全力办理。

后： 要能够那样，就好。此外一些琐碎的事用不着我吩咐了，你们都是有经验的。总之要能够临机应变，一呼百诺，说要什么就有什么。在预定的节目内的，固然要准备，就是在预定的节目外的，也要有见机的准备。国王的脾气你们也是很清楚的！万一有什么差池，责任是要落在你们的头上。

女等： 是，我们知道。

后： 好的，那么你们可以下去了，假使上官大夫到了，赶紧把他引到这儿来，说我在等他。

女等：（应命）是。（分别由左右阶下堂，再行鞠躬，复向左右首侧道下场。）

　　　　南后一人由阼阶下堂，在中雷中来回踯躅，若有所思。有间，女史甲引靳尚由左翼侧道上。靳尚是一位瘦削的中年人，鹰鼻鹞眼，两颊洼陷，行动颇敏捷。

女甲： 启禀南后，上官大夫到了。

　　　　南后回顾，靳尚趋前行礼。

靳： 敬请南后早安！

后：（略略答礼，向女史甲）你可以下去。

　　　　女史甲应命，鞠躬由原道下。

后：(登上右翼总章右房之阶段上)上官大夫,我昨天晚上托你的事情,怎么样了?

靳：启禀南后,我是早就应该来禀报的。昨天晚上太迟,今天清早又奉了命令要准备中午的宴会,竟抽不出时间来。刚才国王出宫外去了,我疑心他是去找三闾大夫,所以我特地跑到屈原那里去探望了一下。好在国王并不在那儿,恐怕是到令尹子椒那里去了!

后：(略有愠色)你怎这样的啰唆! 我是在问你昨天晚上去会张仪的事情啦!

靳：是的,南后,你听我慢慢地向你陈述吧。我跑到屈原那里去,是怕国王到了他那里,又受了他一番鼓吹。国王如果要他今天中午来陪客,那事情就不大好办。好在我跑去看,国王并不在他那儿,我是刚从那儿跑回来的。我想国王一定是到令尹子椒那里去了。要那样就毫无问题,即使国王要叫令尹子椒来陪客,也是很好商量的。令尹子椒,那位昏庸老朽,简直是活宝贝啦……

后：哎,你赶快把我所问的事直截了当地回答吧,你到底要兜好多圈子!

靳：是,是,很快就要说到本题了。因为事体很复杂,也很要紧,要慢慢把头绪理清楚,说来才不费事。南后,慢工出细活啦。

后：(生气,愈着急)哎,我看你这个人的话,真是大牯牛的口水,太长!

靳：(故意,略呈惶恐)是,是,是,我就说到本题了。(向四下回顾了一下,把声音放低了些)我昨天晚上到张仪那里去,我把南后送给他的礼物,亲手交给了他。我说:"阁下,南后命我来向阁下问安,送了这点菲薄的礼物,以备阁下和阁下的舍人们回魏国去的路费,真是菲薄得很,希望阁下笑纳。……"

后：你不必把我当成张仪,不要这样重皮叠髓地说! 张仪到底表示了些什么态度?

靳：张仪的态度吗? 是,我看他接受了你的礼物,他很高兴。他说:"请你回去禀报南后,我张仪实在是万分感激。这次由秦国来,没有多带盘费,舍人们的衣冠都破烂了,简直不能成个体统,得到南后这般的厚爱,实在是万分感激。望你多多在南后面前为我致谢。……"

后：哎呀呀,你又把你自己当成张仪了,真是糟糕！到底张仪对于我所要
求的事,他表示了什么意见？

靳：他表示了很多意见啦,南后,你听我说吧。我对他说："南后问你是不
是很快地便要到魏国去？"他说："是呀。"我又说："南后听说你到魏国
去,有意思替敝国的国王,选些周郑的美女回来,南后是非常感激
的。"……

后：我怎么会感激？谁要你这样对他说？

靳：唉,南后,你怎得聪明一世……唉,不好说得。

后：你说我"糊涂一时"吧！我没有你糊涂！

靳：你想,我在张仪面前,怎好直说出你不高兴？你从前对待魏美人的办
法,我是记得的,你恕我再唠叨一下吧。从前我们的国王有一次喜欢
那位魏国送来的美人,你对她也不表示你的嫉妒,反而特别加以优
待,显示得你比国王还要喜欢她。因此国王也照常的喜欢你,说你丝
毫也不嫉妒。后来你就对那位魏美人说："国王什么都喜欢你,只是
不喜欢你的鼻子。你以后见国王的时候,最好把鼻子掩着。"那魏美
人公然也就听了你的话。到后来国王问你："那魏美人见了我为什么
一定要掩着鼻子？"你就说："她是嫌国王有股臭气。"这样就使得我们
的国王把那魏美人的鼻子给割掉了。你那个办法是多么精明呀！

后：哼,谁要你来恭维！我现在的年纪已经不比当年了,我急于要知道张
仪的态度,而且急于要想方法来挽救,你偏偏在那儿兜圈子。你是有
意和我作弄吗？

靳：南后,你用不着那么着急,事情已经有了把握,所以我才这样按部就
班地告诉你。假使没有把握,我实在是比你还要着急呢。

后：哼,你讲,你究竟有什么把握？你讲！你直截了当地讲！

靳：那张仪毕竟是个聪明人,他经我那么一提,倒有点出乎意外。他问
我："那真是南后的意思吗？"我说："南后确实是那样告诉我的,大概
总不会是假的吧。"他踌躇了好一会儿,接着又说:他往魏国倒并不是

本意。因为他从秦国带来的要求,国王不肯接受:国王不肯和齐国绝
交,不肯接受秦国的土地,他就没有面目再回到秦国去,所以也就只
得跑回魏国了。(稍停)他就这样把他的真心话说了出来,所以这个
问题据我看来,倒不在乎他到不到魏国去找中原的美人,而是我们要
设法使他能够回到秦国。

后： 你反正还是啰唆,这算得有什么把握呢? 国王已经听信了屈原的话,
要和齐国重申和亲的盟约,已经叫你们在草拟国书了。而且国王回
头就要给张仪饯行送他回到魏国,你有什么把握能够使他回到秦
国呢?

靳： 把握是有的。我们所当争取的也就是这个中午了。我同张仪商量过
一下,我们的意见是应该就在这短期间之内打破国王对于屈原的信
用! (口舌带着热情地流利了起来)这件事情,须得我同你两个内外
夹攻。国王的性情和脾味我们是摸得很熟的。我自己是早有成竹在
胸,不过在你这一方面,要望你把你的聪明多多发挥一下啦!

后： (呈出适意的神气)哼,你有什么成竹在胸,你不妨讲给我听听。(步
下阶来)

靳： 南后,我希望你把耳朵借给我。

　　　　　南后以耳就靳尚,靳尚与之低语有间。

后： (略略摇首)可是,你这把握,并不十分可靠。

靳： 所以要希望你后援啦。

后： 哼,我老实告诉你,我也早就有我的把握的。我所关心的就是张仪的
态度。只要他和我们扣在一起,有心回秦国,那问题就好解决了。

靳： 是,南后,你的把握,好不也让我知道一些?

后： 那可不必。"机事不密则害成",你回头慢慢看好了。三闾大夫是很
快就会到我这儿来的。

靳： (惊异)怎么? 屈原会到这儿来?

后： 是的,我叫子兰去请他去了,他是一定会来的。

靳： (狐疑地)那么,南后,我简直不明白你的意思了。

后： 我的意思,我也并不想要你明白。我认真告诉你:国王确实是到令尹子椒那里去了。去的时候我同他说过,回头我要派你去请他回来。你到子椒那里,一方面也正好趁着机会,把你想要说的话对他说。你等子兰回来,便可以走了。(突生警觉)外面已经有人的脚步声,你留意听。(又低声补说)还有,你引国王回来的时候从那边进来,(指着左翼)一定要叫两名女官先把门打开,再揭开帘幕,转身下去,你们再走进来。千万照着我所吩咐的做,不准有误。

　　　　靳尚点头,二人缄默倾听,向左翼侧道方面注视。

屈： (在内)子兰,南后是在什么地方等我?

兰： (同)妈说,在青阳内室呢,你跟定我来吧。

　　　　二人由左翼侧道出场。见南后,即远远伫立。

兰： 妈,我把三闾大夫请来了。

后： (呈出极喜悦的面容,向屈原迎去)啊,三闾大夫,你来得真好。我等了你好一会儿了。

屈： (敬礼)敬请南后早安,南后有什么事需要我?

后： 大大地需要你帮忙啦。国王听信了你的话,不和齐国绝交,张仪是决心回魏国去了。回头国王要替他饯行,我们准备了一些歌舞来助兴,这是非请你来指示不可的。我们慢慢商量吧。(回向靳尚)上官大夫,你的任务,主要是在外面周旋,你须得叫膳夫庖人作好好的准备。说不定国王还要歃血为盟呢,珠盘玉敦的准备也是不可少的。

靳： (鞠躬)是,我一定要样样都准备得很周到。我便先行告退。(向南后行礼,又向屈原略略拱手)三闾大夫,我刚才到你府上去来。

屈： (还礼)遗憾,有失迎迓。

靳： 你那可爱的婵娟姑娘把我的话告诉了你吗?

屈： 婵娟已经传达了,谢谢你。

后： (向子兰)子兰,你去把那扮演《九歌》的十位舞师给我叫到这儿来,要他们通统都装扮好。

兰： 知道了,妈。

　　向南后及屈原打拱,随靳尚由右翼侧道下。

后：(向屈原)三闾大夫,你听我说。我这个孩子真是难养呢,左脚不方便,身体又衰弱,稍一不注意便要生出毛病。这一向又病了几天,先生那儿的功课又荒废了好久啦。

屈：那是不要紧的。公子子兰很聪明,只要身体健康,随后慢慢学都可以学得来。

后：做母亲的人一般总是抱着过高过大的希望,一面要孩子的身体好,一面又要孩子的学问好。不过有时候这两件事情实在也难得兼顾。所以我在一般人看来,恐怕对于我的孩子不免有点娇养吧? 好在先生是他的老师,有你这样一位好老师,他将来一定可以成器。

屈：多承南后的奖励。子兰公子,我是把他当成兄弟一样在看待,我只希望他身体健康,心神愉快,将来能够更加用功。我自己是要尽自己的全力来帮助他的。

后：多谢你啦,三闾大夫,那孩子真真是幸福,得到你这样一位道德文章冠冕天下的人做他的老师。事实上连我做母亲的人也真真感觉着幸福呢。

屈：多承南后的奖励。

后：子兰的父亲也时常在说,我们楚国产生了你这样一位顶天立地的人物,真真是列祖列宗的功德啊。

屈：(愈益恭谨)臣下敢当不起,敢当不起!

后：屈原先生,你实在用不着客气,现在无论是南国北国,关东关西,哪里还找得到第二个像你这样的人呢? 文章又好,道德又高,又有才能,又有操守,我想无论哪一国的君长怕都愿意你做他的宰相,无论哪一位少年怕都愿意你做他的老师,而且无论哪一位年青的女子怕都愿意你做她的丈夫啦。

屈：(有些惶惑)南后,我实在有点惶恐。我要冒昧地请求南后的意旨,你此刻要我来,究竟要我做些什么事?

后：啊,我太兴奋了,你怕嫌我过于唠叨了吧? 我请你来,刚才已经说过,就是为了歌舞的事情。我是已经叫他们把你的《九歌》拿来歌舞的。经你改编过的那些歌辞,实在是很优美。我是这样布置的,你看怎么样呢?(指点)在那明堂内室的左右二房里面陈列乐器,让乐师们在那儿奏乐。唱歌的就在这西边的总章右房,跳神的就从那东边的青阳左房出现。单独的跳舞在房中各舞一遍,一共十遍;最后的轮回舞在这中霤跳舞,把《礼魂》那首歌反复歌唱,唱到适度为止。你觉得这办法好不好呢?

屈:　那是再好也没有。

　　　　南后与屈原对话中,子兰引舞者十人由右翼侧道登场。舞者均奇装异服,头戴面具,与青海人跳神情景相仿佛。舞者第一人为东皇太一,男像,面色青,极猛恶,右手执长剑,左手持爵。第二人为云中君,女像,面色银灰,星眼,衣饰极华丽,左手执日,右手执月。第三人为湘君,女像,面白,眼极细,周身多以花草为饰,两手捧笙。第四人为湘夫人,女像,面色绿,余与湘君相似,手执排箫。第五人为大司命,男像,面色黑,头有角,手执青铜镜。第六人为少司命,女像,面色粉红,手执扫帚,司情爱之神也。第七人为东君,太阳神,男像,面色赤,手执弓矢,青衣白裳。第八人为河伯,男像,面色黄,手执鱼。第九人为山鬼,女像,面色蓝,手执桂枝。第十人为国殇,男像,面色紫,手执干戈,身披甲。十人步至明堂内室前,整列阶下,身转向外。

兰:　(俟南后与屈原对话告一段落)妈,这十个人我把他们引来了。

后:　好的。(略作考虑)我看索性叫那些唱歌的,奏乐的,也通统就位,预先来演习一遍。三闾大夫,你觉得怎样?

屈:　那是很好的,待我下去吩咐女官们,叫她们就位好了。

后:　(急忙拦住他)不,不好要你去。子兰,你去好了。还要叫没有职务的女官们都不准进来!你也不准进来了!

屈:　子兰走路太辛苦……

　　　　但屈原话犹未说完时,子兰已跛着由右首侧道跑下。

后:　小孩子还是让他勤劳一下的好,这不是你素常的教条吗?(回顾十人)我看,你们坐下去好了,站着不大美观。本来是要让你们由那东边的青阳左房出场的,你们现在已经出来了,就坐在那儿好了。(十人坐下)每一个人的独舞是要在房中跳舞的,时间不够,我看就只跳那最后的一轮合舞好了。(又回顾屈原)三闾大夫,你觉得怎样?

屈：那样要好些,的确时间是不够了。

后：是的,国王恐怕也快回来了。他是到令尹子椒家里去了。你是知道他的,他平常每每喜欢做些出其不意的事。有好些回等你苦心孤诣的把什么都准备周到了,他会突然中止。但有时在你毫无准备的时候,他又会突然要你搞些什么。真是弄得你星急火急。我看他的毛病就是太随自己高兴,不替别人着想。就说今天的宴会吧,也是昨晚上才说起的。说要就要,一点也不能转移。你看,这教人吃苦不吃苦?

屈：南后,你实在太辛苦了。我在家里丝毫风声也不知道。刚才上官大夫到我家里来,才把消息传到了。我丝毫也没有出点力,心里很惶恐。

后：三闾大夫,你不必那样客气啦。我本来也想早些通知你的,请你来指导我们。不过我又想这样琐碎的事情不好来麻烦你。你们做诗的人,我自信是能够了解的,精神要愈恬淡,就愈好。你说是不是?

屈：有时候呢——(想说"有时候是这样,"但未说完。)

后：所以我决心不想麻烦你。我想到你的《九歌》,那调子是多么的活泼,多么的轻松,多么的愉快,多么的娓婉呀!那里面有好些辞句是多么的芬芳,多么的甜蜜,多么的优美,多么的动人呀!我想你做出了那样的好诗,一定是很高兴的。你使我们大家都高兴了,我们也应该使你更加高兴一下。因此我也就决心自己亲自来编排一次,让你看看你所给予我们的快乐是多么的大呀。

屈：啊,南后,你实在是太使我感激了。你请让我冒昧地说几句话吧:我有好些诗,其实是你给我的。南后,你有好些地方值得我们赞美,你有好些地方使我们男子有愧须眉。我是常常得到这些感觉,而且把这些感觉化成了诗的。我的诗假使还有些可取的地方,容恕我冒昧吧,南后,多是你给我的!

后:(表示极其喜悦的情形)哦,真是那样吗? 我真高兴,我真幸福,我真感激你啦! 不过我自己是明白的,你不一定完全满意我。像我这样的人,你怕感觉着不太纯真,不太素朴,不太悠闲贞静吧? 是不是?

屈:(踌躇着苦于回答)……

后:你不说,你的心我也是知道的。不过这是我的性格。我喜欢繁华,我喜欢热闹,我的好胜心很强,我也很能够嫉妒,于我的幸福安全有妨害的人,我一定要和他们争,不是牺牲我自己的生命,便是牺牲他的生命。这,便是我自己的性格。(略停)三闾大夫,你怕会觉得我是太自私了吧?

屈:(仍苦于回答)……

后:我看你不要想什么话来答复我吧,你不答复我,我是最满意的。你的性格,认真说,也有好些地方和我相同,你是不愿意在世间上作第二等人的。是不是? (略停)就说你的诗,也不比一般诗人的那样简单,你是有深度,有广度。你是洞庭湖,你是长江,你是东海,你不是一条小小的山溪水,你不是一个人造的池水啦。你看,我这些话是不是把你说准确了?

屈:(颇觉不安)南后,我实在不知道怎样回答你的好。不过我自己的缺点很多,我是知道的,我是很想尽量地减少自己的缺点。

后:也好。或许你能够甘于寂寞,但我是不能够甘于寂寞的。我要多开花,我要多发些枝叶,我要多多占领阳光,小草小花就让它在我脚下阴死,我也并不怜悯。这或许是我们的性格不同的地方吧。(在二人对话之中,唱歌及奏乐者已全部由内门入房就位,透过帘幕,隐约可见。至此南后始转过意念)哦,这样的话说得太多了,歌舞的人都已经准备停当了,三闾大夫,我看我们就叫他们开始跳神吧。

屈:好的,就让他们跳《礼魂》。

后:(向房中奏乐及歌唱者)你们听见了吧,要你们试奏《礼魂》之歌。(又向舞者)你们可以站起来了。等我站到明堂的台阶上去,用手给你们一挥,你们的歌、乐、舞三种便一齐开始。要你们停止的时候也是这样。(向屈原)三闾大夫,我们上阶去。

南后先由西阶(右首宾阶)上,屈原改由东阶(左首阼阶)上,相会于正中之阶上。舞者十人前进至舞台前,向后转。房中人均整饬作准备,注视南后。

南后将左手高举,一挥,于是歌舞乐一齐动作。舞者在中雷成圆形旋转,渐集拢,又渐散开。歌者在房中反复歌《礼魂》之歌。

唱着歌,打着鼓,

手拿着花枝齐跳舞。

我把花给你,你把花给我,

心爱的人儿,歌舞两婆娑。

春天有兰花,秋天有菊花,

馨香百代,敬礼无涯。

歌舞中左侧青阳左房之正中后门被推开,女官甲、乙走出,将房前帘幕向左右分揭套于柱上。对歌舞若无闻见者然,复由后门退下。

南后复将左手高举,一挥,歌舞乐三者一齐停止。

后:啊,我头晕,我要倒。(作欲倒状)三闾大夫,三闾大夫,你快,你快……(倒入屈原怀中。)

屈:(因事起仓促,且左右无人,亦急将南后扶抱)……

楚王偕张仪、子椒、上官大夫出现于青阳左房,诸人已见屈原扶抱南后在怀,但屈原未觉,欲将南后挽至室中之座位。

后:(口中不断高呼)三闾大夫,三闾大夫,你快,你快……(及见楚王已见此情景,乃忽翻身用力挣脱)你快放手!你太出乎我的意外了!你这是怎样的行为!啊,太使我出乎意外了!太使我出乎意外了!(飞奔向楚王跑去)

屈原一时茫然,不知所措。

楚王及余人由东房急骤下阶,迎接南后。南后由左阶奔下,投入楚王怀抱。

后： 太出乎我的意外了！ 太出乎我的意外了！

王： 你把心放宽些,不要怕！ 郑袖呀！

后： 啊,幸亏你回来得恰好,不然是太危险了！ 我想三闾大夫怕是发了疯吧？ 他在大庭广众之中,便做出那样失礼的举动！

屈： (此时始感觉受欺,略含怒意地)南后,你,你,你怎么……

王： (大怒)疯子！ 狂妄的人！ 我不准你再说话！

屈： (怒形于色,无言)……

后： (气稍放平)啊,我真没有料到,在这样大庭广众当中,而且三闾大夫素来是我所钦佩的有道德的人。

王： (拥扶着南后)你再放宽心些,用不着害怕,用不着害怕。

楚怀王扶南后上阼阶,余人亦随后上阶。

屈： (见楚怀王走近身来,拱手敬礼)大王,请容许我申诉！

王： (傲然地)我不能再容许你狂妄！ 唬,你这人真也出乎我的意外！ 我是把你当成为一位顶天立地之人,原来你就是这样顶天立地的！ 你在人前夸大嘴,说我怎样的好大喜功,变换无常,我都可以容恕你。你说楚国的大事大计,法令规章,都出于你一人之手,我都可以容恕你。你说别人都是谗谄奸佞,只有你一个人是忠心耿耿,我都可以容恕你。但你在大庭广众之中,在我和外宾的面前,对于南后竟做出这样狂妄滔天的举动,我怎么也不能容恕！

屈： (毅然)大王,这是诬陷！

王： (愈怒)诬陷？ 我诬陷你？ 南后她诬陷你？ 我还能够相信得过我自己的眼睛啦。假使方才不是我自己亲眼看见,我也不敢相信。哼,你简直是疯子,简直是疯子！ 我从前误听了你许多话,幸好算把你发觉得早。你以后永远不准到我宫廷里来,永远不准和我见面！

屈： (沉着而沉痛地)大王,我可以不再到你宫廷里来,也可以不再和你见面。但你以前听信了我的话一点也没有错。你要多替楚国的老百姓设想,多替中国的老百姓设想。老百姓都想过人的生活,老百姓都希望中国结束分裂的局面,形成大一统的山河。你听信了我的话,爱护老百姓,和关东诸国和亲,你是一点也没有错。你如果照着这样继续下去,中国的大一统是会在你的手里完成的。

　　楚怀王屡欲爆发,但被南后从旁制止。

　　南后、张仪及余人均采取冷笑态度。

屈：(愈益沉痛)但你假如要受别人的欺骗,那你便要成为楚国的罪人。

王：(怒不可遏)简直是一片疯话!……这……这……这……

后：(从旁制止)你让他把疯话说够吧。

屈：(同前)你假如要受别人的欺骗,一场悲惨的前景就会呈现在你的面前。你的宫廷会成为别国的兵营,你的王冠会戴在别人的马头上。楚国的男男女女会大遭杀戮,血水要把大江染红。你和南后都要受到不能想像的最大耻辱。……

王：(暴怒至不能言)这……这……这……

后：(奚落地)南国的圣人,不能再让你这样疯狂下去了。(回顾令尹子椒及靳尚)你们两人把他监督着带下去,不然他在宫廷里面不知道还要闹出什么乱子。

王：(怒不可遏)把他的左徒官职给免掉!

椒：(鞠躬)是。

靳：(同时)我们遵命。

　　二人上前挟持屈原。

屈：(愤恨地)唉,南后!我真没有想出你会这样的陷害我!皇天在上,后土在下,先王先公,列祖列宗,你陷害了的不是我,是我们整个儿的楚国呵!(被挟持至西阶,将由右翼侧道下场,仍亢声斥责)我是问心无愧,我是视死如归,曲直忠邪,自有千秋的判断。你陷害了的不是我,是你自己,是我们的国王,是我们的楚国,是我们整个儿的赤县神州呀!……

后：(闻屈原言为之切齿,似恨复似畏)……

王：唉，简直是发了疯，简直是发了疯。（扶南后坐左席）你不用害怕，好生休息一下。

后：（振作了起来）不，大王。我并不怕他，我怕的是对于张仪先生太失礼了。

王：（此时仿佛才忽然记起张仪在自己身边）啊，是的，张先生，真是太失礼了。请坐，请坐。（肃张仪就右席。）

张：（拱手谦让）岂敢，岂敢。

   张仪就座，楚怀王亦就正中座位。

张：请恕客臣冒昧，这位高贵的人就是南后郑袖吗？（对郑袖作拱手状。）

王：（忙作介绍）呵，是的，是的，这就是我的爱妃郑袖。（向南后）这位就是秦国的丞相张仪先生啦。我们在子椒那里碰了头，所以便把他拉来了。

   二人相互目礼。

张：我今天第一次拜见了南后，要请南后和大王再恕客臣的冒昧，我才明白——（欲语，但又踌躇。）

后：张仪先生，你有什么话就请不客气的说吧，反正我是南国的女人，不懂中原的礼节的。

张：（再作道歉状）要请恕我的冒昧，我今天拜见了南后，我才明白——屈原为什么要发疯了。

王：（大喜，狂笑）呵，哈哈哈……真会说话，真会说话。

后：（微笑）张仪先生，你真是善于辞令。

张：真的，客臣走过了不少的地方，凡是南国北国，关东关西，我们中国的地方差不多都走遍了。而且也过过各种各样的生活，以一介的寒士做到一国的丞相，公卿大夫，农工商贾，皂隶台舆，蛮夷戎狄，什么样的人差不多我都看过了。但要再请恕臣的冒昧。（又作一次道歉状）我实在没有看见过，南后，你这样美貌的人呵！

王：（愈见高兴）呵，哈哈哈……我原说过，天地间实在是不会有第二个的。

张：没有，没有，实在没有。

王：昨天你还在替中原的女子鼓吹，你不是说"周郑之女，粉白黛黑，立于街衢,见者人以为神"吗?

张：唉,那是客臣的井蛙之见喽,所谓"情人眼里出西施"啦。我自己是周郑之间的人,我所见到的多是周郑之间的女子,可我今天是开了眼界了。(又向南后告罪)南后,请你再再恕我的冒昧,你怕是真正的巫山神女下凡吧?

后：(微笑)张仪先生,你真是善于辞令。

王：好了,好了,你们两位不必再互相标榜了。(起立,执张仪手一同起立)总之,张仪先生,我很佩服你。你说凡是一口仁义道德的人,都是些伪君子,真是一点也不错。我看你是用不着到魏国去了,我也不希望你去给我找什么美人。我是不再听那个疯子屈原的话了,你能够使秦王听信你的话,对于我特别表示尊敬,我很满意。我一定要和齐国绝交,要同秦国联合起来,接受秦国商於之地六百里。

张：那真是秦楚两国的万幸!

王：(又至南后前执其手,使之起立)今天你实在是辛苦了。疯子屈原做的东西,我现在再也不能忍耐。今天的跳神可以作罢。(稍停又一转念)就是今天的宴会也可以作罢。我们同张仪先生此刻到东门外去散步,也不要车马,我们到东皇太一庙去用中饭,那倒是蛮好玩儿的。(回向张仪)好,张仪先生我们就走吧。这些鬼鬼怪怪的东西(指中雷中之跳神者,因未奉命不能退场,只三三两两或坐或立,散布于庭中。东皇太一与云中君坐东房阶上,山鬼立于其侧。大司命与少司命坐西房阶上,国殇立于其侧。东君与河伯倚东房之柱而立。湘君与湘夫人倚西房之柱而立)就尽他们来收拾好了。

　　　　三人行至阶前。

　　　　令尹子椒与靳尚复由右首出场,在阶下向楚怀王敬礼。

椒：启禀大王,屈原已经解除了他的职位。放他走了。

靳：他走的时候仍然叫不绝口,把冠带衣裳通统当众撕毁了。

王：(复厉声大怒)哦,真是疯子!你们把这些鬼鬼怪怪的东西,通统给我撤消下去!

Chu Yuan (Act II)

SCENE: *The palace court. In front are four huge, parallel pillars; in the centre is the inner chamber, flanked by chambers on each side, with steps leading to them. Behind, on the wall are curious and ancient frescoes, and on both sides between the chambers hang transparent curtains. There is a door in the centre of the back wall on which is a golden animal face with a ring in its mouth. There are also bright paintings on the doors and on the walls. (This is the south side: the pillars are red and the curtains yellow.)*

On the right is the right chamber, decorated as is the front, with staircases, pillars, curtains and frescoes. (This is the west side: the pillars are red and the curtains white.)

On the left is the left chamber, similarly decorated. (This is the east side: the pillars are red and the curtains green.)

The court is in front, while the structures in the centre and those on the left and right are not connected, but have corridors leading to the court in the centre.

At the back of the stage is the king's throne, of considerable height and size, with a seat on each side.

When the curtain rises Queen Cheng Hsiu is standing on the middle steps watching her maids as they prepare the court. They spread a tiger-skin on the king's throne and tiger-skins on the ground before it, placing leopard-skins on the left and right seats, and leopard-skins on the floor before them.

There are also maids in the left and right chambers, polishing bells, cymbals, harps and lyres.

The queen is about thirty-four or thirty-five, beautiful and nimble in movement. When the maids have finished their work she looks over it, and appears satisfied.

QUEEN: You have been quite quick. I was afraid you would not be in time, but now it is all right; everything is ready.

ONE MAID: If it please Your Majesty, shall we draw the curtain of the two chambers?

QUEEN: No, wait until the feast has started. Are all the singers and dancers ready?

ANOTHER MAID: They are all ready. The singers are waiting on the west side and the dancers on the east.

QUEEN: Very good. Let them take care not to come late or miss their cues.

BOTH MAIDS: Yes, we shall be sure to watch them carefully.

QUEEN: Let me see, I think you should divide your duties. You (*pointing to one maid*), look after the music in the hall, and the serving of wine. You (*pointing to the other maid*), look after the singing and dancing at the foot of the steps. Each of you choose some reliable people to help you. If you make everything go very smoothly today, I shall certainly reward you; but if you do badly, then you know my temper!

BOTH MAIDS (*looking frightened and yet pleased*): Yes, we shall do our best.

QUEEN: In that case all will be well. As for the details, you don't need me to instruct you; you are both experienced. On the whole you just want to suit your actions to the occasion, and be ready when I call. Of course, you will have to prepare the programme which has been decided on, but you should also be ready to meet any occasion that arises outside the fixed programme. You know the king's temper well enough! Should anything go wrong, the blame will fall on your heads.

BOTH MAIDS: Yes, we know.

QUEEN: Very well then, you may go. If the minister Chin Shang comes, bring him here at once, and say that I am waiting for him.

BOTH MAIDS: Yes.

(*They leave the court by the right and left-hand steps, bow and exeunt by the corridors on either side. The queen herself descends from the court by the left-hand steps and walks about in the centre court, deep in thought. Presently a maid leads in Chin Shang from the passage on the left side. Chin Shang is a lean, middle-aged man, with hooked nose, sunken cheeks and deep-set eyes. He moves quickly and lightly.*)

MAID: Your Majesty, the minister Chin Shang is here.

(*The queen looks round. Chin Shang advances and bows.*)

CHIN SHANG: Is Your Majesty well?

QUEEN (*inclines her head slightly. To the maid*): You may go. (*The maid assents, bows and leaves by the same passage. The queen ascends the steps of the right-hand chamber.*) My lord, what of the business I entrusted to you last night?

CHIN SHANG: If it please Your Majesty I should have come earlier to report, but it was too late last night, and this morning I had orders to prepare for the feast at noon. Also just now when the king went out of the palace I suspected that he had gone to see Chu Yuan, so I went there specially to find out. The king was not there, however. He had probably gone to see Counsellor Tze Chiao.

QUEEN (*slightly annoyed*): How long-winded you are. I was asking you about your interview with Chang Yi last night.

CHIN SHANG: Yes, Your Majesty, let me tell you in detail. The reason that I went to see Chu Yuan was because I was afraid that the king might have gone there and been influenced by him again, and I feared the king might ask him to the feast today at noon, for that would make things very difficult. However, when I went there the king was not there. I have just hurried back from there, and I suppose the king must have gone to the counsellor's house, in which case all will be well. For even if the king asks the counsellor to come to the feast, we shall have no trouble. The counsellor is a complete fool.

QUEEN: Well, quickly, tell me straight out what I asked you. How many other digressions are you going to make?

CHIN SHANG: Yes, yes, I am just coming to the point. It is because this is extremely complicated and at the same time extremely important that we must unravel it slowly, for then it will be easy to explain. Your Majesty, a slow artisan produces skilled work.

QUEEN (*angry and impatient*): Ah! Your words are like the slobber of a buffalo — too long!

CHIN SHANG (*pretending to be a little alarmed*): Yes, yes, I am coming to the point. (*Looking round and lowering his voice.*) Last night I called on Chang Yi. I presented in person the presents Your Majesty gave me, and I said, "Sir, the queen asked me to send her best regards to you, together with this very humble gift, in order to help towards such expenditure as you and your retinue may incur on your journey to the land of Wei. It is very little, but I hope that you will deign to accept it."

QUEEN: There's no need to take me as Chang Yi; no need to go over all that again. What was Chang Yi's attitude?

CHIN SHANG: Chang Yi's attitude? Oh, yes, I believe when he received the presents you sent him, he was very pleased. He said, "Please inform the queen that I am extremely grateful, the more so since I come from the state of Chin, with scant travelling expenses, and my followers' shabby clothes present a very poor appearance. I am indeed most grateful for Her Majesty's munificence. Please express my humble thanks to the queen ..."

QUEEN: Really, now you are taking Chang Yi's part. This is too stupid. What was Chang Yi's actual reaction to my request?

CHIN SHANG: His reaction was most complex, Your Majesty, if you will just listen. I said to him, "The queen asks if you are going to the state of Wei soon." And he said, "Oh, yes." Then I said again, "The queen heard that when you go to the state of Wei you intend to choose some beautiful girls for our king, and the queen is most grateful to you ..."

QUEEN: Why should I be grateful? Who told you to say that?

CHIN SHANG: Ah, Your Majesty, how is it that sometimes you are so clever — well. I had better say no more.

QUEEN: I suppose you mean that now I am stupid? I am not so stupid as you are.

CHIN SHANG: Just consider, how could I say frankly to Chang Yi that you were displeased? I still remember how you treated that last girl from the land of Wei, if you will excuse my mentioning it again. There was a time when the king favoured the girl sent by the state of Wei, and you, instead of expressing your jealousy, went out of your way to be kind to her, so that it seemed as if you liked her better than the king. Therefore the king remained fond of you and praised you, saying that you were not in the least jealous. Then you said to that girl, "The king likes everything about you except your nose. In future when you see the king, you had better cover your nose." And the girl took your advice. Later the king asked you, "Why must that girl cover her nose when she sees me?" You said, "She imagines that Your Majesty smells." So the king cut off the girl's nose. That was a very clever plan!

QUEEN: Who wants your flattery? I am not so young now, and I am impatient to know Chang Yi's reaction, and to find a way to meet it; but you are deliberately talking in circles. Are you trying to make a fool of me?

CHIN SHANG: Your Majesty, don't be so impatient. Everything is all right. That is why I am telling you in the proper order. If it were not so, I should be more impatient than you are.

QUEEN: Well, go on. What do you mean by all right? Speak up! Give me a direct answer.

CHIN SHANG: Chang Yi is a clever man. After my hint he was surprised, and he asked me, "Is that really the queen's opinion?" I said, "The queen told me so, so it probably is." He hesitated for some time, and then he told me he had not originally intended to go to the state of Wei, but as the king would not accept the proposals he brought from the state of Chin, and would not sever relations with the state of Chi in return for the land ceded by the state of Chin, then he had no face to go back to the state of Chin but must go to the state of Wei. (*Pause.*) Thus he told me the truth. So the problem, from our point of view, is not whether he will go to the state of Wei or not, to look for a beautiful girl, but how we can make him go back to the state of Chin.

QUEEN: You are still talking too much. How is that all right? The king has taken Chu Yuan's advice and means to renew the friendly alliance with the state of Chi; he has been asking you to write the request, and he is just about to give Chang Yi a farewell feast before seeing him off to the state of Wei. Then how can you make him go back to the state of Chin?

CHIN SHANG: It is all right; our task is at noon today. I have talked it over with Chang Yi, and it is our opinion that in this short time we must discredit Chu Yuan in the eyes of the king. (*Speaking more vehemently.*) In this matter you and I must cooperate. We are familiar with the king's nature and temperament. I have a plan in mind, but you on your side must see to it that you display all your cunning.

QUEEN (*appearing pleased*): Well, what is the plan you have in mind? You may as well let me know. (*Walks down the steps.*)

CHIN SHANG: Your Majesty, listen to me.

(*The queen inclines her head towards Chin Shang, who whispers in her ear.*)

QUEEN (*shaking her head dubiously*): But this plan of yours is not absolutely reliable.

CHIN SHANG: That is why I want your help.

QUEEN: Well, to tell you the truth, I have my own plan. What concerns me is Chang Yi's attitude. Provided he is on our side and wants to go back to the state of Chin, the problem will be simple.

CHIN SHANG: Yes. Your Majesty. Won't you tell me something of your plan?

QUEEN: Better not. "Without secrecy, a plan will fail." Just wait and see. Chu Yuan is coming here presently.

CHIN SHANG (*surprised*): What? Is Chu Yuan coming here?

QUEEN: Yes, I have sent Tze Lan to invite him; he will certainly come.

CHIN SHANG (*dubiously*): In that case, Your Majesty, I am at a loss to understand you.

QUEEN: I don't want you to understand. To tell you the truth, the king has indeed gone to see Counsellor Tze Chiao. When he went, I told him that later I would send you to invite him back. When you go to the counsellor's house, you can also take the opportunity to tell him what you wanted to tell him. As soon as Tze Lan comes back you can go. (*Suddenly cautious.*) There is somebody outside. Listen carefully. (*Whispers.*) Another thing, when you bring the king back, come in by that door. (*Pointing to the left.*) You must first tell two maids to open the door and draw the curtain, then let them go away before you enter. At all costs you must do as I say. There must be no bungling!

    (*Chin Shang nods; the two listen in silence, looking towards the corridor on the left.*)

CHU YUAN (*within*): Tze Lan, where is Her Majesty?

TZE LAN (*within*): My mother said she would be in the court. Come with me.

    (*The two enter from the corridor on the left side, and halt on seeing the queen.*)

TZE LAN: Mother, I have brought His Excellency Chu Yuan here.

QUEEN (*Looking very pleased, advances towards Chu Yuan*): Ah, my lord, how good of you to come! I have been waiting for you for some time.

CHU YUAN (*bows*): I hope Your Majesty is well. What does Your Majesty want of me?

QUEEN: I need your help very urgently. The king has taken your advice and will not sever relations with the state of Chi, so Chang Yi has decided to go to the state of Wei. The king is going to give him a farewell feast, and we are preparing some songs and dances as entertainment; this is where I need your advice. We shall discuss it presently in detail. (*Turning to Chin Shang.*) My lord, your main duty is outside, to see that the cooks have everything ready. It is also possible that the king may want to pledge the agreement, so we shall need the sacrificial vessels too.

CHIN SHANG (*bows*): Yes. I shall have everything very well prepared. I shall take my leave, then. (*Bows to the queen, nods slightly to Chu Yuan.*) My lord, I went to your house just now.

CHU YUAN (*returning the bow*): I am sorry that I missed you.

CHIN SHANG: Did Chan Chuan give you my message?

CHU YUAN: She did, thank you.

QUEEN (*to Tze Lan*): Tze Lan, go and call the ten dancers for the performance of the "Nine Odes." Let them all be prepared.

TZE LAN: I understand, Mother.

　　(*Bows to the queen and exits with Chin Shang by the corridor on the right.*)

QUEEN (*to Chu Yuan*): Sir, listen to me. This boy of mine is very spoilt; his left foot is lame and his health is poor, so that whenever we relax our vigilance a little he falls sick. He has been ill for several days again, and fallen behind with lessons with you again.

CHU YUAN: That is of no consequence. The prince is very intelligent, and provided his health is good he can learn gradually.

QUEEN: Mothers are always very ambitious for their children, on the one hand wanting them to be healthy and on the other wanting them to shine in their studies. But sometimes these two things are incompatible. So, from the ordinary point of view, I may be spoiling my son. We are lucky, though, to have you as his tutor. With such a good tutor I am sure he will turn out all right.

CHU YUAN: Thank you for the compliment. I treat the prince as my own younger brother, and I only want him to have good health and to be in good spirits, so that he can be more diligent. I shall do my best to help him.

QUEEN: Thank you so much, my lord. The boy is really lucky to have such a virtuous, learned and brilliant tutor. In fact I, his mother, am grateful for such good fortune.

CHU YUAN: Thank you for your praise.

QUEEN: His father too is always saying that we owe it to the good deeds of our ancestors to have such an eminent man as you in our state.

CHU YUAN (*even more polite*): You have praised me too much, far too much.

QUEEN: Chu Yuan, you really need not be polite; for where can we find another like you, whether in the south or the north, or east or west of the Pass? Your literary achievements are so great, your character is so lofty, and you have such talent and integrity, that all the rulers in the world must want to have you as their minister, all the young people must want to have you as their teacher, and all the girls must want to have you as their husband!

CHU YUAN (*ill at ease*): Your Majesty, I am rather embarrassed. May I ask Your Majesty what you wanted me here for?

QUEEN: Ah, I was carried away; you must find me too talkative. I asked you here, as I said just now, to help me with the singing and dancing. I have ordered them to sing and dance your Odes. Those songs rewritten by you are really very beautiful. Tell me what you think of my arrangement. (*Pointing.*) In the right and left chambers of the inner hall I shall have the musical instruments set out, and the musicians will play. The singers will appear from the right-hand chamber on the west side, and the dancers from the left-hand chamber on the east side. They will each dance separately in the middle room, making ten dances in all, and then they will dance in circles in the court and sing the last song again and again, until it is fitting to close. What do you think of this plan?

CHU YUAN: It could not be better.

    (*While the queen and Chu Yuan are talking, Tze Lan leads the ten dancers in from the corridor on the right. All the dancers wear strange costumes and masks, somewhat like the dancers in Chinghai. The first dancer represents the Eastern Emperor, with a fierce green mask, grasping a long sword in his right hand and a goblet in his left. The second dancer represents the Lady of the Clouds with a silver-grey face, star-like eyes, dressed in magnificent garments, holding a sun in her left hand and a moon in her right. The third represents the Goddess of the Hsiang River, white-faced, almond-eyed, wearing a costume decorated with flowers and herbs, holding a reed-organ. The fourth represents the Lady of the Hsiang River, green-faced, dressed for the most part like the last dancer, but holding double pipes. The fifth represents the Great Fate, black-faced, horned and holding a bronze mirror. The sixth represents the Young Fate, Goddess of Love, rosy-faced and holding a broom. The seventh represents the Lord of the East, God of the Sun; he is red-faced, holding bow and arrows, wearing a blue tunic and white skirt. The eighth represents the God of the Yellow River, yellow-faced and holding a fish in his hand. The ninth represents the Spirit of the Mountains, a blue-faced woman holding a cassia bough. The tenth represents the Fallen Warrior, purple-faced, grasping a shield and spear, and clad in armour. The ten dancers walk to the hall and stand in a line before the steps, facing the audience.*)

TZE LAN (*when the queen and Chu Yuan stop speaking*): Mother, I have brought the ten dancers.

QUEEN: Good. (*Thinking.*) I think we might as well have the singers and musicians come to their places too, and have a rehearsal. What do you think, my lord?

CHU YUAN: A very good idea. I will go and tell the maids to call them.

QUEEN (*hastily stopping him*): No, you must not go. Tze Lan, you had better go. And tell the maids who have no duties not to come out. I don't want you to come back either.

CHU YUAN: Tze Lan walks with such difficulty ... .

(*But before he has finished speaking Tze Lan has already hurried off, limping, down the corridor on the right.*)

QUEEN: Young people should have exercise; isn't that your usual teaching? (*Looking round at the ten dancers.*) I think you had better sit down. It does not look good for you all to stand. Originally I meant you to appear from the left-hand chamber on the east side; but since you have come out, you had better sit there. (*The ten dancers sit down.*) Each individual dance should be danced in the chamber; but since there is not enough time for that I think we had better just go through the last dance together. (*Turning to Chu Yuan.*) What do you think, my lord?

CHU YUAN: That would be better, for there is really not enough time.

QUEEN: Yes, the king will be coming back soon; he has gone to see Counsellor Tze Chiao. You know what he is like: there is no telling what he will want. Often, when you have taken great pains in preparation, he will suddenly call everything off; and sometimes when you have not prepared anything he will want something, and want it at once. I think his trouble is that he only thinks of himself and never of other people. Take today's feast, for instance; it was only mentioned yesterday evening, but when he wants a thing he must have it, and nothing else will satisfy him. Can't you imagine how troublesome it is?

CHU YUAN: Your Majesty, you have really been to great pains; but I knew nothing about it at home. I only heard it when Chin Shang came to my house; so I have not been of the least assistance, and I feel very ashamed.

QUEEN: Don't be so polite, my lord. I wanted at first to tell you earlier, to have the benefit of your advice; but then I thought it would be wrong to trouble you for such a trifle, because you poets, if I read you aright, like to remain as tranquil as possible. Isn't that so?

CHU YUAN: Sometimes — (*Meaning to say "Sometimes that is so," but does not finish.*)

QUEEN: So I decided not to trouble you. Speaking of your Odes, what lively tunes those are, how delightful, how gay and how tender! And the lines are so fragrant, so sweet, so beautiful and moving. I think after you have written such good poems you must be very happy. You make us all happy, so we ought to make you happier; that is why I decided to supervise the dance myself, so that you might know what great happiness you have given us.

CHU YUAN: Your Majesty, I am really too indebted to you. If I may presume to say a few blunt words, many of my poems are given to me by you. Your Majesty, you have so many qualities calling for our admiration, that in many ways you make us men ashamed. This is what I have always felt, and I have translated such feelings into poetry. If my poems have any good points — Your Majesty must excuse my presumption — they are all given to me by you.

QUEEN (*apparently overjoyed*): Oh, is it really so? How happy I am! How lucky I am! How grateful to you I am! Only I know very well you can't be entirely satisfied with me. I suppose you consider a person like myself not very simple, nor very innocent or quiet. Am I right?

CHU YUAN (*hesitates, at a loss how to reply*): ….

QUEEN: Even if you do not speak, I know what you think. Only this is my nature, which I cannot help. I like splendour, I like excitement; my will to conquer is too great, and I can be very jealous. When someone endangers my happiness and safety I must fight against him, until either I sacrifice my own life or his. This, I think, is my nature. (*Pause.*) I suppose, sir, you consider me too selfish?

CHU YUAN (*still at a loss for a reply*): ….

QUEEN: You need not think of a reply, for when you don't reply I am most satisfied. Actually your nature is in many ways like mine. You do not want to play second fiddle in any society. Isn't that so? (*Pause.*) Your poems, again, and not as simple as those of other poets, for you have range and depth. You are the Tungting Lake, you are the Yangtze River, you are the Eastern Ocean. You are not a small mountain stream or an artificial lake. Tell me, have I described you accurately?

CHU YUAN (*very ill at ease*): Your Majesty, I really do not know how to reply. I have many defects, and I know them; but I am doing my best to overcome those defects.

QUEEN: Well, perhaps you may be content with solitude, but I am not. I want to blossom, I want to flourish, I want a greater place in the sun, and if the small herbs and flowers die beneath my feet, I feel no pity for them. This may be the difference between our characters. (*While they are talking, all the musicians and singers take their places in the different chambers, where they are visible through the curtains. Now the queen remembers the business in hand.*) Oh, I have been talking too much, and all the singers and musicians are ready. My lord, I think we may as well tell them to begin the dance.

CHU YUAN: Good, let them dance "The Last Sacrifice."

QUEEN (*to the musicians and singers in the chambers*): You have heard: you are to rehearse "The Last Sacrifice." (*To the dancers.*) You may stand up. When I am standing on the stairs of the hall and wave my hand at you, the singing, music and dancing must start. When I want you to stop, I will raise my hand again. (*To Chu Yuan.*) My lord, let us go up the stairs.

(*The queen ascends the western steps, while Chu Yuan ascends the eastern steps, meeting in the centre. The ten dancers come to the front of the stage, and stand facing inwards. The performers in the chamber are ready, looking at the queen. The queen raises high her left hand, and makes a motion, whereupon the singing, dancing and music start together. The dancers make a circle in the court, coming together and scattering again, while the singers in the chamber sing the ode "The Last Sacrifice":*)

> The rites performed, the wizards strike the urn,
> Pass round the sacred herbs and dance in turn;
> With grace the lovely damsels dance and sing:
> "Asters for autumn, orchids for the spring,
> Through endless years this sacrifice we bring."

During the singing and dancing, the back door of the left-hand chamber is opened, and two maids enter and lift the curtains on both sides, attaching them to the pillars; then, paying no attention to the music and dancing, they withdraw through the back door. The queen again raises her left hand and makes a motion, whereupon the singing, dancing and music stop simultaneously.)

QUEEN: Oh, I feel faint, I am falling. (*She pretends to fall.*) My lord! My lord! Quickly, quickly! (*Falls into his arms.*)

CHU YUAN (*taken by surprise, and seeing that there is no one else at hand, supports the queen*): ...

(*The king of Chu appears in the left-hand chamber with Chang Yi, Tze Chiao and Chin Shang. They see Chu Yuan holding the queen in his arms, but Chu Yuan does not see them as he prepares to carry the queen to a seat in the chamber.*)

QUEEN (*calling incessantly*): My lord! My lord! Quickly, quickly! (*When she is sure that the king has seen them she suddenly turns about, and thrusts him away.*) Quickly let me go! You astound me! What kind of behaviour is this? Indeed you amaze me! (*Runs towards the king.*)

(*Chu Yuan is dazed and does not know what to do. The king and the others hastily descend the steps from the eastern chamber to meet the queen, who runs down the left steps and flies to the king's arms.*)

QUEEN: I am really amazed! I am really horrified!

KING: Calm yourself! Don't be afraid, Cheng Hsiu.

QUEEN: Ah, luckily you came just in time, otherwise I shudder to think what might have happened! I'm afraid the minister Chu Yuan must be mad to behave so shamelessly in public.

CHU YUAN (*only just realizing that he has been deceived. Angrily*): Your Majesty — what do — what do you mean?

KING (*furious*): You madman, you lunatic, I forbid you to speak!

(*Chu Yuan remains angry and silent.*)

QUEEN (*slightly calmer*): Ah, I really could not have foreseen it, in the public court of all places, and when the minister is a man whose moral character I have always respected.

KING (*embracing the queen*): Calm yourself! There's no need to be alarmed, no need to be alarmed.

(*The king helps the queen up the steps, followed by the others.*)

CHU YUAN (*seeing the king approaching, bows*): Your Majesty, will you allow me to speak?

KING (*arrogantly*): I cannot allow any more madness! Ha, you indeed astound me. I have always considered you a great man, but this is what you really are! You boast openly that I am changeful and wilful; but that I could forgive you. You say that all important affairs and policies, laws and regulations of our kingdom are dictated by you; but that I could forgive you. You say that all others are flatterers and slanderers, and you alone are loyal; but that I could forgive you. But in public, before me and my guest, to behave in such an insolent manner to the queen, that I cannot forgive!

CHU YUAN (*resolutely*): Your Majesty, this is a conspiracy.

KING (*more angry*): Conspiracy? Am I conspiring against you? Is the queen conspiring against you? I can still believe the evidence of my own eyes. Had I not seen it with my own eyes just now, I should not have believed it. You are really mad, quite mad! I have taken your advice in the past, but luckily I have seen through you before it is too late. From now on, I forbid you to set foot in the palace, or ever to see me again!

CHU YUAN (*quietly and with feeling*): Your Majesty, I need never come to your palace again nor see you again. But you were not wrong before when you listened to my advice. You should think more of our people, more of the people of China. All men want to live as human beings, all men long for the time when disunion shall end and China become a peaceful, united country. When you took my advice about caring for the people and allying with the kingdoms east of the Pass to resist the power of Chin, you were not wrong at all. If you pursue this policy, you will bring about the unification of China.

(*The king wants to interrupt, but is stopped by the queen, who is listening cynically with Chang Yi and the others.*)

CHU YUAN (*with more feeling*): But if you let yourself be deceived by others, you will become the destroyer of our kingdom.

KING (*unable to suppress his anger*): Arrant nonsense! ... What ...

what ...

QUEEN (*stopping him*): Let him finish his raving.

CHU YUAN (*continues*): If you let yourself be deceived by others, you will live to know calamity. Your palace will become the enemy's camp, your crown will be put on the head of an enemy horse, your people will be massacred until the rivers run red with blood, and both you and the queen will suffer indescribable indignities.

KING (*too angry to speak*): What ... what ... what ...

QUEEN (*sarcastically*): Sage of our land, your frenzy has gone too far. (*Turning to Tze Chiao and Chin Shang.*) Take him away, otherwise he may cause further trouble in the palace.

KING (*nearly bursting with rage*): Dismiss him from his office!

TZE CHIAO (*bows*): Yes, Your Majesty.

CHIN SHANG (*at the same time*): We shall carry out Your Majesty's orders.

(*The two men approach Chu Yuan and lay hands on him.*)

CHU YUAN (*indignantly*): Ah! Your Majesty, I could never have thought that you would plot against me in this way. Let heaven above, earth below and all our royal ancestors bear witness! You have plotted not against me, but against our entire kingdom! (*He is dragged to the western steps towards the exit on the right side, but he still calls out.*) I have done nothing to be ashamed of! I can look on death without flinching! Which of us is right and which wrong, which loyal and which treacherous, future generations will decide. What you have plotted against is not me but yourself, our king, our country and all China!

(*When the queen hears Chu Yuan's words, she bites her lips, hating and fearing him.*)

KING: Well, he is certainly mad, he is certainly mad. (*Helping the queen to sit on the left-hand seat.*) Don't be afraid; rest a little while.

QUEEN (*pulling herself together*): No, Your Majesty, I am not afraid of him; I am only afraid that we are being too discourteous to His Lordship Chang Yi.

KING (*only just remembering Chang Yi's presence*): Yes, indeed. My lord, we are too discourteous. Please sit down. (*Invites Chang Yi to sit on the right-hand seat.*)

CHANG YI (*bowing*): It is all right, quite all right.

(*Chang Yi sits down, and the king also sits on the throne in the middle.*)

CHANG YI: Please excuse my presumption, but is this noble lady the Queen Cheng Hsiu? (*Bowing to the queen.*)

KING (*hastily introducing them*): Oh Yes, yes. This is my favourite Cheng Hsiu. (*To the queen.*) This is Lord Chang Yi, Prime Minister of the state of Chin. We met in Tze Chiao's house, so I asked him to come here.

(*The two bow to each other.*)

CHANG YI: Today is the first time I have seen the queen. Please excuse my presumption again; but I only now realize ... (*Wanting to speak, but hesitating.*)

QUEEN: My lord, please don't stand on ceremony. I am a southerner, and do not understand court etiquette.

CHANG YI (*still apologetically*): Please excuse my presumption; but after seeing the queen today, I realize why Chu Yuan should lose his reason.

KING (*very pleased, laughs, aloud*): Ha, ha, ha! Very well said, very well said!

QUEEN (*smiling*): My lord, you have a ready tongue.

CHANG YI: It is true. I have been in many places, south and north, east and west of the Pass; I have travelled practically all over China under varying circumstances, rising from the rank of a poor scholar to that of prime minister of a state; I have met all kinds of people: nobles and knights, peasants and artisans, merchants, officers and barbarians. But, if you will excuse my presumption, Your Majesty (*again looking apologetic*), I really have never seen anyone so beautiful.

KING (*still more pleased*): Aha! I always say there can't be another like her in the whole world.

CHANG YI: No indeed, certainly not.

KING: Yesterday you were still praising the women of the Middle Plain. Didn't you say that the girls of the land of Chou and Cheng are so beautiful that when they stand in the streets people think they are goddesses?

CHANG YI: Alas, that was due to my ignorance: that is what is called partiality. I come from those districts, and I had seen only the women of those districts. Today, however, I have seen what real beauty is. (*Again apologizing to the queen.*) Your Majesty, please excuse my presumption again, but you must be the reincarnation of the Goddess of the Witch Mountain.

QUEEN (*smiling*): My lord, you are very ready with your tongue!

KING: All right, all right; no need to praise each other any more. (*Standing up and taking Chang Yi's hand so that he rises too.*) At all events, Lord Chang Yi, I have the greatest respect for you. You say all who talk in a high-sounding way are hypocrites. That is quite true. I think you need not go to the land of Wei, and I don't want you to find me any beautiful girls. I shall pay no more attention to the advice of that lunatic. I am very pleased that you could persuade the King of Chin to show special deference to me, and I shall certainly sever relations with the state of Chi and ally with the state of Chin, accepting the two hundred square miles of the district of Shang Yu in the kingdom of Chin.

CHANG YI: That is indeed the good fortune of both our states!

KING (*coming to the queen, takes her hand to help her up*): Today you have worked hard; and as for the songs made by that lunatic, I can't bear the thought of them. So let today's dance be cancelled. (*Pauses while he reflects.*) And today's feast can be cancelled too. Let us go for a walk now outside the East Gate with Lord Chang Yi, without taking our carriages. We will have lunch in the Temple of the Eastern Emperor. That should be quite interesting. (*Turning to Chang Yi.*) Well, Lord Chang Yi, let us go. As for these lunacies, let the others take care of them.

(*He points to the dancers in the court who have not yet received orders to leave, but are sitting or standing in small groups, scattered about. The Eastern Emperor and the Lady of the Clouds are sitting on the steps of the eastern chamber, the Spirit of the Mountains beside them. The Great Fate and the Young Fate are sitting on the steps of the western chamber, with the Fallen Warrior standing beside them. The Lord of the East and the God of the Yellow River stand leaning against the pillar by the eastern chamber; the Lady of the Hsiang River and the Goddess of the Hsiang River stand leaning against the pillar of the western chamber. The king, queen and Chang Yi walk to the steps. Tze Chiao and Chin Shang appear on the right-hand side and bow to the king beneath the steps.*)

TZE CHIAO: Your Majesty, we have taken away Chu Yuan's insignia of office, and let him go.

CHIN SHANG: We should also add that when he went out he was shouting incessantly; and before he left, in front of everybody, he tore his robe to shreds.

KING (*furious again*): What a lunatic! Have all this ridiculous show removed!

CURTAIN

杨宪益、戴乃迭译事年表

杨宪益译事年表[①]

1915 年

1 月 10 日,杨宪益出生在天津花园街 8 号大公馆。

1932 年

尝试以诗体翻译莎士比亚、希腊女诗人 Sappho(今译:萨福)等人的诗歌。

1938 年

与戴乃迭合译《离骚》,当时未出版。

翻译唐诗若干首,刊发在牛津大学学生杂志《契尔威尔》(*Cherwell*)和《伊希斯》(*Isis*)上。

[①] 主要参考:陈志明,编. 杨宪益先生大事年表//杨宪益. 杨宪益自传. 薛鸿时,译. 北京:人民日报出版社,2010:373-385;文明国. 杨宪益先生大事年表//杨宪益. 从《离骚》开始,翻译整个中国:杨宪益对话集. 北京:人民日报出版社,2011:276-289。根据现有传记和研究文献,本书著者对部分地方有增添、修订。该篇"杨宪益译事年表"中所有注释为本书编者根据历史文献查证后的修订信息。

1943 年

接受梁实秋邀请,受聘国立编译馆,开启夫妻二人携手合作的翻译生涯。当时的国立编译馆只有人从事将西方经典翻译成中文的工作,还没有人进行中文外译。梁实秋希望杨宪益夫妇能去领导一个部门,专门从事将中国经典翻译成英文的工作。

开始与戴乃迭合译《资治通鉴》。

1944 年

用笔名在重庆一家报纸副刊上发表所译英国诗人罗伯特·赫里克《致羞涩的情人》一诗。

开始与戴乃迭合译《老残游记》。

与戴乃迭合译陶渊明诗歌、唐五代诗歌、唐变文、南北朝佛学论争文、苗族创世诗等,但当时未出版发行。

与戴乃迭合译艾青、田间诗,郭沫若,阳翰笙戏剧等,但当时未出版发行。

1947 年

与戴乃迭合译《老残游记》(*Mr. Decadent*),由南京独立出版社出版。

1948 年

所译《近代英国诗钞》在中华书局出版。

与戴乃迭合译《老残游记》(*Mr. Derelict*),英国乔治·艾伦—昂温出版公司(George Allen & Unwin Ltd.)出版。

1951 年

将苏联历史学家格列科夫院士(Boris Dmitrievich Grekov)论基辅罗斯的一本书和其他短论文的英译本译成中文。由于译稿散失,这一部分历史学译著最终没有能够面世。

1952 年

与戴乃迭合译宋庆龄《为新中国奋斗》(*The Struggle for New China*)，由外文出版社出版。

1953 年

与戴乃迭合译《离骚》《阿 Q 正传》，由外文出版社出版。

1954 年

与戴乃迭合译《柳毅传——唐代传奇选》《王贵与李香香》《太阳照在桑干河上》《白毛女》《渡荒》《周扬文艺论文集》《鲁迅短篇小说选》等，由外文出版社出版。

与罗念生等合译阿里斯多芬著《阿里斯多芬喜剧二种》，由人民文学出版社出版。

1955 年

与戴乃迭合译《长生殿》《屈原》(五幕剧)，由外文出版社出版。

1956 年

与戴乃迭合译《鲁迅选集》(1 卷)、《柳荫记》《打渔杀家》，由外文出版社出版。

所译萧伯纳戏剧《匹克梅梁》与《凯撒和克莉奥佩特拉》两种，收入人民文学出版社《萧伯纳戏剧集》(3 卷)。

1957 年

与戴乃迭合译《鲁迅选集》(2 卷)、《中国古代寓言选》《儒林外史》《杜十娘怒沉百宝箱——宋明平话选》《十五贯》(昆曲)、《白蛇传》(京剧)，由外文出版社出版。

所译维吉尔《牧歌》由人民文学出版社出版。

1958 年

与戴乃迭合译《搜书院》(粤剧)、《秦香莲》(评剧)、《汉魏六朝小说选》《关汉卿杂剧选》《中国古典文学简史》《中印人民友谊史话》,由外文出版社出版。

所译阿里斯托芬《鸟》由香港中流出版社出版。

1959 年

所译田间诗歌《少女颂》("The Girl")在《中国文学》(*Chinese Literature*)1959 年第 6 期刊载;所译赵树理《新食堂里忆故人》("A New Canteen and Old Memories")在该杂志第 12 期刊载。

与闻时清合译儒勒·凡尔纳《地心游记》,由中国青年出版社出版。

与戴乃迭合译《鲁迅选集》(3 卷)、《中国小说史略》(鲁迅著),由外文出版社出版。

开始翻译《史记》。

1960 年

借调至中国社会科学院(当时称中国科学院哲学社会科学部),翻译荷马史诗《奥德修纪》、法国古典史诗《罗兰之歌》等。

所译郭沫若撰《反帝斗争的连锁反应》("The Chain Reaction of the Anti-imperialist Struggle")在《中国文学》1960 年第 7 期刊载;同期还刊载了所译肖三、袁水拍、郭小川三人所创献给古巴的组诗三首:《古巴,我给你捎句话》("Cuba, I Salute You")、《加勒比海一枝花》("Flower of the Caribbean")和《为"诗歌号飞机"送行》("We Send off Our Avion de Poesia");所译李野光诗二首《早啊,非洲,新的非洲》("Good Morning, Africa, New Africa!")和《致阿尔及利亚》("We Support You, Africa!")在该杂志第 11 期刊载;所译杨朔《海市》("Mirages and Sea-Markets")在该杂志第 12 期刊载;所译恽代英、邓中夏、叶挺、李少石、黄诚、陈然等《革命烈士诗选》:《狱中诗》("In Prison")、《过洞庭》("Crossing

Lake Tungting")、《囚歌》("The Prisoner's Song")、《寄母》("To My Mother")、《诗一首》("Poem")、《我的自白书》("My Confession")在该英文杂志第 12 期刊载。

1961 年

与戴乃迭合译《老残游记》(*Mr. Decadent：Notes Taken in an Outing*)，由香港复兴出版社出版。

《史记》翻译工作完成(或为 1962 年)①。开始翻译《红楼梦》。

与戴乃迭合译《鲁迅选集》(4 卷)、《故事新编》《不怕鬼的故事》(程十发绘图)等，由外文出版社出版。

所译晋剧《打金枝》(*A Princess Gets Smacked*)在《中国文学》杂志 1961 年第 8 期刊载；所译川剧《评雪辨踪》(*Footprints in the Snow*)在该杂志同年第 10 期刊载；所译徐迟《直薄峨嵋山顶记》("Climbing Mount Omei")在该杂志同年第 11 期刊载。

1962 年

与戴乃迭合译《刘三姐》《海市》(刘白羽、阳朔等著)，由外文出版社出版。

1964 年

所译纳·赛音朝克图《白色的海》("Emerald Waves and a Silver Sea")在《中国文学》杂志 1964 年第 1 期刊载；所译刘伯温寓言二则(《狙公》与《卖柑者言》)在该杂志同年第 4 期刊载。

---

① 因历史原因，该书译毕很长一段时间未能刊印。20 世纪 70 年代初，杨宪益被告知译稿遗失，据说"文革"期间被某位编辑卖给或送给了香港某位书商，并在香港印制发行，但没有署杨宪益夫妇的名字。

1965 年

《中国文学》杂志 1965 年第 2、3、6、7、8、9、10、12 期相继刊载其所译古典诗词与现代诗歌计 30 余首。

《红楼梦》翻译工作停止,其他翻译工作停止。

1966 年

《中国文学》1966 年第 3、6 期刊载其所译现代诗歌 8 首。

1972 年

在"文革"中受到冲击。1968 年 4 月 27 日,和妻子戴乃迭双双被捕,在狱中度过 4 年。1972 年 5 月,出狱。继续翻译《红楼梦》。此后几年一直从事该书翻译工作。

1973 年

与戴乃迭合译的《无声的中国:鲁迅作品选》,由牛津大学出版社出版。①

1974 年

与戴乃迭合译《野草》,由外文出版社出版。

1975 年

与戴乃迭合译《史记选》,由香港商务印书馆出版。

1976 年

《红楼梦》全部译完。

---

① 因当时的社会环境,国外出版社与中国大陆沟通不畅,所选文稿均为杨宪益、戴乃迭合译鲁迅作品,但书上仅署戴乃迭一人。

与戴乃迭合译《朝花夕拾》,由外文出版社出版。

1978 年

与戴乃迭合译《红楼梦》第一卷,由外文出版社出版。

1979 年

与戴乃迭合译《红楼梦》第二卷、《史记选》,由外文出版社出版。

所译荷马《奥德修纪》由上海译文出版社出版。

1980 年

与戴乃迭合译《红楼梦》第三卷,由外文出版社出版。

1981 年

所译《罗兰之歌》由上海译文出版社出版。

与戴乃迭合译《呐喊》《彷徨》,由外文出版社出版;《中国文学》杂志社"熊猫丛书"推出夫妇合译的《三部古典小说节选》《聊斋故事选》等。

所译茅盾《〈我走过的道路〉序》(Preface to *The Road I Travelled*)在《中国文学》杂志 1981 年第 7 期刊载;所译《萨都刺诗词四首》("Sadula's Poems")在该杂志同年第 10 期刊载。

1982 年

发起并主持"熊猫丛书"系列,重新打开中国文学对外交流的窗口。这套丛书里,既有夫妇俩合作翻译的《诗经》《聊斋志异》《西游记》《三国演义》《镜花缘》等中国古典文学经典,也收录了他们翻译的《芙蓉镇》《沉重的翅膀》以及巴金、沈从文、孙犁、新凤霞、王蒙等人的现当代文学作品。

修订重译的肖伯纳著《卖花女》,由中国对外翻译出版公司出版。

所译邓魁英《罗隐和他的〈谗书〉》("The Late Tang Writer Luo Yin")在《中国文学》杂志 1982 年第 2 期刊载,同期刊载的还有其所译罗隐《〈馋书〉七则》("Selections from *Slanderous Writings*")；所译纪昀《〈阅微草堂笔记〉十一则》("Selections from *Notes of Yuewei Hermitage*")在该杂志同年第 4 期刊载；所译《刘鹗和他的〈老残游记〉》("On *The Travels of Lao Can*")在该杂志同年第 12 期刊载。

1983 年

所译《龚自珍诗文选》("Gong Zizhen's Writings")在《中国文学》1983 年第 5 期刊载，同期刊载的还有其所译黄裳学术研究文章《沈从文的〈中国古代服饰研究〉》("A Study of Chinese Costume")；所译著名音乐人侯德健歌曲《龙的传人》("The Descendants of the Dragon")在该杂志同年第 9 期刊载。

与戴乃迭合译《老残游记》(*The Travels of Lao Can*)，由中国文学出版社出版。

1984 年

所译《黄永玉寓言十六则》在《中国文学》1984 年春季刊刊载。

携戴乃迭再次访问英国，作为访问学者，在牛津大学莫顿学院交流一个学期，将埃斯库罗斯《被缚的普罗米修斯》译成中国的韵文，但只译了大约一半。

1985 年

所译唐弢《西方影响与民族风格——中国现代文学发展的一个轮廓》("Western Influence and National Style: A Brief Survey of the Development of Modern Chinese Literature")在《中国文学》1985 年春季刊刊载。

所译古罗马普劳图斯著《凶宅》、与王焕生和范之龙合译《一坛金子》和《福尔弥昂》纳入《古罗马喜剧三种》由中国戏剧出版社出版。

1986 年

《中国文学》杂志社推出与戴乃迭合译的英译本《汉魏六朝诗文选》。

1987 年

与申慧辉等合译《圣女贞德》，由漓江出版社出版。

1991 年

外国文学名著丛书编辑委员会编订出版杨宪益所译普劳图斯著《古罗马戏剧选》，由人民文学出版社出版。

1999 年

妻子戴乃迭因病辞世，享年 80 岁。杨宪益此后搁置译笔。

2002 年

所译《凯撒和克莉奥佩特拉》由人民文学出版社出版。

2005 年

与戴乃迭合译的《老残游记》(*The Travels of Lao Can*)由外文出版社出版。

2009 年

9 月，获颁中国翻译协会"翻译文化终身成就奖"。

11 月，辞世。享年 95 岁。

戴乃迭译事年表

1919 年

1 月 19 日,出生于北京。

1937 年

入读牛津大学走读生学院(Society of Home Students),攻读法国文学。

经中文教授休斯先生介绍加入中国学会,结识学会主席杨宪益,帮助杨宪益组织中国学会的会议并担任秘书。

从法国文学专业转读中国文学,随休斯研读《诗经》《论语》《易经》、唐代传奇和佛教书籍等。

1938 年

与杨宪益合译《离骚》,当时未出版。

1940 年

从牛津大学毕业,获二等荣誉学位,成为牛津大学汉学科荣誉学位第一人。

经中央大学(后来的南京大学)校长罗家伦推荐,往重庆中央大学柏溪分校任教,被聘为英语系讲师。

1941 年

与杨宪益赴贵阳师范学院任教,被聘为英文系教授。

1943 年

与杨宪益一同接受国立编译馆聘任,开启夫妻二人携手合作的职业翻译生涯。

开始与杨宪益合译《资治通鉴》。

1944 年

开始与杨宪益合译《老残游记》。

与杨宪益合译陶渊明诗歌、唐五代诗歌、唐变文、南北朝佛学论争文、苗族创世诗等，但当时未出版发行。

与杨宪益合译艾青、田间诗，郭沫若、阳翰笙戏剧等，但当时未出版发行。

1947 年

与杨宪益合译《老残游记》(*Mr. Decadent*)，由南京独立出版社出版。

1948 年

与杨宪益合译《老残游记》(*Mr. Derelict*)，由英国乔治·艾伦—昂温出版公司(George Allen & Unwin Ltd.)出版，英译者署名 G. M. Taylor（戴乃迭婚前所用英文名字）。

1949 年

受聘中央大学外文系英文组教授。

1950 年

11 月 25 日，在南京大学校刊委员会编印的《南大生活》上发表文章《对目前抗美援朝运动的看法》。

独译《原动力》(*The Moving Force*)①，由北京 Cultural Press 出版。

---

① 《原动力》一书为女作家草明（原名：吴绚文）创作的新中国第一部反映工人阶级精神风貌的经典作品，1949 年 5 月初版，英译本于 1950 年推出，并未署名。本信息来源自 1951 年 5 月 11 日，戴乃迭发表在《南大生活》的文章《我要以实际行动来表示对新中国的热爱》。

1951 年

5 月 11 日,在《南大生活》发表文章《我要以实际行动来表示对新中国的热爱》。

独译朝鲜前线通讯 4 篇,在《中国文学》1951 年第 1 期上发表。

1952 年

与杨宪益合译宋庆龄著作《为新中国奋斗》(*The Struggle for New China*),由外文出版社出版。

1953 年

独译《李家庄的变迁》《雪峰寓言》,由外文出版社出版。

与杨宪益合译《离骚》《阿 Q 正传》,由外文出版社出版。

1954 年

与杨宪益合译《柳毅传——唐代传奇选》《王贵与李香香》《太阳照在桑干河上》《白毛女》《渡荒》《周扬文艺论文集》《鲁迅短篇小说选》等,由外文出版社出版。

独译《少年先锋队员的故事》,由外文出版社出版。

1955 年

与杨宪益合译《长生殿》《屈原》(五幕剧),由外文出版社出版。

独译《阿诗玛》,在《中国文学》1955 年第 3 期上发表。

1956 年

与杨宪益合译《鲁迅选集》(1 卷)、《柳荫记》《打渔杀家》,由外文出版社出版。

独译《罗才打虎》与新疆青年作家小说 2 篇,分别在《中国文学》1956 年第 1、4 期上发表。

1957 年

与杨宪益合译《鲁迅选集》(2 卷)、《中国古代寓言选》《儒林外史》《杜十娘怒沉百宝箱——宋明平话选》《十五贯》(昆曲)、《白蛇传》(京剧),由外文出版社出版。

独译《阿诗玛》《三里湾》,由外文出版社出版。

独译《在冬天的牧场上》《三里湾》,分别在《中国文学》1957 年第 2、3 期上发表。

1958 年

与杨宪益合译《搜书院》(粤剧)、《秦香莲》(评剧)、《汉魏六朝小说选》《关汉卿杂剧选》《中国古典文学简史》《中印人民友谊史话》,由外文出版社出版。

独译《大林和小林》(张天翼),由外文出版社出版。

独译朱自清散文 5 篇、《哥哥下乡去了》,分别在《中国文学》1958 年第 1、5 期上发表。

1959 年

与杨宪益合译《鲁迅选集》(3 卷)、《中国小说史略》(鲁迅),由外文出版社出版。

与他人合译《毛泽东诗词》,由外文出版社出版。

独译《红旗谱》《百合花》《莫干山纪游词》《捣米》《宝葫芦的秘密》《张天翼和他的小读者》等各类作品近 20 篇,在《中国文学》1959 年第 1 至 12 期上发表。

1960 年

独译毛泽东诗 3 首、闻一多诗 4 首、张永枚诗 2 首、新民歌 13 首、康朗甩诗 2 首等诗歌近 40 首,在《中国文学》1960 年第 1 至 11 期上发表。

1961 年

与杨宪益合译《老残游记》(*Mr. Decadent: Notes Taken in an Outing*)，由香港复兴出版社出版。

与杨宪益合译《鲁迅选集》(4 卷)、《故事新编》《不怕鬼的故事》(程十发绘图)等，由外文出版社出版。

《史记》翻译工作完成(或为 1962 年)①。开始翻译《红楼梦》。

独译《红旗谱》，由外文出版社出版。

独译《绿林行》《你追我赶》《童年的悲哀》《惠嫂》《三家巷》(节选)、闻捷诗 2 首、罗淑小说 2 则等文学作品 13 篇(首)，在《中国文学》1961 年第 3 至 11 期上发表。

1962 年

与杨宪益合译《刘三姐》《海市》(刘白羽、阳朔等著)，由外文出版社出版。

独译《葛梅》《鱼的艺术——和它在人民生活中的应用及发展》《微神》《山地回忆》《东方之珠》等各类作品 9 篇，在《中国文学》1962 年第 2 至 12 期上发表。

1963 年

独译《老社员》《鄂伦春组曲》《祖国,我生命的土壤》《〈呼兰河传〉序》《红色娘子军》等各类作品 20 篇，在《中国文学》1963 年第 1 至 12 期上发表。

1964 年

独译《旷野上》《沉船》《迎接朝霞》《迎冰曲》《"奴隶村"见闻》《难忘的

---

① 因历史原因，《史记》译毕很长一段时间未能刊印。20 世纪 70 年代初，杨宪益被告知译稿遗失，据说"文革"期间被某位编辑卖给或送给香港，并在香港印制发行，并没有署杨宪益夫妇的名字。

人》等各类作品 22 篇,在《中国文学》1964 年第 1 至 12 期上发表。

1965 年

《红楼梦》翻译工作停止;其他翻译工作停止。

与他人合作改写、注释的简写本《青春之歌》译本由商务印书馆出版。

独译《农奴》《姑嫂》《修房曲》《草原纪事》《青年马龙》《特殊性格的人》等各类作品 23 篇,在《中国文学》1965 年第 1 至 12 期上发表。

1966 年

独译《赤道战鼓》(七场话剧),由外文出版社出版。

独译《游乡》(独幕剧)、《新型的小喜剧》《我们的工程师》《雪路云程》《竹鸡坡纪事》等各类作品 13 篇,在《中国文学》1966 年第 1 至 7 期上发表。

1970 年

与詹纳(W. J. F. Jenner)合作编选、翻译鲁迅等人著《现代中国小说选》(*Modern Chinese Stories*),由牛津大学出版社出版。

1972 年

在"文革"中受到冲击。1968 年 4 月 27 日,和杨宪益双双被捕,在狱中度过 4 年。1972 年 5 月,出狱。继续翻译《红楼梦》,此后几年一直从事该书翻译工作。

1973 年

编选、翻译《无声的中国:鲁迅作品选》(*Silent China*:*Selected Writings of Lu Xun*)①,由牛津大学出版社出版。

---

① 因当时的社会环境,国外出版社与中国大陆沟通不畅,所选文稿均为杨宪益、戴乃迭合译的鲁迅作品,但书作上仅署戴乃迭一人。

1974 年

与杨宪益合译《野草》,由外文出版社出版。

1975 年

与杨宪益合译《史记选》,由香港商务印书馆出版。

1976 年

《红楼梦》全部译完。

与杨宪益合译《朝花夕拾》,由外文出版社出版。

1978 年

与杨宪益合译《红楼梦》第一卷,由外文出版社出版。

1979 年

与杨宪益合译《红楼梦》第二卷、《史记选》,由外文出版社出版。

独译《宝葫芦的秘密》,由外文出版社出版。

独译《坚强的人——访问巴金》《奴隶的心》《从森林里来的孩子》《含羞草》、艾青诗、黄永玉诗等各类作品 30 余篇(首),在《中国文学》1979 年第 6 至 12 期上发表。

1980 年

与杨宪益合译《红楼梦》第三卷,由外文出版社出版。

独译《萧萧》《丈夫》《桂生》《太阳下的风景——沈从文与我》,在《中国文学》1980 年第 8 期上发表。

1981 年

与杨宪益合译《呐喊》《彷徨》,由外文出版社出版;与杨宪益合译《三部古典小说节选》《聊斋故事选》等,由中国文学出版社出版。

与杨宪益合译《鲁迅小说全集》，由美国印第安纳大学出版社出版。

与杨宪益合译《明代短篇小说选》，由香港 Joint Pub. Co. 出版社出版。

独译《边城及其它》《春天里的秋天及其它》《新凤霞回忆录》，由中国文学出版社出版。

独译《蝴蝶》《自言自语》《新凤霞回忆录》《关于鲁迅的讽刺诗》《同路易·艾黎的对话》《鲁迅与宋庆龄》等各类作品 15 篇，在《中国文学》1981年第 1 至 11 期上发表。

1982 年

独译《湘西散记》《北京的传说》《李广田散文选》，与他人合译《当代女作家作品选》《黑鳗》《孙犁小说选》《三十年代短篇小说选》（2 册）、《三十年代小说选》，由中国文学出版社出版。

独译《风云初记》，由外文出版社出版。

独译《纪念鲁迅学术讨论会》《〈湘西散记〉序》《关于〈九叶集〉》《花鸟舅爷》《老渡船》《评〈阅微草堂笔记〉》《北京的传说》等各类作品 22 篇，在《中国文学》1982 年第 1 至 12 期上发表。

1983 年

与杨宪益合译《老残游记》《诗经选》，由中国文学出版社出版。

与杨宪益合译《中国古典文学史大纲》，由香港三联书店有限公司出版。

与他人合译《王蒙小说选》，由中国文学出版社出版。

独译《单口相声故事传》《芙蓉镇》，由中国文学出版社出版。

独译《单口相声故事 5 则》《单口相声故事 2 则》《以苦为乐》《南湾镇逸事》，在《中国文学》1983 年第 1、2、5、8 期上发表。

1984 年

与杨宪益合译《唐宋诗文选》，由中国文学出版社出版。

与他人合译《五十年代小说选》《郁达夫作品选》，由中国文学出版社出版。

独译《浮屠岭》《条件尚未成熟》《"九十九堆"礼俗》《血红的九月》《矛盾交响曲》《银风筝下的伦敦》《寓言16则》，在《中国文学》1984年夏、秋、冬季刊上发表。

1985 年

与他人合译《古华小说选》《绿化树》《茹志鹃小说选》《老舍短篇小说选》，由中国文学出版社出版。

独译《绿化树》《祖母绿》《烟壶》《高女人和她的矮丈夫》《北京人》(选)，在《中国文学》1985年春、夏、秋、冬季刊上发表。

1986 年

与杨宪益合译《汉魏六朝诗文选》《明清诗文选》《唐代传奇选》，由中国文学出版社出版。

与他人合译《北京人》《邓友梅小说选》《张洁小说选》，由中国文学出版社出版。

独译《鸭巢围的夜》(节选)，在《中国翻译》1986年第2期发表。

独译《北京人》(选)、《单家桥的闲言碎语》《树王》在《中国文学》1986年春、秋、冬季刊上发表。

1987 年

独译本《沉重的翅膀》(*Leaden Wings*)，由英国首家专门针对女性读者的出版社维拉戈出版社(Virago Press)出版。

与他人合译《人到中年》《冯骥才小说选》《叶圣陶作品选》《茅盾作品选》，由中国文学出版社出版。

独译《减去十岁》《人人之间》，在《中国文学》1987年春、冬季刊上发表。

1988 年

与他人合作编译《龙的传说》《流逝》《玛拉沁夫小说选》,由中国文学出版社出版。

独译《一个不正常的女人》《清高》,在《中国文学》1988 年春、秋季刊上发表。

1989 年

与他人合译《菉竹山房》《村仇》《中国优秀短篇小说选(1949—1989)》,由中国文学出版社出版。

独译《菜园》《知识》《一个爱国的作家》《杨柳》《蜀道奇遇记》《天堂里的对话》《谈〈天堂里的对话〉》,在《中国文学》1989 年夏、秋、冬季刊上发表。

1990 年

与他人合译《闻一多诗文选》,由中国文学出版社出版。

独译《黄豆芽,绿豆芽》,在《中国文学》1990 年冬季刊上发表。

1991 年

与 Deborah J. Leonard 和 Zhang Andong 合译张洁中短篇小说集《只要无事发生,任何事都不会发生》(*As Long As Nothing Happens, Nothing Will*),由美国格罗夫·韦登菲尔德出版社(Grove Weidenfeld Press)出版。

独译《窑工老吕》《家丑》《转运汉巧遇洞庭红》,在《中国文学》1991 年春、夏、冬季刊上发表。

1999 年

11 月 18 日,在北京阜外医院因病辞世,享年 80 岁。

图书在版编目(CIP)数据

中华翻译家代表性译文库.杨宪益、戴乃迭卷 /
辛红娟编.—杭州:浙江大学出版社,2020.1
ISBN 978-7-308-19883-7

Ⅰ.①中… Ⅱ.①辛… Ⅲ.①杨宪益(1915—2009)
—译文—文集 ②戴乃迭(1919—1999)—译文—文集 Ⅳ.
①I11

中国版本图书馆 CIP 数据核字(2019)第 288464 号

中華譯學館 莫言題

杨宪益　戴乃迭卷
辛红娟　编

出 品 人	鲁东明
总 编 辑	袁亚春
丛书策划	张　琛　包灵灵
责任编辑	祁　潇
责任校对	吴水燕　陆雅娟
封面设计	闰江文化
出版发行	浙江大学出版社
	(杭州市天目山路 148 号　邮政编码 310007)
	(网址:http://www.zjupress.com)
排　　版	浙江时代出版服务有限公司
印　　刷	浙江海虹彩色印务有限公司
开　　本	710mm×1000mm　1/16
印　　张	33.25
字　　数	554 千
版 印 次	2020 年 1 月第 1 版　2020 年 1 月第 1 次印刷
书　　号	ISBN 978-7-308-19883-7
定　　价	88.00 元

中華譯學館·中华翻译家代表性译文库

许　钧　郭国良　总主编

第一辑